D0935624

Freedom, Corruption and Government
IN ELIZABETHAN ENGLAND

by the same author

THE QUEEN'S WARDS
ELIZABETH I AND THE UNITY OF ENGLAND
THE ELIZABETHAN NATION

CONTROL OF RAW MATERIALS

as editor or joint editor

SHAKESPEARE'S WORLD
ELIZABETHAN GOVERNMENT AND SOCIETY
TUDOR TIMES (ENGLISH HISTORY IN PICTURES)
THE REFORMATION CRISIS
ELIZABETHAN PEOPLE: STATE AND SOCIETY

Freedom, Corruption and Government
IN ELIZABETHAN ENGLAND

JOEL HURSTFIELD

*Astor Professor of English History
in the University of London*

091731

HARVARD UNIVERSITY PRESS

CAMBRIDGE, MASSACHUSETTS

1973

Central Bible College Library
Springfield, Missouri

THIS COMPILATION FIRST PUBLISHED 1973
INTRODUCTION AND COMPILATION COPYRIGHT © 1973 BY JOEL HURSTFIELD

'Was there a Tudor despotism after all?'
© 1967 by Joel Hurstfield
'The paradox of liberty in Shakespeare's England'
© 1972 by Joel Hurstfield
'Church and state, 1558–1612: the task of the Cecils'
© 1965 by Joel Hurstfield
'The succession struggle in late Elizabethan England'
© 1961 University of London
'Political corruption in Modern England'
© 1967 Historical Association
'Corruption and reform under Edward VI and Mary' (1953),
copyright jointly held by Longman Group Ltd and Joel Hurstfield
'The political morality of early Stuart statesmen'
© 1971 Historical Association
'Tradition and change in the English Renaissance'
© 1967 Thames and Hudson
'County government: Wiltshire c.1530–c.1660'
© 1967 University of London
'Office-holding and government mainly in England and France'
© 1968 Cambridge University Press
'Gunpowder Plot and the politics of dissent'
© 1970 by Joel Hurstfield

ALL RIGHTS RESERVED

Library of Congress Catalog Card Number 73-76380

SBN 674-31925-7

PRINTED IN GREAT BRITAIN

Contents

TO

J. E. NEALE

Magistro Severo Amico Iucundissimo

Author's Note

I have been at work on the material for this book over the last ten years or so. It has been written at intervals, between other books and articles, because I felt that the only way I could tackle it was by exploring certain major themes by taking soundings, as it were, into different periods and different aspects of Tudor society. But I have never lost sight of the central task, which has been to search into the minds and experiences of sixteenth-century Englishmen, to see what they felt about freedom, corruption and the nature of government. When I considered that I had completed work on a particular issue, I submitted the article for publication to editors of journals or, in some cases, to the publishers of commissioned books.

I gratefully acknowledge permission to reproduce the essays in this volume granted by the following: Athlone Press, for 'The succession struggle in late Elizabethan England', from *Elizabethan Government and Society*; Cambridge University Press, for 'Office-holding and government in England and France', from the *New Cambridge Modern History*, Vol. III; the Ecclesiastical History Society and *Studies in Church History*, for 'Church and state, 1558–1612: the task of the Cecils'; the English Association and John Murray Ltd and Humanities Press, New York, for 'The paradox of liberty in Shakespeare's England,' from *Essays and Studies 1972*; the Historical Association and *History*, for 'Political corruption in modern England: the historian's problem' and 'The political morality of early Stuart statesmen'; Longman Group Ltd and *English Historical Review*, for 'Corruption and reform under Edward VI and Mary: the example of wardship'; the Royal Historical Society, for 'Was there a Tudor despotism after all?', from *Transactions of the Royal Historical Society*, 5th series, vol. 17, 1967; Thames and Hudson Ltd, for 'Tradition and change in the English Renaissance', from *The Age of the Renaissance*

(1967); the Victoria County History Committee of the Institute of Historical Research, University of London, for 'County Government: Wiltshire *c.*1530–*c.*1660', from *Victoria History of the Counties of England: Wiltshire*, vol. 5 (1967), pp. 80–110; University of Minnesota Press, for 'Gunpowder Plot and the politics of dissent'.

I should also like to thank The Clarendon Press for permission to quote from *Cranfield: Politics and Profits under the Early Stuarts* by Menna Prestwich.

I acknowledge with gratitude the scholarly care and patience of Miss Jane Berkoff of Messrs Jonathan Cape Ltd in seeing this book through the press, and the typing and other assistance given me by Mrs Katie Edwards of University College, London.

For the sake of unity and continuity I have in a few places extended the range of this book beyond the specific dates of the reign of Elizabeth; and I have throughout left the essays in their original form, save for minor textual alterations.

University College London   J.H.
June 1972

Introduction:
The boundaries of freedom

A historian, in writing about the past, cannot altogether escape being caught up in the issues and controversies he is studying. His aim is detachment but, even with the best will and the best skill in the world, no man can wholly accomplish it. The men of the past subtly weave their web around him; and he may find himself participating in their conflicts as though they were his own. There is, however, another hazard no less important in its effects; and that is built into the material he uses. He may understand the words that men spoke and wrote without grasping the assumptions which underlay their speeches and writings. For the assumptions, being assumptions, are not normally put into words. Yet these assumptions, so elusive to the historian writing about another age, are fundamental to his understanding, for they provide the quality and texture of society itself.

I can explain this more fully by means of a modern example. If I were to write a book today about freedom in twentieth-century England, I would not include a section discussing whether slavery is right or wrong. That is because my readers and I share the assumption that it *is* wrong. If I write about reform of the law, I do not include any lengthy discussion on the death penalty because many of my fellow Englishmen and I are agreed that capital punishment should not be imposed—though that would not have been the case ten years ago. Probably my readers and I have common assumptions also about war and peace, cruelty to children and to animals, and about the treatment of the old and the infirm. (On the other hand, we may operate from different bases in talking about democracy, unemployment or political and social corruption.) In short, our assumptions are sufficiently well known not to need to be formally stated. And

if this is so when I am writing a work on politics and government, it is far more so when I am making a speech or writing a
letter.

But when I am studying the Elizabethans, I am doing so at a
distance of four hundred years. How can I know when I read
their speeches and letters what they assumed about liberty
or government, quite apart from the particular points they
were discussing? Of course, their statutes and lawsuits, their
pamphlets and letters will tell me something; and slowly and
painfully I may move forward to the roots of their society,
to the assumptions they lived by. Failure to do so has, I think,
led to a great deal of historical controversy, not all of it
fruitful.

In earlier books I have, on a number of occasions, argued that
the historian is not only concerned with the constitution and
machinery of government, though he must master these, but
with the gap, narrow or wide, between the will of a government and its power. To these questions I revert in the pages
which follow. But, in recent years, my dominant concern—I
almost write obsession—has been to discover something more
about liberty, order and corruption in the Tudor context. The
papers now collected in this volume represent my attempts
during the past decade to explore these questions, more especially
during the Elizabethan period. I wanted to try and find out
what the Tudor monarchs and their subjects thought these
things meant; how much freedom and order they wanted; how
far they fell short of their aims, and why. By what means could
governmental authority be imposed on the people, and how
corrupt was Tudor society? To none of these questions have I
presumed to give a definitive answer. But I have suggested
certain interim conclusions, and I hope that I have indicated some
lines of research which could be profitably pursued. The historian
engaged in the study of freedom, for example, must always ask
himself two questions in respect of a past society. The first is:
how free were they in their own terms? The second is: how free
were they in our terms? The historian who professes no interest

in this second question has gone too far in isolating the present from the past.[1]

My own developing views have been modified by a number of influences. The first is the reading of the documents themselves. History is, as it were, a 'cumulative' subject. As the historian comes to feel at ease with the materials of his period, so they develop, enlarge and make more complex the notions he has received from his predecessors and from his own earlier researches. This often forces him to question the 'establishment' view, however assiduously that view may be pressed and however fierce the denigration of dissenting opinion. His intimacy with his materials obliges him to ask new questions, and the answers which emerge may undermine the received notions about the past. Some historians have the interesting experience, throughout their lives, of coming upon documents which marvellously confirm the conclusions they had themselves presented many years earlier. Such discoveries may be encouraging to the discoverer but I doubt whether they serve any greater purpose. For the historian who is too busy defending an entrenched position will lose his capacity to go foraging into the open country.

Certainly, as I look back and read some of the things I once wrote about freedom and consent in the sixteenth century, for example, I find that I can no longer use the words in the senses I did then. For many historians (including of course myself) have, it seems to me, used these words outside their historical context. Or, to put it another way, we have used sixteenth-century words on two levels, the Tudors' and our own.

The word 'consent' is central to one of the themes of this book. To our ears, consent means voluntary agreement freely entered into by two or more persons or groups of people. It must be voluntary and it must be agreed: otherwise there is no consent. When we use the word in politics we mean that the people have had an opportunity to participate freely in the choice of the

---

[1] The best recent general discussion of some of the problems arising from the relations between freedom and government is in Sir Isaiah Berlin's *Four Essays on Liberty* (Oxford, 1969).

government (though the choice may be limited to one of two parties) and that they can in due course participate again in maintaining or changing the government at the next election. Political consent assumes, also, freedom to criticize the government and its actions throughout the whole period of its existence. And this may be more important than any election. If these conditions prevail then I live in a society and under a government based on consent.

Now, if I suggested that these conditions could or should have been established in the sixteenth century, I should be guilty of an absurdity and a manifest anachronism. But, and this is the crux of the matter, sixteenth-century writers like Sir Thomas Smith[1] used the word consent, and they believed that they lived in a society based on it. So did others. But this was a hierarchical society: in theory there was a place for everyman, and everyman knew his place. It was based on both paternalism and patronage. In politics and much else the master gave consent on behalf of his servant, and most servants accepted it. A lord lieutenant of Wiltshire found himself obliged to warn his suitors in search of patronage that though some must govern others must obey.[2] Elizabeth's lord treasurer held the same view: 'All must not be like,' said Lord Burghley, 'some must rule, some obey.'[3] Most people who thought about the question at all would have agreed with this view of consent. But doubts existed: the Anabaptists, the Family of Love, the Levellers and the Diggers did not grow up out of nowhere; and they held some unconventional views about who gave consent on behalf of whom.

However, let us accept that most people acquiesced in the notion of consent as promulgated by the Tudor governing class. Do we then simply report the matter and rubber stamp these acceptable views? Surely the historian goes on to point out that elections were not free, that most people did not have the

[1] Sir Thomas Smith, *De Republica Anglorum*, ed. L. Alston (Cambridge, 1906), p. 49; below, p. 41.
[2] A. H. Dodd, 'The pattern of politics in Stuart Wales', *Trans. Hon. Soc. Cymmrodorion* (1948), p. 10; below, p. 241.
[3] See below, p. 84.

vote, that publication of religious and political dissent was usually prohibited and that there was a steady stream of propaganda, issuing from government sources, to justify the official policies. Some obvious examples are the preambles to statutes and proclamations, and the official account, setting forth the nature of his treason, issued on the morrow of the execution of a public figure. I do not for one moment deny that many — but by no means all — of the controls and restraints were essential for national security and survival. Nor do I suggest for one moment that the Tudors could or should have established the modern principles and machinery for consent. But I must also, at the same time, say that they are using the word consent in their sense and not in ours. I would add the generalization that where freedom of expression, of publication, of election do not exist, then no matter in which period or country it is found, this is not a society based on freedom.

This is no mere exercise in semantics. It is a basic problem of historiography. For it raises the fundamental question: does the historian base his conclusions on what contemporaries say of their own society or does he employ an independent set of criteria? Should the historian adopt a contemporary and changing scale for each period he studies or should he, slowly and painfully, move forward towards a series of general historical principles, which will enable him to understand the nature of liberty, corruption and other features of past societies? I think that he should continue to search for generalizations. If he has a contribution to make to the social sciences — as I believe he has — then it lies in his capacity to offer generalizations about society, seen over the long perspective of time.

The second influence on my writing is exterior to my Tudor studies. I spent some years in a government department, as the result of which I wrote a book on an aspect of policy and its implementation.[1] During this period I saw official and unofficial documents, ranging from cabinet minutes to the most insignificant correspondence on the most trivial matters. More

[1] *The Control of Raw Materials* (1953). All books are published in London, except where otherwise stated.

important, I saw policy in the process of its making, and more important still to my training as a historian, I saw records in the process of manufacture. I could see the relationship between internal departmental discussion, a parliamentary draft and an official 'handout' – the publicity material which accompanies ministerial and parliamentary decisions. Of course, the processes of government in the sixteenth century were different from our own; but the problems of government, in some of their fundamentals, were similar. The lesson I learned was a simple one, familiar to some historians, yet surprisingly unfamiliar to others. It was that one must distinguish between what a government says and what it does; between the statute and the means by which it was made; between the form of government and the realities; between the propaganda and the practices.

What I learned in a government department, I learned, too, from the experiences of living in a changing world and in an age of political and social revolution. For here also one learned always to observe the distinction between the paper constitution and the political practice. We could all name modern states which have constitutions worthy of Athenian democracy at a moment of perfection, constitutions in which the liberty of the individual is protected in the most sonorous language, and which at the same time operate all the apparatus of police control with great skill and devotion. In short, we have learned in our own day to distinguish, as that great Elizabethan, Peter Wentworth, put it, between the name of liberty and the thing itself.[1]

Here we run into a different problem. England has never had a violent revolution; her public buildings have not been burned down, her records have survived. And, as everyone knows, it is government rather than private records which survived in abundance, and in sometimes continuous series. We have plenty of unofficial documents and some of those have been extensively used. But, until recent years, historians, theses supervisors and postgraduate students have been mainly, and understandably, attracted to the official records, to the machinery of government. The result is that we know a vast amount about the mechanics

[1] J. E. Neale, *Elizabeth I and Her Parliaments 1559–1581* (1953), p. 319.

of government, and the technical processes of the constitution, much less about the processes of social change, or the relationship between the government and the community it governed. When a historian argues that royal power rested on popular support,[1] he presents to the historian of a later generation almost intractable problems. How do we know that Henry VIII enjoyed public support, as compared with acquiescence, and how can we discover what public opinion was, and how it was made? We are back once more at the problem of consent.

No one alive today who is aware of the problem of consent can fail also to be aware of the importance of communication and the techniques of communicators which have developed in the present generation. The first revolution in communication, that of printing, deserves to be widely discussed.[2] The second, in broadcasting and television, has not yet worked itself out and the consequences are impossible to assess. But no less important in its effects is the rapid growth of a whole army of communicators, including the advertising copywriters and the public relations officers. Some believe that these professions render some kind of public service; others hold that they are mere parasites on the common weal. But for the historian what is most important is the ancestry of this profession, and the part the early communicators played in creating public opinion and in making government opinion acceptable to the nation as a whole. Already some important work has been done in this field[3] and we know something, for example, about how public support or acquiescence was won. This, of course, is quite apart from the use of statutes *in terrorem*.

[1] G. M. Trevelyan, *History of England* (1926), p. 366; below, pp. 29–30.

[2] See e.g. H. S. Bennett, *English Books and Readers, 1475–1603* (2 vols., Cambridge, 1952, 1965); Eleanor Rosenberg, *Leicester: Patron of Letters* (New York, 1955); Elizabeth L. Eisenstein, 'The advent of printing and the problem of the Renaissance', *Past and Present*, no. 49 (1969), pp. 19–89, and no. 52 (1971), pp. 135–144.

[3] W. G. Zeeveld, *Foundations of Tudor Policy* (1948); R. C. Strong and J. A. Van Dorsten, *Leicester's Triumph* (Leyden, 1964); Frances Yates, 'Queen Elizabeth as Astraea', *Journal of Warburg and Courtauld Institute*, x (1947), 27–82; R. C. Strong, 'The popular celebration of the accession day of Queen Elizabeth I', ibid., xxi (1958), pp. 86–103.

Our difficulty in writing about the Tudor period lies in discovering just how much support, active or passive, was given to the government, and how much of it was a response to the continual pressure of propaganda, misrepresentation, persuasion of various kinds, threats and a heavy, though not always successful, censorship. What can be said in our present state of knowledge is that there is no simple equation to explain the relationship between government and people, and that there is a complicated balancing of forces between the will of a state and the needs and desires of its people. But the measure of a free society is in the diversity of its sources of knowledge and opinion. A social order which is hostile to diversity is itself hostile to freedom.

Freedom and consent: what do they mean in the Tudor context? How shall we define them? The first section of this book attempts to discover how these things appeared to the practising politicians and writers of the time; and more particularly I have been concerned to see what links there are between freedom and equality. In the second section I explore these and related questions in the field of religion; and from there I turn to the problem of corruption, to see how far we can define it in the period. (And here I add that, though I dissent from some of Mrs Prestwich's conclusions in her excellent book, I greatly value her close examination of the available sources.[1]) I devote my last section to surveying the pattern and balancing of forces within English society.

There is no acknowledged frontier between what the individual has liberty to do and what the state has authority to restrain. But the sixteenth century has a special interest in that respect because it was the first period since classical times in which the frontier began to be vigorously disputed all along its length. Once again in our own day fierce battles have erupted at many established positions and no man can say where, in the end, the line will hold. The essays which follow, concerned as they are with a past age, offer no solutions to the problems which confront us; but

[1] See below, pp. 183–96.

they may perhaps shed light on some of the questions which need to be asked.[1]

★　　★　　★

This book is dedicated to Sir John Neale, my teacher and life-long friend. With some of the arguments presented here, I believe he will agree. With others he will perhaps disagree. But from him in the lecture-room I first heard the doctrine: 'There are no pundits in history. Each scholar must be free to reach his conclusions in the light of his reason and research.' I hope that this book will show to him that I never forgot the lesson he taught me; and that I believe now, as ever, that the study of history flourishes best amidst diversity of opinion.

---

[1] While this book was in the press, my friend, Professor G. R. Elton published an article, 'The rule of law in sixteenth-century England', (in *Tudor Men and Institutions*, ed. A. J. Slavin, Baton Rouge, 1972) which is, in part, a reply to my 'Was there a Tudor despotism after all?'. I propose to comment on his article in a later work: it must suffice here to say that it is extremely welcome that the whole issue of liberty in Tudor England is once again open to discussion. Historians have perhaps, in the recent past, been inclined to attach a disproportionate importance to contemporary official opinion.

Part I · Liberty and Authority

I

Was there a Tudor despotism after all?

In the reign of James I, Sir Walter Ralegh, a prisoner in the Tower and under sentence of death, occupied some of his leisure in writing a *History of the World*. Unfortunately, he never got beyond 130 B.C.; but in his Introduction he did pause to comment on more recent history. Now that Elizabeth I was dead, he felt able to speak quite freely about her father:

> Now for King Henry the Eight: if all the pictures and patterns of a merciless prince were lost in the world, they might all again be painted to the life, out of the story of this King. For how many servants did he advance in haste (but for what vertue no man could suspect) and with the change of his fancy ruined again, no man knowing for what offence? To how many others of more desert gave he abundant flowers, from whence to gather Hony, and in the end of Harvest burnt them in the Hive?[1]

Now, as it happens, this is not the isolated opinion of an embittered and disappointed man who had been a failure in politics. King James I – who agreed with Ralegh in nothing else – agreed with him in this.[2] So did Sir Robert Cecil.[3] So did many historians writing in the eighteenth and nineteenth centuries. It was not until the middle of the nineteenth century, when James

NOTE: First published in *Transactions of the Royal Historical Society* (1967), 5th Ser., xvii, pp. 83–108.

[1] W. Ralegh, *The History of the World* (1687), p. viii.
[2] See the passage cited in G. R. Elton, 'Henry VIII's Act of Proclamations', *Eng. Hist. Rev.* (1960), lxxv, p. 228.
[3] *Proceedings in Parliament, 1610*, ed. Elizabeth R. Foster (New Haven and London, 1966), i, pp. 231–2.

Anthony Froude was publishing his *History*, that a new picture began to be drawn.[1] In Froude's books Henry VIII emerges not as an autocrat forcing a revolution on a subject people but as the authentic voice of English liberty and independence, both the architect and the saviour of the English nation. But the effect of Froude's *History*, as of everything else he wrote, was to stir a controversy rather than to resolve a doubt. It would, in any case, be of little profit to ponder over the posthumous reputation of Henry VIII were it not that it raises much larger questions of freedom, authority and self-government. The question which our predecessors asked, as we do today, is: did the people of sixteenth-century England consent to the government which ruled over them?

This is not just a modern question thrust anachronistically on a past age. Englishmen of the sixteenth and seventeenth centuries were much concerned with this fundamental problem of self-government. 'What is it that you would have?' asked Oliver Cromwell, at the height of his power, of the irrepressible Ludlow who presumed to criticize him. 'That which we fought for,' was the answer, 'that the nation might be governed by its own consent.'[2] He was merely expressing with a soldierly brevity what, eighty years before, Peter Wentworth was saying in the House of Commons in his magnificent Elizabethan prose.[3]

When I was an undergraduate, the conception that Tudor England was governed by a despotism was the received doctrine, although it was beginning to show signs of strain. Now, apparently, the position is quite otherwise. 'Tudor despotism' — I am quoting from an undergraduate essay presented to me earlier this year — 'which was supposed to be a fusion of "Lancastrian constitutionalism" and "Yorkist tyranny" has long joined the other two terms in the dustbin.' From that opinion I ventured to dissent; but it is not simply to register my dissent that I have prepared this paper. My own recent work has increasingly pressed

[1] J. A. Froude, *A History of England, from the fall of Wolsey to the defeat of the Spanish Armada* (1856–70), many times reprinted.

[2] *The Memoirs of Edmund Ludlow*, ed. C. H. Firth (Oxford, 1894), ii, p. 11.

[3] Cited in J. E. Neale, *Elizabeth I and her Parliaments* (1953), i, pp. 318–25.

doubts upon me about the accepted notions of Tudor rule. Somehow one must analyse and explain the enormous gap between the constitution and the political reality; between those who wielded authority and those who merely legalized its use; between the language of law and the facts of life. This surely is the historian's problem: where in fact lay the roots of power?

The notion that the sixteenth century saw the rise of a Tudor despotism derived in part from the belief of historians as to what had been happening in the fifteenth, a belief which I shall attempt, all too briefly, to summarize. To Stubbs and his contemporaries, the first half of the fifteenth century saw an extraordinary exercise in self-government, which they designated the Lancastrian experiment.[1] According to this seductive thesis, the usurping Henry IV, anxious to make his government acceptable, made a bid for middle-class support as represented in the House of Commons. Here, then, under the Lancastrians was the first, premature essay in parliamentary government, a fragile, insecure thing which collapsed in the disordered years of Henry VI. There followed the factious struggle of the aristocracy and the chaos of civil war until, under the Yorkists, and more especially under the Tudors, a nation, weary alike of constitutional experiment and internal warfare, gladly yielded up its powers to a new monarchy. Hence strong, centralized government was established (or re-established) and this was the Tudor despotism.

In all this there is a great deal of mythology. The Commons, it was later argued, did not foreshadow the democratic spirit of Victorian parliaments; the members were rather the instruments of aristocratic patronage than the assertive representatives of local opinion; and there was no dramatic decline from self-government into autocracy.[2] If, then, the 'Lancastrian experiment' was no more than an exploded myth, the same discredit therefore attached itself to the 'Tudor despotism', which was

[1] W. Stubbs, *The Constitutional History of England* (Oxford, 1878), iii, chapter xviii. See also the valuable re-assessment of Stubbs in Helen M. Cam, 'Stubbs seventy years after', *Camb. Hist. Journal* (1948), ix, pp. 129–47.
[2] See e.g. G. O. Sayles, *The Medieval Foundations of England* (1958), pp. 464–5 and references given on p. 465.

under fire for other reasons as well. For the fifteenth century, however, the pendulum has begun to swing back, in the writings of Professor Roskell, Sir Goronwy Edwards and others, not towards the notion of an experiment but to acknowledge a greater maturity in the House of Commons than recent critics would allow.[1] But the concept of a Tudor despotism did not share in this recovery. As every schoolboy knows, it was shattered beyond repair; and it is only on a quiet Saturday afternoon in Chelsea, and in the company of a handful of scholars — all personal friends — that I would presume to ask whether the demolition squad has been too zealous in its work.

But first I must define my terms. If by despotism we mean only that form of society in which the government is supreme and unchallenged; in which no divergent expression is possible; and in which all aspects of life are entirely under the control of one central power; then we shall seek in vain for it in any past or present society. However harsh a regime, it could be acquitted of the charge of despotism. For all governments are no stronger than their weakest human link; and every government, however tyrannical, encounters resistance, either voluntary or involuntary, from some at least of the people it governs. But if we regard despotism as authoritarian rule in which the government is resolved to enforce its will on a nation and to suppress all expressions of dissent; and if this is a society in which the people have few means of influencing decisions on major issues; then we may find despotisms — of varying degrees of efficiency — at many stages during the evolution of modern society.

The kind of despotism which historians discovered in the sixteenth century varied according to their knowledge of the period and their sensibility to the colour and texture of Tudor English. For it was in the sixteenth century that Englishmen were for the first time speaking a language closely identifiable with our

[1] J. S. Roskell, *The Commons in the Parliament of 1422* (Manchester 1954) and his article 'Perspectives in English Parliamentary History', *Bull. of the John Rylands Library* (1964), xlvi, pp. 448–75; J. G. Edwards, *The Commons in Medieval English Parliaments* (1958); A. L. Brown, 'The Commons and the Council in the reign of Henry IV', *Eng. Hist. Rev.* (1964), lxxix, pp. 1–30.

own, or at least easily mistaken for it. The study of semantics is no part of the training of a historian and we are liable, therefore, to fall into every linguistic trap that lies hidden below the thin surface of the documents we handle. I have constantly to remind myself that, although a Tudor politician spoke our language, he did not think our thoughts. If we take merely these dynamite words, liberty, representation, parliament, law, kingdom, empire, not a single one of them meant to him what it means to us. In most cases, the meanings which these words have acquired would have been repulsive to the governing classes of Tudor England. Or if not repulsive, then as incomprehensible as would have been Sir Edward Coke's views on Magna Carta to the barons of thirteenth-century England. If, then, we use phrases like limited monarchy or the supremacy of statute we should tread warily for we have somehow wandered into a minefield.

To John Richard Green, writing in 1874 his *Short History of the English People*, 'the character of the monarchy from the time of Edward the Fourth to the days of Elizabeth, remains something strange and isolated in our history'. Parliament was reduced to submission, liberty was 'almost extinguished', 'justice was de-graded'. 'To careless observers of a later day the constitutional monarchy of the Edwards and the Henries seems suddenly to have transformed itself under the Tudors into a despotism as complete as the despotism of the Turk.' 'Such a view', he adds gravely, 'is no doubt exaggerated and unjust.' No doubt it is. But, according to Green, this was no government by consent, save in this respect: landowner and merchant alike dreaded the return of war and disorder. So 'the landed and monied classes clung passionately to the Monarchy, as the one great force which could save them from social revolt ... It was to the selfish panic of both landowner and merchant that she [England] owed the despotism of the monarchy.'[1]

If there is something *simpliste* in all this, Bishop Stubbs writing his Oxford lectures seven years later saw Henry VIII and his government in much the same light, although the language is

---

[1] J. R. Green, *History of the English People* (1878), ii, pp. 6–7, 21. I am quoting from the fuller version which appeared soon after the *Short History*.

more temperate. 'From the very beginning of his reign', he writes, 'he is finding out what he can do; from the fall of Wolsey, and especially after the sacrifice of More, he is coming to regard what he can do as the only measure of what he ought to do: he is becoming the king for whom the kingdom is, the tyrant whose every caprice is wise and sacred.' Elsewhere he speaks of the system as 'the Tudor dictatorship'.[1] Some seven years after this, Maitland, lecturing at Cambridge, saw the power of Henry VIII within a subtle and more complex constitutional pattern. Like Green and Stubbs, he considered that the House of Lancaster was 'in a measure identified with a tradition of parliamentary government' and that the House of York was 'bound up with a claim to rule in defiance of statutes'. Yet, Maitland emphasizes, the constitutional restraints remain. The king has 'no theoretic claim to be above the law'.[2] His powers are still within the framework that Fortescue set out in the generation before the accession of the Tudors.[3] But theory and practice are parting company. The constitutional restraints are being turned into organs of royal government. 'The King', says Maitland, 'is beginning to find out that parliamentary institutions can be made the engines of his will.'[4] This is, of course, still autocracy but it is autocracy within a parliamentary framework.

Maitland wrote as a constitutional historian, as did A. F. Pollard when, in 1902, he brought out his masterly study of Henry VIII. But to the skills of a constitutional historian he added high skills also as a biographer. Although he came closer than any other historian to understanding the king, he did not fall under his spell — or perhaps I should say, because of this understanding. He saw Henry as an able ruler, ruthless, egotistical yet with a profound sense of the national interest which he bound up with his own. 'His dictatorship', writes Pollard, 'was the child of the

---

[1] W. Stubbs, *Seventeen Lectures, on the study of medieval and modern history* (Oxford, 1886), pp. 246, 262.

[2] F. W. Maitland, *The Constitutional History of England* (Cambridge, 1955), pp. 194–9.

[3] John Fortescue, *De Laudibus Legum Angliae*, ed. S. B. Chrimes (Cambridge, 1942); *The Governance of England*, ed. C. Plummer (Oxford, 1885).

[4] Maitland, op. cit., p. 199.

Wars of the Roses and his people ... were willing to bear with a much more arbitrary government than they would have been in less perilous times. The alternatives may have been evil but the choice was freely made.' *The choice was freely made.*[1] Here is the basic assumption to which I shall shortly return. But to Pollard Henry was none the less a despot who believed that autocracy was the only means to safeguard the nation; and to this end the whole apparatus of the state was directed. 'No king was so careful of law,' he writes, 'but he was not so careful of justice. Therein lay his safety, for the law takes no cognizance of justice, unless the injustice is also a breach of the law, and Henry rarely, if ever, broke the law.'[2] Pollard did not disguise the price that was paid. 'The nation purchased political salvation at the price of moral debasement; the individual was sacrificed on the altar of the State; and popular subservience proved the impossibility of saving a people from itself.'[3] Yet built into Pollard's thesis was as we can see, the doctrine of popular consent. '*The choice*', he said, '*was freely made.*'

The critical qualifications in Pollard's analysis were lost in the work of some of his successors. G. M. Trevelyan, writing in much more general terms, saw parliamentary consent as an active expression of the popular will. His *History of England*, published in 1926, is not a work of original research but it was widely read and reflects the revival of a romantic attitude to the Tudor period as a whole. 'In the Tudor epoch', he writes, 'the nation asserted its new strength and ... claimed the right to do whatever it liked within its own frontiers.' All this was 'embodied in the person of the Prince. This is the general cause of the Kingworship of the Sixteenth Century.' 'The plenary powers of the new State', Trevelyan believed, 'could in that age have been exercised only by the King.' King and Privy Council, he says, taught the parliamentarians and the justices of the peace the work of government, so long neglected. 'Parliament', he writes, warming up to a

---

[1] A. F. Pollard, *Henry VIII* (1930), p. 429. See also C. H. Williams, *The Making of the Tudor Despotism* (2nd edn, 1935), chapter VIII.

[2] Pollard, op. cit., pp. 435–6.

[3] Ibid., p. 438.

wholly misleading analogy, 'was ready to be the scholar and servant of royalty, like a prentice serving his time and fitting himself to become partner and heir.' So Henry VIII 'set the new Monarchy in alliance with the strongest forces of the coming age'.[1] And then, looking again at the position at the end of the century, Trevelyan saw in it the fulfilment of the early prospects. That individual liberty did not exist he fully acknowledged, yet he managed to find in Tudor England the basic conditions of acceptance. 'England was not a despotism. The power of the crown rested not on force but on popular support.'[2] Here in its full splendour and conviction was the doctrine of consent. The hand is the hand of Trevelyan but the voice is the voice of Froude.

A good deal of this is a flight of fancy on the part of Trevelyan; yet it reflected views widely held among historians. But in a general work of this sort his account was vague, question-begging and inevitably brief. As is often the case in such a discussion, the evidence is implicit rather than explicit; but the argument is familiar. That is, the Crown had no standing army, no adequate revenue, no effective administrative machinery, no reliable system of communications – all of them essential to a strong government which aims to enforce its will on the nation as a whole. Therefore, so the argument runs, the government could not have imposed its will and could only have survived because it gave voice to the will of the community. These then are the two central assumptions of modern historical writing: that the government could not exercise the force necessary for an autocracy and that it survived because its will was based on popular consent freely given. If, however, it can be shown that the government *did* have means for imposing its will and secondly, if there are doubts as to whether it rested on popular consent freely given, then the whole subject of Tudor despotism is once again open for debate among historians.

I have said that Trevelyan's arguments are general and implicit. In the work of Dr G. R. Elton, on the other hand, the relations between the Crown and Parliament are analysed in the course of a

---

[1] G. M. Trevelyan, *History of England* (1926), pp. 269–70.
[2] Ibid., p. 366.

deep study of an extensive range of governmental documents. On the basis of his evidence, which we shall examine shortly, Dr Elton writes:

> Thus the political events and constitutional expansion of the 1530s produced major changes in the position of Parliament. Long and frequent sessions, fundamental and far-reaching measures, revolutionary consequences, governmental leader-ship—all these combined with the Crown's devotion to statute and use of Parliament to give that institution a new air, even to change it essentially into its modern form as the supreme and sovereign legislator.[1]

The best summary of Dr Elton's standpoint is given in his textbook on sixteenth-century England, where he writes: 'Whatever may have been the case before Cromwell's work—whatever Wolsey may have stood for—there was no Tudor despotism after it. Wittingly or not—and the present writer has no doubt that it was done wittingly—Cromwell established the reformed state as a limited monarchy and not as a despotism.'[2] With these words, it may be said, the obsequies upon the notion of a Tudor despotism were finally spoken. Tudor despotism was not only dead but buried.

Or was it? In any discussion of the nature and aims of early Tudor government we are at once confronted with the problem of Thomas Cromwell. In this we are fortunate in having R. B. Merriman's *Life and Letters of Thomas Cromwell*,[3] published in 1902, and the various articles and books by Dr Elton, of which the most important is his *Tudor Revolution in Government*, published in 1953.[4] Merriman's book is valuable for what he prints of Cromwell's papers rather than for what he says himself; for

---

[1] *The Tudor Constitution*, edited and introduced by G. R. Elton (Cambridge, 1960), p. 234.
[2] G. R. Elton, *England under the Tudors* (1955), p. 168.
[3] R. B. Merriman, *Life and Letters of Thomas Cromwell* (2 vols., Oxford, 1902).
[4] G. R. Elton, *The Tudor Revolution in Government* (Cambridge, 1953). See also his important *Policy and Police: the enforcement of the Reformation in the age of Thomas Cromwell*, which appeared in 1972.

his views are extreme and his evidence not always strong enough to sustain them.[1] But it was an important pioneer work.

For a more detailed presentation of Cromwell's position, however, we must turn to Dr Elton's paper, 'The political creed of Thomas Cromwell', read before this Society in 1955,[2] and some of the materials presented in his *Tudor Constitution*, published in 1960.[3] In his paper, Dr Elton rejects the view that Cromwell was hostile to Parliament and favoured autocracy, and rejects, too, the alternative view that he was not seriously interested in Parliament as an expression of constitutional rights. On the contrary, Dr Elton argues, Cromwell believed in the supremacy of statute, that is, of the Crown in Parliament. As part of his evidence, Dr Elton, who has counted the statutes as well as the pages of the statute book, shows that far more public Acts were passed in the eight years of Cromwell's dominance than in the twenty-two years which preceded it, and only seventy-nine less than in the whole reign of Elizabeth. Or again, Cromwell's eight years require 409 pages of the printed *Statutes of the Realm* while Elizabeth's whole reign takes up no more than 666 pages. I am myself reluctant to attempt to measure the quality of parliamentary government by weight; and I am not at all sure that the more statutes passed means the greater limits upon the Crown's power. After all, four of Henry's marriages were ended either by nullification or execution, or both, and each needed a lengthy statute.

More important is a famous passage, cited by Dr Elton, in which Cromwell made an amusing comment to a correspondent about the deliberations of the House of Commons during 1523, deliberations which stretched on over seventeen weeks. Cromwell wrote:

... by long tyme I amongist other haue Indured a parlyament which contenwid by the space of xvij hole wekes wher we communyd of warre pease Stryffe contencyon debatte

---

[1] See e.g. Merriman, op. cit., i, pp. 89–94.

[2] G. R. Elton, 'The political creed of Thomas Cromwell', *Transactions of the Royal Historical Society* (1956), 5th Ser., vi, pp. 69–92.

[3] *The Tudor Constitution*, ed. Elton, esp. pp. 21–2, 283–6.

murmure grudge Riches pouerte penurye trowth falshode Justyce equyte discayte opprescyon Magnanymyte actyuyte force attempraunce Treason murder Felonye consyli ... and also how a commune welth myght be ediffyed and also contenewid within our Realme. Howbeyt in conclusyon we haue done as our predecessors haue been wont to doo that ys to say, as well as we myght and lefte wher we begann.[1]

Dr Elton tells us that he finds it 'a little difficult to understand why writer after writer has taken this amusing note to show contempt for Parliament'.[2] I do not share Dr Elton's difficulty. As I see it, this is the comment of a bored, impatient, cynical man who has suffered beyond endurance the unquenchable eloquence of the politicians. 'We might suspect even from this letter', writes Dr Elton, 'that Cromwell was fascinated by the work and potentialities of Parliament.' With respect, I should like to suggest that the fascination is somewhat muted; and that he is saying that the whole business dragging on over the last seventeen weeks has been a total waste of time. Robert Cecil, Earl of Salisbury, another vigorous minister, would have shared his opinion. The 'wisdom of former ages', he said, 'affected not long parliaments; they are neither good for the king nor the people'.[3] Cromwell, like Cecil, wanted legislation not deliberation.

But this is evidence at the perimeter of the argument. More central to our problem is the matter of the Statute of Proclamations of 1539.[4] It must first be emphasized that we are talking about the statute — which is what the government got at the end — and not the bill — which was what the government wanted. The bill has not survived: all that we know about it is that it ran into stubborn resistance, long remembered; and all historians agree now that the demands of the government must have been larger than Parliament or the statute would allow. It should, secondly, be

---

[1] Merriman, op. cit., i, p. 313.

[2] Elton, 'The political creed of Thomas Cromwell', pp. 79–80.

[3] *Proceedings in Parliament, 1610*, ed. Foster, i, p. xi and ii, p. 301.

[4] 31 Hen. VIII, c.8. Large excerpts from it are printed in *Tudor Constitutional Documents*, ed. J. R. Tanner (Cambridge, 1922), pp. 532–5, and in *The Tudor Constitution*, ed. Elton, pp. 27–30.

stressed that the statute, in its final form, gave no large extension to royal authority. It used to be thought that it stood at the apex of the Tudor advance to autocracy; but, under scrutiny, the statute turns out to be rather a tame affair. It did not give the Crown's proclamations the force of law, save in a limited sphere, and it restrained the Crown from issuing proclamations which conflicted with the common law. The statute gave very little to the Crown that it did not already possess. On this, too, all historians are now agreed.

But to earlier historians this celebrated statute seemed to present the gravest threat to the survival of self-government in England. The king's will as expressed in proclamations (so it was thought) would carry the force of law: statute would be superseded, consent would be unnecessary, Parliament would atrophy. The central doctrine of Roman civil law—*quod principi placuit legis habet vigorem*—would be the dominant theme of English government and society. So Merriman and those who followed him believed.[1] How are we to explain this? I think that this error arose because earlier scholars paid too much attention to the preamble and too little to clause II, which is the most important enacting clause. As we re-read the preamble, it is easy to see how the older interpretation of the statute arose:

Forasmuch as the King's most royal Majesty for divers considerations by the advice of his Council hath heretofore set forth divers and sundry his Grace's proclamations, as well for and concerning divers and sundry articles of Christ's religion, as for an unity and concord to be had amongst the loving and obedient subjects of this his realm and other his dominions, and also concerning the advancement of his commonwealth and good quiet of his people, which nevertheless divers and many froward, wilful and obstinate persons have wilfully contemned and broken, not considering what a

[1] Merriman, op. cit., i, pp. 123–5. But Maitland saw the significance of the supremacy of statute, namely that these powers derived from Parliament. Maitland, *The Constitutional History of England*, pp. 253–5. But once bestowed, how can these powers be withdrawn if the king does not choose to summon Parliament? See below, pp. 37–8, 39.

King by his royal power may do, and for lack of a direct statute and law to coarct offenders to obey the said proclamations, which being still suffered should not only encourage offenders to the disobedience of the precepts and laws of Almighty God, but also sin too much to the great dishonour of the King's most royal Majesty, who may full ill bear it, and also give too great heart and boldness to all malefactors and offenders; considering also that sudden causes and occasions fortune many times which do require speedy remedies, and that by abiding for a Parliament in the mean time might happen great prejudice to ensue to the realm; and weighing also that his Majesty (which by the kingly and regal power given him by God may do many things in such cases) should not be driven to extend the liberty and supremacy of his regal power and dignity by wilfulness of froward subjects; It is therefore thought in manner more than necessary that the King's Highness of this realm for the time being, with the advice of his honourable Council, should make and set forth proclamations for the good and politic order and governance of this his realm of England, Wales, and other his dominions from time to time for the defence of his regal dignity and the advancement of his common-wealth and good quiet of his people, as the cases of necessity shall require, and that an ordinary law should be provided, by the assent of his Majesty and Parliament, for the due punishment, correction, and reformation of such offences and disobediences ... [1]

These are large claims; but when we come to the enacting clauses we find that most of them have disappeared. Clause II excludes the royal power of proclamations from men's 'inheritances, lawful possessions, offices, liberties, privileges, franchises, goods or chattels'. The Crown shall not by proclamation inflict the death penalty (save for heresy); it shall not infringe common law or statute. It is for these reasons that Professor Adair was able to argue that the statute was a relatively innocuous document

[1] The English is here modernized.

designed to improve the judicial machinery of the prerogative to try certain cases, mainly those involving breaches of the Act of Supremacy. This may have been its effect but was it the design? Since this act is taken by Dr Elton to show that Cromwell was anxious to bring proclamation within the framework of statute, we must be careful to distinguish between design and effect, between the bill and the Act. For if we assume that the intention, that is the bill, was so modest in aim, we are left with more unresolved problems than we faced in the time of Maitland.

We know that the original bill encountered severe resistance in both Lords and Commons. The first bill was thrown out and a new one prepared. But was a modest measure of administrative reform likely to suffer so stormy a passage? And why did so innocent a piece of legislation leave so nasty a taste in the mouth that the Protector Somerset hastened to repeal the measure in the first, fine, careless rapture of the new administration?[1] And here we come to the central puzzle—though it contains within itself its own explanation—why are the large claims of the preamble so profoundly at variance with the minimal powers claimed by the subsequent clauses?

We know from many of the statutes that the function of the preambles was to justify and explain whatever new powers the government was hoping to assume by means of the Acts; that they were propaganda devices to state and defend a case; that they were declarations of intent. If that is so, then our statute of 1539 explains itself. The preamble is the declaration of government claims and intentions; the enacting clauses are all that it was left with. Professor Adair is, of course, right when he says that the resulting act brought no significant increase in the royal power.[2] But was that all that the government wanted? Certainly, Stephen Gardiner, who was involved in its making, thought otherwise.[3] Nor is the preamble so restricted. It deals with religion but it is

---

[1] I Ed. VI, c.12.

[2] E. R. Adair, 'The Statute of Proclamations', *Eng. Hist. Rev.* (1917), xxxii, p. 45.

[3] *The Tudor Constitution*, ed. Elton, p. 24.

concerned also with 'unity and concord', with 'the advancement of the commonwealth' and—ominous and familiar Tudor phrases—with the 'good and quiet of his people', the 'boldness of all malefactors and offenders' and so on.

It is said, too, that the statute was not a threat to Parliament for two reasons. In the first place, it rested on parliamentary consent. I am at a loss to see the force of this logic. Of course, Parliament was the acknowledged source of this power of proclamations now to be confided in the Crown; but, once the authority had been granted, why summon Parliament? I do not believe in historical parallels but we are here speaking about fundamental constitutional law; and it is worth considering a modern example where the power of proclamation was conferred by a legislative assembly. In March 1933 the German Reichstag conferred on the chancellor, Adolph Hitler, the right to govern by proclamation. The title of the law is itself interesting: it is the *Gesetz zur Behebung der Not von Volk und Reich*.[1] These words are extremely difficult to translate—the nearest I can get is 'Statute to meet emergencies of the Nation and State'—but the meaning is clear enough. To protect the German nation in a time of emergency, the chancellor can issue edicts which have the force of law. These powers were to last for four years, after which they were duly renewed by the Reichstag, and then renewed periodically until May 1943, when they were again renewed, but this time by the chancellor in his person. By this last measure, the modern German editor solemnly tells us in a footnote, the chancellor acted unconstitutionally. But certainly it is true that everything that Hitler did before 1943 was within the framework of the law and the constitution although some of his deeds were the most barbarous in the history of mankind. They were autocratic but lawful, despotic but lawful, because the supreme legislature had conferred sovereign law-making powers upon him. We in this country who watched the development of the German constitution, and who read the repeated assertions that Hitler's actions represented the will of the consenting German

[1] Cited in E. R. Huber, *Dokumente zur Deutschen Verfassungsgeschichte* (Stuttgart, 1966), iii, p. 604. I owe this reference to Professor Francis Carsten.

nation, can no longer use the word consent until we know how that consent was obtained.

It is argued, secondly, that proclamations were not in any case thought of as a substitute for parliamentary legislation. We return to the preamble, where we read – and this is by no means limited to ecclesiastical matters – 'considering also that sudden causes and occasions fortune many times which do require speedy remedies, and that by abiding for a Parliament in the mean time might happen great prejudice to ensue to the realm'. *By abiding for a Parliament.* This may, of course, be read simply as the right to take emergency measures during the few weeks required to summon and assemble a Parliament. But to pass emergency – or controversial – measures through Parliament might require a great deal more time than this. Implicit in the preamble, then, is the assumption that the Crown in its person can act as legislator at such times as it alone determines that an emergency exists. The Crown in its person as legislator is a despotism.

My evidence so far has been drawn from the preamble which, I have argued, says quite different things from the enacting clauses. In the light of these clauses we must, of course, reject Merriman's view that the statute was 'the most drastic of the measures which Cromwell adopted to strengthen the power of the Crown'.[1] But supposing, in the light of the preamble, we alter the word 'adopted' to 'proposed', have we not a fair description of the ambitions revealed in the preamble?

We are fortunate in that Cromwell elsewhere gives us a clue to his processes of thought. In 1535 – so he told the Duke of Norfolk – he had sought the opinion of the senior judges as to whether proclamations were valid to stop the carrying of coin out of the country. The lord chief justice replied in the affirmative. I quote Cromwell's account of it: 'the Kynges hyghnes by the aduyse of his Cownsayll myght make proclamacyons and vse all other polecyes at his pleasure *as well in this case as in anye other lyke*'. These proclamations, Cromwell was informed, 'sholde be of as good effect as any law made by parlyament or otherwyse'.

---

[1] Merriman, op. cit., i, p. 123.

'Which oppynyon', Cromwell blandly concluded, 'I assure your grace I was veray gladde to here.[1]'

This passage has been taken by Dr Elton to mean that 'Cromwell continued to prefer a statutory basis to a common law one'. And this, he adds, is 'a common feature of the legislation passed in the fifteen-thirties and under his aegis'.[2] What is in dispute, however, is whether these methods led to a limited monarchy and prove, therefore, that his aims were not despotic. It is this assumption—that the use of statute is somehow hostile to despotism—which, I suggest, the evidence does not sustain. Of course Cromwell preferred to support every extension of the royal power by statute: that made it all the more powerful and all the more secure; and it gave it the illusion of popular consent. To the simple question, why did the government of 1539 use Parliament in trying to give authority to its proclamations? the answer is also simple: there were no other means open to it if it wanted to gain these powers lawfully. But is a thing less tyrannical because it is lawful? Hitler's destruction of German liberty was fully buttressed by law. Was Henry VIII's use of an Act of attainder to destroy Cromwell any the less despotic because he used parliamentary processes? It is well to be reminded by Pollard that Henry VIII would do nothing unless it was lawful or could be made lawful.

In the case of the Statute of Proclamations some of the pieces in the jigsaw puzzle are missing; and all who have written on it have inevitably had to use some measure of speculation. But such evidence as we have supports the view that Gardiner was right when he saw in the debate pressure on the Crown to respect Parliament and the common law; that the members of the House of Commons were right when they disputed the bill, blocked it, mutilated it; that John Aylmer was right when, twenty years later, he described those who opposed the bill as 'good fathers of the countri and worthy commendacion in defending their liberty';[3] that James I was right when, long after-

---

[1] Merriman, op. cit., i, p. 410.
[2] Elton, 'Henry VIII's Act of Proclamations', p. 220.
[3] Cited by Elton, 'Henry VIII's Act of Proclamations', loc. cit.

wards, he declared that 'the king's seeking in that point was tyrannical'.[1] We note the word 'seeking'. James I was referring to the strength of the bill, not the weakness of the Act. And so are we.

The historian of government is concerned with aims no less than achievements, with the failures of governments no less than with their successes. In asking ourselves whether there was a Tudor despotism we are also asking whether the government was trying to establish a Tudor despotism. I think that the events of 1539 mark a failure on the part of the government and may have been the first premonitory signs, as far as the king's minister was concerned, that the sands were running out.

But we have still to face the issue of consent. Whatever one's views on Cromwell's aims in using parliamentary legislation, the fact is that all these measures were dependent on the consent of both Houses; and we must look, therefore, at the nature of consent in sixteenth-century England. It would be unreasonable for us to argue that Tudor Parliaments should have been entirely representative bodies elected by universal suffrage. But it is equally unreasonable to argue as though they were. The material we have considered so far shows no evidence that Henry VIII, Cromwell or anyone else in authority saw in Parliament anything other than a useful instrument for providing revenue, for giving teeth to a strong policy, and for adding the weight of Parliament to the powers and decisions of the Crown. But where in all this is *consent*? And consent by *whom*? Those who argue that the Tudor Crown was not despotic must prove that the people, or their representatives, were actively involved in the decisions of government. If they were not, then decisions were made elsewhere. It is necessary then to ask all over again the basic question which nineteenth-century historians were asking, to which they got an answer, and which for various reasons we stopped asking altogether, although new material and approaches are now available to us. Our question is: how representative was Parliament and how freely did the representatives—if they were such—speak? Upon the answers to these questions, the rest of my paper must stand or fall.

[1] Cited by Elton, 'Henry VIII's Act of Proclamations', loc. cit.

The method of Tudor representation in Parliament is so well known that it need only be briefly rehearsed.[1] The best contemporary statement on the structure of Parliament is in Sir Thomas Smith's *De Republica Anglorum*, written in 1565.[2] After declaring that Parliament (we may take this to mean the Crown in Parliament) is supreme in legislation, he writes '... everie Englishman is entended' — i.e. understood — 'to bee there present, either in person or by procuration and attornies, of what preheminence, state, dignitie, or qualitie soever he be, from the Prince (be he King or Queene) to the lowest person of Englande. And the consent of the Parliament is taken to be everie man's consent'.[3] Taken by whom? As it happens, Smith devotes other chapters to analysing the class structure of England; and there we read of its four main divisions: the monarch; aristocrats, knights, squires and gentry; yeomen; and what Smith describes as 'the fourth sort of men which doe not rule'. He lists these as 'day labourers, poore husbandmen, yea marchantes or retailers which have no free lande, copiholders, and all artificers, as Taylers, Shoomakers, Carpenters, Brickemakers, Bricklayers, Masons, &c'. And he goes on to underline that 'These have no voice nor authoritie in our common wealth, and no account is made of them but onelie to be ruled, not to rule other'. He adds that they play some part in local affairs, as churchwardens, alecunners, constables, and as jurymen, if yeomen are not available; but, in general, matters of commonwealth are out of their range.[4] Now, a most conservative estimate of these men would put them at far above fifty per cent of the male inhabitants of England. At once, our political electorate falls to a minority of the population, and is reduced still further by the fact that some at least of the others held land worth less than forty shillings per annum, the minimum necessary for the county suffrage. In many cases the leading factions in the shire reached agreement as to who should be elected. In the boroughs the electorate was almost invariably

[1] The standard modern account is J. E. Neale, *The Elizabethan House of Commons* (1949). See also *The Tudor Constitution*, ed. Elton, chapter 8.

[2] Sir Thomas Smith, *De Republica Anglorum*, ed. L. Alston (Cambridge, 1906).

[3] Ibid., p. 49.

[4] Ibid., p. 46.

a minority and, in many of these cases, election was by patronage, that is, some nobleman, privy councillor or other worthy had the free and independent nomination of one or both Members of Parliament for the constituency. We don't yet know the figure for this in the early period but we know, thanks to the work of Sir John Neale, that the landed gentry and their patrons had by the end of the sixteenth century captured four-fifths of the borough seats.[1]

Patronage is related to packing but the degree of packing is hard to establish in detail until we have worked out the relationship between ministerial patronage and privy council policy.[2] But this we do know. Thomas Cromwell himself in 1536 forced the Canterbury constituency to repudiate the candidates it had elected and choose his nominees;[3] while of the Parliament of 1539 itself he told Henry VIII that he was about to carry through a nice piece of packing 'forasmoche as I and other your dedicate conseillers be aboutes to bring all thinges so to passe that your Maiestie had never more tractable parlement.'[4] Cromwell may, of course, have been lying. A falling minister may do anything and claim anything in the effort to rehabilitate himself. But, in any case, it reveals what Cromwell would have liked to do and indicates the framework of his concept of government. It is Maitland, surely, who puts his finger on the crux of the matter. '... This very tractability of parliaments', he writes, 'serves in the end to save and to strengthen the parliamentary constitution; parliament is so tractable that the king is very willing that king in parliament should be recognized as supreme — it strengthens his hands that what he does should be the act of the whole nation.'[5] I think that there is a fruitful comparison to be made here between the subsequent histories of the English Parliament and the French Estates General.

I know of no measure instituted by Cromwell, efficient and able

[1] Neale, *Elizabethan House of Commons*, pp. 147–8.
[2] The chronicler Hall believed that in the 1529 Parliament, 'the most parte of the commons were the kynges seruauntes', *Chronicle* (1809 edn.), p. 767.
[3] *The Tudor Constitution*, ed. Elton, pp. 289–91.
[4] Merriman, op. cit., ii, p. 199.
[5] Maitland, *The Constitutional History of England*, p. 252.

minister that he undoubtedly was, which was not aimed at increasing the efficiency and strength of the Crown. What else should an efficient and able sixteenth-century minister aim at—a liberal constitutionalism? Good government, as he indicated to Henry VIII, required a subservient Parliament. Beyond a subservient Parliament would be a Crown which could govern by edict, that is, proclamation. This last prospect was not fulfilled. His power did not measure up to his will. It looks as though the resistance he encountered was greater than he expected; and he was left with an emasculated Statute of Proclamations, unhappy portent of his own crumbling power.

On the basis of what we know, the House of Commons consisted of a minority of a minority of the population, while the members of the House of Lords, as contemporaries were aware, represented no one but themselves. Within the limits of such an institution we may, if we wish, speak of a partnership, provided that we see the House of Lords as becoming increasingly a pocket borough of the Crown, and the House of Commons as elected to a large extent under ministerial and aristocratic patronage.

We turn from what Parliament was to what Parliament did. We know that, if the Crown wanted to impose direct taxation, the consent of Parliament was essential; and we should not minimize the importance of the House of Commons in this sphere. For the power to withhold money was used, in Tudor times, to inaugurate debates on government policy; and, although the government repudiated any right on the part of the Commons to infringe its prerogative, in practice taxation gave the Commons a voice that was heard—but not necessarily attended to—in the higher councils of the state. Nor should anything in this paper be taken to imply that the Commons submissively approved of the legislation proposed to it. Debate could be prolonged, modifications could be substantial, as we have already seen in the Statute of Proclamations. But, when all is said, the first and the last word rested with the Crown. Although Henry VIII could say, in 1543, 'we at no time stand so highly in our estate royal as in the time of parliament,'[1] it is none the less true that all

[1] *The Tudor Constitution*, ed. Elton, p. 270.

Tudor monarchs behaved as though Parliaments were no more than regrettable necessities. 'It is in me and my power ...', said the Speaker in the queen's name in 1593, 'to call Parliaments, it is in my power to end and determine the same; it is in my power to assent or dissent to anything done in Parliaments.'[1] This was no more than a statement of the facts as they had always been.

No less significant is the kind of legislation which did pass, whether by management or a general sense of a common interest. No one now believes that the Reformation was an act of state carried through at the will of the government. But, by contrast, does anyone believe, as Froude did, that it represented an upsurge of the national will? The monarch and a considerable section of his parliamentarians – how far speaking for the nation in this policy we simply do not know – moved step by step towards an Anglican settlement, although they differed among themselves as to what exactly that could be taken to mean. But that settlement required powerful sanctions: to deny the supremacy of the Crown was high treason. And the supremacy was enforced. So was the ideology. Parliament, public office, university education became the preserve of those who were identified with the established church. We sometimes forget that in the second half of the sixteenth century, throughout the whole of the seventeenth century, the whole of the eighteenth and until 1826, when University College, London was founded, university education in England and Wales was restricted to those who could affirm their acceptance of all Thirty-Nine Articles. Or again, that there were nine different treason laws in the reign of Henry VIII alone, hardly a demonstration of a secure government resting equably on the support of the people.[2]

Consent voluntarily given: we are still in search of evidence that this was a free society in which men reached their decisions by the reasonable processes of free discussion. And in this, I think, we can look at the problem differently from our nineteenth-century predecessors. For we have witnessed in our own lifetime

[1] *The Tudor Constitution*, ed. Elton, p. 113.
[2] Cf. Maitland, *The Constitutional History of England*, p. 227.

44

the emergence and misuse of a mass medium of communication of gigantic proportions. We have also seen the rapid growth of a related abuse in the shape of the public relations officer, often a hired propagandist. Now the thing which makes Tudor governments different from all those which went before was the emergence, for the first time, of a mass medium, the printing press, an instrument of enormous power. The word 'propaganda' we owe to the Jesuits but the thing itself is older than the word. We know, too, that the government held a tight grasp on Parliament, the pulpits and the printing press and strove, not always successfully, to silence the expression of dissentient opinion, in both the spoken and the written word. The government fully recognized the danger of dissent and fought it with a powerful body of writers who poured out, often under Cromwell's direction, a stream of pamphlets whose sole object was to justify the king's ways to men. Thomas Starkey, Richard Morrison, William Marshall learned and used the arts of political persuasion; but outside this group, also, there was a steady dissemination of literature in defence of the existing order. We need only list some of the titles of works in circulation: *Exhortation to Unity and Obedience*, *The Obedience of a Christian Man*, *The Hurt of Sedition*, *De Vera Obedientia*. And this is the Speaker of the House of Commons, Richard Rich, a follower of Cromwell, addressing Parliament in 1536. Henry VIII, he said, was 'worthily and rightly to be compared to Solomon on account of his wisdom and justice, to Samson on account of his strength and courage, to Absalom on account of his form and beauty'.[1] In the 1540s convocation discussed the publishing of homilies for the use of uneducated or unreliable clergy; and the first series was issued in 1547, one more channel for the dissemination of officially acceptable opinion. One passage must suffice:

> Take away kings, princes, rulers, magistrates, judges, and such states of God's order, no man shall ride or go by the highway unrobbed, no man shall sleep in his own house or bed unkilled, no man shall keep his wife, children and possessions in quietness, all things shall be common, and there

[1] *Lords Journal*, i, p. 86.

must needs follow all mischief and utter destruction both of souls, bodies, goods and common wealths.[1]

Nor should we forget John Foxe's *Acts and Monuments* which — whatever its intention — did yeoman service to the Tudor conception in Church and state.[2]

To understand the relationship between the Tudor people and their governments, it is essential to take into account that this was minority rule, an uneasy and unstable distribution of power between the Crown and a social elite in both the capital and the shires, and that this governing class, this elite, itself played a double role. It was under pressure to conform and was at the same time the channel of communication for a vast mass of propaganda in defence of the existing order, pumped out through press and pulpit, through preambles to Acts and through proclamations read out in the market-place, through addresses to high court judges in Star Chamber and by high court judges at the assizes, through all the pageantry and symbolism of royal progresses. All this functioned under a heavy censorship which, for all its clumsy ineptitude, struck hard at independent thinking. After 1529 the supervision of book publishing passed from the Church to the privy council. In 1536, 1538 and 1546 proclamations were issued tightening this control.[3] 'Between 1532 and 1547', writes Professor Baumer, 'the government alone prescribed the intellectual diet of the English public, and seldom was the latter permitted to partake of forbidden fruit.'[4] Here was a despotism in the making, sometimes of the Crown over Parliament, more often of the Crown in Parliament over the nation. This is what I mean by the dual role of the elite.

Yet one should not minimize the difficulties facing the Tudor

[1] Cited in F. Le Van Baumer, *The Early Tudor Theory of Kingship* (New Haven, 1940), pp. 104–5.

[2] 'Sacred monarchy was the most operative politico-religious idea of the 16th century, and it was John Foxe who provided a historical justification for the peculiar form of it which underlay the Tudor assumption of supreme authority in both Church and State.' Frances Yates in review of Foxe's *Book of Martyrs*, ed. and abridged by G. A. Williamson, in *Encounter* (1966), xxvii, p. 86.

[3] Baumer, op. cit., pp. 220–21.

[4] Ibid., p. 224.

monarchs and statesmen trying to set up strong, centralized government with only a rudimentary administrative machine, with slender financial resources and even more slender military ones. If, then, our question is: was there a Tudor despotism which managed to hold in submission the whole nation against its will and interests, then the answer must be an emphatic No. There can indeed have been few despotisms in the history of the world to which, by these standards, we could apply the term. But if we formulate our question realistically and ask: did the Tudors break by force every movement of political and religious dissent; did they prohibit the expression of contrary opinion by every means at their disposal; did they evolve a propaganda machine of formidable proportions and of great subtlety and range which was directed to establish that the state policy was always just and right and that the head of the state stood in a special and direct relation to God; did the Crown already possess, or obtain, control of foreign policy, religious doctrine and practice and, at the same time, possess an enormous reservoir of emergency power; were ministers responsible to the Crown alone, being appointed at its will and dismissed (and sometimes executed) at its will? Then indeed an entirely different answer to our question suggests itself.

But no government, however despotic, can be conducted by one man. He needs not only a group of ministers to carry out his will but a sufficiently influential section of his people to support him. That such support was given to the Tudors there is no reason to doubt, but the degree and nature of support we are unable to say: historians are only now beginning to ask questions about the elite in Tudor society. What we do know is that on many occasions the majority of parliamentarians—elected in one way or another—tended to support the government, and, similarly, support was largely given in the provinces. But in the provinces there existed also a measure of resistance in the governing class itself, capable of nullifying the policy it was instructed to enforce. We know this, in particular, in agrarian and ecclesiastical matters. Over and over again, the medieval conception of a king subject to the law disseminated ideas inherently hostile to an autocratic

47

state. It would, of course, be idle to argue that the monarchy pressed forward with its policy in the teeth of opposition from its governing classes. On the contrary, I have argued that, with at least a section of that class behind it, the Crown was able to employ the existing apparatus of government and communication to try to impose official policy on the rest of the nation.

In all this the role of Parliament was complex and ambiguous. It was an active source of strength but a potential source of weakness. In a positive sense it turned the will of the government into the declared will of the nation. That is what Henry VIII was saying when he declared that 'We at no time stand so highly as in the time of Parliament'. But, from the Crown's point of view, support by Parliament must never mean dependence on it. That is why Henry VII made clear that he was king as of right and before his first Parliament was assembled. That is why all the great Reformation statutes affirm that the supreme ecclesiastical powers are the king's as of right, Parliament merely confirming these powers and imposing penalties for dissent. But if a few hundred men are brought together in a hall to approve legislation they will also discuss it and criticize it, as the Tudors learned to their embarrassment and the Stuarts learned to their misfortune. There was one way out of this dilemma: for Parliament voluntarily to give up its authority and vest it in the Crown. At that moment the king in Parliament and the king in his person would become identical and the last constitutional barrier to royal supremacy would fall. That, it seems to me, was the purpose of the Bill of Proclamations of 1539. It failed; and that failure put out of reach the prospects of a full despotism in Tudor England.

My object in preparing this paper was to reopen the whole question as to how far government policy was enforced upon the nation rather than made by it. I have perforce concerned myself mainly with the first half of the sixteenth century; but I hope at another time and place to re-examine the same problem in the reign of Elizabeth I. I have not mentioned a single new document but only material which is perfectly well known to historians. Reading these again, I have asked myself increasingly often in recent times: how is it that this material, and a good deal like it, has come somehow to mean that this was government by consent? How can we call it consent when we know that the avenues of dissent were deliberately closed by policy? It is true, as I have acknowledged, that there was no standing army, but it was always possible to raise sufficient forces to suppress the Pilgrimage of Grace, the Rising in the West, Kett's Rebellion, Wyatt's Rebellion and the Rising of the North. And if English arms did not suffice, there were foreign mercenaries to be called upon, as Warwick did in 1549. This is not for one moment to imply that strong government was not indispensable. I myself believe that without strong government England might have been the scene of civil war and foreign invasion. If the government was to carry its policy through, some kind of a despotism was essential. It is for those who believe that this was a limited monarchy functioning by consent to explain how it managed to survive without the powerful controls essential to an embattled government alone in a hostile world.

During these formative years of the Tudor state, there existed the need and the opportunity to establish strong central government because of the nature of the crisis itself and the public awareness of that crisis. But there was also danger—a danger that, in the drive towards power, the monarchy might so enlarge its authority as to take on the shape of an autocracy, which is, in fact, what happened in France. Of this danger percipient statesmen in England were fully aware: 'Master Cromewell,' said Thomas More to the king's great minister, 'you are nowe entered into the service of a most noble, wise and liberall prince. If you will followe my poore advise, you shall, in your councell-gevinge vnto His Grace, ever tell him what he owght to doe but never what he is able to doe … For if [a] lion knewe his owne strength, harde were it for any man to rule him.'[1] The man who made this remark, and the man to whom it was made, was each in his turn crushed in the path of the advancing Tudor state he served. If the government of Henry VIII failed to establish, in the fullest sense, a Tudor despotism, it was not for want of trying.

[1] W. Roper, *The Life of Sir Thomas Moore, Knighte*, ed. Elsie V. Hitchcock (*E.E.T.S.*, Oxford, 1935), No. 137, pp. 56–7.

2

The paradox of liberty in Shakespeare's England

When, as a schoolboy, I began to read poetry for myself, I turned again and again to those lines and verses which brought the poet into the arena of politics. I think on this occasion of Wordsworth's famous lines:

> We must be free or die, who speak the tongue
> That Shakespeare spake ... [1]

I recall, too, Browning's famous rebuke of Wordsworth when he appeared to have abandoned the liberal cause:

> Shakespeare was of us, Milton was for us,
> Burns, Shelley were with us, they watch from their graves.[2]

Wordsworth, he said, had deserted the noblest ideal of liberty with which the great poets had always been identified.

It is significant that, in the vanguard of these great liberal exponents, stands Shakespeare—or so, at least, Wordsworth, Browning and others always believed. I am not a literary critic but a historian; and one of the questions I have often been forced to ask myself about Shakespeare is: can we, in fact, include him among the great exponents of liberty, and did liberty mean very

NOTE: This paper is a revised version of the Shakespeare Birthday Lecture delivered at the Folger Shakespeare Library, Washington, in 1969. I am indebted to my colleague Mr Basil Greenslade for reading and commenting on the text. It was first published in *Essays and Studies, 1972* (in honour of Beatrice White), ed. T. S. Dorsch, pp. 57–82.

[1] *Poems dedicated to National Independence and Liberty*, Sonnet XVI (1803).
[2] 'The Lost Leader' (1845).

091731

much to the society in which he lived? Did Elizabethan Englishmen understand the nature of individual liberty, did they want it,
do the plays of Shakespeare reflect these interests and aims? I shall
not anywhere say or imply that I know what Shakespeare himself
believed or wanted. But it is reasonable to hold a mirror up to
Shakespeare and see if he reflects to us any of the basic assumptions
of his age. In so doing I shall simply use Shakespeare as a historical
source, as I shall use other books and documents by contemporaries; and I shall try to extract from these difficult and ambiguous materials some idea of the concept of liberty in
Shakespeare's England. I shall also, in the final part of this paper,
consider the reflections of these sixteenth-century attitudes in
modern English society; and I shall ask why it is that, though we
share a common Shakespearean heritage, the role of liberty in
American history is so profoundly different from its historic role
in England.

Liberty, like beauty, exists, I know, in the eye of the beholder.
We who earn our living, and pass much of our leisure, with the
written and spoken word believe that freedom of speech is the
highest currency. We consider that those who try to debase it are
the enemies of the common cultural heritage of the Western
World. But the fervour with which we defend it should not
obscure our appreciation of the chequered story of its emergence.
Liberty of speech is not something that has existed since time
immemorial. Nor was it often in the forefront of men's aims.
When Milton defended free speech in the middle of the seventeenth century he spoke for a tiny minority. Cromwell and his
followers didn't believe in it; the Cavaliers certainly didn't believe
in it; and the vast mass of the people didn't care about it anyway.
Liberty of speech as an end in itself is of comparatively modern
origin; I doubt whether it is older than the eighteenth century.
But since then it has become part of our intellectual assumptions
that freedom of speech is a fundamental and inalienable element
in our lives, that restraints upon this freedom threaten the very
substance of our world.

But there are many people in other places who do not share
what I loosely call these Western intellectual traditions, and there

Central Bible College Library
Springfield, Missouri

are many, too, in our society who have rejected them. They say that we are mistaking the part for the whole; that we overrate freedom of speech and underrate the other freedoms, freedom from want, freedom from false materialist values, freedom from the power of an entrenched minority. They say, too, that starving men would readily sacrifice liberty of speech for a square meal under an autocratic government.[1]

I draw attention to these criticisms not because I accept them but because they are made by a large number of sincere and able people and their governments in many parts of the world, and because they are supported by a formidable mass of evidence about the nature and extent of our freedom and about the agencies which mould opinion in a free Western society. But, apart from this, I draw attention to these attitudes because it makes it easier for us to understand that Shakespeare's contemporaries could also dispense with our modern intellectual assumptions about liberty, though for reasons quite different from those of our modern critics.

But before I come to my central theme, I want to make clear that I am concerned with liberty, not independence, which is an entirely different thing. It is the confusion of these two ideals which has put Shakespeare, mistakenly in my view, among the founding fathers of the modern liberal outlook. Throughout modern history, in the overwhelming majority of cases, the movement for national independence has preceded the belief in individual liberty; and it is independence not liberty which figures so prominently in many of Shakespeare's plays. The sense of nationalism, already marked in fifteenth-century England, and vastly enlarged by the English Reformation under Henry VIII, came to its full flowering in the age of Shakespeare. It is in the sixteenth century that England ceased to be an offshore island lying to the north-west of Europe, and became instead an Atlantic power aware and proud of her nationhood, jealous of her independence.

[1] 'Most people still measure freedom', observed Khrushchev, 'in terms of how much meat, how many potatoes, or what kind of boots they can get for one rouble.' Cited in *The Times*, December 19th, 1970.

> This royal throne of kings, this scept'red isle,
> This earth of majesty, this seat of Mars,
> This other Eden, demi-paradise,
> This fortress built by Nature for herself ... [1]

These are familiar words, every schoolboy knows them. But if it is true that these lines could only have been written by Shakespeare, it is also true that they could only have been written in the sixteenth century.

Henceforth those twenty-two miles of water which separate England from the continental land mass became less of a channel of communication in a common culture and religion, and more a moat preserving England against European pressure during the time of English imperial expansion overseas, on the American continent and beyond. It is only in the present generation that the process has been reversed and England, turning away at last from anachronistic concepts of empire, has begun to resume her role as an integrated member of a European society.

With national independence I am not concerned on this occasion; though it would be fruitful to inquire why in Shakespeare's plays there is so much which evokes the highest emotions of national independence and so little which proclaims the glories of personal freedom. But it is personal freedom which we must here consider; and I turn first from Shakespeare's plays to Shakespeare's countrymen.

Freedom implies government by consent and, therefore, the right to dissent. It implies the right to say, write, and do, what I please, in order to accomplish what I seek, provided that I do not use force or the threat of force to achieve my purposes. If, however, my critics can prove that my words or deeds can do positive harm, my freedom of speech or action will be reduced or even withdrawn. To this extent I live under restraint. But my freedom is not only limited in this way. I have given up other things as well. I cannot control all my income because some of it I must give up as taxation. I cannot build a house where I like nor can I

---

[1] *Richard II* II, i, 40ff. In this and all subsequent references to Shakespeare's plays, the edition used is *Complete Works*, ed. Peter Alexander (Collins, 1951).

even control the house in which I live because, if the government decides to build a six-lane motorway over the land on which it stands, and is unwilling to make a detour to suit my convenience, they will pull my house down, give me a sum of money and tell me to go and live elsewhere. In these, and in many other ways, I have lost some part of my freedom; yet this is a situation which, however reluctantly, I accept. I do so because I believe that the society I live in is based on consent. By consent I mean not simply the right to put in – or, more likely, throw out – the government every five years. I mean much more: I mean the right to organize movements, parties, demonstrations, protests; the right to speak and publish what I please in defence of my interests or ideals. I mean, in short, the continuous exercise of my right to inquire and to dissent. For, if I have not the publicly recognized right to *dissent*, then my nominal *consent* at elections is a mockery of the term.

Since consent is central to my theme, I ask whether Shakespeare's contemporaries consented to the government which ruled over them. We are fortunate in that one of these contemporaries commented on this very question in his study of the society and government of his day. Sir Thomas Smith, scholar, politician, civil servant, ambassador to France, sets before us, in a famous passage in his book, *De Republica Anglorum*, a detailed description of parliamentary authority and procedure. He tells us that matters are debated and issues are decided in the two Houses of Parliament. Bills which have been approved, and have received the royal assent, become law. 'Anything there enacted', writes his contemporary William Harrison, 'is not to be misliked but obeyed of all men without contradiction or grudge.' This is taken as the voice of the whole nation, for all men are represented there.[1]

But every Tudor historian knows that this was the *form* of authority and that real power lay elsewhere. He knows that only a fraction of the population had the suffrage and that, in any case, elections rarely took place. The results in the county seats were, in

---

[1] Sir Thomas Smith, *De Republica Anglorum*, ed. L. Alston (Cambridge, 1906), pp. 48ff.; W. Harrison, *Description of England*, ed. G. Edelen (Folger Shakespeare Library, Ithaca, 1968), pp. 149f. See also above, pp. 41–2.

the overwhelming majority of cases, agreed upon—or as we should say, fixed—by the leading families in the county; in the boroughs elections were usually determined by an oligarchy, or by a single patron. Some four hundred members were elected in this way, and they were drawn from a narrow sector in the upper ranges of society; while the members of the House of Lords went through no process of election whatsoever. Moreover, years went by without Parliament being summoned at all, so its average duration during the reign of Elizabeth I—as Sir John Neale has shown—was three weeks each year.[1] Its powers, too, could be neutralized by the government, which could quash bills or use other devices; and it could be shut down altogether at short notice by the Crown. In any case, a large area of the national interest was held to be outside parliamentary debate or decision.

The more we examine the procedure of consent, the more it is reduced to the limited processes of minority rule. For the men who consented in Parliament, if elected at all, were sent there by a small section of the total community and themselves belonged to a smaller section of those who had elected them. Yet they believed that they had the right to consent on behalf of the nation as a whole, as Sir Thomas Smith said they had; and here was a fundamental distinction between them and us. Smith and his contemporaries held that a man could represent his community by virtue of his station in life. This concept was the product of medieval feudalism and Tudor paternalism. A Member of Parliament consented on behalf of his community much as a father consents on behalf of his family. Neither was elected by those on whose behalf he consented. But to us representation in Parliament is taken to include *election* and we assume that without election no man can claim to represent his community. Yet we forget how recently this has come about. Just over fifty years ago no woman in England had the vote. It was assumed that her views were adequately represented by her husband or some other consenting male. In most other countries until recently large sections of the population had no part in the election. But their consent was assumed. In Tudor England the same assumption was made.

[1] J. E. Neale, *The Elizabethan House of Commons* (1949), pp. 381 and 433.

Power of consent was vested in a much smaller segment of society than today and the representatives owed their powers to their wealth, their social standing and their birth.

Consent, then, freedom of election, functioned only within these constitutional restraints. But there were other controls as well. We now understand better than we once did the marvellous power which an efficient propaganda machine can exercise on behalf of the state or an individual interest; and such a propaganda machine existed in Tudor England. Before the middle of the sixteenth century the printing-press had been harnessed to the political aims of government.[1] Thomas Cromwell quickly learned to exploit it: the pamphlet and the pulpit gave a measure of influence over men's minds and judgments which added a new dimension to the organs of control. Royal progresses played their part too, and so did proclamations, as did what we should call the 'briefing' of the county leaders at quarter sessions and the assizes. This is not to say that these measures always succeeded: printer or preacher might take an independent line. Buf if he did there were heavy sanctions to be called into play. And for the one John Stubbes who lost a hand in the service of political dissent, there were many printers and preachers who did what they were told. For the one Peter Wentworth who sacrificed his liberty in a defiant gesture for freedom of speech, there were many other Members of Parliament who sat silently on their benches in Westminster, or, indeed, vainly counselled him to put a rein on his eloquence.[2]

I have argued so far that the Tudor conception of consent was (at least in theory) different from our own; and that the kind of liberty that a twentieth-century writer regards as the *sine qua non* of his very existence figures only rarely in the works of Shakespeare's contemporaries. His greatest contemporary, Francis Bacon, enlarged his collection of essays from ten in 1597 to thirty-eight in 1612, to fifty-eight in 1625. They covered an ever-

[1] See e.g. W. G. Zeeveld, *Foundations of Tudor Policy* (1948); Frances A. Yates, 'Queen Elizabeth as Astraea', *Journal of Warburg and Courtauld Inst.*, x (1947), pp. 27–82.

[2] J. E. Neale, *Elizabeth I and Her Parliaments: 1584–1601* (1957), pp. 154ff. and *passim*.

widening spectrum of human affairs, including Truth, Death, Atheism, Empire, Counsel, The True Greatness of Kingdoms, Usury, Faction, Judicature and many other large and fundamental issues. Yet he left us no essay on liberty. When we meet the word in Shakespeare's plays we meet it usually in the narrow sense of being set at liberty from prison, or in the more technical sense of privilege, the medieval notion of *libertas*, as indeed it is used in Magna Carta. But when Shakespeare uses the word liberty in a sense nearest our own, it is heavily loaded with irony, scepticism and the deliberate assumption that liberty, licence and mob rule are close companions in political unrest. 'Liberty', says the Duke in *Measure for Measure*, 'plucks justice by the nose.'[1] From him we turn to the famous scene in *Henry VI* where Jack Cade, leader of the rebels, addresses his henchmen:

> And you that love the commons follow me.
> Now show yourselves men; 'tis for liberty.
> We will not leave one lord, one gentleman;
> Spare none but such as go in clouted shoon ... [2]

And then, in the next scene, after the savage battle on Blackheath, Cade congratulates Dick, the butcher of Ashford, for his share in the slaughter:

> They fell before thee like sheep and oxen, and thou behavedst thyself as if thou hadst been in thine own slaughter-house.

Shortly after, Cade adds:

> ... the bodies shall be dragged at my horse heels till I do come to London, where we will have the Mayor's sword borne before us.[3]

This harsh picture of the rebels who murder in the name of liberty is not unexpected, for the peasant wars of Reformation

---

[1] *Measure for Measure* I, iii, 29.
[2] *2 Henry VI* IV, ii, 178ff.
[3] Ibid. IV, iii, 3ff.

Europe, quite apart from England's experience of more modest affairs, formed part of the folk-inheritance of the age. But in *Julius Caesar* it is not the peasantry but members of the governing class who wage battle for liberty. We notice that after the murder of Caesar, it is Cinna who utters the battle-cry:

> Liberty! Freedom! Tyranny is dead!
> Run hence, proclaim, cry it about the streets.

And it is Cassius who reinforces him with:

> Some to the common pulpits, and cry out,
> Liberty, freedom and enfranchisement!

Brutus at first is slow to respond. He uses none of the conspirators' rhetoric, but introduces a note of calm:

> People and Senators, be not affrighted;
> Fly not; stand still. Ambition's debt is paid.

But then, under pressure, he responds, and strikes the same note as his fellows. He bids men bathe their hands and swords in Caesar's blood:

> And waving our red weapons o'er our heads,
> Let's all cry, 'Peace, freedom and liberty!'[1]

Here surely is the moment of supreme irony: peace proclaimed in the market-place with a bloody sword!

When we meet liberty in Shakespeare we meet it in the responding company of violence. I mention these incidents simply to indicate that, though poets like Wordsworth or Browning may have found in Shakespeare an ally in freedom's cause, a mere historian finds the search for liberty in this context difficult and unrewarding. This difficulty arises, I think, because of the relationship between liberty and equality. Freedom of speech and organization depends, among other things, on the principle that

[1] *Julius Caesar* III, i, 78ff.

men have equal rights. (I am not speaking of the doctrine that all men are created equal, which is another matter, and which I shall come to shortly.) If men have equal rights in the sight of the law, then they have equal rights to say and write what they please, subject of course to the equal rights of other men, as I have already indicated. But Shakespeare's England was not based on equal rights, and least of all on any conception of human equality. Magna Carta, it is true, had long ago declared that all freemen had equal rights before the law, but freeman was a technical term and it extended to only a proportion of the people. By the sixteenth century Magna Carta was in any case rarely referred to save by antiquarian political radicals: Shakespeare managed to write his play *King John* without a single mention of it. Englishmen did not regard all men as equal in any sense of the word. They did not even believe that men had equal rights to wear certain kinds of clothes – there was legislation to stop humble folk from aping the dress of the rich[1] – let alone regard men as having equal rights to make speeches or write pamphlets. The Speaker of the House of Commons in his formal request for freedom of speech at the opening of the session always stopped well short of any such request. Tudor society, by any measure, was an unequal society.

In place of equality there existed hierarchy. It is impossible to understand the Tudor way of life – or for that matter a good deal of Tudor literature – without seeing it as a society based on order and degree. I need not cite here the long speech of Ulysses in Shakespeare's *Troilus and Cressida*, where the virtues of this kind of social structure are vigorously expounded. I turn instead to Shakespeare's contemporary, William Harrison, who in his *Description of England* has a section called 'Of Degrees of People in the Commonwealth of England'. Here is clearly brought out the nature of an aristocratic, articulated society, with the orders of nobility and knighthood, followed by esquires, gentlemen,

[1] See e.g. F. E. Baldwin, *Sumptuary Legislation and Personal Regulation in England* (Baltimore, 1926), chapters IV and V. For a recent discussion of this problem see the work of my pupil Joan R. Kent, 'Social attitudes of Members of Parliament with special reference to the Problem of Poverty, c. 1590–1624' (unpublished London Ph.D. thesis, 1970), chapter 7.

yeomen, citizens, husbandmen, artificers, and on to idle serving-men and beggars. And, according to Harrison, each man more or less knows his place.[1] This is, of course, looking at the world through rose-tinted, conservative spectacles. But it was a commonly expressed view.

Hierarchy was the cement of the existing order. It belonged, as Professor Lovejoy argued, to a cosmic concept of the Great Chain of Being, reaching in harmony and order from the godhead to the humblest element in the universe.[2] It was part of a divine logic into which every fragment of life could be fitted. Whether Englishmen of Shakespeare's day were as aware of the Great Chain of Being as are Harvard undergraduates of today who study Shakespeare, I don't really know. Recent scholarship has brought out the complexity and variety of the contemporary responses to these assumptions.[3] But the common opinion was that this was a stratified society and that so it should remain. Men like Lord Burghley, the principal minister of Queen Elizabeth — the Polonius of Hamlet — saw perfectly well that there was a gap between theory and practice: many men did not remain in the station in which they were born. Burghley himself did not. This was a fairly fluid society with a measure of social mobility, too much, in the opinion of great conservatives like Burghley and the queen. And like all conservatives they tried to pretend that nothing had happened. In any case, hierarchical it remained.

Hierarchy preserved and justified the framework of an unequal society. Popularity threatened it. Popularity meant an appeal to the people, to popular opinion: in essence to call in liberty to threaten order. Francis Bacon warned the Earl of Essex against seeking popular support.[4] 'I love the people' — we turn again to the Duke in *Measure for Measure* —

[1] Harrison, op. cit., chapter V.

[2] A. O. Lovejoy, *The Great Chain of Being: a study of the history of an idea* (Cambridge, Mass., 1936). See also E. M. W. Tillyard, *The Elizabethan World Picture* (1948).

[3] W. Sanders, *The Dramatist and the Received Idea: Studies in the Plays of Marlowe and Shakespeare* (1968).

[4] *The Letters and the Life of Francis Bacon*, ed. J. Spedding (1862), ii, p. 44.

> But do not like to stage me to their eyes;
> Though it do well, I do not relish well
> Their loud applause and Aves vehement;
> Nor do I think the man of safe discretion
> That does affect it.[1]

One recalls at this point the revulsion of Coriolanus as he enters Rome and is given a hero's welcome by the crowds.

> No more of this, it does offend my heart;
> Pray now, no more.[2]

Burghley, drawing up a code of behaviour for a rising politician, that is to say his son, Robert Cecil, thought that it might be possible to strike a happy mean: 'I advise thee not to affect nor neglect popularity too much. Seek not to be E. and shun to be R.'[3]

Any consideration of Shakespeare as a historical source for the political thinking of his age — and I emphasize again that this is not taken to mean that Shakespeare himself held these views — must have special regard to *Coriolanus*. For here again and again are raised fundamental questions about the character and legitimacy of popular rule. Coriolanus himself rejects all notion that the people have any right to govern, or indeed any claim to be flattered. But quite apart from his extreme position the play itself provides a contrast between aristocratic rule, in the form of patricians and senators, and popular pressures expressed through the people and their tribunes. To the nobility popular rule is an affront to reason. Coriolanus's mother is said to regard the people as

> ... woollen vassals, things created
> To buy and sell with groats; to show bare heads
> In congregations, to yawn, be still and wonder,
> When one but of my ordinance stood up
> To speak of peace or war.[4]

[1] *Measure for Measure* I, i, 68ff.
[2] *Coriolanus* II, i, 159f.
[3] *Advice to a Son*, ed. L. B. Wright (Folger Shakespeare Library, Ithaca, 1962), p. 13. The initials are normally taken to stand for Essex and Ralegh.
[4] *Coriolanus* III, ii, 9ff.

But even the more tolerant Menenius speaks of them in bitter scorn.

> ... You and your apron men; you that stood so much
> Upon the voice of occupation and
> The breath of garlic-eaters![1]

Anyone who reads Thomas Smith on government with its clear, firm and elaborate account of parliamentary election and voting finds a harsh parody of it in Coriolanus's ironical appeal (voice is the sixteenth-century word for vote):

> Your voices! For your voices I have fought;
> Watched for your voices; for your voices bear
> Of wounds two dozen odd; battles thrice six
> I have seen and heard of; for your voices have
> Done many things, some less, some more. Your voices?[2]

We cannot fail to notice the effect of the mounting irony by repetition of the word 'voices'.

Everything that I have said so far indicates that this was an unequal society. If we want to grasp the sentiments of Shakespeare's Englishman we should, in effect, put from our minds the language of Wordsworth and Browning. We might usefully turn instead to a Victorian hymn; a hymn which was still being sung at school when I was a boy but which, I imagine, if suggested now, would lead to fighting in the streets:

> The rich man in his castle,
> The poor man at his gate,
> God made them high or lowly,
> And ordered their estate.

And ordered their estate. For long, if with diminishing confidence, the Elizabethans clung to this comforting conviction, until their world crumbled beneath them.

---

[1] Ibid. IV, vi, 97ff. See also W. G. Zeeveld, ' "Coriolanus" and Jacobean Politics', *The Modern Language Review* (1962), lvii, 321–34.

[2] *Coriolanus* II, iii, 123ff.

Hierarchy to our modern minds is rightly associated with rigidity, privilege and an ingrained hostility to change. Much of this indeed applies to the men who governed England in the sixteenth century. But if we use the term only in its pejorative sense we lose a great deal of the texture of English life of those days. For, if it was an aristocratic society, this was an aristocracy assumed to be responsible for the community over which it exercised its privilege. Some of these noblemen, it is true, were no more than harsh and selfish power seekers or drunken idlers, some of the gentry brutal, quarrelsome adherents of faction. Yet built into this ruling order was an element of responsibility, forced on the privileged often by the central government, yet inherited too with their lands and their titles. *Noblesse oblige:* I have to turn to a French expression to convey this complex of attitudes which characterized the best elements – but only the best elements – of the English governing class. Put briefly, their wealth and their position were regarded as imposing a trust, a trust conferred upon them to serve the public interest, the welfare of the whole nation. In some respects Lord Burghley tried to follow this ideal. So did the Earl of Huntingdon, so did Sir Nicholas Bacon, father of the philosopher, so did many Members of Parliament, so did leading citizens and gentry whose deeds we now dimly see in the faded and obscure records of local administration. The pamphlet literature of the late sixteenth century, the parliamentary speeches, the sermons contain, it is true, much in them that is shallow, harsh, couched in that self-righteous language beloved of men in any age who defend their own vested interests. But when that is said there remains a good deal in both the literature and the legislation of the period which reaches forward, to a surprising degree, to the social thinking of the nineteenth and twentieth centuries.

This then was the unequal society of sixteenth-century England. It was a place where the publication of political or religious dissent was not permitted; where the practice of the Catholic faith was prohibited; where there were restraints on what men read, what they ate (on Fish Days), what they bought, what they sold, where they travelled. Where in all this, we may ask, was liberty? In every age there are a few men who glimpse all the rich prospects of liberty and seek to preserve it, whatever the cost. Erasmus of Rotterdam came nearer than other men to an understanding of the nature and value of individual freedom. Our own Thomas More as a young man may have held similar views, if *Utopia* is any guide to his thinking; but in his case a combination of middle age and politics — as ever the twin sources of disillusion — quenched his ardour.

But it was not theory which preserved some measure of liberty in Shakespeare's England. Rather it was the government's unwillingness — and more often its inability — to implement the legislation. The anti-Catholic laws were on many occasions not enforced, sometimes on the instruction of the queen; there was likewise a toleration of Puritans in high places. And a good deal of literature hostile to the most eminent men of the day managed to circulate widely. I don't want to suggest for one moment that the queen and her government presided benignly over the widespread expression of diversity of opinion. They did nothing of the kind: they hated criticism and did their best to repress it.

I have come over the years reluctantly to the conclusion that the measure of private freedom in Shakespeare's England was small; that the government tried where it could to condition men's minds and where it could not, to repress diversity of opinion. It did so because it believed that any challenge to its interests or the existing social structure threatened the future order and stability of England. It did so because it was deeply fearful of a restoration of Catholicism in England and therefore submission — so it seemed — to a foreign power. Alternatively, dissent might lead to a Puritan struggle, civil war and a weakened England, occupied by a foreign power. In short, it thought that to preserve social stability and national freedom it must suppress private freedom. This is the recurrent paradox of liberty in the history of the Western World from the Reformation to the present day.

But there is a difference between the history of Tudor England and that of most European countries. It was a hierarchic society as was theirs but in the course of Shakespeare's lifetime there was built into hierarchy the responsibility for making the welfare legislation effective; and both legislation and hierarchy survived. I argue that where a governing class—I mean a class, not just the government—is committed to, and involved in, the welfare of the whole society, there is relative stability; and where there is stability some measure of liberty can survive. But where a governing class is not so committed there is alienation, the divisions harden, distrust leads to violence and where violence determines the issue, we get extreme fluctuations: for governing bodies in their weakness yield everything to force and, when they recover their strength, take all back and repression prevails. In the process true liberty perishes.

Social stability preserved some elements of liberty, and provided the conditions in which liberty could grow. But there were other influences at work. And here we find a curiously contradictory element in the system of government. For, though liberty was restrained, enough of it survived to challenge hierarchy itself. Or, to put it another way, neither monarchy nor aristocracy was allowed to harden into supremacy, rigidity and isolation. They never, as it were, emancipated themselves from their human condition. This was a class system, not a caste system. Nowhere is this better brought out than in the plays of Shakespeare. They appear at one and the same time to accept and reject the divine attributes of kingship, to accept and reject the hierarchic system of the Elizabethans.

The crown is separate, anointed, divine, but the king is also a man. Henry V, walking in disguise on the night before Agincourt, explains to three soldiers that the king has all the ordinary qualities of a man:

> the violet smells to him as it does to me; the element shows to him as it doth to me; all his senses have but human conditions; his ceremonies laid by, in his nakedness he appears but a man ... [1]

In his soliloquy after the soldiers have gone he reverts to the same thought:

[1] *Henry V* IV, i, 103ff.

And what have kings that privates have not too,
Save ceremony — save general ceremony?
And what art thou, thou idol Ceremony? ...
O Ceremony, show me but thy worth!
What is thy soul of Adoration?
Art thou aught else but place, degree and form ...

The king, when all is considered, is a man as are other men, but to him falls the pomp and burden of royalty,

> ... the balm, the sceptre, and the ball
> The sword, the mace, the crown imperial,
> The intertissued robe of gold and pearl ... [1]

In this, as in so much in Shakespeare, the universal man denies the inequality affirmed in form and ritual; just as in the *Merchant of Venice*, his Shylock breaks through for a moment the hierarchy of race and religions.

We are, as it were, looking at Shakespeare's England on two levels: the elaborate order of artifice which is clearly visible to the naked eye, and below it the rough, hard surface of reality, scarred and cracked under the dissolving pressures of change.

It may be that this tension between things as they seemed and things as they were helps us to explain such violence as existed in Tudor England — I do not mean civil war but the sporadic street violence, the quick exchange of blows, the swift hand to the dagger, the vendettas of feuding groups over an acre of disputed land or some imagined insult. When we read of the splendours of Elizabethan culture and achievement, it is of interest to recall that a man might spend the evening in one of the great houses of London holding subtle discourse on literature, or listening to the most exquisite music, yet, if he ventured out at night alone, half a mile from that very house in the capital city of England, he might have his purse stolen and his head broken and might count himself fortunate to escape with his life. The contemporary who, as poet and playwright, was second only to Shakespeare, was killed at the age of thirty in a violent incident in a tavern. What, I have

[1] Ibid. IV, i, 234ff.

sometimes asked myself, did the audience feel as they listened to the almost unspeakable horror and bestiality of *Titus Andronicus*? I do not myself believe that this experience can be explained – or explained away – by the time-honoured cliché of catharsis. It is, rather, a reflection of the dualism in society, the conflict between form and reality, between power and the limitations upon its exercise. In the course of this conflict liberty was preserved.

If we can see this dualism reflected in Shakespeare's plays, we can see it more clearly in the contemporary politics. The courtier Earl of Essex, the perfect image of the gallant nobleman reared to the mystique of royalty, wrote thus in 1598 to the lord keeper of the great seal: 'I owe to Her Majesty the duty of an Earl and Lord Marshall of England.' But, he said, he was being demeaned from his high place to the position of a slave. And now, in the moment of truth, he tore away the enveloping illusion of an infallible Crown: 'What, cannot princes err? Cannot subjects receive wrong? Is an earthly power or authority infinite? Pardon me, pardon me, my good Lord; I can never subscribe to these principles.'[1] This was blunt and crude, and was written at a time of great personal strain. But it had been said with greater eloquence yet equal vigour more than twenty years earlier by that most troublesome Member of Parliament, Peter Wentworth: 'Certain it is, Mr. Speaker, that none is without fault: no, not our noble Queen … It is a dangerous thing in a Prince unkindly to intreat and abuse his or her nobility and people, as Her Majesty did the last Parliament. And it is a dangerous thing in a Prince to oppose or bend herself against her nobility and people … '[2] John Knox's views about the authority of James VI of Scotland and about James's mother, Mary Queen of Scots, as well as about Mary Tudor of England, are too well known to be recalled at this time.

The Rev. Edward Dering, in a famous sermon preached before the Queen of England in 1570, rebuked her for allowing a grave decline in the quality of the Anglican Church which, he said, now

---

[1] W. B. Devereux, *Lives and Letters of the Devereux, Earls of Essex* (1853), i, p. 501.
[2] J. E. Neale, *Elizabeth I and her Parliaments: 1559–1581* (1953), p. 322.

included among its ministers 'some shake bucklers, some ruffians, some hawkers and hunters, some dicers and carders, some blind guides and cannot see, some dumb dogs and will not bark'. And thus he addressed her sovereign majesty: 'And yet you in the meanwhile that all these whoredoms are committed, you at whose hands God will require it, you sit still and are careless, let men do as they list. It toucheth not belike your commonwealth, and therefore you are so well contented to let all alone.'[1]

What was said about kings was said, too, about archbishops and noblemen. The ordered hierarchy was under challenge. If Peter Wentworth had no hesitation in rebuking an archbishop, the Rev. Thomas Wood had none about writing in the frankest possible terms to eminent statesmen like William Cecil, the Earl of Leicester and his brother, the Earl of Warwick. We may take simply as illustration the opening of one such letter from Wood to the Earl of Warwick: 'Many very ill and dishonourable brutes (Right Honourable and my singular good Lord) are spread abroad of my Lord your brother, which I do oft hear to my great grief...' Wood goes on to criticize Leicester's handling of religious matters and to add, too, a reference to his private life; and, he ends, if these rumours are true, 'God's judgments in the opinion of all godly men without speedy repentance is not far off, and therefore had need to be plainly dealt withall...'[2]

You will have noticed that the critics I have cited—and they are drawn from a much larger number—had one thing in common: they were Puritans. And it is this which provides us with our principal clue to the rapid collapse of the ordered society of the Elizabethans. Everyone knows that the Puritan movement, with its increasing moral commitment to austerity, constituted a threat to English drama, and to culture as a whole. Its threat to the state was more enduring because it was fundamental. For here was a basic clash in authority. The Tudor sovereigns owed their power to the long traditions of monarchy, to their supremacy in the

[1] P. Collinson, *A Mirror of Elizabethan Puritanism* (Friends of Dr Williams' Library, 17th Lecture 1964), p. 17.

[2] *Letters of Thomas Wood, Puritan, 1566–1577*, ed. P. Collinson (Special supplement No. 5, *Bull. of Inst. Hist. Research*, 1960), pp. 9f.

Church and to the semi-divine qualities with which anointing endowed them. The Puritans were prepared to recognize the sovereign as head of the Church and state but they acknowledged an authority greater than the monarch: the voice of God as made known to man in the Bible. The rediscovering of the Bible by the Puritans—it was no less—has perhaps not always been given its fullest weight by historians. For the Puritans were perhaps the first Christian sect to use the Old Testament as the Jews did, not simply as a religious source but as a code of private and public behaviour. Here they lighted upon the Sabbath in its primitive form with results which are still familiar to this day to anyone who cares to spend a wet Sunday in Edinburgh or Philadelphia. In the Bible also they entered upon a world which was without bishops, and, for long periods, without kings. And they found, too, that when there were kings who sinned or were in error, they were corrected or deposed by a righteous God acting through the agency of his chosen people. So, armed with the knowledge of God acting through history, the Puritans challenged the bishops, the monarch and, in effect, the existing order. 'Let them', said the Earl of Essex to the lord keeper in the letter I have already cited, 'acknowledge an infinite absoluteness on earth that do not believe in an absolute infiniteness in Heaven ... '[1]

Still more important for our purpose, the Puritans rediscovered a spiritual world without hierarchy, as had Luther and the other Protestants who followed him, a world in which all men were equal in the sight of God. But Luther had always believed that this equality began and ended in Heaven and had nothing to do with the kingdoms of this world. The Anabaptists had gone further and sought to establish equality on earth, at once and in all material as well as spiritual things, with a consequent reign of terror first by them and then to suppress them. The Puritans were not communists as the Anabaptists were. Few of them ever dreamed of the equal ownership of wealth and power. They still envisaged social inequality and held that the 'magistrates', the elite, should act for the people as a whole. But at least the basis of their system was popular and the monarch, like themselves, was

[1] W. B. Devereux, op. cit., i, pp. 501f.

under the law. And they demanded freedom to speak their minds.

This was an erosive doctrine; and it was already possible to see during the last decade of Shakespeare's life, when the Tudors had given place to the Stuarts, that the Puritans and their parliamentary allies were unwilling to acknowledge the divine right of the existing order. This alone could not have destroyed Charles I. Rather it was blunders and intolerance on both sides, and, in the end, deep distrust of a king who was prepared to lie and twist to his subjects provided that he was faithful to the higher authority of God: all these as well brought civil war and the execution of Charles I in 1649.

But I have left out one important ingredient in this process of dissolution. I refer to the printing-press. The long-term effects of the invention of printing in the middle of the fifteenth century were, and still are, ambiguous. Most sixteenth-century governments, including that of England, used it as an instrument of control, by means of pamphlets, proclamations, homilies and other devices. But the voice of dissent used the printing-press too, sometimes as in the famous case of the Marprelate tracts, printed by an itinerant, clandestine press, until it was captured and smashed up by the government. But others appeared, or foreign printers were called to the service of a worthy cause. Our heavily indented coastline, and our proximity to the continent of Europe, meant that there was no effective barrier against a small boat bringing dangerous truths to the faithful. Freedom found an ally in the printer.

All these various forces pressed upon and cracked the constitutional mould of the Stuart government. For a time it was set aside as irreparable and the Puritans, under the Protector Oliver Cromwell, held power. But, while a minority of his followers held passionately to the doctrine of equality, though not of personal freedom, neither the Protector nor his parliamentarians found it viable or indeed desirable. Hence the government of Cromwell moved back to hierarchy and came to resemble in form, but not formalities, the government of the Stuarts. So the logic of the situation called for a return of the Stuarts. Things were never the same again, and there was a further revolution a generation later.

But the Puritans had failed; the old social order, the old complex social hierarchy, resumed its place and function.

And here is one more paradox in this strange story. Had the Puritans triumphed they might have built up a formidable apparatus of repression; and the slender shoots of liberty could have been crushed back into the soil. But they were neither strong enough to win nor weak enough, even in defeat, to be discounted. They survived, a permanent, nonconformist movement which grew in dignity, integrity, idealism, and in its demands for freedom. Greater in defeat than in victory, they passed on to succeeding generations, and in many unexpected guises, the liberal outlook which the nonconformist conscience—at its best—has contributed to the world.

But though the Puritans failed in England they lived to fight the battle anew overseas. To follow this battle, I must make an excursion into American history. Shakespeare's *Tempest* depicts for us a new world free from the encrusted traditions of the old. For many English dissenters, Puritan and Catholic alike, such a new world was, in Shakespeare's lifetime, already in the making. Four years before *The Tempest* was first produced, English colonists had made a successful settlement in Virginia, a settlement which endures to this day. And in *The Tempest* we encounter the first, and purest, version of the American dream:

> Had I the plantation of this isle, my Lord,

says Gonzalo, and then, ignoring ribald interruptions, he goes on

> I' the commonwealth I would by contraries
> Execute all things; for no kind of traffic
> Would I admit; no name of magistrate;
> Letters should not be known; riches, poverty,
> And use of service, none; contract, succession,
> Bourn, bound of land, tilth, vineyard, none;
> No use of metal, corn, or wine, or oil;
> No occupation; all men idle, all;
> And women too, but innocent and pure;
> No sovereignty—[1]

[1] *The Tempest* II, i, 137ff.

No sovereignty. Here at last would be cast off the long, burdensome traditions and organization, and men would be as free as the air they breathed. The paradox of liberty and order would be resolved, or rather, it would become irrelevant. The passage is full of irony and satire but it has certain qualities of the ever-recurring American dream.

We are told that when Moses took the Children of Israel out of Egypt he caused them to tarry for forty years in the wilderness so that the generation which reached the promised land would have shed all memories of subjection and of an older order. For the American colonists, though they endured on the Atlantic many stormy weeks in their long, courageous, hazardous passage from the Old World to the New, the time was not long enough. They brought with them, and re-established, many of the institutions and attitudes of their forefathers. But not all. The Puritan vein was stronger in many of them than in the people they had left behind; and it was enduring. And when, after a century and a half, they rejected once and for all the old dominion, and established a republic, they rejected also not only monarchy but the whole conception of hierarchy.

'We hold these truths to be self evident: that all men are created equal.' Now the Americans possessed a doctrine which the British have never had, before or since, the doctrine of the equality of man. English people were prepared to believe that all men are equal in the sight of God. They came in time to believe that they were equal in the sight of the law. They came in time to seek to get nearer to equality of opportunity. But the equality of man they have never affirmed as state policy.

The English had deposed Charles I but they summoned back Charles II. Two Americans deposed George III but they never restored George IV. Behind this symbolic difference in our histories lies the fundamental difference in our societies. And three generations later, in the time of another great upheaval, Abraham Lincoln turned back to the hallowed sources of American freedom: 'Four score and seven years ago our fathers brought forth on this continent a new nation, conceived in liberty, and dedicated to the proposition that all men are created equal.' Here was the clear identification of equality with liberty, a commitment to equality which the best of every succeeding American generation has acknowledged as binding upon itself. Here, too, I think lies part of the explanation of the troubled conscience of modern America; but that is another story.

With us the chain of events was different. Our Bill of Rights of 1689 was a negative thing: it laid down what the king might not in future do. But the doctrine of equality is never visible in its clauses. For the seventeenth century, like time past and time future, was an age of inequality. Yet liberty was somehow preserved. How did this come about? If liberty is allied with equality, it is also allied with security. For it is only when men feel secure that they move freely and speak freely: and this freedom Englishmen increasingly enjoyed from Shakespeare's day until ours, in fact rather than in form. They owed it to a complex of historical causes; and we have a pre-vision of the essential framework of stability in Elizabethan England. For, by the end of the sixteenth century, Englishmen were coming to see that violence was the product of instability, and that instability derived in part from poverty. In the second half of the sixteenth century the local authorities and the central government moved unevenly, reluctantly, towards a programme of alleviating unemployment and ameliorating the effects of sickness and old age. The Poor Law Acts of 1598, consolidating the experience of more than half a century, set out the main objectives of the welfare legislation which was to survive in England for two and a half centuries. Some, looking to its past, would call the policy interested paternalism, that is, paternalism in the interest of the governing classes; others, looking to the future, could regard it as the blue-print of a welfare state. Whatever it was, it gave to England a larger measure of stability, and therefore the promise of freedom, than was given to other nations in Europe.

But in the nineteenth century it was challenged. Paternalism, poverty relief and various other devices, it was said, had gone too far. At a time of enormous opportunity for economic expansion, when the markets of the world were at Britain's feet, it was said that English industry and trade, and English labour were being inhibited by social restraints. So emerged the doctrines and the practices of *laissez faire*, or free enterprise, which for a time helped bring Britain to the peak of influence and power. But to some the price seemed too high. The slums of Manchester and London, the poverty, the sickness, the despair: these, too, seemed to be the consequence of *laissez faire*; and in despair there was alienation, violence, division, the ultimate prospect of the collapse of the unity of England. To illustrate how some men felt I turn, not to Charles Dickens, but to another novelist, Benjamin Disraeli, writing in the 1840s, a novelist one day to become prime minister of England. There is a famous passage in his novel *Sybil* where an English aristocrat, Egremont, is confronted by a young stranger, soon after the accession of Queen Victoria. Victoria, says Egremont , 'reigns over the greatest nation that ever existed.'

'Which nation?' asked the young stranger, 'for she reigns over two.' And then he goes on to describe an England now divided into two nations:

> ' ... between whom there is no intercourse and no sympathy; who are as ignorant of each other's habits, thoughts, and feelings, as if they were dwellers in different zones, or inhabitants of different planets; who are formed by a different breeding, are fed by different food, are ordered by different manners, and are not governed by the same laws.'
> 'You speak of — ' said Egremont, hesitatingly.
> 'THE RICH AND THE POOR.'[1]

At the very time when Disraeli was writing his novels, another writer was engaged in a major study of the society and economy of Europe. Karl Marx, in his *Das Kapital* and his other works, also depicted England as divided into two nations and foresaw the time when, out of this division, would come a communist revolution and the collapse of capitalism. To Disraeli the coming conflict was abhorrent, to Marx it was welcome. Yet neither Disraeli's fear nor Marx's hope was fulfilled. Why was this so? In search of an answer, I turn again to a politician to put it into words. What

[1] Benjamin Disraeli, *Sybil* (1845 edn.), Vol. I, pp. 149–50.

he said symbolized what was about to happen rather than caused it.

I will call it the doctrine of the ransom. 'I ask,' said Joseph Chamberlain in 1885 at a meeting of the Liberal Party, 'I ask what ransom will property pay for the security which it enjoys?' The speech shocked many who heard him; yet he pointed to the solution which was adopted. Wealth, he said, will have to pay back more and more so that the social services could be maintained. The British welfare state—high taxation and the partial re-distribution of wealth in the shape of the social services — was implicit in all he said. 'I think', said Chamberlain, 'in the future we shall hear a good deal more about the obligations of property, and we shall not hear quite so much about rights.'[1]

I believe, though there is no time to discuss it here, that the re-discovery of social responsibility in the late nineteenth century, merging into the welfare state of the twentieth, saved England from disaster. For they restored in a more sophisticated form the ideas about welfare and social responsibility—of *noblesse oblige*—which Shakespeare could have heard from some of the forward-looking Members of Parliament and pamphleteers in the London of Queen Elizabeth. Here was the doctrine that without social responsibility there is no security and stability, and when there is no security and stability liberty walks in danger.

I have argued in this paper that there were few men in Shakespeare's England who valued liberty above all things but that those few who did had set its value so high that they were prepared to sacrifice life itself to preserve it. 'Sweet indeed is the name of liberty,' said Peter Wentworth, 'and the thing itself a value beyond all inestimable treasure.'[2] Many of his fellow countrymen set less store by liberty but were involved increasingly in the tasks of social responsibility, whether they liked it or not. So in stability freedom could grow. I have argued, also, that since Puritanism was defeated in England but triumphed in America, the doctrine of equality has exercised less influence in our history than in that of the United States. We were forced therefore to search for an

[1] J. L. Garvin, *Life of Joseph Chamberlain* (1932), Vol. I, p. 549.
[2] Neale, *Elizabeth I and Her Parliaments: 1559–1581*, p. 319.

alternative doctrine and found it in an increasing measure of social commitment. The British welfare state was not invented by an English prime minister in 1945 but in the sixteenth century by the Elizabethans. We came — however reluctantly — to believe that by giving up some of our economic and social liberty we would preserve stability and create conditions for freedom to flourish. But we have had to learn this lesson over and over again in a constantly changing world. Thus, the paradox of liberty implicit in Shakespeare's England has become explicit to our own troubled generation who, seeing freedom in danger, may yet, in remembering its past, preserve its future.

Part II · Religion and the Succession

3

Church and state, 1558–1612: the
task of the Cecils

A week before Christmas 1604, Robert Cecil, secretary of state
to James I, and recently elevated in the peerage to a viscountcy,
received from Matthew Hutton, Archbishop of York, a frank
piece of advice. 'Good my Lord Cranborne,' wrote the archbishop, 'let me put you in mynde that you wer borne and brought
up in true religion. Your worthy father was a worthy instrument to banish superstition and to advaunce the Gospell. Imytate
him in this service efectyally.' There followed some unkind
observations about James I's love for the blood sports, and a
further warning about the Roman Catholics, and then a concluding
prayer: 'Thus beseching God to bless your Lordship with his
manyfold graces that you may as long serve his most excellent
Majestie as your most wyse father did serve most worthy Queen
Elizabeth, I bid you most hartely farewell.'[1]

Archbishop Hutton was not the first—nor the last—to put
pressure on Robert Cecil and urge him to do more for the true
faith. But Hutton raised also the whole question of the service of
father and son to the Church. There are indeed many fascinating
questions that we might usefully ask; but here I wish to deal with
only one central theme: what did the Cecils consider was the
proper role of the Church in the state? We know, of course, that
the Anglican compromise forged by Elizabeth I and Burghley—
like the political compromise—worked reasonably well during
her long reign. We know also that the religious compromise, again

NOTE: First published in *Church Studies*, ed. C. J. Cuming (1965), ii, pp. 119–40.

[1] HMC, *Laing MSS*, I, 99–100. To avoid confusion, William Cecil, later Lord
Burghley, is generally referred to throughout this article as Burghley, and his
son, Robert Cecil, later Earl of Salisbury, as Cecil.

like the political compromise, proved increasingly unworkable in the reign of her successor, and that it collapsed in ruins in the reign of his successor. For fifty-four of these years, from 1558 until 1612, the Cecils, father and son, exercised enormous influence on the religious and political scene. Did the son betray the cause for which the father laboured so long and so well?

The Church of England which the queen re-established in 1559 had been made in the reign of her brother between 1549 and 1553. During that period William Cecil was secretary of state. This, of course, does not make him one of the authors of the established Church; but it is reasonable to assume from his actions and attitudes that this brother-in-law of John Cheke and friend of Cranmer was sympathetic to its tenets and organization. Yet under Mary his fate was quite different from that of so many of his fellow Protestants. He did not seek martyrdom, or safety – or purity of faith – in flight abroad; and he was prepared to serve Queen Mary, if not as secretary of state, then in special tasks she chose to allot to him. Looking back long afterwards upon the events of these years, he explained to a member of his household the position he had then taken up. He was, he said, approached indirectly by Queen Mary and offered the secretaryship of state, provided he would change his religion to Roman Catholicism. That he declined to do; but he made it plain that as 'she had byn his so gracious Ladie as he wold ever serve and praie for her in his hart, and with his body and goodes be as ready to serve in her defence as anie of her loyall subjects, so she wold please to graunt him leave to use his conscience to himself, and serve her at lardg as a private man, rather then to be her greatest counsellor.'[1] In this capacity, indeed, he acted as a member of the mission to Brussels to conduct Cardinal Pole back to England.[2] According to this version, he refused to take part in a backstairs intrigue during a parliamentary session and cleared himself also of charges of disloyalty made against him from time to time by his enemies. The queen acknowledged his loyal conduct and (it is

[1] A. Collins, *Life of William Cecil* (1732), pp. 11–12.
[2] Ibid., p. 12.

added) 'used him very graciously, and forbore either to hear his accusors or to disgrace himself'.

There is, of course, a retrospective glow about all this; nor should one ignore the half sentence buried amid this self-righteous modesty, namely, that 'His wit made escape out of danger'. His wit always did seem to make escape out of danger. But the events of these years have an importance beyond their immediate effects, especially in the manner in which Burghley saw them after the passage of time and in the new Elizabethan context. If we take his own words and apply them to religious dissent, Catholic and Puritan, in the second half of the sixteenth century, we are afforded a clue as to what Burghley himself expected of the opposition. In other words, members of the opposition groupings should with body and goods be as ready to serve in the queen's defence 'as anie of her loyall subjects'. It was a principle easier to declare than to uphold: but it lay at the heart of his policy.

But what exactly was the faith to which Burghley adhered? Clearly he was not a Catholic; but equally clearly, I think, he was not a Puritan. And here I must pause to define that term, as troublesome to the historian as were the people who clung obstinately to its ways. It is, of course, an extremely vague term whose meaning was constantly changing from the 1560s, when it began to be used, until 1660 when the Puritan Commonwealth finally collapsed. It meant at the beginning of Elizabeth's reign, very broadly, the attempt to purify the Church of its popish relics, and, as such, aroused a good deal of sympathy in the highest places in Church and state, although never in the heart of the queen. To her, even this most modest desire for further reform was anathema, for it would break that delicate compromise of an Anglican Church which, although Calvinist in theology, was Catholic in much of its ceremonial and all of its organization, except that the queen, not the pope, was at its head. Meanwhile, Puritanism had broadened as a movement to purify the Church and reform its structure. If one looks at the position just before 1570, that is to say, just before the papal Bull of deposition and the coming of the missionaries, then one might say that the queen's policy—in the political sense as far as Catholics were concerned—was largely succeeding. But the price she paid was increasing Puritan intransigence. If the 1570s is the age of the Catholic missionaries, it is also the age of Cartwright and the Puritan doctrinaires. The popish vestments were being enforced by the bishops, one more relic of popery; and the bishops increasingly became the object of Puritan assault, which culminated in the monstrous proceedings of Martin Marprelate. But if the queen could accept Calvinist theology with equanimity, the first hint of Calvinist Presbyterianism was intolerable. I am not suggesting that all Puritans were Presbyterian, but many were—and most were assumed to be. It was the attack on the bishops, and the whole Church organization, which made Puritanism a burning political issue during the remainder of the queen's reign. For if the bishops were usurpers, then the monarch who now stood in the place of the supreme pontiff was by implication an usurper too. If, in these terms, the Church and its head were under threat, then the state and its head were also in danger. So it was that during the last two decades of the reign the Puritan opposition was confronted with the unyielding resistance of the queen allied to her Archbishop of Canterbury, John Whitgift.

Of this godly alliance, Lord Burghley was not a member. There is, moreover, evidence to indicate that his sympathies lay elsewhere. The same was true of his attitude to the Church in the early part of the reign. This and other aspects of his policy have given rise to the view that he was a patron of Puritanism. Since this issue is of considerable *political* importance, both in Elizabeth's reign and in the next, I propose to examine it more closely.

Certainly the evidence of the early part of the reign indicates that Burghley shared the mood of the more active protestant party within the Church; and some of the evidence goes back even further than that. When Catherine Parr, that premature Puritan, sixth and final wife of Henry VIII, wrote *The Lamentation of a Sinner* (the sinner, surprisingly enough, is not her royal husband but herself), it was Burghley who supplied a virtuous introduction to this supremely virtuous work.[1] He was apparently

[1] *Harleian Miscellany*, ed. T. Park (1810), v, pp. 293–313.

well disposed towards Calvin. 'Now is the time', he wrote to Nicholas Throgmorton in 1561, 'for Calvin and all such noble men ... to impugn and suppress the tyranny of the papists.'[1] Later on he patronized a whole embarrassment of Puritan leaders like Peter Wentworth, James Morrice and Robert Beale. He appointed William Travers, one of the ablest of the Puritan preachers, to his lectureship at the Temple, and may also have appointed him as tutor to his son, Robert Cecil.[2] He tried to protect some of the Puritan extremists from the harsh rigours of the Whitgift reaction. All this is significant enough; but far more evidence points in the opposite direction.

For example, the collections of precepts which he drew up, on one occasion for his elder son, on another for his younger, although containing many worthy religious sentiments, have not a sentence to indicate the slightest Puritan inclination. His warning, 'Suffer not thy sons to pass the Alps, for they shall learn nothing but pride, blasphemy, and atheism',[3] is merely one more example of English insularity combined, of course, with the well-known Cecilian prudence. We turn next to his will, since wills sometimes supply valuable clues to a man's faith. In his case it is colourless. We have no reference to the elect, nothing about predestined grace, no bequests to maintain godly preachers; and, finally, he chose as one of the overseers of his will, none other than that hammer of the Puritans, John Whitgift, Archbishop of Canterbury.[4] But already, nearly forty years earlier, the formidable Catherine Bertie, returning from her Protestant exile, detected in Burghley one of the lost leaders of the faithful. 'Wherefore,' she lamented to him, 'I am forced to say with the prophet Eli, "How long halt ye between two opinions?" ... To build surely is first to lay the chief corner stone!' Her parting shot was a brief one: 'Today, not tomorrow!'[5] That was in 1559. But as far as Burghley was concerned the Puritan tomorrow never came. In 1561 Burghley was himself complaining of the Bishop

[1] C. Read, *Mr. Secretary Cecil and Queen Elizabeth* (1955), p. 241.
[2] C. Read, *Lord Burghley and Queen Elizabeth* (1960), pp. 297–8.
[3] *Advice to a Son*, ed. L. B. Wright (New York, 1962), p. 11.
[4] His will is printed in Collins, op. cit., pp. 80–98.
[5] Read, *Mr. Secretary Cecil*, p. 134.

of Norwich that 'He winketh at schismatics and anabaptists. Surely I see great variety in ministration. A surplice may not be borne here. And the ministers follow the folly of the people, calling it charity to feed their fond humour. Oh, my Lord, what shall become of this time?'[1] Less than a decade later Edward Dering, who could tell a good Puritan when he saw one, saw nothing of the kind in Burghley. In a letter to him, which was as self-righteous as it was impertinent, he wrote: 'I thought thus to admonish you, both that you have dealt hardly with God's children and your brethren, and that you should at the last look at so great abominations. If it cannot sink into your heart, or you will not, I am afraid in your behalf, that God's judgement will overthrow you.'[2] Not God's judgment but the queen's threatened Edward Dering in the Star Chamber three years later but he was acquitted; and he died in 1576, too soon for the unfolding struggle in both Church and state. But Burghley lived on for another quarter of a century, the unwilling object of the ministrations of the righteous.

To discover where Burghley stood, it is best to let him speak for himself. I quote him as reported by his contemporary biographer.[3]

He wold saie there cold be no firme nor setled course in religion, without ordre and government; for without a head, theire cold be no body, and if all weare heades there shold be no bodies to set the heades upon. All must not be like, som must rule, some obey, and all doe theire duties to God and the Church, like good pastors and teachers in every function. He held there cold be no government where there was division; and that state cold never be in safety where there was tolleration of two religions. For there is no enmytie so greate as that for religion, and they that differ in the service of God can never agree in the service of theire Contrie.

Church and state: they rest secure on order and degree. If we

---

[1] Read, *Mr. Secretary Cecil*, p. 261.
[2] Read, *Lord Burghley*, p. 114.
[3] Collins, op. cit., pp. 55–6.

turn to John Clapham, Burghley's clerk, we find exactly the same thing put more succinctly. 'In matters of religion,' he tells us, he 'dissented from the Papist and the Puritan, disliking the superstition of the one and the singularity of the other; holding the midway between both, as a mean between two extremities.'[1]

To this outlook Burghley remained constant throughout his long life, as well in the time of his weakness under Mary as in the long years of his power under Elizabeth. It explains his attitude to the Puritans no less than his attitude to the Catholics. It resolves the apparent contradictions of his religious position: his willingness to conform to a Catholic queen, yet later on to urge severe measures against the more extreme Catholics; his sympathy with certain Puritan ideals but his general hostility to the Puritan movement in England. For his religious policy cannot be explained by his religion but by his politics. And in politics he knew clearly and consistently what he wanted. His task was to secure 'order and government' in Church and state. That Burghley was a religious man I do not for one moment deny. But he was essentially an inward man who revealed himself to few; and his religion was, of course, the most inward part of his being. He was also a man with a deep love of scholarship, and it is this which explains his personal friendship with men like Travers. But his personal friendship with a scholar like Travers did not make him a Puritan any more than his personal friendship with a scholar like Cardinal Pole made him a Catholic. He believed that the religion for England in the second half of the sixteenth century was that broad, ambiguous Anglicanism which, if it aroused only a limited enthusiasm, would stimulate only a limited opposition. In this his assessment of the developing situation proved largely correct. But about one thing he was quite clear: he did not believe in religious toleration.

It is the fashion among some historians to speak as though the Elizabethan age saw the coming of religious toleration in England. Hence the enormous emphasis placed upon the time-exhausted cliché that the queen did not want to make windows into men's

[1] J. Clapham, *Elizabeth of England*, ed. Evelyn Plummer and Conyers Read (1951), p. 80.

souls. This expression, apart from having done valuable service to examiners in history, has little to recommend it, either in the familiar form, or in the form in which it was first coined by Francis Bacon as 'not liking to make windows into men's hearts and secret thoughts'.[1] That men were not imprisoned for their beliefs is of course true; but they were imprisoned for what they wrote and they were sometimes executed for what they practised. Men were certainly more free to hold their own faith in London than they were in either Madrid or Geneva. But for how long can a minority of men hold religious beliefs, and pass them on to their children, if they are not free to practise them? Dissenting Protestant ministers were deprived of their livings and, wherever possible, deprived of all means of communication with the men who needed their ministrations. After 1581 everyone had to attend the established Church or pay a fine of £20 a month. All men were ordered to attend the Anglican Church; but the only men who could do so with a clear conscience were Anglicans, and atheists who did not believe in any religion anyway. (Burghley, by the way, once said that the queen's court had 'no small number of epicures and atheists'.[2] He should have known.) After 1585, Catholic priests were, by their very office, declared traitors and executed with the full obscenities of the Elizabethan processes for treason. We sometimes forget that Roman Catholicism survived in England not because of the queen but in spite of her.

Of course this draconic policy can be defended. But it can only be defended for political reasons, for reasons of state. And Burghley approached his religious problems, not simply as a sound Anglican but as a sound statesman. He defended his approach with all the skill of a statesman – and a propagandist. 'William Cecil', wrote his latest and best biographer, Conyers Read, 'was probably more a product of the Renaissance than of the Reformation, more an intellectual than a devotee.'[3] If, then, we look for an explanation of his policy, in terms not of his

---

[1] This is pointed out in Read, *Lord Burghley*, p. 565, n. 49.
[2] Ibid., p. 120.
[3] Read, *Mr. Secretary Cecil*, p. 105.

religion but of his politics, the pattern becomes more clear and, I think, more consistent. He wanted a reformed Church of the highest moral and educational standards, for its own sake as an effective bulwark against the incursions of a better-trained, better-educated Catholic priesthood, and for its important contribution to political and social stability. In this, especially in the early days, he was prepared to go along with the active wing of the Protestants so far as was practicable. In the 1570s it became less practicable, especially as the queen herself resolved not to retreat an inch further from her entrenched position. But he had his own reasons, no less powerful. Here are his words, written in the autumn of 1573:

> There are in sundry parts of her realm entered into ordinary cures of souls, that is, into rectories, vicarages, and such like, and into places of preaching and reading, a number of persons young in years, but over-young in soundness of learning and discretion, which according to their own imaginations and conceits, and not according to the public order established by law, having not only in the common services of the Church, and in the administration of sacraments, made sundry alterations, but also, by their example and teaching, have enticed their parochians, and their auditories, being her Majesty's subjects, to conceive erroneous opinions, in condemning the whole government of the Church and order ecclesiastical, and in moving her Majesty's good subjects to think it a burden of conscience to observe the orders and rites of the Church established by law; a matter pernicious to the state of government, that her Majesty cannot, for the charge committed to her by Almighty God, but by speedy good means procure the stay of the dangers that must needs follow.[1]

We note the familiar expressions, 'not according to the public order established by law,' 'the Church established by law', 'pernicious to the state of government', and so on. Elsewhere, we have his objection to 'singularity and variety', when he

[1] Read, *Lord Burghley*, p. 117.

speaks of his old college, St John's, Cambridge,[1] and again he writes of his duty as Chancellor of the university 'to further all good learning and quietness in that university, that indecent contentions be excluded from thence'.[2] To him Puritanism savoured of what contemporaries called 'popularity', the search for a popular following (implicit in the theory but not necessarily the practice of Calvinism), instead of obedience to the known and established sources of authority in Church and state. Behind 'popularity' lay the threat of popular rule, mob rule, the social disorders of Anabaptism. We should not forget that the middle-aged minister and his middle-aged queen, who held power at this time, had spent their earlier, formative years in one of the most crucial phases in the whole of modern history. This was the time when many places in Europe lay under continuous threat of the upheavals which accompanied – although they were not always caused by – the highly combustible materials of religious dissent.

Order, good learning, quietness: these were at the centre of Burghley's policy; and they meant more than all else. Yet it is the same Burghley who stubbornly opposed Whitgift's ruthless methods. There is, for example, the famous scene in which Burghley listened to Barrow's attack on Whitgift to his face, while Whitgift was Burghley's colleague on a commission. When Barrow, finding time even for a pun, said that the archbishop was 'neither ecclesiastical nor civil' and was in fact the 'second beast' referred to in the Book of Revelations, Burghley politely asked if he could have the reference. Barrow complied, reading a passage beginning at Revelations 13:11, and was then about to begin on the second Epistle to the Thessalonians 2, when the tormented archbishop at last rose to his feet, blazing with anger, and had Barrow thrown out of the room.[3] There is also the well-known controversy in which Burghley rebuked Whitgift for his inquisitorial methods, used to discover and root out the Puritan leadership. 'I desire the peace of the Church,' said Burghley, 'I desire concord and unity in the

[1] Read, *Mr. Secretary Cecil*, p. 359.
[2] Read, *Lord Burghley*, p. 114.
[3] L. H. Carlson, *The Writings of Henry Barrow* (1962), p. 188.

exercise of our religion.' But this, he believed, could not be obtained by turning the Church into an instrument for persecution; indeed concord and unity might thereby be lost. It was as though he believed that Whitgift, at least as much as the Puritans, constituted a danger to peace and unity in the state. He summed it up, as was his wont, in the taut and telling phrase from St Paul: '*omnia licent*, yet *omnia non expediunt.*'[1] It might serve as the best and briefest summary of his whole political career.

Omnia licent, yet *omnia non expediunt*. To Burghley, then, the Church was immensely important in a man's private life, but in the state its powers must be restrained, whether in the shape of Cartwright or Whitgift, new presbyter or old priest. And for the new priests sent hither from the seminaries abroad Burghley called into action the full armoury of a modern state, skilful propaganda no less than savage penal laws. In the 1560s he did all he could to prevent the queen sending a delegate to the Council of Trent. In the period after 1570, when summary trials and executions were being meted out to the Northern rebels, he pressed for the most harsh and exemplary punishment.[2] In the 1580s he was guiding both the work of legislation against the Catholics and the publicity which accompanied it. The clearest exposition of his approach is to be found in his pamphlet published in 1583 under the title *The Execution of Justice in England.*[3] Here his case rested essentially on the independence of the sovereign state (in this case against the call to rebellion of the papal Bull), and he affirmed the state's right to take whatever measures it thought necessary in its own defence. The so-called martyrs for the Church, he argued, were in fact martyrs for the pope, willing or unwilling agents for his political purposes. The declaration that men were executed not for their religion but only for their share in these political aspirations is, of course, a fair declaration of intentions; but it evaded the central issue at the root of the

---

[1] Read, *Lord Burghley*, p. 295.
[2] Read, *Mr. Secretary Cecil*, pp. 463–4.
[3] *The Execution of Justice in England*, ed. R. M. Kingdon (Folger Shakespeare Library, Ithaca, 1965).

problem in his day and in ours. Men were not free to pursue their religion if they were deprived of the service of a priest: the political intention challenged the religious right, just as religious authority challenged the authority of the state. The medieval issues were still unresolved; and Burghley's statecraft brought them no nearer resolution. But he was concerned less with some general political theory which could carry these processes a major step forward than with reducing to a minimum the threat to state sovereignty — and, more important, to stability — offered by those who found their authority in Rome alone or in the Bible alone. This policy would be furthered by maintaining a *via media*.

Having said all this, we must still frankly acknowledge that it does not add up to a political philosophy. Had the queen merely been the secular head of a secular state, it could have been argued with some plausibility that she opposed those forms of religion which in any way threatened the internal neutrality, stability and survival of the state. But she was not asking simply for political conformity and punishing political nonconformity. She was from the start assuming spiritual authority and demanding obedience to it. In the year 1558 mature and experienced men, statesmen and scholars, were being asked to acknowledge that this slip of a girl of twenty-five was by divine authority and the will of the Parliament of England Supreme Governor of the whole Church. There is, so far as I am aware, no process of political philosophy which can justify this relationship of state and Church as assumed in the official position. There are, of course, ways of justifying the queen's position as did Burghley and Robert Cecil. But they were not philosophical but pragmatic. The challenge of the nonconformists in philosophical terms is, I believe, unanswerable. It is no wonder that the Calvinists and the Jesuits, who disagreed in all else, came ultimately to agree on one thing: the separation of Church from state. For them the Church of England offered nothing of a *via media*.

I have for some time had doubts about the attribution to Elizabeth herself of this policy of a *via media*. So far as we can discover, her own concepts of religion became those of a diminishing number of her subjects. (I am not concerned with doctrine here but her concept of the structure of the Church and the place of religion in the state.) The Church she re-founded was, it is true, cast in the Edwardian mould, and the prayer book she approved was that of 1552, deprived only of a few extravagant phrases. But surely here she was in the hands of experienced ministers, themselves sympathetic to the forward-looking protestant wing in the House of Commons. How much room for manœuvre did she have *at that time*? The forty-five years of her reign found her increasingly out of sympathy with vocal Protestant opinion, and in the last twenty years she was closely wedded to the high episcopal party of Whitgift, that spiritual ancestor of Archbishop Laud. But neither in Parliament nor the country was Protestant opposition truly overcome. She made a bid for Catholic support for her Church. How much she gained here it is hard to say but she cast away a large measure of Protestant support which ultimately turned against the monarchy. The opportunities to reform the Anglican Church were missed, the pressures to reform were dammed up only to burst their banks in so disorderly a flood in the next century. These high monarchical claims in both Church and state carried diminishing conviction as the years passed until it fell to Charles I and Laud to demonstrate their absurdity.

In politics it often happens that a statesman, having passed the peak of his achievement, declines both in popularity and skill; he begins to repeat himself while history unfortunately does not. The old slogans wilt a bit. During the last two decades of Elizabeth's reign, in her religious policy as in her political policy, we have one more example that in statecraft as in economics there is a law of diminishing returns.

Via media. If anyone truly understood the political significance of the expression, it was not the queen, nor Leicester, nor Walsingham, least of all Whitgift, but William Cecil, Lord Burghley. He indeed wanted a broad and moderate Church of England and was sufficient of a churchman and a statesman to see how that might come about. But nothing was more difficult during this period than to damp down the fires of religious controversy; and they were still burning in the 1590s when he began the slow transfer of power to his son, Robert Cecil.

In the process of transmitting power, Lord Burghley was also concerned to transmit to his son his concepts of Church, government and society which wisdom, time, and experience had taught him. Throughout his long life he had been generous with his good counsel to his family and friends, counsel which was not always sought or appreciated, and which his son-in-law, the Earl of Oxford, for one, found wholly unwelcome. Of all Burghley's scattered aphorisms, the one which I find most relevant to my context is the last sentence of the last letter he ever wrote. 'Serve God by serving of the queen,' he told Robert Cecil, 'for all other service is indeed bondage to the devil.'[1] That was in 1598. We may put alongside this some words which Cecil himself wrote in about 1601 to King James VI of Scotland. 'I will beseech you to know,' he wrote, '... that *in qua fide puer natus sum, in eadem senex moriar*, so have I ben bredd, so baptised, instructed and lived.'[2] Here, it would appear, we have the virtuous son following in the footsteps of a virtuous father. It comes then as something of a shock when we turn from these noble sentiments to look at some of the less formal correspondence in which Cecil was involved. From amongst many we may choose a letter sent jointly by Cecil and Sir John Wolley to Matthew Hutton, at that time Bishop of Durham but shortly to be promoted to the archbishopric of York. Hutton had been asked to grant a favourable lease of episcopal land to Cecil's brother-in-law, George Brooke, sponsored by Cecil, Wolley and, apparently, the queen. Hutton resisted, complaining that this could be alleged to be a simoniacal payment for the grant of preferment. Now there followed this sharp rebuke from Cecil and Wolley, pointing out (by a most interesting process of reasoning) that simony does not apply where the Crown is involved. The letter concludes: 'Your Lordship shall do well to

[1] J. Strype, *Annals of the Reformation* (Oxford, 1824), IV, p. 480.
[2] *Correspondence of James VI with Sir Robert Cecil and others in England*, ed. J. Bruce (Camden Soc. lxxviii, 1861), p. 33.

advise yourselfe of some better reasone if yow determyne to make denyall ... so wee cannot but admonishe yow that theese nyceties will hardlie be admitted, where suche a prince vouchsafes to intreate ...'[1] To that, the archbishop-elect made a most dignified reply, offering to give up all preferment and retire into private life rather than deny his conscience. 'I never hurt any ecclesiastical living in my life,' he wrote, 'and I am loth to begin now when one of my feet is almost in the grave.' Moreover, he bluntly told them, 'I can tell what simony is, and do detest it as the canker of the church and religion.' His letter ends with a devastating farewell prayer, hoping that Cecil and Wolley will long remain the queen's counsellors, advising her how 'to advance the gospel, maintain the ministers of the word, and to continue a most loving nurse to the church'.[2]

'Theese nyceties' were indeed hardly admitted in numerous other cases, where Sir Michael Hickes, for example, a close friend of Cecil, was actively involved in the business of ecclesiastical promotion, promotion in every sense of that word. I told him, one of his correspondents said of a candidate for a deanery that it 'was as well to paye as praye'.[3] Must we then, in the light of this and of a good deal of other evidence, accept the traditional view that the late sixteenth century saw a decline in public morality; and that the decline was reflected in Church as well as state; and that Robert Cecil was the greatest practitioner in that field?

I think that in the present state of our knowledge, both of state and Church, such a conclusion is premature. But here I am concerned only with an interim assessment of Robert Cecil's role in the formulation of high ecclesiastical policy. Mr Christopher Hill, in his important book *Economic Problems of the Church*,[4] drew our attention to the fundamental, and fatal, breach between the government's theory and practice in this sphere. The Crown, and its ministers, wanted a reformed Church with good administration, able bishops, and a learned ministry. Yet the very government

[1] *The Correspondence of Matthew Hutton* (Surtees Soc., xvii, 1843), p. 94.
[2] HMC, *Salisbury MSS*, v, 95.
[3] A. G. R. Smith, 'Sir Michael Hickes and the Secretariat of the Cecils, circa 1580–1612', p. 187 (unpublished London Ph.D. thesis, 1962).
[4] J. E. C. Hill, *Economic Problems of the Church* (Oxford, 1956).

itself was engaged in despoiling the Church of its wealth, of which only the most glaring example was the pressure upon bishops, or deans and chapters, to let out their lands to the governing classes at ridiculously uneconomic rents on long leases in an age of inflation. On top of this, in the parishes themselves there was the impoverishment of the local benefices by the large-scale diversion of their revenues to lay patrons and their cronies. As a result, such parishes could only sustain a feeble, unlettered clergy, or for decades the pulpit might stand empty. All this was in scandalous contrast to the fanatical devotion and ability of the Catholic priests, on the one hand, and the Puritan ministers on the other. An impoverished Church, it is argued, is a weak and decadent Church; but when at last Archbishop Laud decided to make a stand against the unending depredations of the gentry he added fury to the forces already arrayed against him.

It must be said at once that the Cecils, father and son, were unquestionably involved in diverting episcopal revenues into private pockets, their own if possible. But to them, and to many of their contemporaries, this delectable business was no impediment to their known, and declared, ecclesiastical ideals. To them a bishop was the holder of a public office which, like all public offices, derived from patronage, and was a source of patronage and revenue to the holder. If a teller of the exchequer could be expected to pay some thousands of pounds to obtain office, why should not a Bishop of Durham give some thanks for the bounty which had come his way? A bishop's revenues included profits from leases, wardships, the grant of office. Many of these revenues were employed not for the spiritual ends of a diocese but for the more immediate needs of the members of a bishop's family. If the Bishop of Durham, to his credit, might refuse to taint his conscience with simony, the Bishop of Bath and Wells had a more relaxed approach to ecclesiastical lands. He was busily engaged in enriching his family with long leases at the cost of his successors, while the Dean and Chapter of Wells were busily engaged in feathering each other's nests. There could seem nothing amiss to sophisticated statesmen like the Cecils to divert some of the bishop's revenues into the pockets of hard-working civil servants—which was often the case—rather than into the pockets of the under-employed progeny of bishops. For example, when John Aylmer, Bishop of London, died in 1594, he left his eight children well provided with episcopal lands to the tune of £16,000, at the very time when St Paul's Cathedral badly needed £4,000 spent on repairs.[1] Nor could the transfer of wealth from bishops' families seriously disturb a queen who, in any case, found the whole idea of episcopal marriage repellent to a degree.

The despoiling of the parishes was another matter. There is a good deal of evidence that the Cecils genuinely wanted a learned ministry.[2] But a learned ministry would have had to be paid for, and would have also implied, therefore, a massive blow at the whole system of lay patronage as it existed—and long survived—in the Church of England. The idea of a learned ministry remained for the Cecils, as for many of their successors, a pious hope. To have brought it into being would have required a fundamental reconstruction of the Church of England from top to bottom: a revolution in society no less than in the state. That was out of the question; but in 1610 Cecil was joined with Bancroft in a scheme to provide all vicarages with at least twenty acres of glebe land. At the same time it was proposed that the poorer clergy should have their first fruits and tenths remitted by the king. Here was one serious attempt to raise the incomes—and therefore the standards—of the clergy.[3] But for Cecil 1610 was his year of lost causes; and it came to nothing. Two years later he was dead.

This remained therefore a large and long-term problem. But there were two immediate issues which confronted the government in the passage to a new dynasty and a new century. The one was the intransigent body of Catholic priests and laymen for whom no compromise was possible; the other was the substantial body of vigorously Protestant clergy and their supporters eager to fight again—and with greater hope of success—the battles which their fathers and grandfathers had fought in the last half-

[1] R. G. Usher, *The Reconstruction of the English Church* (New York, 1910), I, pp. 114–15.

[2] e.g. Read, *Lord Burghley*, p. 297; CSP Domestic, 1603–10, 189.

[3] Usher, op. cit., II, p. 257. See also S. B. Babbage, *Puritanism and Richard Bancroft* (1962), pp. 313ff.

century. The Catholic issue (which I personally believe raised throughout the period far less danger to the government than did the Puritan) roused the greater passion. And that passion blazed fiercest around Robert Cecil. 'The ruin of England was sure,' one priest was reported as saying in 1601.[1] 'The government [is] all in the hands of one man, a professed enemy to the Catholics,' and one moreover who was about to marry Arabella Stuart and make himself king of England when the queen died. 'The Earl of Salisbury', said another correspondent in 1606, 'is as violent as ever against Catholics.' The only solution was to insert somebody into his service with the sole purpose of assassinating him. 'If Hector weare gone,' the correspondent added in an enchanting postscript, 'the Trojans would be quietter.'[2] Someone else in the same year resolved to murder Cecil because 'the papists should not prevail as long as he lived'.[3] Yet another plotter, in 1609, proposed to eliminate both Cecil and Archbishop Bancroft, 'as the greatest obstacles and enemies to the holy catholique cause in England'.[4] But was Cecil the sworn enemy and the ruthless destroyer of Catholics as most men believed?

To see this in perspective we must glance back for a moment to a pamphlet which was published long before, in the year of the Armada. Its title is *The Copy of a Letter sent out of England to Don Bernardino de Mendoza*, at that time Spanish Ambassador in France; and the original was said to have been found among the papers of Richard Leigh, a seminary priest who had been executed. In the *Short Title Catalogue* it is in fact attributed to Leigh. It is an appeal for a change in Spanish policy based upon the experiences at the time of the Armada. The Catholics, it said, had been utterly loyal to the queen in the time of danger; and this, it argued, should be the pattern for the future. All that was needed was for the pope to grant a dispensation to English Catholics to attend the Established Church occasionally, and they would be able to live out their lives in freedom, un-

[1] CSP Domestic, 1601–3, 37.
[2] CSP Domestic, 1603–10, 278.
[3] Ibid., 313.
[4] Ralph Winwood, *Memorials of Affairs of State*, ed. E. Sawyer (1725), III, p. 49.

troubled by the intolerable burdens of recusancy fines. We know now, thanks to the work of Conyers Read, that the pamphlet was not written by Richard Leigh, nor was it found among his papers. Its author was, in fact, William Cecil, Lord Burghley.[1] It was an ingenious piece of propaganda designed to drive a wedge between the Jesuit missionaries and the main body of English Catholics. But I think that it was more than a piece of propaganda and reflected a genuine conviction on the part of Burghley that Catholic Englishmen were loyal, as indeed Armada year *had* shown, and, if the Jesuit spearhead were broken, internal religious peace would be in sight. It was that policy which Robert Cecil inherited and pursued to within measurable distance of success. In the last years of the reign the breach between the Jesuits and the secular priests in England widened, as the latter entered into secret negotiations with Cecil for some limited measure of toleration. But the whole issue was distorted and confused by the controversy over the succession; and in any case only a tiny fraction of English Catholic priests felt able to take the Oath of Allegiance in the form presented to them at the beginning of 1603.[2]

During these last years Cecil had been groping towards some kind of a *modus vivendi* with the Catholics. In toleration itself he did not believe; but in the early seventeenth century he came much nearer to accepting that the practice of the Catholic religion should be permitted, provided it was shorn of all political associations and aspirations. This reflected and supported the views of the new king. 'I will never allow in my conscience that the blood of any man shall be shed for diversity of opinions in religion,' James VI had written to Cecil;[3] and the king declared himself indeed ready to acknowledge the Catholic Church as the 'mother church', but marred by 'infirmities and corruptions.' But the king's policy was clumsy and uneven: it made a bid for Catholic friendship while it punished the Catholics intermittently

[1] Read, *Lord Burghley*, pp. 431–3.

[2] For a discussion of this controversy, see my 'The succession struggle in late Elizabethan England', in *Elizabethan Government and Society*, ed. S. T. Bindoff, J. Hurstfield and C. H. Williams (1961), pp. 369–96; below, pp. 115–26.

[3] Cited in A. Cecil, *A Life of Robert Cecil* (1915), p. 231.

with fines. It played into the hands of the extremists—the parliamentary Puritans on the one hand, the Gunpowder Plotters on the other. But when the dust and anger of the Gunpowder Plot had died away, Cecil made a fresh attempt, through the new Oath of Allegiance of 1606. It went much further towards the exemption of loyal Catholics from the penal laws, but its price was a categorical denial of the papal right of deposition, a denial expressed in the most offensive terms. To many Catholics it proved unacceptable; but in the year following the Gunpowder Plot it was as far as the government could reasonably have been expected to go. 'As far as blood goes,' Cecil told the Venetian envoy, 'rest assured, provided the Catholics keep quiet; but as regards property the laws must be enforced; though even here we shall go dexterously to work and far more gently than in the days of the late Queen.'[1] Shortly after, he went further and told the ambassador that 'if the world can be assured that papal superiority will be confined exclusively to affairs spiritual ... I assure you that the next day the king would concede liberty of conscience and permit the exercise of the Catholic religion'.[2] This bold assertion may well have been designed for foreign consumption; but it was the kernel of Cecilian policy. It could never have come from the lips of Burghley. We know also that Cecil greatly tempered the savagery of the recusancy laws.[3] No friend of the Catholics, it remains hard to see Cecil as their bloodthirsty enemy.

He was no bloodthirsty enemy of the Puritans either, but he could hardly be called their friend, for he was impatient of schismatics. He declared himself ready to tolerate divergence of ecclesiastical opinion but intolerant of those who 'dream of nothing but a new hierarchy, directly opposite to the state of a monarchy'. They would 'break all the bonds of unity to nourish schism in the church and commonwealth'.[4] But he was anxious to be scrupulously fair. He had been careful to point out that in

[1] CSP, Venetian, x, 229.
[2] Ibid., 230.
[3] HMC, *Rutland MSS*, I, 420.
[4] W. K. Jordan, *The Development of Religious Toleration in England, 1603–1640* (1936), p. 28.

the forces of discontent gathered round the Earl of Essex in 1601 not a single Puritan had raised his hand against the queen.[1] To the king's policy he loyally subscribed; but there is no evidence that he sought to bring the full weight of the state machine into operation against the Puritans. Rather his appreciation of them was cool, logical, dispassionate.

Yet beneath this cool logic there was a fervour—unexpected, rarely revealed—which, when encountered, at last gives coherence to his life as a man and a statesman. Nowhere is this better displayed than in his last will, composed on March 7th, 1612, two months before his death.[2] It was, of course, common for a testator to make some religious affirmation in his will; and occasionally these declarations show strongly held doctrine. But Cecil's will contains more than this: it is an open declaration to both his friends and enemies of the reality of his Christian faith. After the formal, introductory matter, 'In the name of God, I Sir Robert Cecill, Knight, Earle of Salisburie, Lord High Treasurer of England, knowing and beleeving that all the sonnes of men have but their tymes of pilgrimage on earthe and must at last (though some sooner, some later) leave this transitorie lyef at the hower appoynted by their Creator,' he proceeds to a much fuller exposition of his faith:

First I do acknowledge myself to be a most greevous synner, for which both in generall and particuler I repent me from the bottome of my heart, begge and beseech pardon at the handes of Almightie God for his Sonne Jhesus Christ his sake, the onelie Saviour and Redeemer of all mankynde, noe way trustring [*sic*] or beleving that any workes of myne can be meritorious or coadiutors [helpful] to my salvation. But on the contrarie that all can be done by me a wretched synner is of itself inutile and contemptible in respect of the oft great and greivous offences which nothing but the precious blood of Jhesus Christe shedd upon the Crosse for me and all mankinde can wash awaye by livelie faythe in him.

[1] HMC, *Salisbury MSS*, XI, 148.
[2] Prerogative Court of Canterbury Wills, 49 Fenner.

Having clearly expressed his Protestant faith in divine grace, he turned away for a moment to consider the charges his enemies made against him:

> So because I would be glad to to [*sic*] leave behinde me some such testimonye of my particuler opinion in poynte of faythe and doctrine as might confronte all those who, judging others by themselves, are apt to censure all men to be of little or noe religion which by their calling are ymploied in matters of state and governement under great kinges and princes, as yf there were no Christian pollicie free from irreligion or ympietie, I have resolved to expresse my self and opinion in maner following:
>
> First concerninge the infinite and ineffable Trynitie in Unitie and Unitie in Trinitie and the misterie of reconciliacion in Christ Jhesus as it concernes the Church, the Saynctes, their synnes, their soules and bodies, and lastlie their retribucon in Heaven, in all theis poyntes and everie of them I do assuredlie beleive in my heart (as I have always made profession with my mouthe)[1] whatsoever is conteyned in the Apostles Creede which, bicause it is *summum credendum*, I have always observed as the best rule of necessarie faythe and poyntes of Salvacon.
>
> Agayne, for the Sacraments, as I verelie beleive for Baptisme that it is the ordinarie wayes and meanes appoynted in the Word for our admittaunce into the church without which church whosoever is, is also without salvacon. So, for the Sacrament of the Supper, as I could never render to my self any reasonable accompt of carnall presence in the same either without or within the Elements of bread and wyne because God himself hath taught me that flesh and blood availeth nothing with him but the spirit and lyef, so on the other side I alwaies dissented (yet without scandall) from them that make it but a bare signe or significacon of Christes death; and [I] was ever resolved upon the oracle of my Savior that it is reallye and trulie his

[1] I assume that the passage within parentheses ends here, but the final parenthesis has been omitted in the original.

bodie and blood to all purposes of speciall nourishment and lief and graces whatsoever to him that receives it, yf he be a penitent and true believer (as I hope I am and shall be).

Here surely was the middle path—somewhere between Catholicism and Zwinglianism—in the bitter theological controversy over the Sacrament which was splitting Europe from end to end. With this brief exposition of the Anglican compromise, the statesman writing in the time of his political frustration and despair made his final declaration of faith:

And therefore [I] do heartelie desire to receive this holie Sacrament (yf it please God) for my spirituall comfort and strength, even then when I shall be nearest the end of this my mortall lyef and beginninge of the other in Heaven. Therefore I do here in the sighte of God make profession of that fayth in which I have always lived and hope to dye in, and feare not to be iudged at the greate accompte of all flesh, and purpose to leave it behinde me as full of lief and necessarie fruite as I can for the direccon of my children as their best patrimonie and for the satisfaccon of the world as the truest accompte I can give for my self and my accions.

The story of the first decade of James I's reign—Cecil's decade—is in Church as in state the story of solutions glimpsed and opportunities missed. No one in that brief interval of promise had sufficient of either the will or the power to solve the problems which for half a century had pressed for solution: namely to broaden the Church sufficiently to meet the reasonable demands of the moderate Puritans and to broaden the state sufficiently to meet the reasonable demands of the moderate Catholics. A Church less impoverished in its financial resources would have been less impoverished in its ministers; and a good and learned ministry might have absorbed the talents of Puritan ministers and diverted their activities, and those of their supporters, to the defence and not the destruction of the established Church. In relation to the Catholics, in the last years of the queen, some prospect of a *détente* came into view. In 1606 it came again. If toleration cannot come into the range of practical politics until 'schism is recognized as possible even if not legitimate', as McIlwain rightly argued,[1] then the Oath of Allegiance of 1606 is the first hesitant step towards the recognition of schism, the separation of Church from state. But by calling upon Catholics to declare that a future act of the pope – the deposition of a king – might be *heretical*, i.e. an error in *religion*, it blurred a distinction which was only just beginning to become clear. The Oath was only a first step.

The credit for this first step must go to Cecil, to Bancroft, and to James I himself. But both sides, the government no less than the Catholics, had constantly to look over their shoulders at the stronger forces pressing upon them: on the one hand the Puritans in Parliament, on the other the Jesuits. The result was that each gesture of conciliation had to be accompanied by the vigorous assertion that no concession was intended. But the early experiment failed. The grant of the full rights of citizenship to Catholics and Dissenters was long delayed and came late – too late – in our history; and the whole nation was thereby the poorer. If the policies, first tested in the early seventeenth century, had been carried through, these things might have come much sooner than they did. But Bancroft died in 1610, Cecil in 1612. Thereafter James I passed under the influence of second-rate men, and worse still, under the influence of the Spanish ambassador, Gondomar. Meanwhile, the Puritan opposition grew. The forces in the way of a moderate solution were too powerful and they were exerted from many directions.

I began this paper with the friendly criticisms made of Cecil by the Archbishop of York in his effort to urge him along the path marked out by his father. I should like to end with Cecil's answer to that letter. It is no longer the Cecil of the 1590s bullying a bishop to make over some dubious lease, but Cecil the experienced statesman charged with the heavy responsibility of power in a new reign. He writes with courtesy and modesty. 'Your place and yeares', he says, 'deserve too great a respect and reverence to be forgotten by my father's sonne, whome I have

---

[1] *The Political Works of James I*, ed. C. H. McIlwain (1918), p. xxx.

heard soe often speake of your zealous care and industry.' Then he sketches out his own middle path between the papist 'on the left hand with superstitious blyndnes' and the Puritan 'on the right with unadvised zeale'. (Cecil would not have understood modern historians who speak of the left wing in Parliament, by which they mean the Puritans.) There follows a warning against exaggeration: 'whosoever shal behold the papists with puritane spectacles, or the puritan with papistical, shal see no other certeyntye than the multiplication of false images.' He ends the long passage with a denial that he was a supporter of toleration.[1] But he protested too much. Behind the show of conservative zeal for the established Church there was for Cecil the glimpse of a better prospect, if not yet of toleration then at least of amelioration. In that vision James fully shared. But the king's clumsy handling of Parliament and his even clumsier handling of foreign policy helped to blot out these prospects for a long time to come, Like his predecessor – although for utterly different reasons and in utterly different ways – he appeared to lean further towards the Catholics than parliamentary opinion was at that time prepared to go. The result is a paradox. The Anglican compromise was sustained, not so much by the monarchs, Elizabeth I and James I, who stood successively at its head, as by their ministers, William Cecil, Lord Burghley, and Robert Cecil, Earl of Salisbury, his son.

[1] Strype, *Annals of the Reformation*, IV, pp. 545–9.

4

The succession struggle in late Elizabethan England

'God bless you on earth,' wrote Lord Burghley in March 1598, a few months before his death, to his son Robert, 'and me in heaven, the place of my present pilgrimage.'[1] What blessings awaited Lord Burghley in heaven we do not know; but certainly the next few years brought a whole series of blessings to Robert Cecil on earth. 'I think you happy for your great and honourable fortune,' his elder brother could write to him in September 1602, 'and happier that the Lord has given you grace and judgement.'[2]

By the end of Queen Elizabeth's reign Robert Cecil, although not yet forty, had emerged as the undisputed leader of the government; and it was he who presided over the transfer of power from the Tudors to the Stuarts. Indeed, within a year of Burghley's death a correspondent, writing from London, could declare that the queen was entirely under the direction of Robert Cecil 'who now rules all as his father did'.[3] So there grew up, even in his own day, the legend that by a marvellous combination of skill and intrigue – mostly intrigue – Cecil had by 1603 destroyed or driven into impotence all the men who stood in his way. Since this legend has survived for so long, and in recent years acquired some interesting accretions, it is time that it was tested against the background of the bitter struggle for power during the closing years of the queen's regime. In essence there were two succession struggles during the period: one for the throne itself on behalf of rival claimants, the other for the immense concentra-

NOTE: First published in *Elizabethan Government and Society*, ed. S. T. Bindoff, J. Hurstfield and C. H. Williams (1960), pp. 369–96.

[1] *Cal. S.P. Dom.* 1598–1601, 33.
[2] Ibid., 1601–3, 240.
[3] Ibid., 1598–1601, 251.

tion of power which Burghley had enjoyed for four momentous decades.

The long years of her personal rule had by this last crucial period left the queen a tired woman. In the summer of 1599 it was reported of her that 'when she rideth a mile or two in the park, which now she seldom doth, she always complaineth of the uneasy going of her horse; and when she is taken down her legs are so benumbed that she is unable to stand'.[1] These were the words of an unfriendly critic; but early in the next year Thomas Windebank, her clerk of the signet, recorded the inner conflict which at times paralysed the queen's power of decision.[2] He was writing at a moment of great tension, after the Earl of Essex's precipitate return from Ireland; but it was precisely at such times that a cool head at the centre of power was essential. Instead there was weakness and divided counsel: and in such an atmosphere double-dealing and corruption flourished. 'The people', said Bishop Goodman, looking back from the reign of Charles I, 'were very generally weary of an old woman's government.' He could remember, as a small boy, cheering the queen in Armada year; but at the end of the reign he found things different.[3] When Thomas Holland, Regius Professor of Divinity at Oxford, printed in 1601 his accession-day sermon of two years earlier, he found it necessary to preface it with 'An Apologetical Discourse' against those who opposed the celebration of November 17th as a Holy Day.[4] At the opening of her last Parliament, in 1601, the queen showed the unmistakable signs of physical and spiritual fatigue.[5]

A decade ago, in a famous article, Sir John Neale drew our attention to the decay of government in the declining years of Queen Elizabeth.[6] It was, moreover, particularly tragic, in political terms, that the queen and her lord treasurer grew old together; for thereby continuity of government was gravely

---

[1] Ibid., 252.

[2] Ibid., 394.

[3] G. Goodman, *The Court of King James I*, ed. Brewer (1839), i, pp. 97, 163.

[4] M. MacLure, *The Paul's Cross Sermons*, pp. 220–21.

[5] J. E. Neale, *Elizabeth I and Her Parliaments: 1584–1601* (1957), p. 375.

[6] *The Elizabethan Political Scene* (Brit. Acad. Raleigh Lecture in History, 1948), reprinted in *Essays in Elizabethan History* (1958), p. 59–84.

imperilled. There was no obvious person who could transmit the established concepts of government into the new age. She frankly acknowledged her deep dependence upon him. In the last year of his life she sent him a cordial with her best wishes for his recovery. She added that 'she did intreat heaven daily for his longer life — else would her people, nay, herself, stand in need of cordials too'.[1] Thomas Wilson, a sour commentator on the contemporary scene, wrote a couple of years later in less flattering terms. The factious grip upon power, the advancement of second-rate men at the expense of men of ability, all this 'was first brought by the old treasurer of whom it was written', he said, quoting Spenser, 'that he was like an aged tree that lets none grow which near him planted be'. That policy, he concluded, was being faithfully carried on by his son, Robert Cecil.[2]

Certainly Burghley had nothing to learn in the arts of faction and patronage; but the source of faction — as of authority — lay not in Burghley but in the queen. No one minister was allowed to be the custodian of all her secrets or the delegated authority of all her power. Against Burghley there was Leicester; against Robert Cecil, Essex. But, said Wilson, this division went right through the administration and even reached into the Tower of London itself where the lieutenant of the Tower and the master of ordnance were not on speaking terms. The same conditions prevailed, he added, between the lord deputy of Ireland and the governor of Munster; and such had always been the case.

It did not need Thomas Wilson to point out the peculiarly grave perils of faction in these closing years of the sixteenth century. 'The jarrs continue as they did, if not worse by daily renewing,' wrote John Chamberlain from London, 'and our music runs so much upon discords that I fear what harmony they will make of it in the end. Many things pass which may not be written.'[3] He was referring of course to the growing bitterness of the Essex-

[1] John Harington, *Nugae Antiquae*, ed. Park (1804), i, p. 237.

[2] T. Wilson, 'The State of England, Anno Dom. 1600', ed. F. J. Fisher (Camd. Soc., 3rd Ser., lii), pp. 42–3; cf. R. Naunton, *Fragmenta Regalia* (1808 edn), pp. 178–9.

[3] *The Letters of John Chamberlain*, ed. N. E. McClure (Philadelphia, 1939), i, pp. 67–8.

Cecil rivalry which, two years later, was to fester and burst into rebellion. But it is unfortunate that the dramatic character of this personal struggle has diverted attention from the larger struggle which underlay the whole situation: namely the struggle for the succession. Here indeed was something 'which may not be written'. There had been a thorough – and embarrassing – ventilation of the subject as long ago as 1566.[1] In 1571 an Act had imposed severe penalties upon the publication of any claims to the royal succession, other than what was to be 'established and affirmed' by Parliament.[2] But Parliament, inhibited by the queen, had established and affirmed no successor, so Peter Wentworth's *Pithie Exhortation* on the subject, and his speech in the Commons, had won him a sojourn in the Tower from 1593 until his death four years later. Finally, at the time of the Parliament of 1601, a bill was drafted to prohibit the writing or publishing of books about the succession on the grounds that they bred faction and inspired traitorous acts against the queen.[3]

The English succession at this stage provided the happy hunting ground for the mischief-makers of international politics. The centuries of dynastic marriage had indeed created a situation in which most of the crowned heads of Europe could claim each other's thrones with some degree of plausibility. But in England the position was made more complex by the matrimonial infelicities of Henry VIII. As the result of divorces and marriages there had been provided in the last fourteen years of his reign three different Acts laying down the succession, as well as Henry's last will in which, under statutory authority, Henry himself declared who were in line to succeed. Since, however, the will was alleged to be technically faulty and, in any case, was for a time mislaid (although its contents were known) the whole issue was criss-crossed with uncertainties. What was clear, however, was that the will had excluded the Stuart line and, in effect, left the crown after Elizabeth's death to the dubious claims of the House of Suffolk.

[1] J. E. Neale, *Elizabeth I and Her Parliaments: 1559–1581* (1953), pp. 129–64.
[2] 13 Eliz. c. 1.
[3] *Cal. S.P. Dom.* 1601–3, 115–16.

There were about a dozen people who in the 1590s could present themselves, with varying degrees of optimism, as the future occupants of Elizabeth's throne. (Henry IV of France added one more candidate with the polite observation that, since a bastard of Normandy had succeeded to the English throne in 1066, he could not see why a bastard of his own should not do the same thing when Elizabeth died.[1]) But of all the candidates for promotion we need only consider a short list of five. Under the law of primogeniture, James VI of Scotland had the best claim since he was descended from Margaret, the elder daughter of Henry VII. But James was a foreigner and those who opposed him could therefore allege that this barred the way. If that were so then Lady Arabella Stuart, born in England and the next senior descendant of this elder daughter, took his place. But if Henry VIII's will was valid, this claim was set aside since he had shifted the succession to Mary, the younger daughter of Henry VII. But her marriage to the Duke of Suffolk was itself of doubtful validity, as was that of her elder daughter, Catherine Grey. The Grey line need not seriously detain us here except to notice that, if Catherine's marriage were in doubt, the inheritance passed through her younger sister to the Earl of Derby, married to a niece of Robert Cecil. If all these claimants were set aside, then a whole new series came up for consideration, including Philip II of Spain (descended from John of Gaunt) and, if he should stand aside, his daughter, the Infanta.

'Thus you see', wrote Thomas Wilson, 'this crown is not like to fall to the ground for want of heads that claim to wear it, but upon whose head it will fall is by many doubted.' Out of all these, three candidates received the particular attention of the succession speculators and the chanceries of Europe, namely James VI of Scotland, Arabella Stuart, and the Infanta. Wilson himself was sure 'that the King of Scotland will carry it, as very many Englishmen do know assuredly. But to determine thereof is to all English capitally forbidden, and therefore so I leave it.'[2]

---

[1] *Cal. S.P. Dom.* 1601–3, 148.
[2] Wilson, 'The State of England, Anno Dom. 1600', p. 5.

Thomas Wilson prudently acknowledged the queen's hostility to all this speculation.

But Father Robert Parsons, as leader of the English Jesuits abroad, laboured under no such inhibition; and, from his itinerant exile on the continent of Europe, he felt free to speculate as he pleased about the queen's successors. Where exactly Parsons himself stood became clear quite early in the debate; for, soon after the execution of Mary Queen of Scots, he was engaged in manufacturing genealogical tables to establish Philip II's claim to the throne.[1] His conclusions, under the title *Conference about the Next Succession*, were published in 1594. Whether or not the essay was to be treated as a serious discussion of that delicate problem, it could certainly be expected to sow discord among the queen's subjects. It proved also something of a boomerang for it helped to make a sharp cleavage inside the Catholic priesthood. True, to some priests it confirmed their beliefs that an anti-national, pro-Spanish policy was at this time the only way of making England safe for Catholicism. In others, the English party—or the Appellants as they came to be known—it strengthened their hostility to the Spanish party and emphasized the need to break out of this entanglement and to negotiate direct with the English government some *modus vivendi* for their co-religionists. Certainly Robert Cecil, who had read the *Conference*, and no less certainly read the logic of the situation, showed himself to be an astute politician in his handling of it. In the ensuing battle of wits—in essence between Cecil and Parsons—some of the basic problems of English Catholicism were brought into the open. In the process we get also the first pointer to their ultimate solution.

It is impossible, of course, to do justice to the polemical skill of so experienced a propagandist as Robert Parsons; but for our purpose his arguments may be briefly summarized. There were numerous claimants to the English succession; but their lines were tainted with illegitimacy or heresy, or disputed over by conflicting directions of royal will or parliamentary statute. Only

[1] A. O. Meyer, *England and the Catholic Church under Queen Elizabeth*, tr. J. R. McKee (1916), p. 381.

one candidate stood out from the rest with an incomparably superior claim: the Infanta of Spain. To her rights by inheritance she added the additional qualification of the impeccable orthodoxy of her faith.

It would not be necessary to tarry long over the unrealistic speculations of an *émigré* were it not that it was seriously alleged at about this time (for example at the trial of the Earl of Essex) and repeated in modern historical studies, that these views about the succession were shared by so hard-headed a politician as Sir Robert Cecil, at that time Elizabeth's secretary of state. Cecil was not normally responsive to the persuasion of Father Parsons; but it has recently been argued again that there is a considerable body of evidence from various sources which sustains this thesis.[1] Some of this evidence can be dealt with briefly. Mrs Carmichael Stopes, who is first cited, turns out in effect to have produced a speculation of the most fantastic kind. Essex, she believed, had probably received 'some hint' that Cecil was a Spanish pensioner. However, he did not wish to incriminate others, so at his trial he referred to the pension only in an indirect way by saying that Cecil had spoken in support of the Infanta. In short, Essex allowed his whole defence to collapse rather than state what he believed to be true about Cecil. Moreover, she continued, Cecil took a pension from the King of Spain and secret presents 'during the whole life of James' [*sic*],[2] so 'it is much more than likely he had begun to do so even towards the close of Elizabeth's reign'. This time, apparently, 'was a much more fitting period for the Spanish king to begin to tempt the English courtiers than the commencement of the reign of her legitimate and approved heir'. There is very little comment to be made upon this 'more than likely' explanation except to say that it is worth no more than a straightforward invention of the facts.

To reinforce these guesses we are now offered additional material which, it is said, clearly establishes Cecil's involvement in

[1] The most recent presentation of this view is in L. Hicks, 'Sir Robert Cecil, Father Parsons, and the Succession, 1600–1' (*Arch. Hist. Soc. Iesu*, xxiv), pp. 95–139, from which the evidence discussed in the following pages is taken.

[2] I cite this as given by Father Hicks. Mrs Stopes in fact said, 'during his whole life under James I': *The Third Earl of Southampton*, p. 212.

this Spanish succession plot. The argument is as follows. The bitter rivalry between him and Essex, damped down during the last decade of Burghley's rule, finally flared up into a life and death struggle as soon as the old statesman was in his grave. Essex, by one device or another, had gained the ear of James VI who now looked to him as the rising statesman of the new age. With the intention of making himself doubly secure, Essex warned James of Cecil's hostility and of the latter's plot to frustrate the Stuart succession by bringing over the Infanta of Spain. Cecil, for his part, blackened Essex's name in the eyes of the queen and took, also, more practical steps to discredit his rival by trapping him into accepting the impossible task of subjugating Ireland. Once Essex was there, Cecil completed the manœuvre by sabotaging the Irish campaign through inadequate provision of men and supplies.

This is a familiar accusation, but with all its details we are not here concerned. Since, however, we are now offered 'a revealing letter' which purports to show one more link in the guilty chain of Cecil's duplicity, it deserves a little attention. In May 1599, Sir William Knollys, uncle of Essex, wrote to Cecil about Ireland to draw his attention to the danger arising from shortage of supplies. Part of one sentence from that letter has been quoted to indicate what was afoot, of which this is the correct version as given in the Historical Manuscripts Commission's *Report*.[1]

> I am not of opinion you have reason to hearken to any new demand, though he [Essex] shew a necessary reason touching the carriage horses which are not there to be had, and without which he will not be able to march, but unless you keep touch with him *in the agreements concluded on*, both for his number and the timely supplies, he may allege the same excuses that former governors have done, and *in the end that state must perish of a consumption, and it cannot but so infect England as it may grow into the like danger.*

Apart from minor errors, the quoted extract has left out the last

[1] Hist. MSS. Com. *Salisbury*, ix, 188. The problem of the supply of carriage horses is discussed in L. W. Henry, 'The Earl of Essex and Ireland, 1599' (*Bull. Inst. Hist. Res.*, xxxii), pp. 1–23.

part of the sentence and one significant expression in the middle (I have italicized the omitted passages). As a result, it looks as though Knollys is simply telling Cecil to ignore these urgent demands. It is even more significant that the letter as a whole, from whose context this part of a sentence has been torn, is a strong appeal to Cecil that the government should fulfil its commitments to Essex. 'Truly', wrote Knollys, 'if it be not done in his due time, it were as good not at all, for it is so much treasure and victual lost and Her Majesty's state there growing to be worse and worse.' These needs, in other words, must be fulfilled in the national interest and for that reason 'I am not of opinion you have reason to hearken to any *new* demand' (my italics). In essence he is saying that commitments must be met, in respect of 'the agreements concluded on', rather than new demands entertained. His letter includes a renewed appeal for action or '*in the end that [Irish] state must perish of a consumption, and it cannot but so infect England as it may grow into the like danger*' (my italics). What we are told is a piece of advice to betray Essex turns out on investigation to be an appeal to give Essex the full aid that has been promised. Since the cited extract, implying that Knollys was betraying Essex, has been used to impugn Knollys's evidence at Essex's trial, it has been necessary to establish first what in fact Knollys was saying.

But far more important than this is the new 'evidence', now brought forward, of Cecil's plans to replace James VI by the Infanta as Elizabeth's successor. First we are reminded of the promise by a certain Italian, Filippo Corsini, of the secret, speedy dispatch to Cecil of a portrait of the Infanta and her husband the Archduke.[1] Whether this was for himself or the queen we cannot say; but the purchase of portraits of foreign notables was a widespread practice and it is dangerous to draw from this any conclusions other than that it represents the natural desire of a leading English statesman to have a portrait of a claimant to the throne. That Cecil was interested in the Infanta there can be no question. She had, after all, been strongly urged by Father Parsons and might well be supported by English Catholics abroad — or even at home. She might indeed be raised also as a bargaining counter

[1] Hist. MSS. Com. *Salisbury*, ix, 345, 391, 440.

in the Anglo-Spanish peace negotiations which opened in 1599. Here was a perfectly good reason for the speedy dispatch of the portrait which would, especially at this time, have to be done secretly. The request is therefore no more than a sign that the English government took seriously the claims being put forward on behalf of the Infanta.

But shortly after this, in April 1600, Father Parsons began to receive letters from a correspondent in England which purported to shed light on Cecil's policy about the succession. Who the correspondent was is not stated, nor have the original letters survived. But Spanish translations of them, sometimes with comments by Parsons, were sent to Philip III of Spain (who had succeeded Philip II in 1598), having been passed on by his ambassador in Rome; and these papers are now at Simancas. The correspondent, it is claimed, 'was in contact with the party of Cecil'. The Cecilians, he said, had their own claimant in the person of Anne, daughter of the fifth Earl of Derby. Since this group was not ill-affected to the Catholic religion, the Cecilians might be able to carry many of the Catholics with them. It was therefore necessary to get an indication of his views from the King of Spain so that English Catholics might know where they stood. His majesty, however, would at this stage go no further than a vague promise of support for a Catholic, and then left Father Parsons to his own (diplomatic) devices.

By the autumn of 1600, Parsons's correspondent had, apparently, obtained from the Cecilians a more precise declaration of where their interests lay. They had, he claimed, abandoned any hope that an English subject could possibly succeed. The choice lay therefore between the King of Scots and the Infanta; and it was known that they hated and feared James VI. If, however, they received no guidance from the King of Spain, they would, the report continued, be bound soon to make terms with the King of Scots. At once this brought from Parsons his urgent plea that Philip III should act with all speed. So, at last, in February 1601, Philip acquiesced and declared himself for the Infanta; but he added the strong request that the knowledge of this decision should be withheld from everyone save those 'who can be trusted to promote its successful issue'. If Philip at last began to move, the others involved continued to drag their heels. The Infanta received the proposal coolly. The pope, who looked with great alarm at any increase of Spanish power and feared the Catholic King of Spain more than the heretical King of Scotland, had his own reasons therefore for holding aloof. He had also to consider the King of France with whom the delicate ties of friendship might easily be snapped if it became known that the pope was supporting a Spanish candidate. 'No woman', said the disillusioned Spanish ambassador, was 'more careful not to arouse suspicion in her husband than was the pope as regards the French King.' But the best comment on the situation in general had come earlier from a disappointed Catholic, writing in August 1600. 'The Spanish King's council', he said, 'have often inquired if we cannot find a king of our own, temperate to Catholics, and they would aid. So matters remain unresolved, and we in the briars, not knowing the way out. The Jesuits feed us with words and the Spaniards with hopes.'[1]

Who, in fact, evolved the wishful delusion of Robert Cecil engaged in ushering in the Infanta's rule of England under Spanish–Jesuit patronage we shall probably never know. It may have first taken root in Parsons's own mind since his inventive— if wayward—genius could weave fantasies with irrepressible fervour. Or it may be that his correspondent, some dim purveyor of hare-brained rumours, really persuaded Parsons that he had genuine knowledge of Cecil's political attitude. It may even be that some lesser politician in England, for reasons best known to himself, led some political innocent into a wonderland of his own. Certainly it was common enough for Cecil's enemies to accuse him behind his back of supporting the Infanta. James VI was being bombarded with such information, as earlier he had apparently been told by the Earl of Leicester that Cecil's father was opposed to James.[2] Similarly, James appears to have been told that Essex was opposed to his succession;[3] while the irrepressible Father

[1] *Cal. S.P. Dom.* 1598–1601, 460.
[2] Read, *Lord Burghley and Queen Elizabeth* (1955), pp. 291–2.
[3] Hist. MSS. Com. *Salisbury,* ix, 307–8.

Parsons — that 'broker of kingdoms' as Camden called him — tried to persuade the earl to side with the Infanta![1]

All that we have, then, is a vague, unsupported story (without a single scrap of concrete evidence) from some unidentified correspondent of Father Parsons. And against this must be set the repeated affirmations by Cecil that such charges were untrue, and his public refutation of them at the trial of the Earl of Essex. More important still as an indication of Cecil's attitude is his behaviour after Essex was dead. Now Cecil was without his most dangerous rival, and if he had genuinely feared — as some said — that James would one day avenge himself for his mother's execution, he was in a far better position to further the claims of the Infanta. Instead he devoted all his energies and patience to procuring the peaceful accession of James VI. It seems that we must treat this latest version of Cecil's policy — based upon Parsons's documents — with the same scepticism with which it was received by the Infanta.

But if, amidst the troubled waters of international intrigue, Father Parsons was fishing with his accustomed lack of skill, it would be a mistake to dismiss the result as no more than an insignificant bubble in an extremely muddy stream. For, if we consider the timing of the episode, it has a particularly close relevance to one of the great issues of Elizabethan England, namely that of Catholic recusancy. For the English Catholics — at home and in exile — were now engaged in their own struggle over the succession. In the process the whole problem of the place of Catholics in the English polity would be thrashed out again.

By the last decade of her reign, Elizabeth's relations with her Catholic subjects had reached something like deadlock. For more than thirty years her government had tried by various methods to bring them, at least nominally, within the framework of her Church settlement. In her early years it seemed — at least to the Catholic exiles — that she might be succeeding; that the broken, leaderless remnant of their followers might before very long disappear into the anonymous, enveloping folds of the Church of England. But, as long as the queen's religious policy was

[1] W. Camden, *Elizabeth* (1688 edn), p. 652; *Cal. S.P. Dom.* 1598–1601, 453.

ambiguous, there remained among the optimists some slender hope that she might yet revert to the Roman jurisdiction. To us, looking back, the idea seems unrealistic but to contemporaries it was much more easy to conceive. A return to Rome would not necessarily mean for Elizabeth the abandonment of all that had been gained by the English Reformation: papal authority could be more flexible than its more authoritarian *dicta* might lead some to believe. After all, the Valois kings of France had negotiated a concordat which gave them something like control over a national church and had won their victory without having to fight for it. Philip II had gained the same thing. His dynastic imperialism was often hostile to papal intentions but he remained, albeit with difficulty, a powerful King of Spain at the same time that he was a faithful adherent of the Church.[1] His dynastic interests usually predominated: hence, in the context of his anti-French hostility, he had for more than a decade shielded Elizabeth from the due chastisement of a heretic.

But by 1570 the papal Curia had decided that it must follow a line of its own, without giving too close attention to the diplomatic manœuvres of Philip II. The Bull of excommunication and deposition, issued against Elizabeth in that year, and the vigorous missionary policy which in due course followed, combined to give to Catholicism in England a political significance of grave and growing dimensions. That situation was exacerbated by the peculiar role which Mary Queen of Scots assigned to herself. In face of this the government, under parliamentary pressure, responded with intensified penal legislation. By the 1580s Catholicism was a proscribed religion and its priests were being hunted down as traitors.

It is not necessary to rehearse that legislation here. In 1581 and 1585 it took on its most savage form: non-attendance at church was to be punished at the rate of £20 a month and priests were *ipso facto* to be deemed traitors. But what followed in the next decade should not be underrated. For the act of 1593 alleviated, if only by a little, the further penalties now proposed against

---

[1] For a discussion of this see J. Lynch, 'Philip II and the Papacy', *Trans. R.H.S.*, 5th Ser., xi, pp. 23-42.

Catholics. A priest, who refused to answer as to his identity, could be sent to prison but did not, as proposed, in virtue of this refusal automatically become subject to the death penalty.[1] It was a small alleviation; but it was a sign of the times.

In one sense this was an acknowledgment of deadlock: the government had gone as far as it was able towards eliminating the Catholic resistance to its policy of *gleichschaltung* — and it would go on exacting the heavy penalty of £20 a month for recusancy where it could — but the small hard core of Catholicism would remain. In the north of England it was much more than this. The evidence as it began to come in, for example from Lancashire in the 1590s, drew an alarming picture of the infiltration of Catholic missionaries from top to bottom of Lancastrian society, from the family of the Earl of Derby himself down through the commission of the peace, the gentry and the rest.[2] The Lancastrian recusants, said the Bishop of Chester, 'despise authority ... and are fed by their priests with hopes of a better time shortly'.[3] On the other side of England, Yorkshire had its share of Catholic resistance, probably less than in Lancashire; but in the city of York, for example, headquarters of the Court of High Commission, the brother of the lord mayor himself was known to be a recusant.[4] The ecclesiastical commissioners, said the queen, behave 'as though the laws were instituted not for punishment [of recusants] but to enrich' commissioners. The instructions that 'we have sent hitherto have been written in water'.[5] In Hampshire, recusancy was significant.[6] In Sussex, Lord Montagu and other leading figures were Catholics. In London, the Clink, intended as a prison for active Catholics, had become a propaganda cell for

---

[1] 35 Eliz. c. 2; Neale, *Elizabeth I and Her Parliaments, 1584–1601*, pp. 295–6.

[2] J. S. Leatherbarrow, *The Lancashire Elizabethan Recusants* (Manchester, 1947), pp. 112–15.

[3] *Cal. S.P. Dom.* 1598–1601, 389–90.

[4] A. G. Dickens, 'The first stages of Romanist recusancy in Yorkshire, 1560–1590' and 'The extent and character of recusancy in Yorkshire, 1604' (*Yorks. Arch. J.*), xxxv, pp. 157–81 and xxxvii, pp. 24–48.

[5] *Cal. S.P. Dom.* 1598–1601, 276.

[6] J. E. Paul, 'Hampshire Recusants in the reign of Elizabeth I' (unpublished Southampton Univ. Ph.D. thesis, 1958).

the whole capital.[1] The periodic purges of the commissions of the peace, the martyrdom of priests, the heavy fines and imprisonments, if they had kept the Catholic problem within bounds, had none the less failed to break through the strategically powerful defences of Catholicism in the shires.

In that sense, then, the slight alleviation of 1593 was a recognition that the Catholic revival was too sturdy a movement to be broken by legislation, especially as that legislation was aided only by a rudimentary and corrupt police system and resisted in many places by thoroughly hostile local officials. But this more temperate mood was a sign also of something else. Mary Queen of Scots had been executed; the Armada was defeated. Yet, at two such delicate moments for English security, nowhere in the country had a single Catholic done anything to hinder the government in its defence precautions. By 1590 it had thus become certain that, although in terms of religion the Catholic movement was invincible to the queen, in terms of politics it was invincible to her enemies. The significance of this was not lost either on the queen's government or on the more aggressive of the Catholic missionaries. So the 1590s in effect saw the struggle for the soul of English Catholicism between the government — and more especially Robert Cecil and Richard Bancroft, the Bishop of London — and the Jesuit missionaries, led with such resource and imagination by Robert Parsons. One scene of that struggle was the castle of Wisbech in Cambridgeshire.

Since 1580 this relatively isolated, decaying building on the Isle of Ely had been used as an internment centre for Catholic priests. The total number gathered there was never very large, at most about thirty-five, but they included some notable scholars as well as some lively missionaries. After 1585 the government could, if it wished, have executed newly captured priests as felons; but the moral effect of these martyrdoms had been to inspire rather than terrify the reviving Catholic movement. Executions went on; but some of the most distinguished of the priests were spared the scaffold and sent to Wisbech. Here the conditions of confinement

[1] J. Gerard, *The Autobiography of an Elizabethan*, trs. Philip Caraman (1951), pp. 79–80.

were, at first, probably severe. But as the community grew the prisoners were allowed, within measure, the modest amenities of communal life. They dined together, held discussions, were in some cases allowed servants and could receive guests – as well as gentlemen's sons, sent to them for their education – and were free to go into the neighbouring town. So in time Wisbech developed a character of its own and became a combination of hostel, school, postgraduate seminar in ecclesiastical studies and a propaganda discussion centre. Propaganda, like charity, begins at home; and one of the minor successes of Wisbech was the conversion of the gaoler's daughter to Roman Catholicism. Her father was a virulent Puritan.[1]

But conditions were far from good. Moreover, in spite of the concentration of such diverse talent under one roof – or perhaps because of it – internal feuds began to develop. Such differences are not unknown in any academic community; and here, as else-where, they may have developed simply as the result of discordant temperaments being driven to extremity in the intimate stress of enforced communal life. But once the differences were openly expressed they took shape, not simply in personal attack, but in a struggle over principle. By 1595 two bitterly opposed parties existed at Wisbech which, in the course of the struggle, involved in their affairs the Jesuit order, the papacy, the King of Spain – and Sir Robert Cecil. For a good part of the time the battle was fought over organization; but it became increasingly dominated by the struggle over the succession.

Viewed superficially, the issue was at first simple enough: who was to preside over the Wisbech community? Among the early prisoners had been Thomas Watson, Bishop of Lincoln under Queen Mary, and he had exercised an informal authority over his colleagues there. That authority had passed after his death in 1584 to the Jesuit Thomas Metham, who had continued this unofficial leadership, latterly against some opposition, until his own death in 1592.[2] After this, another Jesuit, William Weston, exercised

[1] T. G. Law, *A Historical Sketch of the Conflicts between Jesuits and Seculars* (1889), pp. xlii–xliii.
[2] P. Renold, *The Wisbech Stirs* (Cath. Rec. Soc., li), pp. xii–xiv.

considerable influence; but by now the friction between the two main groups had burst out into open conflict. Father Weston accordingly withdrew from the communal arrangements and he was shortly joined by eighteen other priests and the one layman incarcerated with them. In the opposing group were twelve priests led by Christopher Bagshaw and Thomas Bluet. According to the latter group Weston's withdrawal had been voluntary and he had allured or bribed others to join him.[1] According to the Jesuits, Bagshaw had forced Weston and his followers to withdraw. The exact details of these factional moves are, however, less important than the efforts of Weston's followers to obtain his official appointment as 'a judge, corrector and censurer'. This office Weston was apparently reluctant to accept; but his supporters prevailed upon Father Garnett, Provincial of the Jesuits in England, who accordingly appointed Weston but was careful to restrict his powers to moral leadership only. The opposition just the same regarded this step as nothing less than a success for the Jesuits in their efforts to impose their will on their fellow Catholics in England.

Even so, the quarrel might have blown over had it not become involved with a comparable struggle in the English College in Rome and, indeed, with the whole question of the Jesuit role in European affairs. For at least a decade there had been intermittent dissension among the English students in Rome, arising in part from hostility to the discipline administered by the Jesuits. But in 1595 the new outburst was the most bitter of all, involved as it was with principle as well as behaviour. That this internal movement in the English College had, as was alleged by the Jesuits, personal links with the dissidents at Wisbech there is no reason to doubt. But it is the date itself which is of the most significance. A year had passed since the publication of Parsons's book on the succession, and the debate among Catholics had taken on a more vigorous form. These dissidents, said the rector of the English College in 1596, 'speak frequently and sharply against the book on the succession to the English throne and against its author ... I know not whether they hate the Society [of Jesus] on account of

[1] Renold, op. cit., p. xiv and text; Law, op. cit., pp. liii–liv.

the Spaniards, or the Spaniards on account of the Society ... '[1]

From now onwards the issue of the succession was to the fore and gave a more acute definition to the existing causes of conflict. These were in part personal, in part administrative. The Jesuits, with heroic self-sacrifice and masterly discipline, sought with characteristic devotion to carry the ideals of the Catholic Reformation, speedily and forcefully, into the lives of priest and layman alike. They carried many of the secular priests with them in these aims; but others resisted. Those who resisted also had their ideals. But what divided them from the Jesuits was their belief that the Protestant settlement in England was, after forty years, secure; that the best way to improve the lot of English Catholics was, therefore, not to attempt to overthrow the Protestant system but somehow to negotiate terms with it. They believed that there were more roads open to English Catholics than the straight and narrow one imperiously pointed out by the Jesuits. Some English Catholics were in essence becoming insular, but not separatist. They believed—ahead of their time as it turned out—that it was better for Catholicism to seek to become a tolerated minority religion than to hurl itself in vain against the established Church. They had imbibed also, along with their Protestant fellow countrymen, the insular patriotic emotions which it seems to have been the especial task of Philip II of Spain to intensify. In short, they hated the Spaniards more than they hated Elizabeth I of England—or James VI of Scotland.

It is unfortunate that this central issue has been obscured in recent historiography by those who have taken at its face value the volume of abuse which the controversy generated in its own day. Much of it was simply the stock-in-trade of contemporary propaganda methods. There is in fact little utility in basing arguments upon the unedifying catalogue of unnatural vice which was drawn up by both sides. For example, whatever his faults, there is no doubt as to the heroic devotion of Father Parsons in a cause to which he gave a lifetime of unremitting service and a variety of skills. On the other side, William Gifford, who rose ultimately to

[1] C. Dodd, *The Church History of England*, ed. M. A. Tierney (1839–43), iii, Appendix, lxxv.

be a respected Archbishop of Rheims, can hardly be dismissed as an irresponsible trouble-maker. Nor can any credence be given to the 'confession' of the unstable Robert Fisher who, after his arrest at Rome, turned against his Wisbech friends and provided Parsons, and his later defenders, with a valuable storehouse of polemical ammunition.[1] Parsons himself said, 'we will not affirm all to be true which he said'.[2] Nor shall we.

During 1598 this division among English Catholics altered its shape but not its content. It became known as the Archpriest Controversy and, amid changing fortunes, dragged on until the end of the reign. Again, in so far as it concerns the organization of Catholic dissent in England, it need not delay us here. Summarized very briefly, the argument now turned on whether, as some of the seculars wished, a bishop should be appointed to officiate as best he could in a heretical country; or whether, by the institution of the office of archpriest, Catholic interests would be better served. Again personal issues broke into theoretical differences of approach. Many of the seculars believed that a bishop would bring with him some measure of local self-determination – once again their approach bears the impress of their insular outlook – while an archpriest would emphasize, rather than mitigate, their dependence upon overseas direction. When, in fact, George Blackwell was appointed archpriest, and appeared from the start to operate under Jesuit guidance, the dissidents now felt themselves to be given over wholly to the dominance of their opponents, and they appealed to Rome. The Appellants, as they came therefore to be known, had possibly planned in any case to carry their dissident opinions to the Curia; but the establishment of an archpriest gave greater point to their discontent. In this appointment they probably overrated the influence of Parsons;[3] and mistook the consequences of the appointment for its cause. Certainly Parsons played his part in defeating the work of the Appellants in Rome in 1598 and, in so doing, added fuel to the smouldering discontents of the Appellants. That, accompanied by the autocratic

[1] The confession is printed in full in Renold, op. cit., pp. 230–63.

[2] Cited in Law, op. cit., p. 98n.

[3] *Letters of Thomas Fitzherbert, 1608–10*, ed. L. Hicks (Cath. Rec. Soc., xli), pp. 127–8.

methods of Blackwell—including his condemnation of members
of the opposition as schismatics—led to the second appeal to
Rome of November 1600, signed by thirty-three priests.[1] Meanwhile a small group of the opposition had taken the dangerous
step of opening negotiations with the Elizabethan government.

When exactly these secret talks began it is impossible to say.
Contacts of some kind existed before the outbreak of the Archpriest Controversy; but it was not only the English government
that was sounded in this connection. While the controversy was
at its height, the Appellants looked also for support from the
French embassy in Rome and from the university of Paris: one
more move in the anti-Spanish struggle. But it was in their
negotiations with Robert Cecil and Bancroft that the Appellants
embarked upon a series of transactions which look at first sight
like nothing less than treason to their cause.

From the autumn of 1598 Bagshaw was supplying the privy
council with information about the Appellants' relations with the
Jesuits.[2] Also, hostile material about the Jesuits was supplied to the
council the following year by another priest, William Watson.[3]
From now onwards, if not earlier, Robert Cecil was kept fully
informed about the state of the Archpriest Controversy. At about
this time also, the English ambassador in Paris, Sir Henry Neville,
transmitted a report from a Catholic, Charles Paget, claiming to
speak on behalf of Catholic laymen in bitter hostility to Jesuit
plans for the succession.[4] However much he may have exaggerated the size of his following, his was not a solitary voice. Nor
was this the only form in which opposition expressed itself. In
the previous year another secular priest, John Bishop, had come
forward and published a treatise against the papal claim to depose
princes;[5] while the Appellants sought an order from the papacy
prohibiting the publication, without ecclesiastical approval, of
books hostile to the English government. From one viewpoint
these moves may perhaps be described as a sign of the patriotic

[1] Meyer, *England and the Catholic Church under Queen Elizabeth*, p. 431.
[2] Law, op. cit., p. lxxix.
[3] Meyer, op. cit., p. 425.
[4] *Cal. S.P. Dom.* 1598–1601, 220–21.
[5] Meyer, op. cit., p. 420.

fervour of a group of English Catholics; but there can be no question that it is besmirched by personal hostility to the Jesuits and the willingness to denounce their activities to the government of Protestant England. The Appellants were, in essence, appealing to Rome and London at one and the same time. In so far as so dangerous and ambiguous a policy can be explained, the explanation lies in their resolution to prevent a Spanish succession to the English throne, and in their hopes of obtaining religious toleration under some other candidate.

They believed that the Jesuits would favour a Spanish succession; that the Jesuits, and those who shared their opinions, had no use for a toleration given by the tainted hands of the heretics. Toleration might indeed sap the will of Catholic resistance. '[As] for a toleration or liberty of conscience in England,' the pope was reported by one of the Appellants to have said, 'it would do harm and make Catholics become heretics; that persecution was profitable to the church.'[1] Yet, in spite of the questionable tactics that they employed, it is possible to see in the Appellants the first overt sign that a group of English priests was seeking a way of life in which they might become patriotic Englishmen while remaining faithful Catholics. By contrast, the Jesuits believed that there could be no peace without Spain. It was a view sincerely held by them and shared by others, including so eminent a layman as Sir Francis Englefield, who had written in September 1596: 'Without the support and troops of Spain it is scarcely probable that the Catholic religion will ever be restored and established in that country [England]. Even the seminaries, powerful as they are in preparing men's minds for a change must fail to complete their object without the aid of temporal force.'[2] In face of this profound conflict of opinion within the Catholic world, the great campaign of denigration conducted by both sides soils the genuine idealism which lay at the basis of both. Here was the tragedy at the heart of English Catholicism. Because of it both sides played with the dangerous fires of treason, in one case against the state, in the other against their Church.

[1] Law, op. cit., p. cvi.
[2] Ibid., p. xiv n. 3.

For the next few years Cecil and his colleagues were holding conferences with the dissidents, before whom was held continuously the bait of religious toleration. In return for this they would assume the welcome task of breaking the Jesuit hold upon English Catholicism and identify themselves with an anti-Spanish policy. In contrast, the instructions to the archpriest are significant. His task was 'not only to preserve union during the lifetime of the Queen but, much more, to procure a Catholic successor after her death, in conformity with certain briefs which His Holiness has already most prudently addressed to the Catholics'.[1] In allying himself with the opponents of the archpriest, therefore, Cecil was in effect allying himself with that wing of the Catholic movement which stood solidly against the Infanta's succession to the English throne. By 1600 that alliance, however tenuously, had been formed; and the date is important. For it was at this very time that Parsons began to receive letters from his correspondent in England implying that the Cecilians wanted a pronouncement on behalf of the Infanta. It is thus possible now to estimate the value of the evidence about Cecil's involvement in the Infanta plot. For Parsons's story is meaningless without its context of the archpriest controversy and the bitter struggle going on in Rome between the two elements of the English Catholic movement.

Parsons had, by 1600, won no permanent victory against the Appellants and their policy of seeking an understanding with Cecil. It was at this stage, therefore, that Parsons called upon his second line of defence. The Infanta theory, whatever dubious value it had amid the harsh diplomatic realities of 1600, had other services to render. For example, by claiming the Cecilians as allies of the Infanta, at the very time when Cecil was negotiating with the Appellants, Parsons would sow confusion in their ranks and damage the incipient agreement now under negotiation. He would also prove to Rome that the Appellants were a discredited minority who had no notion of Cecil's real plans and who were in fact a barrier to an effective alliance between Cecil and the Jesuits to bring over the Infanta. He would also discomfort and embarrass French diplomacy which was, at this very time, being

[1] Ibid., p. lxi.

asked to support the Appellants against the hispanophile Jesuits. Also, if the story ever reached the queen's ears, it would discredit Cecil as well as his plan for a *détente* with the Catholics. In practice, the Cecil–Infanta story was more important as a move in the internal struggle between the Jesuits and the Appellants than as a serious proposal to the pope or the King of Spain.

It is not surprising that, at the very time when Parsons was filling the diplomatic bag of the Spanish ambassador in Rome with his report of Cecil's conversion to the Spanish cause, similar tales were being whispered in the ear of James VI. (That unfortunate king was the recipient of a number of far-fetched stories during the long years that he was waiting for his inheritance, including one – from Parsons! – that the Appellants were opposed to his succession.[1]) The Spaniards, James VI was warned by the friends of Essex, could rely upon the help of Cecil. Essex repeated the story in the streets of London when he said that the Crown of England was sold to the Spaniard, and he repeated it also at his own trial. Then at last he received the contemptuous refutation of Cecil himself: 'I have said that the King of Spain is a competitor of the crown of England, and that the King of Scots is a competitor, and my Lord of Essex I have said is a competitor; for he would depose the Queen and call a parliament and so be king himself.'[2] His own defence – as well as his actions – carries far greater conviction than the allegations of Essex or of the anonymous correspondent of Father Parsons. Certainly it convinced James VI and thereby inaugurated that secret correspondence between monarch and minister which was to last until James VI peacefully took his seat on the English throne.

The struggle between Cecil and Essex, which came into the open soon after Burghley's death in 1598 and ended only with the death of Essex two and a half years later, was not in any direct sense a struggle over the succession to the throne. It was rather a struggle for power itself during the lifetime of the queen. As such

[1] Law, op. cit., p. cvii.
[2] *Correspondence of King James VI of Scotland with Sir Robert Cecil*, ed. J. Bruce (Camd. Soc., O.S., lxxviii, 1861), p. xxxiii.

it divided England and then, as since, aroused a good deal of sympathy for the defeated candidate. Cecil won because he was the more skilful politician; because, from the start, he held a firm hand on the government machine and enjoyed the confidence of the queen; because the queen blocked Essex in his desire and need for office for himself and his followers until in the end he fell into a trap of his own making by going to Ireland; because, finally, faced with bankruptcy, and in the midst of unendurable nervous tension, he called upon the London mob for aid. But at no stage during these intervening years is there any documentary evidence that Cecil himself planned the downfall of his opponent, nothing comparable to Essex's own plan to replace Sir Walter Ralegh, the captain of the guard, and Sir Robert Cecil, the secretary, by his own nominees, Sir William Russell and Sir Henry Neville (or Thomas Bodley).[1] Cecil could, of course, do his damage verbally since he had the ear of the queen throughout, while Essex was forbidden the royal presence. But if Cecil did this, it was certainly no worse than what Essex did on his behalf to James VI. In fact, the real damage had been done long before 1598, and by Essex to himself, whose conduct at court had deprived the queen of the confidence she had in him as a statesman. 'Mr Secretary [Cecil] did you good service in Council, and the queen liked it well,' Sir Henry Ley had told him in 1598. But he added a warning: 'Your honour [prestige] is more dear to you than your life, yet consider that she is your sovereign, whom you may not treat upon equal conditions.'[2]

The Essex rebellion derived from the impossible situation in which Essex found himself in the last years before 1601. Denied access to the source of patronage and influence, he must either see his power sterilized and his following shrink for want of supplies, or he must break through to gain access to – if necessary, control over – that source. That is what Cecil meant when he charged him with wanting to be king of England. 'It resteth with me in my opinion', noted the shrewd John Harington of the Earl of Essex before the storm broke, 'that ambition, thwarted in its

[1] *Cal. S.P. Dom.* 1601–3, 2.
[2] Ibid., 1598–1601, 88–9.

career, doth speedily lead on to madness — His speeches of the queen becometh no man who hath *mens sana in corpore sano.*'[1] Essex in the end was caught in the ineluctable dilemma of power inherent in the existing political structure. Cecil was no doubt shrewd enough to see the consequences for Essex of such a dilemma; but it was quite unnecessary for him to invent one. That Cecil was alarmed by the rebellion is also clear enough: a full year after it had been crushed the government was still examining witnesses, still looking for the roots and offshoots of conspiracy.[2]

The elimination of Essex provided the opportunity for Cecil to establish contact with James VI. Now at last he could give the quietus to the scandalous reports, spread by his enemies, that he favoured the Infanta. But if the succession problem was in one sense eased, in another it was made more dangerous. For now Cecil had to engage in a secret correspondence with a foreign monarch. If it ever came to the notice of the queen, whose opposition to announcing a successor was still unshakeable, it might lay Cecil open to the charge of disloyalty — or something worse.

There is, of course, a good deal to be said, especially in the earlier part of her reign, in favour of Elizabeth's policy of refusing to acknowledge a successor. The only feasible one then, in spite of her notorious performance as Queen of Scots, would have been Mary Stuart. To have acknowledged her might well have prompted rebellion on behalf of an English candidate against a Catholic Scot. After Mary's death in 1587 Elizabeth did not change her policy; she was still anxious, perhaps, not to rouse an anti-Scottish faction which might have tried to make things impossible for James — and for Elizabeth. Whatever the political reasoning behind it, in this policy Elizabeth was consistent throughout her life. Mingled with it there were, of course, the understandable personal feelings of an old and popular queen who hated to see her own shadow lengthen while the sun rose in Scotland. But it was a dangerous policy, for the risk was always present

---

[1] J. Harington, *Nugae Antiquae*, i, p. 179.
[2] *Cal. S.P. Dom.* 1601–3, 152–3.

that James might ally with some political irresponsible who promised him present joys rather than distant prospects. That surely was what the friends of Essex were doing when they invited him to save Essex – and England – by bringing an army south in 1600.[1] Fortunately, James had none of the adventurous spirit of his mother and, at the last, shrank back from what would have been an act of war. But it was a near thing. And it was not the first time that there were rumours that James VI 'would attempt to gather fruit before it is ripe'.[2]

Long before, in the summer of 1592, James had drawn up a clear statement of his views on the English succession. At this stage, he said, he did not contemplate invading England to obtain his inheritance. Scotland itself was not at peace; and he could not move south leaving a disorderly baronage to wreak havoc behind him. Accordingly, he continued, 'in the meantime I will deal with the Queen of England fair and pleasantly for my title to the Crown of England after her decease.' If his title was recognized – 'as it is not impossible, howbeit unlikely' – 'we have attained our design without stroke of sword'. If not, then he would bide his time and – after notifying the King of Spain! – would obtain the English crown without waiting.[3]

This wild scheme was never put into practice. In 1600, when it might have been, James was eight years older and had grown either more shrewd or more cautious. But even in 1601, when Cecil had established contact with James VI, a dangerous situation remained. Looking back at it, years afterwards, Cecil defended his policy of backstage negotiation with James. 'For what could more quiet the expectation of a successor,' he asked, 'so many ways invited to jealousy, than when he saw her ministry, that were most inward with her [the queen], wholly bent to accommodate the present actions of state for his future safety, when God should see his time?' But this plan of his carried dangers too. However much the queen trusted him, he said, 'if Her Majesty had known all I did ... her age and orbity, joined to the jealousy of her sex,

---

[1] D. H. Willson, *King James VI and I* (1956), p. 151.
[2] *Cal. S.P. Dom.* 1589–1601, 201; cf. ibid., 343.
[3] Willson, op. cit., p. 111.

might have moved her to think ill of that *which helped to preserve her*'.[1]

Very conscious of these dangers, Cecil went so far as to dismiss Simon Willis, his private secretary, 'partly for his pride' but 'principally because I was loath he should have come to some discovery of that correspondency which I had with the king our sovereign, which without great difficulty I could not have avoided'. Hence 'he might have raised some such inferences thereof as might have bred some jealousy in the queen's mind'.[2]

So Cecil, from the spring of 1601, bent himself to two tasks: to instruct James in the duties which would one day await him in London and, secondly, to ensure that James was never again tempted to seize power before his time.[3] He urged him to pay no serious attention to the 'pamphlets and projects of priests and fugitives, who are always labouring to set up one golden calf or other'. Now James began to sing a different tune. 'Yea, what a foolish part were that in me', he wrote, 'if I might do it to hazard my honour, state and person, in entering that kingdom by violence as an usurper.' Rather than climb over hedges to pick unripe fruit, he said, earlier in the letter, he would prefer to enter the garden by the gate 'and enjoy the fruits at my pleasure, in the time of their greatest maturity'.[4] How different this was from his speech to the Scottish Parliament in 1599! Then he had declared that 'He was not certain how soon he should have to use arms; but whenever it should be, he knew his right and would venture crown and all for it'.[5]

This change, in so short a space of time, was a tribute to Cecil's statesmanship. And, although the king later on forgot his debt, his peaceful succession was the clearest manifestation of Cecil's achievement. But new problems arose for Cecil as Sir Walter Ralegh, his friend and collaborator, began to play the Essex in a separate correspondence with James VI. The exact nature of this

[1] A. Collins, *Sidney Papers*, ii, p. 326; my italics.
[2] Ibid., loc. cit.
[3] See e.g. *Correspondence of James VI* (Camd. Soc., O.S., lxxviii), pp. 12–14.
[4] Ibid., p. 62.
[5] Ibid., p. xlv.

new intrigue has never been fully explained, nor is it known why the breach came in the first place. Ralegh may have had an understandable suspicion that Cecil was barring his entry to the privy council. Since government was still conducted on a personal basis, with a good deal of the discussion between monarch and minister unrecorded, it is impossible to say what influence Cecil exerted in this matter. In a letter to Sir George Carew, Cecil did say that he would oppose the promotion of Ralegh to the council unless he gave up the captaincy of the guard to Carew.[1] But this was not a declaration that he would or could veto Ralegh's promotion; nor did he in fact possess any such powers. Elizabeth had indeed, years before, barred Ralegh's entry to high office and, even allowing for the undoubted greatness of that errant genius, she was probably right. But, to Ralegh and his friends at Durham House, it seemed that Cecil was destroying an alliance which had held so fast during the Essex rebellion. And certainly, in his correspondence with James VI, Cecil under provocation wrote harshly of his old friend. He thought fit to remind that virtuous monarch that Ralegh held dangerous views on religion, and that he and his friends were just 'gaping crabs'.[2] It was a squalid business, the more so as it was conducted amidst an outward show of friendship between the two sides; and nobody emerged from it with his hands clean. The situation derived from the feverish, nerve-strung conditions of these closing years, and from the discordant temperaments of the two rivals. It led ultimately to the destruction of Ralegh's political career. Elizabeth had, in any case, judged him incapable of the highest office; so did James. So probably did Cecil. Whatever may be said about the tragedy of Ralegh in personal terms, in the matter of public affairs the two monarchs and Cecil took a just measure of him. Apart from this, if Ralegh stood in the way of mutual confidence between James and Cecil, and the plans for an easy and peaceful succession, then Ralegh must be dropped. Once Cecil had reached this conclusion, it was

[1] *Letters from Sir Robert Cecil to Sir George Carew*, ed. J. Maclean (Camd. Soc., O.S., lxxxviii), p. 86.
[2] *Correspondence of James VI* (Camd. Soc., O.S., lxxviii), p. 18; Helen G. Stafford, *James VI of Scotland and the Throne of England* (New York and London, 1940), pp. 267–73.

not in his nature to allow personal friendship to stand in his way, or to move him to save a falling colleague.

Nothing in this article has argued that Robert Cecil was a man of virtue or unchallengeable integrity. From other evidence at our disposal it is clear that he was afflicted as much as any man with the weaknesses of the time: a taste for intrigue and a greed for wealth and power. But the evidence that we have examined so far does establish that in his political skills, in his judgment of the diplomatic scene, in his supreme sense of the possible, this little, crippled statesman—her pygmy, as Queen Elizabeth elegantly described him—stood head and shoulders above his contemporaries. Only his statesmanship, cool, patient, flexible, saved England from the dangers which threatened the nation in the closing years of the old queen. Above all, he saw clearly what was necessary to achieve a peaceful transfer of power. Without passion —perhaps without feeling—he pursued this single aim.

In the process he went a long way towards restoring unity to a factious realm. If his negotiations with the Catholics were basically political in aim, namely to draw the teeth of the Spanish wing, there was possibly present also a genuine desire for accommodation, for some working agreement with the moderate Catholics. The outcome of the long discussions was at first sight disappointing; and only thirteen priests felt that they could accept the conditions of the queen's proclamation of November 5th, 1602. That proclamation publicly rejected all notion of religious toleration but it hinted that some consideration would be given to the priests who took the oath required.[1] This consideration could not possibly mean very much; but the thirteen who declared their allegiance at the end of January 1603 believed that they had found a means of serving God and Cæsar. They were a tiny minority. Even some of those who had hitherto taken part in the negotiations withdrew before what they felt was too great a victory for Cæsar. Yet it remains true that these thirteen pointed a way to the solution which was adopted by their fellow Catholics when the intense feeling of the Counter-Reformation era had died down.

---

[1] *Tudor Royal Proclamations,* ed. P. L. Hughes and J. F. Larkin (1969), iii, pp. 250-55; *Cal. S.P. Dom.* 1601-3, 260-61.

It may be that the thirteen priests were in too much of a hurry. Had all Catholics done the same at that time, the Jesuits' fears might have been fulfilled: that is, having come to terms with the English state, the Catholics might have been tempted to come to terms with the English Church. The Jesuits undoubtedly played their part in maintaining the integrity of English Catholicism. But when the Jesuits' work had borne its fruit the heirs of the Appellants showed how it could be enjoyed in peaceful relations with the secular government. Whether or not Robert Cecil cared or thought about this distant prospect, he did at least play his part in the more immediate task of limiting the help that a Spanish candidate for the succession could expect from Catholics in England. 'I will affirm truly unto you', he wrote to James VI, 'that most of them do declare their affection absolutely to your title, and some of them have learnedly written of the validity of the same.'[1]

Meanwhile, amid all the complex negotiations about the succession, Cecil was immersed in the urgent economic questions of these years of depression, as the queen's reign drew to a close. Since these questions are not directly involved in the struggle over the succession, the policies Cecil favoured are not considered here. When more is known about them it may be that they will be seen as part of a general programme of national reconstruction to which he had directed his mind. We know that new policies were evolved for fiscal feudalism;[2] new methods were planned for dealing with concealed lands;[3] even the lease of sweet wines, previously held by Essex, was given to a group of people 'to husband it for the queen'.[4] Again, none of this can be taken to mean that Cecil was prepared to become a poor man in the service of the state. He was, of course, fully alert to his private interest, but also alert increasingly to the necessities of a powerful modern state.

The last two years of the queen's rule were indeed Cecil's years. His mind and will are seen in every policy which was tested out.

[1] *Correspondence of James VI* (Camd. Soc., O.S., lxxviii), p. 35.
[2] J. Hurstfield, *The Queen's Wards* (1958), pp. 311–25.
[3] *Cal. S.P. Dom. 1598–1601*, 493–4.
[4] A. Cecil, *A Life of Robert Cecil* (1915), p. 139n.

But his greatest contribution was undoubtedly as the servant of the two monarchs, Elizabeth I and James VI: by a paradox a faithful servant to both, yet above all to the national unity. The measure of his success is that there was no longer any doubt in England as to who would come in. Even before the queen's health finally broke, eyes had turned to Scotland. 'I find some less mindful of what they are soon to lose than of what they may perchance hereafter get,' wrote John Harington on December 27th, 1602.[1] He was no better than the rest; and there was something more than piety in his New Year's gift to James with the words: 'Lord, remember me when thou comest in thy Kingdom.'[2]

Three months later the queen was dead and, within a few days, John Chamberlain was describing the undignified haste to Scotland in search of advancement: 'There is much posting that way, and many run thither of their own errand, as if it were nothing else but first come first served, or that preferment were a goal to be got by footmanship.'[3]

Many men travelled north in the first exciting days of the new reign: Cecil himself was summoned to meet his monarch, for the first time, at York. But all men were engaged on a peaceful mission. Thanks to him, more than to any man, not a single gun was fired in anger as the king made his long progress to his southern capital.

[1] J. Harington, *Nugae Antiquae*, i, p. 321.
[2] Ibid., i, p. 326.
[3] *Letters of John Chamberlain*, i, p. 189.

Part III · Corruption

5

Political corruption in modern England: the historian's problem

William Lambarde, the Elizabethan antiquary, tells of a conversation he had with the queen in 1601, near the end of her life. She had asked him to tell her about 'olden times' as revealed in the ancient records in the Tower of London which he had been studying. She listened to him and then sadly drew a contrast with conditions in her own day. In the past valour determined the issue, but now other things. 'In those days', she said, 'force and arms did prevail; but now the wit of the fox is everywhere on foot so as hardly a faithful or virtuous man may be found.' And then, as she turned away from him to go to her prayers she said, 'Farewell, good and honest Lambarde.'[1] It is as though she felt that the worthy Lambarde, pottering about among his ancient records in the Tower, was just about the only honest man left in late Elizabethan England.

We might be tempted to dismiss her words as no more than the bitter outburst of a disillusioned monarch who had reigned too long. But, as it happens, there is a good deal of other evidence of the same kind for this very period, which seems to reinforce her opinion. 'The number of justices of the peace are grown almost infinite to the hindrance of justice,' said the lord keeper of the great seal in 1595, '... there are more justicers than justice ... many insufficient, unlearned, negligent and undiscreet.'[2] It is of this period, too, that we have, in a bitter poem 'The Lie', by Sir

---

NOTE: First published in *History*, lii (1967), pp. 16–34. An earlier version was read at the Anglo-American Conference of Historians in London, in July 1963.

[1] J. Nichols, *The Progress ... of Queen Elizabeth* (1823), iii, p. 552.
[2] J. Hawarde, *Les Reportes del Cases in Camera Stellata, 1593–1609*, ed. W. P. Baildon (1894), p. 20. I owe this reference to Mrs Alison Wall.

Walter Ralegh, a scorching indictment of court, politics and society. Here indeed are but fragments of the literary evidence from a much larger mass revealing the decay of the times as contemporaries saw it. And it is no wonder that historians, impressed by this and much comparable evidence, have seen the Elizabethan *fin de siècle* as one of the dark periods of political morality.

Before leaving this kind of evidence, however, it is necessary to consider some further material. For example, on one occasion when writing to William Cecil, Sir Francis Walsingham referred to 'this corrupted age'.[1] And here is a memorandum on trade: 'Merchants have grown so cunning in the trade of corrupting, and found it so sweet, that since the [first year of] Henry VIII there could never be won any good law or order which touched their liberty or state but they stayed it, either in the Commons, or higher House of Parliament, or else by the prince himself.'[2] And finally here is one of the best and most brief summaries of the fruits of office:

> For two year a treasurer, twenty winter after,
> May live a lord's life, as lewd men tellen.[3]

We have considered, in all, six examples of observations by contemporaries on the corruption of the age in which they lived. They are cited as literary sources in the special sense that they are descriptive accounts of the contemporary scene; they are conveying an impression that their age is corrupt. But we notice that they offer no evidence. They are unsupported statements that no judge could allow and no historian should accept. This is not to say for one moment that the age was not corrupt, but merely to comment on the nature of the evidence. Secondly, it will be noticed that I gave the rough dates of my first three quotations, which all came from the turn of the sixteenth century. They could therefore be used as 'evidence' that that age was corrupt. But none of the last

[1] J. Strype, *Annals of the Reformation* (Oxford, 1824), iii, pt. i, p. 208.

[2] 'Considerations delivered to the Parliament, 1559', printed in *Tudor Economic Documents*, ed. R. H. Tawney and Eileen Power (1924), i, p. 328.

[3] Cited in J. Ottway-Ruthven, *The King's Secretary and the Signet Office in the XVth Century* (Cambridge, 1939), p. 10.

three which I have just quoted in fact belongs to the end of the sixteenth century. Walsingham's remark about 'this corrupted age' is for the year 1582; the complaint about merchants corrupting government belongs to 1559; and the doggerel about the treasurer living high on the spoils of office is not from the Tudor period at all but belongs to the beginning of the fifteenth century.

We could vastly extend the range of this evidence and find similar passages for any century, medieval or modern. Allegations of corruption were constantly being made by politicians and pamphleteers; and if we relied on their words we should emerge with a powerful impression of the progressive debasement of mankind. Human progress would become a rake's progress of growing wealth overtaken by galloping corruption. For example, the remark that two years at the treasury brings twenty years of ill-gained opulence could just as easily have been made by anyone living at any time in the sixteenth, or the seventeenth, or the eighteenth century. Must we, then, assume that these three hundred years were centuries of corruption, moderated here and there by inexplicable bouts of conscience? Is it true, then, that each man had his price, and it was only the price which varied somewhat from one generation to another?

It is possible to offer an alternative interpretation. Because the very word corruption is vague and extraordinarily difficult to define, it has, quite understandably, become the stock-in-trade of political controversy. Either by direct accusation or by innuendo, it is the easiest charge to make and the most difficult charge to refute. This arises from the very nature of public office itself. For when men assume public office they usually do so for two reasons: first, because they wish to serve the public in office and second, because they wish to enjoy the benefits of office either in prestige, power, wealth or all three. The sweets of office are very sweet indeed; and we should be lacking in realism if we denied the simple fact that statesmen are also human beings with the normal desires of ambitious men. But our problem is to determine which profits of office are legitimate and which are not legitimate, that is to say, which are corrupt. Men have tried to set frontiers to political probity across which worthy – or prudent—

men do not stray. But the frontiers of corruption are themselves vague and undefined: and where frontiers are vague wars are liable to break out and the air grow thick with propaganda and with charge and counter-charge.

But the historian cannot escape his responsibilities. If he wishes to use the word corruption he must be clear as to what he means. The onus of proof rests upon him. He cannot simply take the word of a contemporary. In this search for a definition, it must be confessed, he gets little help from the authorities. None of the volumes in the *New Cambridge Modern History* has an index entry under corruption. The same is true of the modern volumes of the *Oxford History of England*, with the exception of the volume by Sir George Clark on the later seventeenth century – and this is not, I assume, because the later Stuarts were uniquely corrupt. In the subject index at the British Museum there are virtually no entries under corruption with the exception of a few under bribery at elections. The same is true of the subject index of the London Library. This is not to say that there are not numerous volumes, or chapters in volumes, which shed light on corruption. But the problem itself has not been submitted, for the modern period, to detailed analysis and definition. Hence our readiness to accept contemporary opinion at its face value.

This is not to minimize the value of contemporary opinion. After all, the contemporary actually feels where the shoe pinches; and if he tells us that the shoe pinches, he is the one who knows. But does he always know *why* the shoe pinches? In Tudor England, when corn was scarce and prices rose, the consumer cried out against the middleman who, it was said, was corruptly cornering corn. Sometimes, of course, he was; but often he was simply doing some of the essential work of wholesale or retail distribution, and the blame for the shortage of corn really lay not with the corrupt middleman but with the bad weather or the bad roads, or, more generally, because the rising population was outstripping natural resources. What the contemporary offers us is a subjective impression of causes. This itself may be of historic importance because it may lead to very real political consequences. What he says may be entirely correct or, on the other hand, no more than the stale repetition of slander, bandied about by contemporaries and in due course passed on by them to historians. If it is true that there is no smoke without fire, it is also true that there may be a vast amount of smoke with very little fire. When the contemporary speaks of political corruption as a *cause* of current ills, he may be less qualified to speak than is the independent and critical historian. For the historian has access to material which the contemporary cannot normally hope to see; and his emotions are not usually engaged by the parties and people in office. Can the historian, then, get much nearer than the contemporary to an objective assessment of the situation; and, if he can, what criteria of corruption are available to him?

I

The expression corruption may be used in many contexts: corruption in morals, in art, in literature, in music. The historian's primary concern is with the state and society, and in this essay we are in search of a definition appropriate to this sphere. For the moment we may therefore adopt a brief definition to furnish provisionally our terms of reference. If we assume that the object of the state is the welfare of all its members, we may define corruption as the subversion of that object for other ends.

We are at once faced with the problems of evidence and of criteria. This involves three separate processes. We must, firstly, find evidence that money or favour had been given. It is not enough to show that contemporaries *said* that a man was taking bribes. Examples must be brought forward which establish that the man was involved in specific transactions of this kind. Secondly, we must show that on accepting such sums, or in anticipation of them, the recipient damaged the state. Thirdly, we must then explain how and why this came about. The first process is one which involves the examination of sources. The second is one of interpretation of the evidence in terms of criteria. The third requires the placing of these events within the general historic situation. It may then become necessary, for example, to explain why, in the history of political morality, the sixteenth century appears to represent one turning point, and the middle of the nineteenth century another.

For the evidence itself, clearly, a mere quantitative measure of documents about the taking of gifts, which reflect corruption, is no measure of the degree of corruption itself. We may take the Cecil papers as an example. For the sixteenth-century Cecils, there have been preserved from their day to this a vast quantity of private documents, which are still at Hatfield House; and Michael Hickes, who worked with the Cecils, kept a good many more, which are now at the British Museum. There is no comparable collection of private documents on such a scale for an English statesman until we come to recent times. In both these collections there are a substantial number of documents which refer to the giving and taking of gifts. And far more of these belong to the late sixteenth century, when Robert Cecil was in power, than to the earlier decades when his father, Lord Burghley, held high office. Does this mean that the late sixteenth century was more corrupt than the years which preceded it and indeed the centuries which followed? Robert Cecil was a cynic and discussed with his intimates the gifts he took; and some of these discussions have survived among his papers. His father was a hypocrite and he kept his thoughts very much to himself. Does this mean that Robert Cecil was more corrupt than his father, or merely more frank? Is it not likely that a corrupt man will destroy incriminating documents rather than preserve them? Of that, too, we have evidence in the case of Lord Burghley.

But, leaving that aside, there is no question that many gifts were passing to and fro. The evidence for this is substantial for the sixteenth century and for other periods. And here we are faced with our second problem, the problem of *interpretation*. Is the term corruption subjective? Is it governed by convention and as conventions change do our notions of corruption change with them? There are some interesting clues to this problem in the history of the British civil service in modern times. It has become a well established principle that the civil servant does not take gifts from members of the public with whom he is dealing, or is likely to be dealing. For example, if a civil servant, engaged in negotiating with a firm about a government contract, accepted a gift of five shillings from that firm he would be liable to criminal proceedings. This, of course, is the exact opposite of the situation in the sixteenth century, when a merchant or industrialist who went to see a civil servant *without* taking a gift was wasting his time. Yet if today a civil servant, who may not take a gift of five shillings, goes to a lunch paid for by the same firm, at many times five shillings, as the result of which, at least momentarily, he may take an optimistic view of the world in general and of that firm in particular, he lays himself open to no charge whatsoever.

In the eighteenth century it was common enough to pay electors for their votes. If any parliamentary candidate today gave five shillings to a single elector he would at once be the subject of a serious criminal charge. But if he tells the same elector that, if returned to power, he will increase the elector's pension or reduce his tax by fifty pounds, he has committed no criminal offence and may indeed emerge as a self-styled benefactor of mankind. Or again, in England during the Second World War it was held that to deal on the black market was a corrupt and unpatriotic thing. Yet twenty miles away, across the Channel in France, to deal on the black market was, I have been informed, a patriotic and worthy deed because it added to the difficulties of the Germans. I am not in any way challenging this process of reasoning, although it seems to be palpably absurd. I am merely drawing attention to one of the difficulties of the historian of corruption, for the word changes its meaning with time and circumstance. Danton, in 1789, held the view that in time of revolution all things are lawful provided that they further its cause. Lawful things included the taking of substantial gifts without worrying excessively as to their source, even if they came from the monarchy itself. Yet Danton utterly repudiated any notion that he was thereby corrupt. In his ideals as a revolutionary he considered himself incorruptible.

If then we consider merely a few from among numerous examples, we are struck by the variety of experiences which, according to time and circumstance, appear to fall on one or other side of the line which divides corrupt men from their more honourable contemporaries. Let us suppose, then, that we accept

Danton's view as a working hypothesis in our search for a definition of corruption. That is to say, if a man is faithful to his own ideals, whatever they may be, do all things thereby become lawful, and does the charge of corruption fall to the ground? If we accept this, then the word corruption changes its meaning from man to man, and from day to day. It leaves us without any independent criterion of value to the historian. We acknowledge thereby that the whole notion of corruption is but a subjective thing. It happens, however, that statesmen, historians and others have from time to time tried to set forth principles which in some rough way may serve as guides in this field. But the field tends to be law, rather than politics.

II

Corruption in law and in politics are two separate but related things. We start with the legal problem because it presents less difficulties. A statute of 1346 required that a common law judge on assuming office should swear on oath that he would not take 'gift nor reward of gold nor silver, nor of any other thing which may turn to your profit, unless it be meat or drink, and that of small value, of any man that shall have any plea or process hanging before you, as long as the same process shall be so hanging, nor after for the same cause'.[1] Five hundred years later, when Macaulay was discussing the proposals for an Indian penal code, he set forth the same principles. 'The receiving of large presents by a public functionary', he wrote, 'is generally a very suspicious proceeding.' But 'the meat or drink' of the 1346 statute he was prepared to allow, that is,

> a lime, a wreath of flowers, a slice of betel nut, a drop of atar of roses poured on his handkerchief, are presents which it would in this country [i.e. India] be held churlish to refuse, and which cannot possibly corrupt the most mercenary of mankind. Other presents of more value than these may, on account of their peculiar nature, be accepted, without

[1] 20 Edward III, c. 6.

affording any ground for suspicion. Luxuries socially consumed according to the usages of hospitality are presents of this description. It would be unreasonable to treat a man in office as a criminal for drinking many rupees-worth of champagne in a year at the table of an acquaintance; though if he were to suffer one of his subordinates to accept even a single rupee in specie, he might deserve exemplary punishment.[1]

We notice that Macaulay acknowledges that there is no complete consistency in interpretation. Many rupees' worth of champagne, poured down the throat of a senior official — although he has not paid for it — has no ill consequence whatsoever, other than perhaps a touch of the liver the following morning. But a single rupee in currency bestowed upon a junior official is to be met with exemplary punishment. In the case of a judge, however, Macaulay is quite categorical. He must take no gifts of any kind from any party to a lawsuit in a case pending before him. Here is a criterion which it is worth testing against the career of Francis Bacon who, as lord chancellor, was charged in 1621 with corruption.

What had Bacon done? Certain suitors came forward to show that he had received gifts from interested parties in a lawsuit, sometimes while the case was before him, sometimes at the end of a suit. The moral implication was of course clear enough: on the receipt, or in anticipation, of gifts, Bacon's judgment had been corrupted. Bacon admitted the gifts but he vigorously denied that they had in any way influenced his judgment.[2]

Freely recognizing that he had taken gifts, Bacon divided them into three kinds. There were, first, those taken on the understanding that justice would be perverted in the interest of the donor: here Bacon stoutly affirmed, 'I take myself to be as innocent as any born upon St. Innocent's Day, in my heart.' There were, second, gifts received when the judge understood

---

[1] *The Works of Lord Macaulay* (1866), vii, p. 472.
[2] *The Letters and the Life of Francis Bacon*, ed. James Spedding (1874), vii, pp. 213ff.; S. R. Gardiner, *History of England, 1603–42* (1883), iv, p. 88.

that the case was ended but had not taken enough care to see whether the whole business was over. Here he admitted that he might be in some degree at fault. There were, third, payments made when the matter was really settled and which could have no possible effect upon the issue. These, he argued, involved no corruption of any kind.

At first sight this reads like special pleading and legalistic hair-splitting designed to exculpate a corrupt judge. Yet, if we examine the cases which were brought in evidence against him, and ignore Bacon's glosses upon them, one is impressed by a consistent element which runs through nearly all of them: that Bacon appears to have kept the gift and the judgment in two separate compartments of his mind. For example, a certain Christopher Awbry, whose suit in Chancery seemed to be making slow progress, was advised to give the lord chancellor £100. That he did; but still his cause tarried. So he took to writing letters to the lord chancellor, all of which were ignored, except the last to which his lordship gave Awbry the short answer: 'If he importune him, he will lay him by the heels.'[1] In another case, Edward Egerton presented Bacon with £400 and found that the verdict which the lord chancellor subsequently gave was in no wise especially favourable to his cause.[2] Both Awbry and Egerton joined in the outcry against Bacon. But surely their complaint was that justice—not the injustice they sought—had been done. In the case of the litigious Lady Wharton who paid Bacon £300, the judgment was given before the money was received so she might perhaps have kept her money in her purse.[3] It looks again as though justice had not been subverted for money. Macaulay wrote bitterly of Bacon as the man 'who first summoned philosophers to the great work of interpreting nature [but] was among the last Englishmen who sold justice'. So Macaulay turned away in disgust 'from the checkered spectacle of so much glory and so much shame'.[4] But there is another way

[1] Spedding, op. cit., vii, p. 222.
[2] Ibid., loc. cit.
[3] Gardiner, op. cit., iv, pp. 72ff.
[4] *Works*, vi, p. 245.

of looking at it. 'May it not fairly be supposed,' asked S. R. Gardiner, '... that the misdeeds of the great Chancellor were attributable to contempt of forms, to the carelessness of haste, and to an overweening confidence in his own integrity?'[1] There may, however, have been some who benefited by bestowing a bribe, and they, naturally, did not come forward: but we are without evidence.

There was one exception which falls completely outside this category: the Steward case.[2] George Villiers, the royal favourite, was in some way indebted to a Dr Steward, who had lost his case in a trial before Bacon as lord chancellor. Villiers wrote a note to Bacon asking him to reconsider the matter, and then wrote another, more peremptorily. The case was reopened and Steward was accordingly relieved of some of the burdens of the earlier verdict. This was a corruption of justice; and there is no other word for it. But this, so far as I am aware, is the only case involving Bacon in which it has been shown that justice was corrupted for personal favour. But the corruption of justice is relatively easy to identify and to define: it is the distortion of a trial or a verdict in return for money or some other reward. Clearly, since the anticipation of a gift may distort a trial, for a judge to accept a gift before, during or after a lawsuit, from any party involved is corruption. This applies *whenever* a gift is taken, and Bacon's artificial distinction breaks down. Bacon therefore was corrupt.

III

If we turn from law to the complex problems of politics and administration, subjects with which the historian is much more frequently concerned, we are confronted with a far more elusive problem. Public office is the delegation by the state of some fraction of its power. It often becomes something which can be

[1] Gardiner, op. cit., iv, p. 99.
[2] E. A. Abbott, *Francis Bacon, an account of his life and works* (1885), pp. xxivff., 268f.; Spedding, op. cit., vi, pp. 441ff., vii, pp. 5f. and Appendix I. I have here modified the view I expressed in *The Queen's Wards* (1958), p. 184.

bought and sold. It can be used and abused. And the historian of the modern period, whichever part of Europe or the overseas empires he studies, finds the air thick with rumours of corruption. There are, in fact, several separate but related ways in which corruption may enter into the affairs of government. The first is the familiar method of the dishonest civil servant, the man who cooks the books on his own behalf and at the government's expense. For example, John Beaumont did this in the middle of the sixteenth century, and the procedure was simple enough. Many people owed sums to the Court of Wards in return for grants of wardships or leases of lands. When the debtors came in to pay their dues, Beaumont gave them receipts, pocketed the money and omitted to enter the payment on the official accounts. As a result he diverted nearly £12,000 into his private pocket. It was only when he was promoted to a judgeship and his successor began to call in the 'unpaid' debts that the whole business was revealed and Beaumont moved from the Bench to the Tower.[1] This could happen at any time in history. But when, as in the sixteenth century, accountancy was primitive and control was poor, the government was very vulnerable.

Another corrupt process was associated with informers. This time it was the rudimentary, or non-existent, machinery for law enforcement which made the government dependent upon informers who were supposed to report breaches of the law in return for which they received part of the fine. In practice, they had at hand a means for blackmailing ordinary people by threatening to bring them before the courts.[2]

But these malpractices are easy to identify: they are corrupt and there is no dispute about it. When a government extends the range of its economic and social controls it makes possible the

[1] See my 'Corruption and Reform under Edward VI and Mary', *E.H.R.*, lxviii, pp. 25ff., below, pp. 167–9; *The Queen's Wards*, pp. 199ff., 208f.

[2] Ibid., pp. 36ff. and *passim*, and my 'County Government, 1530–1660', Vict. County Hist., *Wiltshire*, v, p. 101, below, pp. 276–7; G. R. Elton, 'Informing for profit', *Camb. Hist. J.*, xi, pp. 149ff., reprinted in his *Star Chamber Stories* (1958), pp. 78ff.; M. W. Beresford, 'The common informer, the penal statutes and economic regulation', *Econ. Hist. Rev.*, 2nd Ser., x, pp. 221ff.; M. G. Davies, *The Enforcement of English Apprenticeship* (Cambridge, Mass., 1956).

rise of a whole army of contact-men, informers and other parasites who batten on the innocent—and the avaricious. In any case, when governments attempt to do more than they have ever done without the organization to do it properly, this kind of corruption grows in volume. In the sixteenth century the work of the municipality, the gild and the local church authorities passed increasingly to the state. So did the complaints about corruption.

Much more complex a problem arises in the case of the appointment to public office, and in its abuse for private gain. Closely associated with the first of these processes, the grant of office, is the exercise of patronage and it is necessary, therefore, to consider the relationship between patronage and corruption. Is patronage inherently a corrupt thing?

The whole subject of patronage has only recently begun to attract the attention of historians, whether in the form of bastard feudalism, as applied by Plummer to the fifteenth century,[1] clientage as applied by Sir John Neale to the sixteenth,[2] or the well-known forms of political, economic and cultural patronage with which we are familiar from the Renaissance—or earlier—to the present day. Patronage may mean no more than the recommendation of someone for office or promotion, an essential stage in any governing system, private or public. But it shades imperceptibly into clientage, the building up of a body of dependants, a closed circle centred on the patron and with interests and objects other than those of the generality. Patronage and clientage can often be considered separately but in many cases they are fed from the same source. Patronage as such is neither good nor bad. It exists and has always existed, because in some contexts it is the only way of making an appointment.

We may again take as an example the modern British civil service. Until the reforms of the mid-nineteenth century, appointment was wholly by patronage. The civil service was more or

[1] C. Plummer in his Introduction to John Fortescue, *The Governance of England* (Oxford, 1885), p. 15. See also K. B. McFarlane, 'Bastard feudalism', *Bull. Inst. Hist. Res.*, xx, pp. 161ff.

[2] See especially *The Elizabethan Political Scene* (British Academy Raleigh Lecture, 1948), reprinted in J. E. Neale, *Essays in Elizabethan History* (1958), pp. 59ff.

less a closed circle to those without connections; and office was granted to relatives, dependants, friends, without too close a regard to their abilities or their worth. The reforms brought in a system of open competitive examination in many branches of the government service. Assessments were now made by independent examiners and, strictly speaking, there was no opportunity for personal intervention by men of influence. Here, at least in theory, there is a dispassionate impersonal procedure for appointing the most suitable candidate for the vacant post. But could any comparable system for entry by examination be devised for appointments to industry or commerce or the universities?

And even in the civil service, although *entry* is now by open competitive examination, clearly *promotion* is not and cannot be, save in certain junior grades. In the senior posts it is entirely out of the question: no competitive examination could possibly be evolved. Promotion, in the civil service as elsewhere, is based on two things: on a man's ability and the recognition of that ability by his superiors. In essence, his superiors are fulfilling the role of patron. They are using their powers of patronage to bestow official advancement. Of course, such a system leads to errors of judgment; but there are various checks and balances which can minimize the effects of these errors. Its faults are only the faults inherent in human judgment and prejudice. But the system of patronage whether in the civil service, the arts, commerce, industry or the universities, is a system under which honourable men are seeking the best candidates for the post. As such it carries no taint of corruption.

Was the same true of Elizabethan patronage? It had, as always, a dual function. One of these was essential if the queen's government was to go on, namely vacant offices had to be filled, and this was done by recommendation, influence, patronage. But it was also a system of internal power politics by means of which the magnates built up a following at court and in the country. Among Elizabethan letters we often find the remark 'he is someone whom I may command', that is to say, he will support me in any dispute which may arise either in the capital or the provinces. In return for this support the magnate provided the client with office (itself a source of income), letters of introduction and all the other services which a great man at the centre of power could render. The Earl of Leicester operated such a system, on the whole successfully. The Earl of Essex tried to operate such a system also, with disastrous results. When he was deprived of his powers of rewarding his followers, his system and his authority collapsed with them. His only hope of regaining authority in 1601 was by a desperate show of force; and that was pitifully inadequate. But it was the Cecils who organized patronage in its most influential and enduring form, for it served the father and the son for more than half a century, from 1558 when the father became secretary of state until 1612 when the son died.

Both father and son grew wealthy in the public service, that is to say, office was to them a form of service and of income; and the same was true of many of their followers. Each of the Cecils, in his day, held the offices of lord treasurer and Master of the Wards; and there is no reason to doubt that in the exchequer, as in the Court of Wards, high office to them meant both public duty and their private gain. In short, because government taxation was notoriously inadequate and therefore official salaries were absurdly low, they collected substantial additional salaries in this dubious and devious way. Whether we describe this as corruption or not will depend in part on whether we consider that there was some alternative way in which the Crown could pay its high officers of state salaries appropriate to their rank and responsibilities.

Was the political system corrupted with it? The historian is never short of evidence of officials of all ranks taking gifts. Yet he must guard himself against the trap of assuming that all gifts were bribes. Many of them undoubtedly were. But a gift is different from a bribe in that a gift is no more than a payment to an official in the processes of administration because that is the accepted convention. It is an informal fee. A bribe is a gift intended to corrupt an official so that he will favour the suitor and thereby subvert the public interest for private gain, his own and that of his suitor. In a sense, all gifts are potentially corrupt. For, even if all officials take gifts in the course of their administrative duties, the man who does not offer a gift will probably suffer for his deviation. But, generally speaking, such gifts, when they are universal and built into the whole revenue system, are not bribes: they do not favour the giver and they do not subvert the recipient. When all men tip the waiter, the waiter is not corrupted.

Looking far back across the intervening experience of four centuries—and with all the advantages of hindsight—we think that an alternative system was to be found in an all-embracing machinery for taxation providing for a properly salaried ministry and civil service; but nobody in Europe saw it in this way then or for centuries to come. How could they, when even increases of official fees produced an outcry? How could they, when taxation was stubbornly resisted from all quarters, when one government after another went bankrupt because government revenue failed to come within striking distance of tapping the national income or of meeting government expenditure?

A more serious criticism of the Cecils was that, to ensure their grip upon power, they surrounded themselves with second-rate men on whom they bestowed office, and they kept out men of ability so that no rival might emerge to challenge their supremacy. Edmund Spenser said it;[1] so did Thomas Wilson;[2] and so did Francis Bacon.[3] We must remember, of course, that appointments were made by the Crown, not by the ministers; and both Elizabeth and James I had, especially in this field, minds and wills of their own. Yet, although the work has not yet been completed on either William or Robert Cecil, my interim impression is that there is some justice in the charge. There were no really distinguished men in their service, although some of them subsequently won some measure of distinction. Most of them were no more than what contemporaries called 'pen-clerks'; and a strong system of clientage was established. In the light of this, the system carries the taint of corruption for it

[1] *The Ruines of Time*, lines 449ff.
[2] Thomas Wilson, 'The State of England, Anno Dom. 1600', ed. F. J. Fisher (*Camden Miscellany*, xvi, p. 42).
[3] Spedding, op. cit., vi, pp. 6f.

sacrificed the public to the private interest, the need for a first-class body of public servants to the interests of a leader of faction.

When we turn from the ministers to the monarchs it is a different story. Queen Elizabeth had a very real affection for favourites. Yet she tried to keep her emotional life separate from her political judgments. She succeeded in the case of Ralegh: she never advanced him to her privy council. In her treatment of Essex she was a failure, with near-disastrous consequences for late Elizabethan England. But it is the early seventeenth century which shows us, under the Stuarts, this whole system in decay. With the death of Robert Cecil in 1612, truly second-rate men moved into positions of power, men like Robert Carr, Earl of Somerset, and George Villiers, Duke of Buckingham. We look in vain, from now onwards until the Rebellion, for any long tenure of office by men of outstanding ability at the centre of power. For, as criteria, ability gave place to physical charm, and political and administrative talents were rated as inferior to superficial personal attributes. Patronage had been corrupted into favouritism. Patronage is not inherently corrupt. Favouritism is, because it sacrifices the long-term needs of the state to the ephemeral tastes of the monarch.

IV

But how had this system come about in Western Europe? And why do we hear these gathering complaints of corruption? In the pre-Reformation period there was, of course, political corruption but we hear far less about it. This change in emphasis is in part due to a change in the structure of government itself. In the first place, the medieval bureaucracy consisted largely of churchmen. For their services they were rewarded with benefices, which they usually held *in absentia* since they were away at the seat of government. In short, the service of the state was paid for by the Church, that is, with ecclesiastical office, not directly by the public at large. More important, such bureaucracy as existed was extremely limited because the activities of government were themselves extremely limited. It provided none of the social services; its diplomatic service was either non-existent or primitive; it had the most rudimentary legislative machine; and, compared with modern times, it rarely resorted to taxation. For all these reasons the civil servant scarcely made an impact upon the public and his demands were relatively few. The ordinary person was more likely to be in contact with the manorial or gild official, the ecclesiastical representative of the bishop, or sometimes with the sheriff. And about all these officials there were complaints in plenty. Certainly there were complaints against the central government also; and, in a conflict within the ruling class – for example in the reign of Edward II – there were loud cries against a corrupt Throne. But, in the main, the cry was against the Church: against the papacy itself, growing, it was said, powerful and splendid by the abuse of political power; against the bishops and their officials in England, extracting the last penny from their oppressed flocks; against the mercenary friars who bartered an escape from purgatory in return for hard cash. But with the representative of the secular state the ordinary man's contacts, save in times of crisis, were brief or non-existent.

In the modern period, both these assumptions have ceased to apply. After the Reformation, in both Protestant and Catholic countries, the power of the Church – and, more important, its wealth – usually diminished. Secondly, the bureaucrats were usually laymen. Therefore the burden of payment for these officials passed to the state. Meanwhile, the state assumed ever-increasing administrative responsibilities – consider for example the rise of the diplomatic service, the secular responsibility for welfare or the enormous administrative commitments of the Spanish Empire in the New World. And these burdens had to be carried with grossly inadequate funds, and in a time of inflation. What alternative had these governments but to leave the officials to collect their own fees in one way or another, without asking too many questions about how these things were done? Let the public which received the services pay the officials who provided them.

Offices continued to multiply. Since the sixteenth century not a single generation in England has seen any long-term recession in the growth of the bureaucracy. One explanation of what has happened attributes this growth to the inherent capacity of a bureaucracy to enlarge itself.[1] There is, of course, some truth in this; and it is a long-standing complaint. 'The abuse of the Court of Wards [is] great,' declared a seventeenth-century Member of Parliament. He had 'known the Clerk of the Wards sit there in a rug gown: now twenty clerks. And where clerks increase the grievance of the subject groweth.'[2] But sometimes this is too superficial an explanation. And this subjective hostility to bureaucracy has too often obscured the realities of the situation. The rise of a bureaucracy has led to a better division of labour in the upper ranges of government and administration, and this is essential to its proper functioning. In most cases the 'clerks' were as essential to progress in past centuries as a technical assistant at work on an electronic computer is essential for scientific progress in our own day. These are the modern bureaucrats who are continuously increasing in numbers. It is quite true that some administrators increase their satellite staff for prestige reasons, and it is also true that kings of France multiplied offices simply in order to sell them. But these are exploitations and distortions of a general trend. Bureaucracy grew because the state assumed responsibility for an ever-increasing sector of human affairs. And the civil servants had to be paid.

From this growth in the bureaucracy, it might have been deduced that a larger part of each generation would have been absorbed into the government service and therefore become defenders of the existing order. In fact the reverse happened. The expansion of the bureaucracy occurred at a time when the educational system was itself expanding in a manner unparalleled until the twentieth century. Between the middle of the sixteenth century and the middle of the seventeenth the schools and universities were opening their doors to a much larger proportion

[1] C. N. Parkinson, *Parkinson's Law, the pursuit of progress* (1958).
[2] Cited in my *The Queen's Wards*, pp. 190f.

of the middling classes.[1] From the universities each year were streaming many more educated young men than could possibly be absorbed into the available offices in Church and state. For the many who failed to gain a place the explanation was simple enough. Appointments were in the hands of a small governing clique and their dependants who maintained a tight grip on the distribution of office and the rewards which went with it. Public careers were not open to men of talent but to the hangers-on of privilege. In many cases this was true; and this was corruption. It was a relatively narrow social and political group of elites, at the centre of government and in the counties, which controlled patronage and advancement. And, as Parliament grew increasingly important, some men sought also to control elections, by persuasion, force and fraud in the sixteenth and seventeenth centuries, and by the familiar process of bribery of voters in the eighteenth. This too was corruption.

Given these general conditions, it is possible to see special influences at work in the early modern period. Certainly as we move from the sixteenth into the seventeenth century, we move from the relatively frugal court of a spinster queen to the extravagant one of a purse-free king; from a monarch who might suddenly sweep down upon administrative waste to one who let everyone make hay, whether the sun shone or not. 'If', said James I to the Venetian ambassador, 'I were to imitate the conduct of your republic and to begin to punish those who take bribes, I should soon not have a single subject left.'[2] As a result, we hear increasing complaints about extravagance and corruption. But those complaints did not end with the English Rebellion. Quite the reverse: we find them as a constant background to political controversy, with charges made with varying degrees of justification. Pepys was accused of corruption; so was Danby. So were

---

[1] M. H. Curtis, *Oxford and Cambridge in Transition, 1558–1642* (Oxford, 1959) and 'The alienated intellectuals in early Stuart England', *Past and Present*, No. 23 (1962), pp. 25ff.; L. Stone, *The Crisis of the Aristocracy, 1558–1641* (Oxford, 1965), pp. 672ff. and 'The educational revolution in England, 1560–1640', *Past and Present*, No. 28, pp. 41ff.; Joan Simon, 'The social origins of Cambridge students, 1603–40', ibid., No. 26, pp. 58ff.

[2] Gardiner, op. cit., iii, pp. 74f.

Walpole, Henry Fox, the Duke of Newcastle. Gifts were made to obtain office; the treasury was emptied to pay for sinecures; votes in the constituencies and in Parliament were bought like chattels. It would be easy to speak of two centuries of corruption lasting until the reforms of the nineteenth century. 'If it were a fault', said Walpole, 'to get an estate in the Treasury, he knew some had got great ones in meaner offices there, than his.'[1]

But the situation was much more complex than this. 'The key to the whole problem of corruption under Charles II', writes Professor Andrew Browning, 'is to be found in the single word "compensation".'

> Representatives of Cavalier families which had suffered in the service of Charles I expected compensation. Representatives of Roundhead families which had been required (unjustly in their opinion) to restore part of their gains also expected compensation. Everybody who had held a lucrative office of any kind and had been deprived of it expected compensation. The innumerable creditors of the Government expected payment, which in practice was apt to be indistinguishable from the compensation accorded to others. In the whole of England there must have been few men of position without claims on the Crown such as their own age would have admitted, while thousands had claims which would be considered valid according to the standards of any age.[2]

But compensation established a link and those who handed out these rewards, at second or third stage removed from the Crown, fastened a link between themselves and their followers which joined them in faction. In the absence of true party politics, where issues of principle unite men in a common cause, faction grows. And faction is the sacrifice of public policy for private interest. In such circumstances clientage flourishes; and clientage channels

[1] Cited in J. H. Plumb, *Sir Robert Walpole* (1960), ii, p. 123.
[2] A. Browning, *Thomas Osborne, Earl of Danby and Duke of Leeds, 1632–1712* (Glasgow, 1951), i, p. 168.

office, interests and power away from the needs of the state. It is also the use of public funds for personal political advancement. 'No revenue', wrote Edmund Burke in 1779, 'is large enough to provide both for the meritorious and undeserving; to provide for service which is, and for service which is not, incurred.'[1]

When we come to Burke's writings on economical reform towards the end of the eighteenth century we are within sight and sound of the governing principles of our own day. It is a time also of heartsearching when, after the loss of the American colonies, men sought for alternatives to extravagance and sinecures. The nineteenth century saw a profound change in the texture of government, and in the public attitude to government. These changes derived from many causes of which I want to select two for special consideration. The first concerns the revenue system. From the early nineteenth century, and more particularly from its middle years, a system of income tax was evolved which at last began to make available to government substantial sums to meet its cost. The evolution of a modern, salaried civil service for the first time became possible and, though old style patronage remained the main system of recruitment, the end of that was also in sight. At the same time, the coming of parliamentary democracy on a wide franchise gave the nation as a whole an interest in government and a concern with the money which more and more of them had to pay towards the cost of government. More people were *involved* in government than ever before in English history. The civil service, whether in the colonies or at home, could not much longer remain a system of outdoor relief for the governing classes. It was becoming instead a life profession for men of education, deeply concerned in the welfare of those whose lives they administered. Administration was separated from politics, patronage moved away from faction.

This administrative change was accompanied by another which I find difficult to explain. There was a change in social attitudes leading to a relatively new approach which we describe as Victorian, a phenomenon by no means restricted to the countries over which Victoria reigned or the period during which she

[1] E. Burke, *Speeches* (1816), ii, p. 6.

lived. About the Victorian attitude there is a good deal to be said, much of it uncomplimentary. It could be smug, self-righteous yet ruthless, hypocritical. It imposed a moral censorship which cramped the spirits of some of its most original minds. It was ambiguous; and its imperialist double-talk is well displayed in the best and the worst poetry of Rudyard Kipling. But it had other qualities as well. When Dr Arnold of Rugby laid his heavy hand upon the public schools he returned to the puritan vein of the seventeenth century against which Englishmen of the eighteenth and early nineteenth centuries had reacted so violently and for so long. I mention Arnold merely as one of many examples of the new influences at work. Yet along with repression and intolerance, the new age brought other things as well, a stronger sense of public service and responsibility; it trained men who pressed upon politicians the responsibility of the state for the welfare of its citizens. It absorbed the ideas of Jeremy Bentham and his followers who had been hammering away at the need for efficiency in government administration. Slowly, unevenly, reluctantly, the basic assumptions of the early modern period yielded to the pressures and the demands deriving from a new social framework.

It is these eighteenth- and nineteenth-century developments which have obscured the historical issue. We have, as historians, been too ready to look back on the past with Victorian eyes — to fall victim to the anachronism of judging one age by the standards of another. We treat these new, nineteenth-century traditions of public service as though they reached far back into antiquity. The expression corruption can, with some justification, be used in many spheres since the mid-nineteenth century when it has taken on some precision, when public servants are paid fair salaries from public funds and are in no way dependent upon political patronage. To use the word corrupt of gifts taken in these circumstances is legitimate. But before then its use is full of hazards: it begs the question it appears to answer. It ignores the economic and social structure of a past age; it underrates the problems of financing and administering government in a relatively under-developed community.

Even in the more limited field of taxation we are still, in our own day as before, confronted with a mass of ambiguities which offer rich rewards to those who can exploit them. Moreover, as governments have tightened their grasp, so more efforts have been devoted by the taxpayer to evading their reach. For example, in the year 1593 the lord treasurer was reported in the House of Commons as saying that in the City of London, the tax assessments were ludicrous.[1] We might indeed postulate it as a general law that the means of collecting taxes always lags behind the means of evading them. In recent times, a veritable bye-industry has developed to deal with these matters.

But the modern tax evader, who finds a way round the law, is apparently not corrupt, only the sixteenth-century civil servant who collected a little taxation for himself. Was the monopolist who taxed the consumer in the early seventeenth century less corrupt than the auditor who re-directed some of the royal income into his private purse? 'Our laws have been a long time like to spiders' webs,' said an Elizabethan Puritan, 'so that the great buzzing bees break through and the little feeble flies hang fast in them.'[2] But if we decide to treat the use of public revenue for private gain as corruption, then we must not only consider men like Sir Robert Cecil and Sir Robert Walpole but a vast miscellany of people, most of them not in the public service, who diverted public revenue into private purses. It is for reasons such as this that I believe that the word corruption, with its high moral overtones, all too often obscures rather than illumines the issues which confront historians.

V

I have argued that the question as to whether there was more or less corruption in the sixteenth century than in the Middle Ages is impossible to answer without taking account of the whole structure of society. Society was different and so was the corruption which afflicted it. But I have suggested that the rise of the

---

[1] Simonds D'Ewes, *Journals of all the Parliaments* ... (1693), p. 483.
[2] Cited in M. M. Knappen, *Tudor Puritanism* (Chicago, 1939), p. 345.

modern state brought the ordinary man into much closer contact than ever before with the machinery and men of secular government. This was partly because controls passed from gild and Church to the central authority but, more important, because the government did more things to, and on behalf of, the individual citizen. All this meant a continuous enlargement of the government service; and more jobs sometimes meant more jobbery. Patronage and clientage flourished. But more jobs also meant the need for more money at a time when an antiquated exchequer and outdated fiscal doctrines made it impossible to raise more than a fraction of the sums required. Unable to tax the subject to pay for the ever-growing government service, the Crown left the civil servants to raise their own fees — in every sense of the word! I have tried to show that, in this special context, the word corruption is irrelevant and confusing, until the nineteenth century. The king's government had to go on.

Secondly, the post-Reformation political system made possible a concentration of power which had been inconceivable in the Middle Ages. The power enjoyed by Henry VIII — even with its built-in weaknesses — was unparalleled before. And even when, then and later, that power was diffused among a governing class, it was still centred on the Throne and it was exercised by a numerically small sector of the nation. It was this group which controlled the distribution of influence, patronage, the profits of office. Government was still personal well into the eighteenth century and, in some respects, beyond. That is why the influence of individuals was important and the quality of government could change with the individual or group who wielded power. I have tried to show that the inherent revenue and administrative weaknesses of the system made it *potentially* corrupt. But it was the impact of a controlling individual or group which could in fact *make* it corrupt. It would be absurd to speak of one age as incorruptible and another as thoroughly corrupt. But it is possible to see evidence where one age is more corrupt than another. And here the personnel of government may be important. To underestimate the influence of personality in a system of personal government is as misleading as to overestimate it. I have never believed that Elizabeth I was all-virtuous and all-wise; and I have written enough elsewhere in criticism of her policies. But her influence was paramount and, in spite of her mistakes, she kept under restraint until almost the end the inherent tendencies of the system towards corruption. Under James I these restraints gradually died away. That is why I consider that the Jacobean age was more corrupt than the Elizabethan. Other historians will, no doubt, have other comparisons in mind.

I have attempted in this paper, in the negative sense, to argue that the word corruption is not helpful in the historical context unless the historian has first made up his own mind about the meaning of the term and has evidence that, in fact, corruption has occurred. For this, literary evidence is clearly not enough. Secondly, the expression is applicable not simply where money has changed hands, but where the public interest is sacrificed. I have therefore indicated the principal areas of conduct where the expression is just and appropriate. These are where gifts are accepted while holding judicial office; where state revenues are diverted into private purses; where appointment and advancement in the public service are by favouritism, or for reasons other than the public interest. On the other hand the taking and giving of gifts — loosely called bribes — cannot, before the nineteenth century, be described automatically as corrupt, without each case being examined on its merits. I was forced to embark on this investigation because, in my study of Robert Cecil and the charges of corruption made against him, I found that I could not get much further until I was quite clear myself as to what I meant by the term corruption. It may be that later researchers into political corruption will criticize and amend some of the principles which, in this preliminary inquiry, I have tried to discover and express. If that should happen, then we shall all be the gainers. For it is time that, as historians, we gave our minds to this central problem of government and society.

6

Corruption and reform under Edward VI and Mary: the example of wardship

The feudal revival of the early sixteenth century was part of the heroic effort of the Tudors to make their monarchy economically secure;[1] and, in the vigour of his feudal assertions, the first of the Tudors was the boldest of them all. After him, Henry VIII passed a Statute of Uses[2] in 1536 and erected a Court of Wards[3] in 1540 in order to shelter what had been won and to gather into the feudal net still more of his subjects. But his machinery of government was unequal to his ambitions. In the last years of his rule, and in the early years of Edward VI's, the Court of Wards passed through a period of decay from which, only at the end of Edward's reign and under Mary, it began to recover. In the history of royal wardship from 1540 to 1558 we have a microcosm of mid-sixteenth century administration as a whole; and we can see in the ample records of the Court of Wards a reflection of the larger issues at stake.

During the eighteen years between its creation and the accession of Queen Elizabeth, the Court of Wards had two distinguished and able Masters at its head. Sir William Paulet,[4] its first

NOTE: First published in *English Historical Review*, lxviii (1953), pp. 22–36.

[1] D. M. Brodie, 'Edmund Dudley: minister of Henry VII', *Trans. R. Hist. Soc.*, 4th Ser. (1932), xv, pp. 133–61; R. Constable, *Prerogativa Regis*, ed. S. E. Thorne (New Haven, 1949); J. Hurstfield, 'The revival of feudalism in early Tudor England', *History*, n.s. xxxvii, pp. 131–45. W. C. Richardson's valuable *Tudor Chamber Administration, 1485–1547* (Baton Rouge, 1952) appeared while this article was in the press.
[2] 27 Hy. VIII, c. 10.
[3] 32 Hy. VIII, c. 46.
[4] Created Baron St John in 1539, Earl of Wiltshire in 1550 and Marquess of Winchester in 1551.

Master, had held the office jointly with Thomas Englefield from November 1526 until December 1534 when Paulet had become sole occupant.[1] When his department was elevated to the status of a fully constituted court in 1540, he retained his post; and though greater honours and heavier burdens came his way, he remained Master of Wards until the beginning of Mary's reign.[2] In May 1554 he was succeeded by the trusted servant of Mary, Sir Francis Englefield,[3] who remained in office until his dismissal by Elizabeth shortly after she came to the throne.[4]

Paulet's career as a finance officer of the Crown was one of the longest in English history. He had become comptroller of the household as early as 1532 and by the time of his death in 1572 he had risen to the summit and borne the full burden of the lord treasurership for some twenty-two years. He had served in succession Henry VIII and his three children; but neither the religious changes of the reigning monarchs nor the disputes of faction had interrupted his career. He was Master of Wards for a generation, his tenure of office being exceeded only by that of Sir William Cecil himself. When Englefield succeeded Paulet the Court of Wards had passed out of its formative period but had not yet won for itself a secure place in Tudor government. What mark, we may ask, did these two Masters leave upon its administration and policy?

One obvious aid to such an understanding would be an annual balance sheet of its revenues. Unfortunately, for the greater part of Henry VIII's reign our records falter and, where they exist at all, they offer us many of the pitfalls which beset students of the financial records of the time.[5] Yet, meagre and hazardous though they are, they do enable us to make rough calculations at certain dates of the net revenues from wardships, that is the profits left

---

[1] *L. and P.* iv, pt. 2, g. 2673 (3), vii. g. 1601 (29).

[2] Ibid., xv, g. 942 (112), xvii, g. 1154 (72).

[3] *Cal. of. Pat. Rolls*, Mary, i, 249.

[4] Dasent, *Acts of the P.C.*, n.s. vii. 29–30 and 47.

[5] There are three other receiver-general's accounts for Henry VIII, but two of them, Wards 8, 107 and Wards 11, 3, 9, are officially described by the Public Record Office as 'unfit' and the third, Wards 9, 361, is inadequate for our purpose.

after the various expenses had been paid.[1] During the whole of
Henry VIII's reign we can do this for only six years, three before
the establishment of the Court of Wards, when there was an
Office of Wards in London functioning under its Master, and
three after its establishment. The earliest receiver-general's
account upon which such calculations can be based is for the
year 1523-4 and it shows the net revenue at £3,134;[2] seven years
later it had fallen slightly to £3,003.[3] Our next account brings us
to the period shortly before the establishment of the Court of
Wards, the year 1536-7, when the profits reached £3,590, an
increase of some 20 per cent over twelve years.[4] When we
look at the position five years later, in 1541-2, we find a further
increase, with the revenue at £4,466; but this total included
profits from liveries (£967), for the first time entered in the
receiver-general's accounts, so that, in effect, the revenue from
wardships had fallen slightly.[5] A year afterwards, however, the
combined total had undoubtedly risen and reached £5,452.[6] When
we come lastly to 1545-6, three years later, we find that the revenue
had almost doubled and stood at its highest so far, £10,550.[7]

For the other years of the reign our records are silent. But when
we come to Edward VI we begin a full and continuous series of
receiver-general's accounts which take us right through the history
of the Court of Wards until its submergence during the civil wars
of the seventeenth century. For Edward VI's reign, however, one
proviso must be made. John Beaumont, the receiver-general, had
been appointed by Henry VIII in January 1545 and held the

[1] From the gross revenue for each year I have deducted the various expenses
which the receiver-general had to meet as well as those 'arrearages' which were
the cash in hand carried over by him from one year to the next. I have given all
figures to the nearest pound.

[2] Wards 8, 72.

[3] Wards 8, 73.

[4] Wards 8, 74.

[5] Wards 8, 108. It should be noted that it is impossible to obtain any reliable
estimate of the profits from liveries before 1541-2. After this date they are
incorporated in the grand totals of the receiver-general's accounts. If, however,
we excluded this item, the broad trend would still remain the same.

[6] Wards 8, 109.

[7] Wards 9, 362.

position until the end of December 1550, having shortly before that been appointed Master of the Rolls.[1] During this period, as he subsequently confessed, he robbed the Crown of £11,823 by omitting from his receipts various sums paid into the Court.[2] If we accept his confession as a full record of the extent of his defalcations, then on an average he falsified his accounts to the tune of some £2,000 during each year of his office. We should bear this figure in mind when we consider the profits officially recorded for the period.

In the opening year of Edward VI's reign we see a significant fall in the net revenues compared with the last full year under Henry VIII. In fact they dropped by 39 per cent and were no higher than £7,638.[3] A year later they had fallen still further and were as little as £6,595.[4] Only in the third year had they recovered this lost ground and in fact gone up to £9,125.[5] But it was not until the fourth year of Edward's reign, and the final year of Beaumont's receivership, that they at last reached and passed the figure recorded under Henry VIII and stood at £13,316.[6] The next year they continued their rise, reaching £14,892,[7] and in the last year of Edward's reign they more or less held their ground at £14,596.[8] It is not without significance that the royal income from wardship did not reach the highest figure of the reign until the late receiver-general had been transferred to another sphere. But even then the contribution was not impressive. In an inflationary crisis, made worse by corruption, the Court of Wards could bring scant comfort to the weak governments of Edward VI.

Meanwhile, many who lived under the shadow of a feudal wardship took steps to 'smother their tenures' where opportunity served. With the various devices for concealment and evasion we

---

[1] *Cal. of Pat. Rolls*, Edward VI, iii, 311 and 329.

[2] Wards 9, 365, fos. 210ʳ–216ᵛ, 218ʳ–219ᵛ and 235ᵛ–236ʳ (and enclosures).

[3] Ibid., fos. 2ʳ–39ᵛ.

[4] Ibid., fos. 48ʳ–93ᵛ.

[5] Ibid., fos. 102ʳ–156ʳ.

[6] Ibid., fos. 166ʳ–236ʳ. (This section includes also the confession of Beaumont.)

[7] Ibid., fos. 238ʳ–297ᵛ. This, however, includes a repayment by Beaumont of £1,597, which was not, in fact, part of this year's profits on wardship.

[8] Ibid., fos. 302ʳ–353ᵛ.

are not in this article concerned. They were a perennial problem throughout the Tudor period. There were, however, other means of resistance. I have shown elsewhere that under pressure of a gathering economic crisis the governments of the 1540s had had to sell land quickly on what was fast becoming a buyer's market.[1] They had therefore perforce abandoned over large areas of land their original plan to impose a tenure in chief by knight-service upon the lands they sold. They agreed instead to the establishment of socage tenures virtually free from the feudal incidents. Then, in a significant statute of 1549 the government gave further ground.[2] Hitherto when a jury in its return had stated that 'the land was held of the king but by an unknown tenure', such land was officially deemed to be held of the king by knight-service in chief. The same had applied where the jury reported that 'they did not know of whom and by what tenure the land was held'. Now the Crown agreed that in such cases of uncertainty a fresh inquiry should be held. In renouncing its original claim the Crown was in fact admitting that for the future any uncertain tenure might, through a second inquisition, be interpreted against the Crown interests, in flat contradiction to the recent trend.[3] This was a major concession to those resisting the feudal claims of the Crown and was a further demonstration of a weak government and a loosening grip.

Weakness also played into the hands of the receiver-general of the Court of Wards. The career of John Beaumont exemplifies the corruption and decay of the Henrician system of government during the minority of Edward VI. Nor was Beaumont content to exercise his talents in the field of wardships alone. When Master of the Rolls and a judge in Chancery he descended to forgery and induced, or compelled, a jury to perjure themselves on his behalf. He also concealed the felony of one of his servants.[4] But he had

---

[1] 'The Greenwich tenures of the reign of Edward VI', *Law Quart. Rev.*, lxv, pp. 72–81.

[2] 2 and 3 Ed. VI, c. 8.

[3] For a flagrant example of how a tenant had suffered through an uncertain tenure, see S. P. Dom. Addenda, Ed. VI, iii, no. 50.

[4] Journal of Edward VI in *Literary Remains of King Edward VI* (Roxburghe Club, 1857), ii, p. 422, June 4th, 1552.

undoubtedly excelled himself in the office of receiver-general of the Court of Wards in which, as Edward VI recorded in his journal, 'he hade bought land with my money, had lent it, and kept it from me to the [*sic*] 9000 *li* and above more then this twelmonth, and 11,000 in obligacions'.[1] There were in fact two separate abuses to which Edward was referring in this elliptic passage. The first was the receiver-general's practice of keeping in his private possession the balance in hand, instead of paying it to the Crown each year as the statute establishing the Court of Wards required. His carry-over at the end amounted to £9,765 and this he had usefully employed in speculation. But the mounting debt he at least acknowledged in his accounts. The second, and more serious, abuse was his suppression of all record of some of his revenue. This, as we have seen, he did to the tune of £11,823; and, as Beaumont's own confession shows, he had begun it all in Henry VIII's reign. The procedure by which it was accomplished was simple enough. He had not recorded in his official receipt books many of the sums paid into the Court of Wards and, for all practical purposes, they had therefore remained his private property. As is well known, Beaumont was not an isolated example of financial malpractices which came to light when the Protector Somerset was overthrown. Lord Paget, Richard Whalley, Sir Thomas Holcroft, Sir John Thynne, Sir William Sharington, Lord Arundel and Sir Martin Bowes were all at about this time charged with serious abuses of their financial offices.[2] But it was Beaumont's misuse of his position of high responsibility which shocked even the case-hardened judges of the Star Chamber with 'so many foul matters as we think have seldom appeared in any one man'.[3] When William Damsell succeeded Beaumont he unfolded, by accident or intention, the mis-

---

[1] Journal of Edward VI in *Literary Remains of King Edward VI*, loc. cit.

[2] Ibid., pp. 422–3; F. C. Dietz, *English Government Finance, 1485–1558* (Illinois, 1920), pp. 180–81.

[3] 'The Lords of the Council to the [?] Duke of Northumberland', printed in *Illustrations of British History*, ed. E. Lodge, 2nd edn (1838), i, p. 175. Perhaps Beaumont was already feeling the net tightening around him when he wrote to Cecil in November 1550 complaining about slanders against himself (S. P. Dom. Ed. VI, xi, no. 2).

demeanours of his predecessor.[1] Perhaps Paulet, now lord treasurer, also became interested in them when he embarked upon a complete survey of the revenue.[2] It is noteworthy, however, that those who had to face these charges belonged to the entourage of the fallen Protector and that they paid at the same time for their political errors as for their official abuses. It may be also that political loyalty to the new Protector cast a veil over the financial disorders of those who were not brought to book. But the heavy sentence upon Beaumont, as well as the details of his confession in the Court of Wards records, leave no suggestion that he was the innocent martyr for a vanquished cause.[3] On February 11th, 1552, he was arrested and imprisoned in the Fleet.[4] On May 28th, after interrogation, he made his confession.[5] On this, Northumberland observed that the result provided no adequate measure of his crimes;[6] and the fuller confession extracted from him is to be found amongst the receiver-general's accounts for the reign.[7] At the time of his earlier confession in May 1552 he had agreed to surrender all his property[8] and in the following October the Crown formally took possession.[9]

The condition of the records under Beaumont indicates in no

---

[1] Those whose payments were concealed by Beaumont may well have been asked by the new receiver-general to pay once again their 'arrears'. In that case, their replies must have provided a considerable volume of evidence about Beaumont's financial methods.

[2] Dasent, *Acts of the P.C.* iii, 29, 11 May 1550. See also ibid., p. 157, 16 November 1550.

[3] The fact that Beaumont, like so many others, had prudently sued out a pardon at the beginning of Edward VI's reign (*Cal. of Pat. Rolls*, Edward VI, ii, 152) could, naturally, be of little help to him.

[4] Dasent, *Acts of the P.C.* iii, 478.

[5] Printed in Strype, *Ecclesiastical Memorials* (1822), ii, pt. 2, pp. 498–9.

[6] Northumberland's comments on the original confession are to be found in his letters of May 30th and 31st, printed in P. F. Tytler, *England under the reigns of Edward VI and Mary* (1839), ii, pp. 108–10. See also Brit. Mus. Harl. MS. 2143, fo. 7ʳ. I am indebted to Lady Neale for this reference.

[7] See above, p. 166, n. 6.

[8] Strype, op. cit., p. 498.

[9] Dasent, *Acts of the P.C.* iv, 152. The *D.N.B.*, *sub* Beaumont, points out that by 'either a curious oversight or an intentional act of grace' his wife was not joined with him in the penalty and was able, therefore, to enter upon her estate tail without loss.

uncertain manner how ill-informed and misinformed the Crown was as to the state of its own revenues. Part of the fog which obscured this vital information derived from the highly defective system of accountancy which prevailed. In the Act which established the Court of Wards it was laid down that the accounts should be audited annually by the Master, attorney and one or both of the auditors of the Court. In other words, the finances were to be checked by an internal audit only. Secondly, the receiver-general was instructed to pay to the 'King's use', within a month of the annual audit, all sums of money left in his hands;[1] this instruction was honoured more in the breach than in the observance, as is shown under Beaumont by the rising tale of 'arrearages' (that is, cash in hand) with which the receiver-general 'charged himself'.

Under pressure of a mounting burden of debt the Crown tried time and time again to come to grips with the situation and to keep itself better informed. The Court of Wards had barely come into existence when the privy council wrote in October 1540 to the Master, as well as to heads of other financial departments, asking for 'an abbrevyate of all the offices and fees with the names of them that have them at this present'.[2] Five years later, in December 1545, the Crown was seeking to make an even more ambitious survey, through a specially appointed commission to analyse all the royal revenues and to take drastic steps to recover the king's debts.[3] Within six months there was a new commission to see that the king's profits from his revenue courts were in fact paid to him; and the direction to the commissioners observed, amongst other things, that much was being lost through the favour or prejudice of the Crown officials.[4]

In just over a year there was yet another commission, issued by a new and penurious king, to make a full examination of the Crown revenues.[5] In March 1552 with the lamentable story of the activities of Beaumont recently laid bare before it and with

[1] 32 Hy. VIII, c. 46.
[2] Nicolas, *Acts of the P.C.* vii, 59 and 60 n. 1.
[3] *L. and P.* xx, pt. 2, g. 1068 (28).
[4] *L. and P.* xxi, pt. 1, g. 1166 (71).
[5] S. P. Dom. Ed. VI. ii, nos. 9 and 31. See also *Cal. of Pat. Rolls*, Edward VI, i. 93.

other scandals in the offing, the government appointed a commission, charged amongst other things with the 'overseeing of the courts';[1] but before its report had come in the privy council had issued in May new instructions to the treasurers of the exchequer, Augmentations, the Duchy of Lancaster and of the Wards

> not onely to stay from payment of suche monny as is and shall be in theyr charge [except on direct instruction from the privy council] ... but allso that they and every of them doo with diligence advertise unto theyr Lordshippes in writing, as well what monny is presently in theyr handes of the revenues of every theyr offices, as what they suppose and doo looke shall cume to theyr handes of the receypt of the same revenues due at the Annunciation of Our Lady last past.[2]

In July a new commission was ordered to collect from the treasurers their cash in hand and to take Draconian steps against the king's debtors.[3] A few months later William Cecil included amongst his memoranda, perhaps for consideration by the privy council, 'the discharge of excessyve chargs in the courts of the revenues'.[4] In December there was still one more commission, this time to inquire whether Crown lands had been properly valued before their sale;[5] whilst by the death of Edward VI or shortly after, the government had drawn up a full and detailed register of the gifts, exchanges and purchases of Crown lands during the reign with the relevant details of price, value, reserved rents and other matters.[6] One of the last statutes of the reign

---

[1] *Literary Remains of King Edward VI*, ii, p. 406 and note.

[2] Dasent, *Acts of the P.C.* iv. 62.

[3] *Cal. of Pat. Rolls*, Edward VI, iv. 355–6.

[4] S. P. Dom. Ed. VI, xv, no. 10, 29 September 1552. See also no. 13, 3 October 1552.

[5] *Cal. of Pat. Rolls*, Edward VI, iv. 397–8.

[6] S. P. Dom. Ed. VI, xix. For a full report of the important commission of Ed. VI and some of its acid comments on the existing system of the Court of Wards, as well as other departments of state, see Brit. Mus. Harl. 7383, fols. 1ʳ–72ʳ (reproduced also in Brit. Mus. Add. MS. 30198). I am indebted to Professor W. C. Richardson for the references.

observed of the royal treasurers that they 'have not so justlye, spedely, neither dulye made yerely paimentes of suche some and somes of money as hathe been by them and every of them received';[1] and with this polite understatement of the mal-practices of Edward's ministers we may for the moment leave them.

With the financial crisis deepening, Mary's reign opened with precise instructions to the receiver-general of the Court of Wards in future to hand over his balances to Sir Edmond Peckham, the treasurer of the Mint;[2] and these instructions, at least in Mary's reign, appear to have been obeyed.[3] The receiver-general's 'arrear-ages', from now onwards, no longer stood at thousands of pounds as they had done recently but were either entirely liquidated or negligible.[4] At about the same time Paulet officially confirmed an internal reform introduced earlier, under which the number of clerks of Wards was reduced from two to one on the grounds that Thomas Anton, at present sole clerk, had proved adequate to the task.[5] This decision in itself offered no immediate economy but was a clear indication of Paulet's resolve to hold the door, so far as he was able, against the periodic multiplication of offices which afflicted successive Tudor governments. In May 1554, the officers of the Court of Wards were specially commissioned to survey the receiver-general's accounts, and to simplify them once and for all by removing the long procession of desperate debts which cluttered up the records.[6] In 1555 plans were made, in preparation for the assembly of Parliament, to estimate the Crown income from the various sources.[7] At the beginning of 1557, under a new commission, a thorough investigation of the royal income was

[1] 7 Ed. VI, c. 1.

[2] S. P. Dom. Mary, Addenda, vii, nos. 4 and 5.

[3] The money was not always paid into the same treasury; it might go to the cofferer, the treasurer of the chamber, or to some other finance officer of the Crown.

[4] In Elizabeth's reign they began to rise again and culminated in another first class scandal when the receiver-general, George Goring, died in 1594. (See Wards 9, 108, fos. 509ᵛ–510ᵛ and H.M.C. Salisbury, *passim*.)

[5] S. P. Dom. Mary, Addenda, vii, no. 11.

[6] Pat. Roll. 1 Mary, pt. xi, m. 37ᵈ.

[7] S. P. Dom. Mary, vi, no. 22.

instituted with instructions to reach back into Henry VIII's reign in search of false statements and fraud.[1]

Meanwhile the average annual receipts from wardships rose markedly during Mary's reign. At first there was a temporary setback and the net revenues fell to £12,888,[2] but they were soon moving upwards again to reach their peak in her fourth year at £20.020.[3] In the last two years they declined again somewhat, but even so the income did not fall below the *highest* figure of Edward's reign. In her last year it was £15,293.[4] Under a new Master, Sir Francis Englefield, and a recently appointed receiver-general, Sir William Damsell, the Court of Wards had entered upon one of the most successful phases of its Tudor history.[5] So the reign of Mary drew to a close with the Wards records and revenues in better shape; but there was still, as the government seemed fully aware, a yawning gap between its rights in theory and its receipts in practice.

The fact that the Court of Wards flourished under Mary has, apart from its economic, social and political significance, a special relevance to an important administrative issue of her reign. As a result of the reforms of Paulet and his colleagues, the new financial courts, with one exception, were abolished and their functions absorbed by the exchequer. First the Court of General Surveyors had been joined to the Court of Augmentations in the last month of Henry VIII's reign.[6] Then at the end of Edward VI's reign the amalgamation of this court with the other revenue courts erected by Henry VIII, or their abolition, was authorized by Parliament.[7] At the beginning of Mary's reign renewed authority was obtained from Parliament[8] and implemented in January 1554 by letters

[1] *Cal. of Pat. Rolls*, Mary, iii, 313.
[2] Wards 9, 365, fos. 371^r–417^v.
[3] Wards 9, 367, fos. 179^r–238^v.
[4] Ibid., fos. 333^r–378^v.
[5] A further confirmation of this trend is the rise in salary awarded to Damsell in recognition of the increased revenues of the Court of Wards (H.M.C., Salisbury, i, 136). The remark in this source that Damsell was receiver-general when the Court was established is an error.
[6] *L. and P.* xxi, pt. 2, g. 771 (1).
[7] 7 Ed. VI, c. 2.
[8] 1 Mary, st. 2, c. 10.

patent.[1] The solitary exception to this process was the Court of Wards, though it too was included within the permissive authority of the statutes. If we knew what sheltered the Court of Wards from the fate of the other financial courts we should probably be able at the same time to shed further light on its earlier history; but unfortunately no records of discussion specifically on the matter at this crucial time have, so far as I am aware, survived.[2]

It is possible, however, to speculate about the motives which influenced Mary and Paulet in their final decision to continue the separate existence of a Court of Wards. When Sir William Damsell was appointed its receiver-general on January 17th, 1554, his patent included the provision that, in the event of the Court being abolished, he would retain his office with the revenues.[3] But when Sir Francis Englefield was appointed Master on May 1st, 1554, there was no reference in his patent to the possible abolition of the Court and no provision was made for his compensation should that take place.[4] It is unlikely, if such a dissolution was still in prospect, that the queen would have made no provision for the Master, a man who was senior in office to the receiver-general and, in the person of Englefield, much closer to her counsels and favour. It looks, therefore, as though some time between January 17th and May 1st, 1554, it was decided not to terminate the independent existence of the Court of Wards; and this perhaps provides a clue to one of the causes, though not the most important, which gave it a new lease of life. The queen was honouring and rewarding one of her most trusted servants; and that very trust she reposed in him must have made her view with confidence the continuance under him of an important department of state, in

[1] The letters patent dissolving these courts do not appear to have been enrolled but the instruction, dated January 19th, 1554, that letters patent be issued is calendared in *Cal of Pat. Rolls*, Mary, i, 73. It is clear, however, from other references in this calendar that the courts were dissolved on January 23rd, 1554, and their functions absorbed into the Exchequer the following day.

[2] The commission of inquiry of Edward's reign (see above p. 171, n. 6) comments on Court of Wards procedure but does not weigh up the pros and cons for dissolution.

[3] *Pat. Roll*, 1 Mary, pt. ii, m. 15.

[4] Ibid., pt. x, m. 7.

spite of the great scandal associated with it in the preceding reign. With Englefield at its head and with Paulet not far away at the exchequer, it was reasonable to hope that no new Beaumont would dare arise to exact his heavy tribute from the Crown. If such hopes influenced Mary's mind at this critical moment in the history of the Court of Wards, its administration during her reign justified these hopes.

Apart from personal considerations, there were weightier causes for this decision. There had grown up within the Court of Wards special techniques for dealing with the complex and delicate issues inseparable from wardship. Whereas the Courts of Augmentations and of First Fruits and Tenths dealt exclusively with land and revenue questions, not fundamentally different from the other revenue questions arising in the exchequer, the problems which came before the Wards officials were of an entirely different category. It is true that land questions formed an integral part of their work; but they had to deal also with grants of wardships, marriages, abuses of guardianship, licences to widows to re-marry, the suing of livery and the administration of the affairs of idiots and lunatics. Some of these functions had in origin little direct connection with the exchequer and had been derived in some cases from Chancery, in others from the Master of Liveries and the pre-1540 Office of Wards. Since 1540 these administrative segments had been welded into one homogeneous department and little would be gained in the future from transferring them to a division of the exchequer, with whose work and interests they could have little in common. Administrative continuity rather than over-centralization seemed to offer better prospects if the Crown's claims were to be pressed to the full and the *expertise* gathered together in the Court of Wards were to be effectively used. And, apart from all this, it was a court of law with a tradition and experience peculiarly its own for dealing with the bewildering ramifications of feudal law. Again, prudence would seem therefore to support its continued autonomy. Perhaps these, and other, considerations had been suggested to Edward VI's mind when he referred amongst his private memoranda of October 13th, 1552, to the proposal to bring the Courts of Augmentations and First Fruits into the exchequer but said nothing about the Court of Wards. He felt, however, that something would have to be done about the 'superfluous fees' both here and in the Duchy of Lancaster.[1]

The full reasons for the reprieve of the Court of Wards during the first half of 1554 may be for ever lost in obscurity; but the consequences of the reprieve were far-reaching. At that time the Court of Wards was only fourteen years old and, had it suffered the same fate as the other financial courts, it might have left little trace on Tudor administration and society, even had the rights of wardship survived. But now it was to extend the period of its life sevenfold and, in the ninety years which followed, the reformed Court of Wards was to become of increasing moment in the financial and administrative structure of the state.

Whatever pleasure or hopes the queen and her ministers derived from the survival of the Court of Wards, it is hardly likely that they were shared by her subjects. Already under Edward VI there had been vigorous criticism of its purpose and functions. 'There was never such marrying in England as is now!' cried Latimer in his sermon before the king in March 1549. 'I hear tell of stealing of wards to marry their children to. This is a strange kind of stealing: but it is not the wards, it is the lands they steal!'[2] Moreover, their education seemed to be sorely neglected. 'I trow there is a Court of Wards', he had observed in his Sermon of the Plough the previous year, 'why is there not a school for the wards as well as there is a Court for their lands.'[3] Latimer's language seems moderate compared with the bitter outburst of Henry Brinklow in his *Complaynt of Roderyck Mors*, written a few years earlier: 'Oh mercyful God, what innumerable inconuenyencys come by sellyng of wardys for maryage for lucre of goodys and landys.' It led amongst other things to adultery and divorce which were, he said, clearly on the increase. 'Now God confound that wicked custome; for it is to abhomynable, and stynkyth from the earth to heauyn, it is so vyle ... For Christys blode sake, seke a redresse

[1] *Literary Remains of King Edward VI*, ii, p. 544.
[2] *Sermons by Hugh Latimer*, ed. G. E. Corrie (1844), i, pp. 169-70.
[3] Ibid., i, p. 69.

for it!'[1] Perhaps the most significant comment came from Sir Nicholas Bacon, himself attorney of the Wards from 1547 until 1561.[2] Viewing the activities of the Court of Wards and its guardians at such close quarters, he seems to have been driven in Mary's reign to draw up a drastic plan of reform.[3] Echoing Latimer's sermon, or perhaps expressing an opinion held widely amongst reformers, he proposed to deprive guardians of the care of their wards at the age of nine so that they could be sent to a specially established school for wards. He had tried once, when Englefield was Master, to get his scheme adopted but his plan, like Latimer's, had fallen on stony ground. Now, in May 1561, a few months after his resignation as attorney of Wards and Cecil's appointment as Master, Bacon was sending him his plan: 'knowinge your good inclynacon to the thinge and your place, I ame in great hope of good successe thereof.' Whatever Cecil's inclination, once again the scheme came to nothing.

Bacon's covering letter drew attention to the irresponsible and selfish treatment to which wards were subjected, 'a thinge hitherto preposterouslie proceedinge'.

That the proceedinge hath bin preposterous [the letter goes on] appearethe by this: the chief thinge and most of price in wardeship is the wardes mynde, the next to that his bodie, and the last and meanest his lande. Now hitherto the chief care of gouernance hath bin had to the land, beinge the meanest, and the boddie beinge the better, verie small, but to the mynde beinge the best none at all, which mee thinkes is playnelie to sett the carte before the horse.

---

[1] Henry Brinklow, *Complaynt of Roderyck Mors*, ed. J. M. Cowper (1874), p. 18. Thomas Starkey makes even the gentle Pole, shortly before the establishment of the Court of Wards, describe the practice of selling wardships and marriages as 'a plain servitute and injury' and a 'bondage' which was 'unreasonable among civil people'. Thomas Starkey, *A Dialogue between Reginald Pole and Thomas Lupset*, ed. Kathleen M. Burton (1948), pp. 110–11.

[2] *L. and P.* xxi, pt. 2, g. 771 (13); *Cal. of Pat. Rolls*, Eliz. ii, 6.

[3] Brit. Mus. Add. MS, 32379, fols. 26ʳ–33ᵛ; see also J. P. Collier, 'On Sir Nicholas Bacon, Lord Keeper; with extracts from some of his unprinted Papers and Speeches', *Archaeologia*, xxxvi, pp. 339–48.

Originally, he understood, one of the purposes of feudal wardship was to enable the ward to be brought up by his lord according to the highest standards. 'Now by abuse it is come (as you knowe) to that, that the greater the personage is to whome the warde apperteynes, the lesse Curtesie for the most parte is had of the wardes bringinge vpp.' Bacon's anxieties had also expressed themselves in a more practical shape. In 1553 he had obtained from Queen Mary a special grant by which his own heir, should he succeed under age, would pass under the guardianship of the child's uncles, Thomas and James Bacon.[1] This precaution is easily understandable. Bacon had been a purchaser of ecclesiastical lands which, as he well knew, often brought military tenures in their train and, as he knew also, 'those tenures haue of late daies and contynuallie doe greatlie encrease'. If he had any doubts about this, which is unlikely, there was always a *memento mori* in the shape of Staunford's *Prerogativa Regis*, written in 1548, dedicated to Nicholas Bacon and full of the most sweeping feudal assertions on behalf of the Crown. Not surprisingly, Bacon was alarmed at 'what great hurte and lacke groweth to euery warde particulerlie, yea and what to the whole comon welthe generallie'.[2] He had himself been the recipient of wardships[3] but what sort of a guardian he made we do not know. It is clear, however, that he was genuinely anxious to introduce these overdue reforms 'as the best peece of service that ever I went about to doe in the Court of Wardes'. Though his ambitious project fared no better with Cecil than with Englefield, perhaps he derived some small compensation from the permission he received during the twelve months which followed to found two grammar schools, one in London (this time with Cecil's help) and the other in Suffolk.[4] He had, long before, proposed that some of the wealth of the dis-

---

[1] *Cal. of Pat. Rolls*, Mary, i, 3. Cf. the case of Matthew Kniveton (S. P. Dom., Mary, Docquet, 38, i, 5 November 1550).

[2] He may also have recalled that one of his predecessors as attorney of the Wards, John Sewster, had died leaving a minor heir to the mercy of the Court of Wards (*L. and P.* xxi, pt. 2, g. 771 [32]).

[3] *L. and P.* xviii, pt. 2, g. 449 (74); xix, pt. 1, g. 610 (23); Wards 9, 365, fo. 122^r; *Cal. of Pat. Rolls*, Ed. VI, i, 56.

[4] *Cal. of Pat. Rolls*, Eliz. ii, 104 and 226–7.

solved monastic lands should be used to establish a kind of embryonic University of London;[1] but that vision of Bacon's was too remote from the harsh realities of Henrician England.

The prevailing discontent over royal wardship is easy to understand when we examine in detail some of the practices of the Court of Wards during this period and the guardians who operated under its aegis. That royal wardship provided the happy hunting-ground for courtiers and officials the records amply demonstrate.[2] Most of the senior officers of the Court appear to have used the available opportunities for picking a few plums for themselves;[3] and the feodaries in the shires had their ears even closer to the ground. For example, Robert Rawson, feodary of the East Riding of Yorkshire, calmly wrote to a Mrs Levening that he had obtained the wardships of her daughters and that she must keep them 'uncontracted' in marriage until she received further instructions. He added, however, that he was prepared to dispose of the wardships at a reasonable price.'[4] The Levening heiresses were evidently ladies of charm or wealth: a few months later we find a suitor writing to a member of the Countess of Rutland's household offering £10 to her ladyship if she could get him the wardships.[5]

We have also examples of the familiar practice of disposing of wardships while the father was still alive. When George Chalcot of Dorset lay dying, a certain Peter Kydwelly was applying for the wardship of the heir. Kydwelly was apparently unable to tell the clerk of the Wards either the full name or the age of the heir, but what he was able to tell was from Kydwelly's point of view

---

[1] *D.N.B*, *Sub* Nicholas Bacon.

[2] e.g. Wards 9, 154, 155, 212.

[3] For Paulet, see *L. and P.* xviii, pt. 1, g. 346 (5), xx, pt. 2, no. 706(89), *Cal. of Pat. Rolls*, Mary, ii, 88; for Philip Paris, receiver-general, *L. and P.* xvii, g. 137 (59); for Richard Lee, his successor, ibid., xix, pt. 2, g. 690 (7); for John Sewster, attorney, ibid., xviii, pt. 2, g. 449 (66, 67), xix, pt. 2, g. 166 (13); for Richard Goodericke, his successor, ibid., xxi, pt. 2, no. 770 (24); for John Perient, auditor, ibid., xxi, pt. 1, no. 148 (57); for Thomas Anton, clerk, ibid., xxi, pt. 2, no. 770 (23).

[4] Ibid., xvii, Appendix no. 8 (1).

[5] Ibid., no. 8 (2).

more important, the value of the lands: £40 per annum.[1] More disconcerting perhaps was the case of Sir Giles Strangeways, also of that county. When he was reported to be dying in August 1546, the wardship of his grandson and heir was granted by direct authority of the Crown to Sir Richard Rich. But before Rich could enjoy this royal favour, a clerk was amending the record with the laconic observation: 'the said Sir Gilis at the entre hereof was sike and lyke to dye and nowe is recouered ageyne'. It was only a temporary recovery; but death tarried long enough to deprive Rich of his quarry, for when a clerk came once more to amend the document he recorded that Sir Giles was 'sithen that tyme ded and his heire apparant maried in his lyf'.[2] This final transaction had also a touch of irony. The immediately preceding entry in this volume shows Sir Giles—over whose dying body the battle of the wardship was being fought—himself buying a wardship! Not all anticipatory wardships were necessarily to the disadvantage of the wards. Sometimes, as we have seen in the case of Bacon, they were insurance policies taken out by the parent or some other relation to forestall an outside suitor for the wardship. For example, a Mrs John Browne of Frampton, in Dorset, was able through the good offices of Sir John Paulet, son of the Master of Wards, to prepare for her future widowhood by obtaining the promise of the guardianship of her son when it should fall due.[3] When, if ever, she got the wardship we do not know. Mr Browne was 'very sycke and like to die shortly' from 1549 until at least 1553,[4] after which he, and the wardship, disappear from our records.

Too often, however, the arrival of complete strangers in the Court of Wards during a father's lifetime was contrary to the best interests of the heir. If the toleration of such practices by the Court of Wards was difficult to defend, no less disturbing was the grant of a wardship to William Tooke, later its auditor, three months

[1] Wards 9, 154, Dorset (Chalcot).
[2] Wards 9, 154, Dorset (Strangeways).
[3] Ibid., Dorset (Browne). A similar arrangement was made on behalf of a certain George Gyffard of Bucks, in May 1555; he had to pay £60 for the privilege (*Cal. of Pat. Rolls*, Mary, ii, 293–4).
[4] Wards 9, 155, Dorset (Browne).

before the heir came of age;[1] or the royal claim to a wardship, not because the land was held of the Crown but because it was held of the attainted Duke of Norfolk, whose property was now in the king's hands.[2] This was sound enough in medieval feudal law but increasingly out of keeping with the society of a new age. On top of all this there was the ill-defined right of prerogative wardship which still further lengthened the reach of the Crown, as the case of Lord Dacre of the South during this period exemplified.[3] Any examination of the Wards records reveals a solid mass of evidence that the growing hostility to royal wardship found its origins in the insecurity and dangers which threatened all tenants by knight-service in chief.

Yet the period provides also a number of examples of the Crown exercising its rights in the interests of the ward. Thus, when Lord Dacre of the North was found in 1550 to have obtained control of Lord Scroope, a ward, Dacre was instructed to deliver him 'for the benefit of his Majesties lawes shall be denyed to none, myche less to the Lord Scroope'.[4] John Hastings, another ward, was granted his own wardship in 1541 by direct authority of the Crown and without charge, partly because of his father's service to Henry VIII; but the Master was instructed even so to estimate 'what the value of the same marige is in case you hadd sold the same in our behalf'. This Paulet duly calculated at £20.[5] In 1546 by another act of clemency the Crown cancelled the debt of £48 6s. 3d. owing to the Court of Wards by a war widow who had lost her husband in battle against the Scots.[6] But these and other acts could only mitigate some of the consequences of a tenure by knight-service. They could not restrain the zeal of the Crown officials in their pressure upon the luckless heir or the

---

[1] *L. and P.* xix, pt. 1, g. 141 (2) and g. 610 (53), Robert Higham (Essex). There had to be two inquisitions (Chancery I.P.M., lxii, no. 65 and lxix, no. 81) before Tooke could claim the wardship and he got it just in time. He received it in January 1544 and by May Higham, Tooke's ward, had sued out his livery.

[2] *Cal. of Pat. Rolls*, Ed. VI, i, 306, Edmund Whyte, Norfolk.

[3] *L. and P.* xvi, nos. 978 and 1028.

[4] Dasent, *Acts of the P.C.* iii, 123.

[5] Wards 9, 149, fo. 102^r.

[6] *L. and P.* xxi, pt. 1, no. 963 (126).

cupidity of informers and suitors who found in the Court of Wards an attractive annex to the land market.

What had happened to the Court of Wards during the first eighteen years of its existence? Like other Tudor institutions it betrayed marked weaknesses of policy and administration during those last years of Henry VIII's rule as the reins of government began to slip from his hands. During the Edwardian minority its history was a chequered one though it began to recover towards the end. When, however, the story of the life and career of one of the great figures of the sixteenth century, William Paulet, Marquess of Winchester, comes to be written, some cognizance will have to be taken of the fact that the receiver-general of the Court was able to dig deep into its revenues under the very eyes of Paulet, at that time its Master. Then, under Mary, it entered upon a period of reform in administration which was soon reflected in increased profits to the Crown. At the time of her death in 1558 it had Englefield at its head, while the late Master, Paulet, was nearby at the exchequer. In this year also, the Court of Wards, in handing down its decision in Tyrell's case, had invalidated 'the use reserved out of an use' and thereby blocked another loophole from the feudal incidents.[1] Englefield's religion was soon to deprive him of office but Paulet was to stay at the treasury for many years; and, after a brief interlude under Parry, the Court was to pass under the long mastership of Sir William Cecil. What he and the new queen made of this extraordinary institution was to shape the lives of many thousands of her subjects as well as leave its mark on our economy and polity for a century to come.

[1] See e.g. W. S. Holdsworth, *History of English Law* (2nd edn, 1937), iv, p. 472.

7

The political morality of early
Stuart statesmen

'Men are not gods.' Every historian, in the course of the long
apprenticeship he serves, learns this discouraging truism. By the
time that he has finished writing his first book he has met wise
statesmen who are not good men, and good men who have
become unwise statesmen. But he has given up looking for the
political saint. And he may have stopped asking questions about
political morality.

One of the many interesting aspects of Mrs Menna Prestwich's
book, *Cranfield: Politics and Profits under the early Stuarts*,[1] is that
throughout its length it is intimately involved with the problem of
political morality. In the process, all the leading figures of Jacobean England pass in review; and, to put them to the test, the
author has built up a formidable apparatus of economic analysis.
They are all tried and found wanting; and it is legitimate, therefore, to ask: what are her criteria for judgment about political
morality?

To this question we shall return shortly. But it is first essential
to state that hers is a valuable contribution to the study of the
period, indispensable henceforth to anyone who, through desire
or need, tries to understand the labyrinthine processes of seventeenth-century exchequer finance. The author in the course of a
busy and successful career as a university teacher devoted many
years to the research and writing of this book; and she thereby
vindicates once again the case for rejecting the pressures put upon

NOTE: First published in *History*, lvi (1971), pp. 235–43.

[1] Menna Prestwich, *Cranfield: Politics and Profits under the early Stuarts, the career
of Lionel Cranfield, Earl of Middlesex* (Clarendon Press, Oxford, 1966, xx, 623 pp.).
All page references given in the text refer to Mrs Prestwich's book.

some historians for the premature publication of a major work, regardless of the exacting standards of modern historical scholarship. The author is to be congratulated on bringing to conclusion a fundamental contribution to a crucial aspect of English history.

Mrs Prestwich makes clear, and with a wealth of evidence, the qualities which brought Cranfield from city merchant with modest means, at the end of Elizabeth's reign, to the lord treasurership, in the last years of James's, and, at the end, to impeachment for corruption. The qualities which brought him forward were a cool, logical brain, a marvellous commercial intuition and endless patience, 'the nerve to wait for prices, buying low and selling high, a quick eye for speculation, and resourcefulness in seeking markets' (p. 53). He grasped from the beginning that the psychological root of successful commerce lay in confidence, and that confidence depended on honouring one's debts. 'At my hand content my debt royally,' he wrote, as a young merchant to a subordinate. 'Let no man come often for his money.' All this was not necessarily accompanied by straightforward dealings in the market: he knew how to dispose of poor quality kerseys or dubious pepper (pp. 53, 55, 56, 58). But again this was done shrewdly, circumspectly and with all the trappings of decency.

Prudence, skilful speculation, tough dealing with debtors and rivals, a strict economy in public and private affairs—he cut his wife's housekeeping allowance by twenty-seven shillings, 'for so much she received of Lewis Wallington for one piece of jean fustians'—these qualities, as Mrs Prestwich rightly observes, equipped him well to become 'so useful a minister to an improvident king' (p. 54). And minister in due course he became, after the failure of Salisbury's Great Contract in 1611: a somewhat inauspicious beginning for his public career under the patronage of Henry Howard, Earl of Northampton, friend and enemy of Salisbury, as indeed Northampton could be to most men.

The decade which began in 1613 saw Cranfield's advance to the surveyor-generalship of the customs, on through the ordnance office, the navy commission, the treasury commission, the

Wardrobe, the Court of Wards and finally to the lord treasurer-ship from 1621 and the earldom of Middlesex. The highest peak was followed by the sharpest descent: in 1624 he was impeached by Parliament. There followed the long sterile years of his en-forced retirement: his talents rusting, his fortune dwindling, he lived on, a sour observer of a declining age. He had been the businessman writ large, transferring the lessons he had learned in his private affairs to the affairs of state. But, however comparable the situation may be, and however skilfully a man may have conducted his private affairs, he finds in the world of politics larger forces than in European commerce and he meets forces over which he has little control. That was Cranfield's experience. But when the time came, after his short period at the pinnacle of power, he was in fact brought down by Parliament on the charge of corruption.

Corruption? Here the modern biographer and the seven-teenth-century parliamentarians pose the same problem for the historian. When we take a reckoning of Cranfield's career, of the pluses and minuses, of the public service and the private gain, of the massive but unsuccessful effort to cut the king's suit according to the nation's cloth, while picking up a yard or two for his own use, do we then confirm the verdict of the 1624 Parliament that he was a corrupt man? Mrs Prestwich is both prosecuting counsel and justice of appeal; and in neither capacity does she consider that any case has been made out to vary the judgment. It may, therefore, seem presumptuous for one who lacks her intimate knowledge of the Cranfield manuscripts to question her con-clusions. But it still remains possible that, using her own evidence, a variant interpretation of that evidence may arise. It is with this central theme of corruption that the remainder of this article is concerned. I emphasize that this is not a matter of moral con-demnation but part of a search for a viable generalization.

It is helpful to readers of the book that Mrs Prestwich has, as it were, embarked on a trial run before her assessment of Cran-field, by attempting, on a more limited scale, a judgment of Robert Cecil, Earl of Salisbury. The reputation of both men must rest upon their work for the national finances, for both held the two key posts of Master of Wards and lord treasurer. Both in a sense were failures. Salisbury tried, in a massive conversion scheme, to barter the king's feudal rights, and his own office of Master of Wards, for a secure and predetermined annual income for the Crown. His work was thwarted by the House of Commons, and sabotaged by a faction of the king's advisers. There are several opinions about the Great Contract, as this scheme was known; and contemporaries as well as recent historians have vigorously debated the issue.[1] But there is no doubt about the parallel with Cranfield, who also tried, without the dramatic occasion of a Great Contract, to reconstruct the national finances. He cut savagely at the sprawling, overgrown pension list and ran clean into the powerful resistance of the whole Buckingham tribe. He struck at the office-holders and tax-farmers, as he tried desperately to enlarge the royal share of their income; and he made numerous enemies for life. 'But the fact that the courtiers, backed by injured office-holders, felt it imperative to unseat him', writes Mrs Prestwich, 'is proof of his drive and determination' (p. 330). He alienated by his commercial policy powerful Commons men like Sir Edwin Sandys; and he lost the support of lesser officials in the departments under him by curbing their profits and tightening his control (pp. 436–7). He, too, like Salisbury, was thwarted and thrust from power by the parliamentary opposition and by the treachery of some of the king's ministers. But though Mrs Prestwich would acknowledge that the careers of the two lord treasurers had something in common, any comparison she would make between them would be unfavourable to Salisbury. It is necessary, therefore, to consider in some detail the charges she makes against him.

'Salisbury', she writes, 'swam with the tide, and then frightened, tried both to utilize the monarchy's prerogative powers and to call for conciliation' (p. 467). There are criticisms that can be made of Salisbury but 'frightened' is a strange epithet to apply to a

[1] e.g. S. R. Gardiner, *History of England, 1603–42* (1883), vol. ii, chapter xiii; F. C. Dietz, *English Public Finance, 1558–1641* (2nd edn, 1964), pp. 134–42; J. Hurstfield, *The Queen's Wards* (1958), pp. 317–25, 351–2; R. Ashton, *The Crown and the Money Market, 1603–1640* (Oxford, 1960), p. 186.

statesman who fought subbornly every inch of the way, almost alone, against king, against court, against Parliament—almost against reason—to carry through a daring project of financial reform. Weakness also Mrs Prestwich finds in Salisbury. In the matter of pensions, his were the halcyon days when he 'had been so helpful to those whom he thought had influence with the king' (p. 26). But did any, in the king's lifetime, manage to stem his insane bounty? Salisbury protested against it, in vain, as did Cranfield. Both failed.

But these charges are less important than her basic one: that Salisbury was corrupt. 'Salisbury', she writes, 'had acquiesced in the extravagance of the king, and he had shared in the profiteering and corruption which penetrated the interstices of government to a degree far beyond that of Elizabeth's reign' (p. 47). She refers to the profits accruing to him from the silk farm, from the Great Farm of 1604, possibly from the alum monopoly. On top of that there were substantial profits from wardships and considerable sums as gifts from suitors anxious to benefit from Salisbury's extensive patronage. The evidence for a good deal of this is, of course, well known; and, so far as I am aware, it has never been disputed by historians. In piling up this evidence, it was therefore hardly necessary to enlarge it with a rumour, which she brings up in three separate places in the book, to the effect that Salisbury's proposal to abolish the Court of Wards would have brought him £20,000 (pp. 21, 35, 421n.). A rumour does not become the truth by being quoted three times.

It has, of course, been pointed out by the present writer and others that Salisbury grew rich in the public service; that he was a pluralist in his official posts; that he made considerable profits from those offices.[1] But any interpretation of his life must take into consideration his attempts to restrain the king's extravagance and to carry through the Great Contract, his sacrifice of health and strength, of future income and of the support of the king in a desperate attempt to force through a major administrative and

---

[1] Hurstfield, *The Queen's Wards*, chapters 15 and 16; L. Stone, 'The fruits of office: the case of Robert Cecil, first Earl of Salisbury, 1596–1612', in *Essays in the Economic and Social History of Tudor and Stuart England*, ed. F. J. Fisher (1961).

financial reform. This could not wholly redeem the lust for wealth and power which marked a good part of his career. But it cannot be ignored in any attempt to assess him as a man and a statesman. Nor should Mrs Prestwich underrate the tremendous drive behind Salisbury's scheme to increase revenue through impositions. Sir Julius Caesar, chancellor of the exchequer, who was ready indeed when opportunity came to plunge a knife into Salisbury's back, wrote of his increase of impositions in 1608 that it 'will prove the most gainful to the king and his posterity of any one day's work by any lord treasurer since the time of King Edward III'.[1]

But quite apart from the unsupported rumour that he would gain from the dissolution of his office of Master of Wards, Mrs Prestwich condemns his whole policy on wards throughout his mastership on the grounds that he kept the prices too low. She notes that Salisbury increased the royal revenue from wardships. 'But', she goes on, 'it is a reflection both on his father's administration and on his efforts that the figure reached in 1613 [just after Salisbury's death] was almost identical with that of 1560 ... but meanwhile there had been a threefold [general] price rise' (p. 35). It was not only the general prices which had risen threefold: the protest against wardships had risen threefold (and more) and had become one of the great battle-cries of the House of Commons. The surprising thing is not that wardship prices were no higher than the 1560 level but that wardships still existed at all. For this the fact that the price rise was controlled under Cecil is, in part, the explanation.

There was, of course, a rise in wardship prices under his successors, especially in the years leading up to the Civil War. But perhaps Mrs Prestwich has forgotten what Clarendon, looking back, wrote about this raising of prices, the very policy which, according to her, Salisbury should have adopted. Clarendon is writing about the mastership of Cottington, who held office from 1635 until 1641, and who

[1] Cited in Dietz, *English Public Finance*, vol. ii, p. 120.

had raised the revenue of that court to the King to be much greater than it had ever been before his administration; by which husbandry, all the rich families of England, of noble-men and gentlemen, were exceedingly incensed, and even indevoted to the Crown, looking upon what the law had intended for their protection and preservation to be now applied to their destruction; and therefore resolved to take the first opportunity to ravish that jewel out of the royal diadem, though it was fastened there by the known law upon as unquestionable a right as the subject enjoyed any thing that was most his own.[1]

Is there any connection between the forcing up of wardship prices and the disaffection of the landed classes on the eve of the Civil War? Clarendon, as a practising politician, saw one clearly enough. Salisbury, the incomparably more sophisticated politician than Cottington, seems, like Clarendon, to have seen the point.

Politics is the art of the possible. Salisbury was nothing if he was not a politician of the most subtle and experienced kind. If any man could have seen that there was a limit beyond which you could not press the gentry in these heavy, anachronistic and repulsive death-duties, it was Salisbury. Mrs Prestwich would dismiss his whole policy as deriving from fear, weakness and greed. Political realism may offer a more convincing explanation.

It is this inability to give the devil his due which throws doubt on Mrs Prestwich's interpretation of the last years of Salisbury's career. When she compares Salisbury with Cranfield, she writes: 'But Cranfield fell from power the victim of outraged courtiers, while Salisbury remained in office, ensconced in the luxury of Hatfield House, the monument to his circumspection and gains' (p. 33). I assume that Mrs Prestwich is writing these words under

[1] E. Hyde, Earl of Clarendon, *The History of the Great Rebellion*, ed. W. D. Macray (Oxford, 1888), vol. i, pp. 198–9, cited in H. E. Bell, *An Introduction to the History and Records of the Court of Wards* (Cambridge, 1953), whose chapter on 'The Agitation against the Court' is especially relevant to this problem. See also Prestwich, *Cranfield*, p. 42, where the author shows that Caesar himself was aware of the danger of great increases. It is hard to see therefore why Salisbury was wrong in keeping the increase of price under control.

poetic licence since she is clearly aware that he spent at most a few days (shortly before his death) at Hatfield (p. 47). The only luxury he was ensconced in at Hatfield is his marble tomb in the parish church. Elsewhere she writes ' ... it should be remembered that Salisbury died in office while Cranfield was soon driven into the political wilderness' (p. 340). Mrs Prestwich makes altogether too much of the fact that Salisbury died in office while Cranfield was impeached. Is it seriously suggested that after the collapse of the Great Contract, defeated as it was by the king's friends at court and the king's enemies in the Commons, and with the king himself contemptuous and abusive, Salisbury — unlike Cranfield in defeat — could now look forward to a brilliant career at the treasury? John Chamberlain had no doubt that Salisbury had wrecked his career; and this comment is in fact to be found quoted in Mrs Prestwich's book: 'Howsever he had fared with his health,' wrote Chamberlain, 'it is verily thought he would never have been himself again in power and credit.'[1] So much for the delights of being 'ensconced in the luxury of Hatfield'.

The difficulties which Cranfield had to face, and his manner of dealing with them, are frequently, throughout the book, contrasted with those facing Salisbury; and, indeed, some of Cranfield's troubles are attributed to Salisbury. Custom-farming, on which Mrs Prestwich has a good deal to say in criticism, was renewed by Salisbury in 1604; and on page 345 we learn that 'Cranfield was the prisoner of the system inaugurated by Salisbury as a minister and man, was, apparently, not much better. sex, we learn again that 'Middlesex was the prisoner of the system inaugurated by Salisbury'. This, clearly, Mrs Prestwich considers an important statement since she says it twice and it is relevant, therefore, to ask: what system was it that held Cranfield in its grip?

Cranfield, though in Mrs Prestwich's opinion better than Salisbury as a minister and man, was apparently, not much better. Even his manner of speech offends. He was 'sententious', 'sanctimonious', had a 'propensity to bully'. He was sycophantic, but

[1] John Chamberlain, *Letters*, ed. McClure, vol. i, pp. 350–1; Prestwich, *Cranfield*, p. 47.

underneath 'there was a core of integrity'; but Mrs Prestwich has second thoughts about this: perhaps it was not integrity but 'possibly just officiousness which was ultimately to ruin his court career' (pp. 56–7, 105, 197). Yet, though there is no love lost between author and statesman, Mrs Prestwich sees a great drive behind his policy to make an extravagant king solvent. He embarked on this heroic task by a series of separate but concerted attacks. He would set a limit to court pensions, which, in two decades, had become a major source of financial debility; would ensure that tax-farmers bought their privileges at more favourable terms to the Crown; force up the revenues from the available sources, for example, wardships; and generally tighten control over government expenditure, which included imposing restraints upon the wilder diplomatic adventures of Buckingham and the Prince of Wales. These were tremendous problems whose origins lay far beyond the Stuart period: to solve them would indeed be to carry through a revolution in administration which would, almost certainly, have changed the constitutional history of England. Cranfield failed: the heavy gates of his prison refused to swing open in spite of the great pressures he put upon them. For the prison which held him fast, as it had his predecessors, was not of Salisbury's making but, as in the case of tax-farming, inherent in the faulty administrative system of early modern England, made worse by the corrosive extravagance of an unteachable king. 'Men in great places', wrote Bacon, 'are thrice servants: servants of the sovereign or state; servants of fame; and servants of business. So as they have no freedom, neither in their persons, nor in their actions, nor in their times.'[1]

Why had Cranfield failed, as Salisbury had failed before him? In the first place government was still essentially personal. If the monarch chose to be lavish in private benefactions or public expenditure, no one could stop him. No one could stop Henry VIII making war on the Continent, or James I showering gifts on worthless men. To oppose the monarch — or his *alter ego*, Buckingham — meant destruction. If any single event ended Cranfield's career, it was his attack on the Buckingham clan, or at least on

[1] Francis Bacon, Essay, *Of Great Place.*

their pensions; and, if any one man could finish Cranfield's career, it was this unprincipled, all-powerful courtier. All this is admirably brought out by Mrs Prestwich in some of the best sections in her book.

But Buckingham or no Buckingham, there were entrenched elements in the existing system which would require more than a Cranfield or Salisbury to dislodge them. Tax-farming may be taken as an example. Everyone will admit that to sell the right to collect taxes to a corporation of private men means that they will in fact get more money than they pay to the Crown. But where money is short, and the civil service weak or corrupt, this is the one device which at least guarantees a basic revenue to the state. Moreover, as Professor Ashton has shown, it is an important way of negotiating loans.[1] It is true that a treasurer may be too generous in his terms to the farmers, and may in the process gain something for himself. But the need to use such devices arises in the first place from the fundamental weaknesses of the whole financial system.

Deeper still lay the whole complex of weaknesses throughout the government machine: duplication, amateurishness, defalcation, the lack of able and committed administrators of the middle rank to hold departments together and loyally to carry out the policy set forth by the lord treasurer. So, in spite of his drive and ruthlessness, Cranfield left his office in no better case than he found it. Mrs Prestwich herself provides the evidence: debts to the Crown could not be recovered; income had drained away through dishonest officials, revenue from land had fallen, pensions increased. '... This hectoring minister, who had thought he could accomplish so much, came to be only a buzzing fly on a chariot wheel' (p. 370). The judgment is a harsh one; but it has a measure of truth.

There remains the problem of political morality which is such an important aspect of Mrs Prestwich's book. Cranfield grew rich, or, rather, richer. She estimates that, during his period as lord treasurer, he had nearly trebled his landed wealth. On the eve of his fall his total income was at least £25,000 per annum

---

[1] Ashton, *The Crown and the Money Market, 1603–1640*.

(pp. 419–20). 'He never neglected his own fortune,' she writes, 'even when performing his great services to the crown' (p. 241). She instances his sugar farm, gained on the cheap; his favourable treatment of himself in the matter of debts to the Crown; his profits from wardships; his sale of exchequer offices; his gifts from tax-farmers and others. This, she argues, is proof of his corruption. And this assumption is made throughout the book, whether the author is discussing Salisbury, Cranfield or any other member of the successive ministries. For there are no heroes in her book, only villains. And some are more villainous than others. There is no difficulty in admitting that the standards of public life declined during this period. Where government is personal, and where the monarch is peculiarly incapable of judging men by their ability but uses the meretricious standards of courtly splendour, there the public interest will be sacrificed. Second-rate men will come to power, able men will be hamstrung in trying to discharge their duties, or will be driven from office. If the criterion is public service, then men like Robert Carr, Earl of Somerset, and, pre-eminently, Buckingham were corrupt. They gave nothing to the public service except wrong judgments and they distorted public policy for private gain. Do Salisbury and Cranfield fit into the same mould?

Mrs Prestwich is too good a scholar to deny that official salaries in the public service were negligible since the public revenue system held these salaries at such absurd levels. Hence the assumption had long since taken hold that perquisites, gifts, favourable leases, cheap wardships were the supplementary income essential to a public servant. And the greater the servant the greater the sources at his disposal; and the greater the sources, the higher his income. By the twentieth-century standards of a Western European state, these are corrupt practices; but the salaries of ministers and civil servants are today realistic and secure. In the seventeenth century they were neither. Of course, these sums of money came directly or indirectly from the royal revenue but, if that is the only way that a man can make sufficient to bring his salary up to pay for his appropriate standard of living, then though the process may be complex and clumsy, it is not inherently corrupt. Would anyone be lord treasurer at the official salary? Nor could one logically argue that if the perquisite is small there is no corruption, if large there is. For corruption is not a question of amount, it is a question of policy.

If, on the basis of Mrs Prestwich's own evidence, Cranfield blasted his career through trying to make the public revenue system work in the Crown's interest and if, as I have suggested, the same is true of Salisbury, then a new factor has entered into the discussion. It is reasonable to argue that they could have made their tenure of the treasurership secure if they had not tried to improve the revenue system. They chose the opposite; and if public service is the criterion for measuring the career of a statesman, then the political morality of these two able men, with all their faults, cannot be dismissed as corrupt. For each in turn sacrificed his career in an unsuccessful—perhaps foolhardy— attempt to force major fiscal reforms on a reluctant king and a hostile court. It is this which puts their large profits from office into perspective. Mrs Prestwich finds it ironical that Cranfield 'saw no reason why the public interest and private profit could not co exist' (p. 106). But Cranfield was not alone in this among his contemporaries. These were the contemporary beliefs. If Mrs Prestwich's forceful judgments are right, then Salisbury and Cranfield were corrupt ministers. But, by the same token, all of their predecessors and successors were. Between the death of Thomas Cromwell and the rise of Oliver Cromwell (or Walpole, or Pitt the Younger), there were no good ministers in English history. This might make a nice quotation to insert in a scholarship examination, but it is less serviceable for any understanding of a complex transitional period in English history.

In the end the historian must choose whether he believes that Salisbury fought like one possessed, using every ounce of his failing strength to force through the Great Contract because he hoped thereby to get a fat pension or whether, believing that it would be his great act of public service, perhaps his last, he wantonly made enemies in court and Parliament alike. The balance of the evidence strongly supports the latter view. The same *mutatis mutandis* could be said of Cranfield. In considering his policy Mrs Prestwich writes:

> He had bent to the winds of the court and he had looked to his own profits, but in the end he refused to support a policy leading to the bankruptcy of the Crown. The principles of good credit on which he had insisted as a young merchant had bitten deep and he wrecked his political career on them. And yet the heroism that comes from realizing that principles exact their price was lacking, for Middlesex was too blinded by an inflated sense of his own abilities to see that his fall was a consequence of his stand (p. 440).

The general argument of the greater part of this passage is sound and shrewd. The last sentence does justice neither to statesman nor author.

Mrs Prestwich's book will inevitably invite comparison with R. H. Tawney's *Business and Politics under James I*, which is a study of Cranfield's commercial and political career, and was published in 1958. It is not relevant in our context to embark on a detailed contrast of the two works so utterly different in their material, their basic assumptions, their judgment of the man. Undoubtedly, Mrs Prestwich's book is the fuller study, and its detailed grasp on the Cranfield papers and other evidence demonstrates her great skill applied with great devotion. Her lengthy study of Cranfield's life after his fall is something which Tawney omitted as outside the career which was his central concern. The works remain complementary but Mrs Prestwich's gets closer in its searching into the dark corners of business and administration. It would not be too bold to suggest that no one since Cranfield's day has understood them as well as she. But there is one fundamental difference of approach. Mrs Prestwich's scholarship is of a high order but her judgment of men is an entirely separate process. Here too she has the most exacting standards, and they demand the unswerving obedience to them by men of a different age where different standards prevailed. The reader cannot escape the impression that the statesmen she discusses all fell short of the mark because that mark lay outside their period and belongs to our times. It is not surprising, therefore, that her book has no heroes but many villains. In this matter, Tawney, for all his commitment to certain principles of social conduct, and for all his dislike of what are sometimes called business ethics, yet wrote of Cranfield with compassion and as a man of his time caught up in the vices of his own age, but also trying to release the institution he governed from their full impact. Tawney's approach is summarized in his preface: 'Merchants and finance ministers function within a framework of international connections, domestic institutions and conditions, and—not least important—political assumptions, aspirations and beliefs, without a grasp of which their activities and vicissitudes are hardly to be understood.'[1] It is the awareness that Cranfield must be *first* measured against the background of his age and state that makes one question (while admiring Mrs Prestwich's scholarship) her final judgment on the man.

Yet, having said this, it remains beyond doubt that this recent study of Cranfield is a fascinating portrait of a statesman, painted with the bold, confident strokes of one who has mastered some of the most complex techniques of administration. Out of this material, sometimes arid and intractable, Mrs Prestwich has made a well-written, stimulating book; and she is to be congratulated on bringing to conclusion a major contribution to early seventeenth-century history.

[1] R. H. Tawney, *Business and Politics under James I, Lionel Cranfield as Merchant and Minister* (Cambridge, 1958), p. vii.

Part IV · English Society

8

Tradition and change in the English Renaissance

In its culture, as in its geography, England in the early sixteenth century lay on the edge of Renaissance Europe. Separated from the continental land mass by a narrow channel of water, at one point not much more than twenty miles across, it somehow escaped, as it did for centuries, the impact of major European developments, or received them late and changed by their sea journey. The structure of English society, too, although it formally resembled the kingdoms of north-western Europe with monarchy, aristocracy, clergy and commonalty, displayed a marked difference from them in the gap between the form and the reality of its class distinctions. To more than one foreign observer, the subtle inflections of its social order, and its traditions and attitudes, seemed insular and self-contradictory.

A Venetian diplomat, *en poste* in London at the beginning of the new century, saw England as a prosperous country with fertile soil and beautiful landscape, and the English as a martial people, yet one inclined to set great store by their physical comforts, especially food and drink. He said that they were a proud people too, who thought well of themselves and rather less of foreigners. They were quick and intelligent rather than educated, regular in church attendance but in many cases sympathetic to novel opinions. (The diplomat here confirms what historians have only recently rediscovered, namely that the Lollards had made greater inroads among Church and people than was at one time believed.) This independence of mood, he believed, extended even to their relations with their monarch, for they were not as devoted to their Crown as were the Scots.

NOTE: First published in *The Age of the Renaissance*, ed. Denys Hay (1967).

The English by nature, apparently, 'hate their present sovereign and extol their dead ones'. The Wars of the Roses had ended only half a generation before but the threat of dynastic war was by no means banished. Henry VII he respected, describing him indeed as the most secure monarch since the days of William the Conqueror. It is interesting and significant to notice, in passing, that while the ambassador refers to the king as 'His Majesty', contemporary Englishmen usually did not: he was known as 'His Highness'; but the style was coming in. Majesty belonged much more to the next reign and a new generation. It belonged also to an outlook more in keeping with the political and cultural trends in Renaissance Europe.

With such a degree of physical and intellectual isolation, it is hardly surprising that the effects of the Renaissance came slowly and late to England. In the middle of the fifteenth century, large-scale intellectual intercourse in print did not yet exist. Communication, whether by land or sea, with the great Italian cities was still primitive; and to these inhibitions were added the hair-raising travellers' tales of the hazards—physical and moral— which lost nothing of their terror to successive generations. Long afterwards, late in Queen Elizabeth's reign, lord treasurer Burghley was to warn his son against crossing the Alps where a man would learn nothing but atheism, blasphemy and vice. In Thomas Nashe's *The Unfortunate Traveller*, published in 1594, we have these monitory tales in their most extravagant form. It is not a one-sided story, however. Our Venetian diplomat unwittingly reciprocates the compliment. The English law-courts, he observes, are extremely harsh; but severe measures are apparently ineffectual. '... There is no country in the world', he writes, 'where there are so many thieves and robbers as in England, in so much that few venture to go alone in the country, excepting in the middle of the day, and fewer still in the towns at night, and least of all in London.'

I

England in the fifteenth century was, and long remained, a place of small towns. London was the only significant exception and even here the population did not exceed 50,000. There were also ancient cathedral towns like Winchester, Canterbury and York; industrial centres like Norwich; ports like Southampton and Bristol. But in most places no traditions of urban culture had ever existed or could even be remotely conceived. On the other hand, aristocratic patronage was equally rare. The heads of the great baronial families looked to war and to internal territorial expansion as their most attractive and rewarding enterprises, not the unlikely prospects of some enduring fame as patrons of art or literature. The English baronage was rural in wealth, influence and outlook. To turn from them, for example, to the cultured patriciate of Florence, is to move from the darkness into the light. Humphrey, Duke of Gloucester, was the exception not the rule. The poets were not members of a cultured group gathered round some provincial court but monks, baronial officials, civil servants. The town chroniclers could on occasion provide fascinating narratives but, for the most part, they were content to record the repetitive trivia of municipal officialdom.

Such other prospects as may have existed of widening the range of patronage were drowned in the intermittent wars with France, lasting until the middle of the fifteenth century, followed by an internal struggle for power between those magnates, or their heirs, who had at last been driven from French territory. This internal poverty, war and instability were, of course, reflected in the court itself where no fifteenth-century monarch (other than Edward IV) had more than a decade of settled power. Even Henry VII, the first of a new and powerful dynasty, had no really secure hold on his throne until the opening years of the sixteenth century. Hence, until the time of the Tudors, any significant court patronage was out of the question.

When we turn from the monarch and the baronage to the other source of power, the Church, the story is comparable. For a large part of the Middle Ages, government had been administered by churchmen and paid for by the Church. The servants of the Crown held bishoprics, deaneries and other ecclesiastical offices, usually *in absentia*. Their stipends as churchmen enabled them to take on the secular duties of administration. Where they had intellectual interests as well, these tended to be part of the thought and culture of the Church and the schoolmen.

All this is not to say that English culture passed through bleak decades of sterility, unease and social disorder. English ecclesiastical architecture, for example, magnificently displayed its vigour and initiative. Merchants, gentry, nobility sometimes raised impressive buildings full of vitality, dignity and enduring beauty. Local gilds produced miracle and morality plays, civil pageants and other lively expressions of a traditional art form. But, over a large field, inspiration came from domestic sources and the impact of Italian culture was at first minimal. What was true of culture in general was equally true of education, whether at school or university. So, when humanism began to make its impact on English life it was both cause and effect. It caused a fundamental redirection in education and produced a profound change in all branches of culture. But, on the other hand, its acceptance and dissemination were the effect of political and social changes and needs, calling for an outlook and training which medieval institutions and doctrines were quite unable to provide.

But although the Church had always known of the advantages to be gained from recruiting educated men to its service, the English nobility and the upper classes in general were much slower to grasp the point. The Venetian ambassador, whom we have already cited, expressed astonishment at the speed with which Englishmen—however wealthy they were—sent their children, aged nine or less, to be boarded out in other men's houses, while they took in strangers' children themselves. When he asked them why they did this, he was told it was so that the children 'might learn better manners'. In his report home, however, the diplomat rejected this explanation and suggested that the real reason was their wish 'to enjoy all their comforts themselves'. They believed themselves to be 'better served by strangers than they would be by their own children'. In any case, they could then 'indulge in the most delicate fare themselves and give their household the coarsest bread and beer, and cold meat baked on Sunday for the week'. If they had their children at home with them 'they would be obliged to give them the same food they made use of for themselves'. Englishmen had, too, great advantages for study with two such well-founded and well-endowed universities at Oxford and Cambridge. Yet, although they were quick at learning, few of them, except the clergy, were 'addicted to the study of letters'. The invasion of the universities by the sons of gentlemen had yet to come. Before the end of the sixteenth century it would be familiar enough.

Yet, in spite of the built-in resistance to alien influences, England in the late fifteenth and early sixteenth centuries was by no means immune to the prevailing winds. Certainly, from the middle of the fifteenth century, churchmen like William Grey (the future Bishop of Ely) and baronial leaders like John Tiptoft, Earl of Worcester, had come back from Italy with new attitudes to culture and perhaps also to society itself. But the central event was the return to England in 1491 of William Grocyn after his period of study in Florence and Rome. It was now that Oxford had its first experience of Greek scholarship, where Grocyn's disciples included Erasmus and More, whose fame would shortly outdistance his own. His fellow Englishman in Italy, Thomas Linacre, took the whole Italian world within his sphere of interest. Bologna, Florence, Rome, Venice, Padua, Vicenza gave Linacre access to classical sources in the arts and sciences, as well as enabling him to study medicine under the leading teachers of his day. On his return he too taught at Oxford, and then in the royal household, becoming in the new reign physician to Henry VIII. Yet Linacre, the founder of the Royal College of Physicians, was, like Grocyn, a priest. For them there was no conflict between ecclesiastical doctrine and classical learning. Erasmus says of his patron, Grocyn, that he was 'exceedingly observant of ecclesiastical rules, almost to the point of superstition, and to the highest degree learned in scholastic theology; while he was, at the same time, a man gifted by nature with the most acute judgment and exactly versed in every description of educational knowledge.' If their influence began in Oxford, it did not end there. It was

Linacre's Latin Grammar which John Colet adopted for his new school, St Paul's, founded in 1510.

No less influential was the work of Richard Fox, administrator, diplomat, scholar, architect, bishop, founder in 1517 of Corpus Christi College, Oxford, and himself a great sponsor of humanist studies in the university. But it is clearly a humanism planted firmly in a Christian context. Nowhere is his mood better revealed – and with it the climate of his whole generation – than in the founding statutes of Corpus Christi, of which the preamble runs:

> In honour of the most precious body of Our Lord Jesus Christ, and of His most Holy Mother, and of all the other saints, patrons of the cathedral churches of Winchester, Durham, Bath and Wells, as also of Exeter, We Richard Fox, by Divine Vocation, Bishop of Winchester, founder, builder, and endower of the College of Corpus Christi in the University of Oxford, first invoking the most dread name of the most holy and undivided Trinity, have framed our Statutes for the same college, and have written them in this original book, for their constant and everlasting remembrance and establishment: and We, the aforesaid, have set our seal thereto in manner following:

It is followed by a clear exposition of the role of learning in society:

> We have no abiding city here, as saith the Apostle, but we seek one to come in heaven at which we hope to arrive with the greater ease and dispatch if while we travel in this life, wretched and death-doomed as it is, we rear a ladder whereby we may gain a readier ascent. We give the name of virtue to the right side of the ladder, and that of knowledge, to the left, and between these two sides lie steps; for either side hath rungs of its own by which we may either soar on high, or sink into the lowest depths. We, therefore, Richard Fox, by Divine Providence, Bishop of Winchester, being

both desirous ourselves of ascending by this ladder to heaven and of entering therein and being anxious to aid and assist others in a similar ascent and entrance, have founded, reared, and constructed in the University of Oxford, out of the means which God of his bounty hath bestowed on us, a certain bee garden which we have named the College of Corpus Christi, wherein scholars, like ingenious bees are by day and night to make wax to the honour of God, and honey, dropping sweetness, to the profit of themselves and of all Christians.

And then, having made provision as to the curriculum of the College, resting on the three pillars of Latin, Greek and Divinity, and for the qualifications of the staff, Fox tried to ensure that his foundation should have access to foreign scholars rather than succumb to a perpetuated insularity in which only Oxford graduates could be appointed to Oxford posts:

And if no person in our College shall be found competent in the judgment of the President and the electors for the office of any lecturer vacating, or if any person in our College be found competent, and yet a stranger shall be found much more learned ... then we will that he shall be preferred to that office and as public lecturer before all the fellows and scholars of our College ... provided only he is born in England, Greece, or Italy, beyond the Po.

Meanwhile, Italian influence of a lesser kind began to make itself felt in England. The papal collectors Giovanni Gigli and Polydore Vergil found patronage at the English court. Vergil's career was, for a time, blasted by the enmity of Cardinal Wolsey; but he lived long enough to see the publication, after the fall of the cardinal, of his *Historia Anglica*, begun many years ago at the end of Henry VII's reign. Another of their countrymen, Pietro Carmeliano, was the first holder of the office of Latin Secretary, established by Henry VII; while some of his lesser contemporaries sought access to the royal bounty with undistinguished Latin compositions in verse and prose.

If, in the intellectual field, English priest, physician, bishop, as well as Italian poet and historian, made characteristic contributions to the Renaissance in this country, it was a cardinal who gave it its greatest impetus in the world of affairs. Wolsey's recruitment of lay scholars and churchmen alike to his service — of the calibre of Richard Pace, Richard Morrison, John Clement, Richard Sampson and Cuthbert Tunstall — ensured for men of the New Learning advancement and reward in the state. At the same time, Cardinal's College, Oxford — not long after his death to become King's College and, in due course, Christ Church — was an impressive monument to the state's hopes of the next generation. Here, too, liberal humanism flourished and, in spite of conservative resistance, Oxford found room also for the beginnings of religious dissent, a process already at work at Cambridge. Thus in this brief interval of moderation, it was possible for some diversity of opinion to be sheltered by the Cardinal of England himself, against the accustomed rigours of the Church. And if the New Learning flourished in Oxford under the high patronage of Wolsey, far away in Padua, in the household of Reginald Pole, kinsman and future critic of Henry VIII, there gathered alumni of Cardinal's College like Richard Morrison and Thomas Starkey to continue their apprenticeship in scholarship or statecraft, or both.

II

Yet, in summoning scholars to positions of influence, the state took serious risks. The Tudor intellectuals, for all their high distinction in a distinguished age, were hardly a success in the upper ranges of government. At the end of the sixteenth century, and in the early seventeenth, we have examples of the all too familiar experience of what happens when an intellectual takes up politics as a career. Sir Walter Ralegh was a failure; so was Sir Francis Bacon. Edmund Spenser got nowhere. All three wrote bitterly about the high cost of the climb to political power: the price to be paid, the sham rewards, the false standards, the disillusionment. In the earlier years of the sixteenth century, we have the most famous case history of all in the rise and fall of Sir Thomas More.

Like his friend Erasmus, More represented the finest expression of the early Renaissance. They brought to bear the full weight of classical scholarship and modern critical techniques upon the literature and tradition of the Church. They were remorseless in their onslaught upon inherited and hallowed superstitions, incisive in style, formidable in the range of their thought and culture. More's *Utopia*, probably completed in 1516, is a brilliant critique of the practice and the fundamental thinking of his own society. But it is much more than a *livre de circonstance*. It reaches beyond Tudor concepts and even Christian doctrine itself to ask what are the basic principles upon which a good society is organized. Here in *Utopia* was the vision of a nation at peace with itself and with its neighbours. Here was a land where men worked freely for all men's welfare and all men had easy access to the wealth they had created. There was no slavery, no oppression of the weak by the strong, no ruthless power based on an intolerable concentration of wealth in few hands. Here was the Christian life, lost to Europe, but rediscovered by the Utopians who were themselves not Christian. *Utopia* was early humanism at its best. But the greatness of its concepts carried the gravest threat to its fulfilment, and indeed to the life, and, more important, the whole way of life of its author. For early Tudor humanism was a compromise: an unworkable one in face of the new political situation which was developing. For the future did not lie with Erasmus and More but with Richard Rich (who betrayed More) and with Thomas Cromwell.

In his recent study of *Utopia*, Professor J. H. Hexter has shown how the driving force behind More had been the belief, in which he followed Erasmus, that true Christian ideals and practice had been perverted by the Aristotelianism of the schoolmen and the social rigidity and inequality of Roman law. The original Christian ideals of poverty, love and spiritual well-being had given place, at least in practice, to private property, material well-being, social hierarchy, usury and all the other abuses which had corrupted the purity of Christian doctrine. So the spirit had been drained out of Christianity and all that remained were the formalities, ritual, a worship of saints amounting almost to idolatry, and all the trappings and rigidities of a narrow creed. Could one bring back to the Church, and at the same time to government, the lost principles of the Christian faith?

The short answer to this question was that one could not. But before we consider the series of events which destroyed all prospects of a society governed by the beliefs of Christian humanism, it is worth examining the inherent strains which were tearing asunder More's compromise. Men like More thought that they had found a way of assimilating the secular approaches of the Renaissance with the teachings of the New Testament. He thought that the humanistic beliefs in the supremacy of intellect and the high classical ideals of the perfectability of man in a man-centred world could somehow be merged with Christian humility, biblical doctrine and a world centred on God, in whom sinful man found his only perfection in the true life of the spirit. Perhaps More's own life represented such a compromise which succeeded. Perhaps even in his own life the compromise was throughout under heavy strain, which might offer some explanation as to why so many of us find it difficult to see him whole, to account for his cynicism mingled with saintliness, his compassion with his persecution of heretics, and his pagan republic which he invented and which was superior to the Christian world he lived in. If the compromise was difficult to fulfil within More's own personality, in early Tudor England it assumed the character of a contradiction in terms and an anachronism. Edmund Spenser tried, half a century later, to rediscover this compromise in his Christian Platonism; but his very greatness as a poet sets him in a world of his own.

It may be that Henry VIII himself was something of a humanist. Certainly he loved the trappings of a Renaissance court, with its elaborate ceremonial, its high patronage of scholarship: a learned prince presiding over a cultured court. He may too have felt genuinely sympathetic to Erasmian aims to rediscover the foundation of Christian doctrine in terms of the original texts. Perhaps, indeed, this amateur theologian saw in himself some remote resemblance to the Platonic philosopher-king. But such humanism as he adopted stopped far short of that Christian poverty and humility which More continued to believe might be attainable amidst the worldly considerations of Tudor society. Decades before, Machiavelli had pointed out how inappropriate Christian ideals were in the practice of politics. 'The religion of the ancients', he wrote, 'beatified none but men crowned with worldly glory, such as leaders of armies and founders of republics, whereas our religion has glorified meek and contemplative men rather than men of action.' The times were changing. If *Utopia* was indeed nowhere, *The Prince* stood with both feet firmly on English soil.

The generation which saw *The Prince* come to power in England and His Highness transformed into His Majesty saw the end of More's world. But, if England was changing intellectually, it was changing physically as well. We are fortunate, therefore, in this period of change, to have the work of one of the greatest of English antiquaries, John Leland, who put on paper in the 1530s his impressive, detailed, scholarly account of the rich diversity of the land, as he saw it with his own eyes. If the discovery of the world is a characteristic of the Renaissance outlook, then Leland set about his discovery of England in the true Renaissance spirit. He was, he told the king,

> Totally inflamed with a love to see thoroughly all those parts of this your opulent and ample realm that ... I have so travelled in your dominions, both by the sea-coasts and the middle parts, sparing neither labour nor costs, by the space of these six years past, that there is almost neither cape nor bay, haven, creek or pier, river or confluence of rivers, breaches, washes, lakes, meres, fenny waters, mountains, valleys, moors, heaths, forests, woods, cities, boroughs, castles, principal manor places, monasteries and colleges, but I have seen them; and noted in so doing a whole world of things very memorable.

It is sad after all this to record that Leland died bankrupt, broken-hearted and insane, his work unfinished. But he left voluminous notes of his itineraries; and we can therefore follow him some of the way. We know that the way was difficult, the roads bad, the population sparse. He found many of the old chartered boroughs in decline but he noted also that some insignificant towns, like Liverpool, were showing signs of growth. He found many of the medieval castles decaying shells except for those like Warwick which had undergone a process of internal reconstruction to meet the needs of comfort rather than civil war. Before he was much older he would know that the monasteries and abbeys had been submitted to faster destructive processes, save those converted into Protestant churches or into the country seats of the new nobility or the gentry, like Woburn in Bedfordshire which went to the rising family of the Russells, future Earls of Bedford.

But Leland's England was not a static society. There was plenty of evidence of movement and change. There was movement along the coast bringing coal from Newcastle and carrying wool textiles from the outports overseas; movement down the Thames estuary to France, Flanders and beyond; movement down the navigable rivers of food, timber, industrial products; movement across country as cattle was brought on the hoof, to be fattened in the home counties for the London food market. And there is plenty of evidence too of the drift to London, already reaching impressive dimensions, that ceaseless process which has lasted on into the present century.

Yet, when all is said, England remained a lightly populated country, and Wales and Scotland even more so. By the middle of the sixteenth century the population of London was approaching 100,000 but that of the rest of the country stood at no higher than about three million. (The population of France was perhaps four times as high.) It was still a country occupied by scattered communities, with some concentrations of people in the cities and ports, but even these were intimately linked with the patterns and rhythms of the countryside. It was a country with a backward economy, a primitive transport system, wasteful agricultural practice and rudimentary industries.

The major force which destroyed the established pattern of English society and culture, as it does in most communities, was the growth of population. How and why this came about is only imperfectly known and the same is true of its extent. But it is clear from the evidence already available that the fall in population which had been going on throughout a good part of the fourteenth and fifteenth centuries was somehow arrested in the course of the fifteenth and then it began to rise; that this rise was followed by a sharper rise for roughly a century from the 1530s and that the process thereafter slackened greatly. We know too that the effects of this rise were exactly those we encounter today in any under-developed economy which experiences the same pressures of population growth. There was a manifest inability of technically backward industries and agriculture to absorb the increased supply of labour available, so there was unemployment, poverty and the continuous threat of social disorder. No less important, though industry could with an effort meet a good deal of the increased demand for its products, agriculture could not: the result was an inflation of food prices which extended throughout the whole economy and was made worse by the heavy debasement of the currency late in Henry VIII's reign. Even though a clumsy attempt was made to arrest inflation in 1551, and a more successful one a decade later, the process could not be fully arrested and its effects lasted on throughout the century and beyond.

Inflation is always a great social solvent. It always leads to a redistribution of power and influence. Hardship it undoubtedly brings: to the wage-earner, to the agricultural day-labourer and, at the other end of the social scale, to the landlord-rentier and the monarchy itself, if they draw a large part of their income from rents where these are held fast by legal and tenurial restraints. But inflation brings benefits too. In moderation it stimulates production and trade, though its bounty is unevenly given. It favours the producer and the merchant; it favours the landlord if he finds some means of breaking through the existing restraints on rents; it favours the lawyers whose professional services are greatly demanded in such times of boom.

Prosperity extends beyond the material world and a new pattern of culture emerges. Mid–Tudor England displayed all the features of a shift in the economic, social and cultural balance of the time. Painting, architecture, literature, the drama were called into the service of the newly prosperous classes, at a time when these classes were in any case adopting the postures of the social leaders of the past. If the College of Heralds was busy manufacturing pedigrees for new aristocrats and new gentry, time and judicious marriages would inject a large measure of truth into the romances of the antiquary. By the end of the century the sources of patronage were much wider than ever before, ranging from the Elizabethan court through the great landed aristocracy on to the greater bourgeoisie of the capital and to the volatile mob who crowded into the Globe theatre to see the latest play by Shakespeare.

III

But before these processes were fully at work there occurred a major upheaval which left its own impress upon the rapidly changing social and cultural scene. The Reformation, which took more than a generation to establish itself, roughly spanning the middle decades of the sixteenth century, exercised an ambiguous influence on the Renaissance in England. It severed old connections with the Continent but established new ones; it released speculative, rational thinking and at the same time tried to suppress it; it greatly reduced ecclesiastical patronage yet gave the Church for a time a more powerful hold on the intellectual movements of the age.

The Venetian ambassador had, at the beginning of the century, seen England as virtually independent of the Holy See. Norman historians, he said, recorded that William the Conqueror did homage to the pope but 'the English histories make no mention of this; and it is a forgotten thing'. Equally forgotten was the tribute arising from King John's submission to the pope. All that was now paid, he said, was Peter's Pence. He cannot have discussed ecclesiastical grievances with many Englishmen. But with these grievances we are not here concerned for they did not cause the breach with Rome. The breach itself derived from a crisis in the monarchy, a crisis shortly to be reflected in another form in the monarchy of France. For if, as Michelet believed, the kings of Renaissance Europe emerged as the new Messiahs they were none the less as vulnerable as the humblest of mortals. France in the second half of the century was convulsed in an exhausting dynastic war as the Valois kingship sank into oblivion for want of an heir. The Tudor dynasty, much more recently established, faced the same threat when, after nearly thirty years of marriage, Henry had no one to succeed him but his daughter Mary. To understand what followed, and indeed much that happened for decades to come, one must be aware that the Wars of the Roses had ended within living memory and that, later on, Elizabethans had the vicarious experience of living through them again as they watched the collapse of government in war-divided France. To reinforce their folk-memory they had the history plays of Shakespeare with the lamentation put into the mouth of Henry VI:

> O piteous spectacle! O bloody times!
> Whilst lions war and battle for their dens ...

It was to guard against these things that Henry VIII broke his allegiance to Rome when he found that there was no other means of ending one marriage and starting another. Here was no planned campaign of advance to a new ecclesiastical order. Rather, an opportunist king felt his way towards this simple objective of a new legitimate marriage, hoping that each threat, each blackmail, each cautious advance would be the last that was needed. But having failed to gain his end with a papal blessing, he found that he gained it more easily against a papal excommunication. In the process the monarchy itself was transformed.

For our immediate purpose we are concerned only with two of the great Reformation statutes, the Act in Restraint of Appeals of 1533 and the Act of Supremacy of 1534. They are worth citing because they seem almost a landmark in the history of English literature as they certainly are in the history of the government, religion and society of England. By now Thomas Cromwell was the closest adviser of Henry VIII, and gathered round Cromwell was that group of writers and publicists who had absorbed many of the new secular ideas abroad in Europe. Moreover, they were writing when the English language was approaching its best period of sensitive, lucid vigour which was soon to make it a wonderful instrument for politician and poet alike. For power of language, rich cadence, and inexorable advance to a grand climax, few contemporary prose passages could have equalled these opening words from the statute of 1533:

> Where by divers sundry old authentic histories and chronicles it is manifestly declared and expressed that this realm of England is an empire, and so hath been accepted in the world, governed by one supreme head and king, having the dignity and royal estate of the imperial crown of the same, unto whom a body politic, compact of all sorts and degrees of people divided in terms and by names of spirituality and temporalty, be bounden and owe to bear next to God a natural and humble obedience ...

And so it goes on, sentence upon sentence, trumpeting to the world that England has returned to her destiny as a great and independent nation, under one supreme monarch answerable to none but God. We notice, too, the appeal to history (false history as it happens), the secular history of Renaissance scholarship, breaking away from the monkish chronicles which record no such triumph for the worldly order, and a good deal which tells a different tale.

The Act of Supremacy of 1534 does not quite reach the heights of the previous measure. It more or less rounds off a revolution which has already been accomplished. But it yields nothing in the bold, confident grandiloquence of its style and content:

Albeit the King's Majesty justly and rightfully is and oweth
to be the supreme head of the Church of England, and so is
recognized by the clergy of this realm in their Convocations;
yet nevertheless for corroboration and confirmation thereof,
and for increase of virtue in Christ's religion within this
realm of England, and to repress and extirp all errors,
heresies and other enormities and abuses heretofore used in
the same, be it enacted by authority of this present Parliament that the King our sovereign lord, his heirs and
successors kings of this realm, shall be taken, accepted and
reputed the only supreme head in earth of the Church of
England called *Anglicana Ecclesia*, and shall have and enjoy
annexed and united to the imperial crown of this realm as
the title and style thereof, as all honours, dignities, preemin-
ences, jurisdictions, privileges, authorities, immunities, profits
and commodities, to the said dignity of supreme head of the
same Church belonging and appertaining.

However many times one reads these passages one cannot
wholly lose the excitement of reading the work of some master
of English prose or escape that sense of involvement in a
revolution in the making. For in spite of all the evidence of the
long roots of the Reformation stretching well back into the Middle
Ages, there is nothing like this in the past which depicts the
emergence of kingship in its full supremacy and with all its
panoply of power over men's lives and thoughts. If ever England
had a Renaissance kingship, it was surely now.

It was now, too, that Italian political literature gained a special
relevance to the English scene when, for example, Thomas
Cromwell set in motion the translation of *Defensor pacis*, a
fourteenth-century treatise in elevation of the secular power,
written by Marsiglio of Padua. Castiglione's *Courtier* and
Machiavelli's *Prince* had to wait some decades for an English
translation; but their work was sufficiently familiar already to
educated Englishmen. At the same time the classical and
biblical texts were being ransacked for evidence of the just and
historic claims of a supreme kingship.

Secular voices of sixteenth-century England were just as loud in their acclaim of monarchy. The Speaker of the House of Commons, Richard Rich, a follower of Thomas Cromwell, addressing Parliament in 1536, had no hesitation in placing Henry VIII, in virtue of his wisdom, justice, strength, courage and beauty in the sacred gallery of Old Testament heroes.[1]

This new doctrine by no means went unchallenged. Thomas More was merely the greatest of those who set a boundary to the advancing claims of royal supremacy. Cardinal Reginald Pole, a kinsman of Henry VIII, found England impossible to live in under the new order, and denounced from Rome this intolerable usurpation of spiritual authority by the Crown. But whether these aggrandized powers were welcome or otherwise to the minds of the king's subjects, their very existence and the enlarged responsibilities of the state called for an enlarged government service, well-adapted for these purposes. This meant both an extension of the range of education and a change in its character. And all this lay at the heart of the English Renaissance.

Long before, when in 1517 Bishop Fox was making his plans to found Corpus Christi College, Oxford, he had thought of a monastic foundation designed to raise standards among regular monks. But Bishop Oldham, his co-founder, emphatically thought otherwise: 'What, my lord, shall we build houses and provide livelihoods for a company of buzzing monks, whose end and fall we ourselves may live to see; no, no, it is more meet a great deal that we should have a care to provide for the increase of learning and for such as by their learning shall do good in church and commonwealth.'

From now onwards it is possible to see, over and over again, this inner conflict of policy throughout the whole field of education. Put in its crudest form, the question could be posed as: should education primarily be directed towards the service of God or of the state? Of course many believed that it could in one sense do both, that is, breed worthy men serving the Christian commonwealth presided over by a God-fearing king. But once

[1] See above, p. 45.

the question of curriculum, instructors, organization, finance had to be faced in detail, then the major problems of definition and aims pressed too hard on the educationists to allow the old order to survive intact. We no longer believe, as was once thought, that on the eve of the English Reformation there flourished under monastic inspiration and control a splendid, wide-ranging educational network which was shattered by the Reformation and the dissolution of the monasteries. Many of the chantry schools, it is true, were outstandingly good but, as Mrs Joan Simon has recently shown, long before the Reformation there had been a growing demand for the new kind of school under secular patronage and to meet secular needs. The belief that Henry VIII and Edward VI, in their destruction of monastic schools and chantries, dealt a severe blow to education can only survive now as a pious legend. Instead, she writes: 'Reformation legislation, following on a long and gradual undermining of ecclesiastical jurisdiction, cleared the ground for much more widespread and rapid developments ... not least so far as the universities were concerned.' This change in emphasis was reflected in the large-scale diversion in the trend of charitable bequests from ecclesiastical to educational purposes, which, as Professor W. K. Jordan has established, is so impressive a feature of the second half of the sixteenth century. All this fits logically into the pattern of political thinking of Thomas Cromwell and his successors.

IV

By the middle of the sixteenth century the belief that education was for clerkly men under instruction from clerkly men, already dying before the Reformation, was a thing of the past. It is possible to see a tripartite system—school, university, Inn of Court—adapting itself to new needs. There were the old grammar schools, often refounded on the basis of ecclesiastical predecessors, like Westminster School, the King's School, Canterbury, the King's School, Worcester. (Winchester and Eton were exempted from the Act dissolving chantries.) But many grammar schools were new, arising from the initiative of town authorities, who often petitioned the Crown for the grant of monastic lands for the purpose, or found the money from other sources. At Hull, Chelmsford and elsewhere, new grammar schools came into existence, including one at Stratford, where Shakespeare may in due course have become a pupil. This process continued. By the end of the sixteenth century there were some 360 grammar schools of which about two-thirds survive.[1] For girls there was no provision for organized education, but private tutors were widely used for them in the families of the governing classes. Of the high level reached, Lady Jane Grey and Elizabeth I are each in their own way exemplars; while the Cooke daughters, children of Sir Anthony Cooke, became the most famous blue-stockings in Tudor England. One of them, Mildred, was to be the mother of Sir Robert Cecil, secretary of state under Elizabeth I, lord treasurer under James I and by then the most powerful man in England. His mother's learning is commended in the contemporary verse:

> Coke is comely and thereto
> In book sets all her care.
> In learning with the Roman dames
> Of right she may compare—

a passage worth quoting if only to indicate how bad Elizabethan verse could sometimes be. Another daughter, Anne, became the mother of Sir Francis Bacon. Thus, in the second generation, the Cooke family gave a lord chancellor as well as a lord treasurer to England.

The two universities at Oxford and Cambridge were attracting more and more the sons of aristocrats and gentry who would stay for a year or two learning the good and bad habits of their class and imbibing a little learning on the way. There were the Inns of Court in London, England's third university, where professional lawyers could be trained but where many more

[1] This passage was written before plans for the massive comprehensivization of schools were put into effect.

young men would attend simply as if it were a finishing school and to learn just sufficient law to prevent them making fools of themselves when they sat as justices of the peace at quarter sessions.

But the important development inherent in these changes is the change in direction of the whole educational outlook. Reforming pressures were brought to bear on schools and universities alike. The new doctrines were to be taught, the Bible was to be read in English. In the universities mathematics, astronomy, cosmography, philosophy moved into positions of importance in the curricula. If theology remained—at least in theory—queen of the arts, she found her court dwindling before the gathering competition of the new sciences. But it was not simply that the students were being taught different things; they were being taught more often and more intensely. The *jeunesse dorée* which, even while at the university, was never far from the sight and sound of the hunt, was caught up none the less in the new educational pressures. If the universities were less crowded by poor men's sons seeking education and advancement in the Church, the gentlemen's sons who were moving in soon learned that scholarship was a means of entry just as much to state office as it had hitherto been in the Church. The most succinct expression of the revolution which was taking place is to be found in the words of the Protector Somerset, written to Bishop Ridley in 1549, about a plan to reform the teaching at Cambridge: 'We are sure you are not ignorant how necessary a study that study of civil law is to all treaties with foreign princes and strangers, and how few there be at this present to do the king's majesty's service therein.' *To do the king's majesty's service.* That was the task confronting the universities.

The intense discussion going on at this time as to the scope and purpose of education reflected both the intellectual and the social crisis of the age. To many scholars, the compromise of Christian humanism continued to be viable. Sir John Cheke (tutor to Edward VI), who was as good a Protestant as Thomas More was a Catholic, believed, as did More, that the new education need shed nothing of its earlier Christian idealism. Cheke, at St John's College, Cambridge, during a period that would later be described as its golden age, saw no conflict between a study of the scriptures and the secular philosophy of the ancient Greeks. 'Eloquence without godliness', wrote Thomas Becon, 'is as a ring in a swine's snout.' But the compromise was under heavy strain. Sir Thomas Elyot's *The Boke named the Governour*, published in 1531, had little regard to theology as essential to a gentleman's education. Indeed intellectual training altogether should be set within limits. 'Continual study', he warned, 'without some manner of exercise shortly exhausteth the spirits vital.' In his view,

> ... The most honourable exercise ... and that beseemeth the estate of every noble person, is to ride surely and clean on a great horse and a rough, which undoubtedly not only importeth a majesty and dread to inferior persons, beholding him above the common course of other men, daunting a fierce and cruel beast, but also is not little succour, as well in pursuit of enemies and confounding them, as in escaping imminent danger, when wisdom thereto exhorteth.

There were other reasons for restricting the educational resources available to the community at large. It may be that one of the reasons that More had preferred to publish his *Utopia* in Latin rather than in English was to prevent his book falling into the wrong hands; certainly Henry VIII lived to regret the speed with which he had hastened to put the Bible in English in every parish church. Cromwell's Injunction of 1538 which had this purpose proclaimed throughout the land was followed, in the time of reaction after his fall, with the statute of 1543 which stringently restricted Bible reading to a small section of the community. For this was the generation which had lived through the Peasants' Revolt in Germany of 1525 when the Bible and Protestant doctrine had appeared to set large parts of Germany ablaze. This was the time of the Anabaptists who menaced the whole established order with their biblical commonwealth in

Münster, a revolutionary, egalitarian society of terrifying proportions. The arch-conservative sitting on the English throne
held the door fast against the very Protestantism which had aided
him in his struggle against the pope.

All this formed part of a larger debate. To men like Archbishop
Cranmer a university education should be free to a man who was
qualified to benefit from it. But this was not a view widely
accepted or seriously applied. It was felt by some that it was
better 'for the ploughman's son to go to the plough, and the
artificer's children to apply the trade of his parent's vocation,
and the gentleman's children are meet to have the knowledge of
government and rule of the commonwealth'. Sir Thomas Smith,
writing in 1565, saw, likewise, education as indeed the distinguishing feature of a gentleman. Trying to define a gentleman, he
acknowledges that it is impossible to do so with any precision,
especially at a time when the class has been inflated by the
climbing zeal of the new propertied men, aided in return for
fees by the College of Heralds. So Smith falls back on certain
general marks of identification. 'For whosoever studieth the laws
of the realm,' he confesses, 'who studieth in the universities, who
professeth liberal sciences, and to be short, who can live idly and
without manual labour, and will bear the port, charge and
countenance of a gentleman, he shall be called master, for that
is the title which men give to esquires and other gentlemen.'

The 'port, charge and countenance of a gentleman' meant
education, wealth, ostentation, courtliness, public service. That
at least was the theory. It is, however, this same Thomas Smith
who tells us elsewhere in the same work of the conditions meted
out to many of the sons of the gentry who had the ill luck to
become feudal wards of the Crown. By some extraordinary
anachronism, by then peculiar to England, heirs to lands held by
a certain outdated (but still formally maintained) tenure, known
as knight-service in chief, became royal wards if they were not
yet of age at their father's death. These wardships were being
bought and sold on the open market because they carried the
right of marriage with them (that is, the right to impose a

marriage upon the ward, or exact a heavy forfeit). Until the heir came of age his care and education were entirely in the hands of his guardian. And this, according to Smith, quoting contemporary opinion, was what happened: a gentleman could be 'bought and sold like an horse or an ox'. This, moreover, was why 'many gentlemen be so evil brought up touching virtue and learning, and but only in daintiness and pleasure; and why they be married very young and before they be wise, and many times do not greatly love their wives.' There was, said Smith, another reason put forward why these children received so little education. 'The buyer will not suffer his ward to take any great pains, either in study, or any other hardiness, lest he should be sick and die before he hath married his daughter, sister or cousin, for whose sake he bought him: and then all his money which he paid for him should be lost.'

This was no isolated allegation. Hugh Latimer earlier had condemned the whole wardship system on moral, social and educational grounds. Sir Nicholas Bacon, Smith's contemporary, denounced the whole business as 'a thing hitherto preposterously proceeding'. Sir Humphrey Gilbert, a decade later, painted a black picture of the education of wards, brought up 'in idleness and lascivious pastimes, estranged from all serviceable virtues to their prince and country, obscurely drowned in education for sparing charges'. And all this, he said, was deliberate. Guardians preferred to 'abase their [wards'] minds lest, being better qualified, they should disdain to stoop to the marriage of such purchasers' daughters'. We should not, of course, set too much store by these charges: they come often from social and educational reformers with specific purposes in mind; and we know from other evidence that their accounts of the treatment of wards are by no means universally true. We know of plenty of cases where guardians lavished every care upon their charges. Lord Burghley, Elizabeth I's Master of Wards, set up a private school for his wards in his own house where the standards of education reached the highest in the country. But there is no doubt that many guardians did abuse their rights, that these abuses reached scandalous proportions, that they aroused a great outcry in the

House of Commons in the early seventeenth century, and that foreigners were astounded that such an extraordinary situation could survive so long. We should bear these conditions in mind when we think of the enormous educational advances of the time.

Yet the broad outlines of change are clear enough and these may be briefly re-stated. In the second half of the sixteenth century more men were going to schools, to the universities and to the Inns of Court. Also, the kind of education now offered was changing in character and purpose: it was training men in the secular arts in the service of the world. It was now that the conditions favourable to Renaissance influences flourished in England: a cultured court presided over by a prince, Elizabeth I, who saw herself in a special role as a patron of the arts; a nobility which, for all its masquerades and formal splendours, was in fact a nobility of service; and below it, a new generation of administrators many of whom had been bred in the universities and Inns of Court precisely with a public career in mind.

It was now, in fact, more than thirty years after it was published in Italy, that Castiglione's *Courtier* was translated and published in England. It appeared in the year 1561 and its translator was Sir Thomas Hoby, husband of yet one more of the celebrated Cooke daughters. It was impossible wholly to anglicize the Italian model. The overwhelming majority of English aristocrats continued, at least until the end of James I's reign, to be firmly rooted in the country. The deracinated 'court' nobleman, familiar enough in France, was virtually unknown until we come to the Scottish aristocrats of the early seventeenth century whom James brought south with him from Scotland, and the London merchants whom he elevated as the reign wore on. But the notion of a courtier had already come to mean the artificial man, with the false and forced political language, the double standards of ruthless ambition, the mailed fist in the velvet glove. Yet when Castiglione's courtier became a naturalized Englishman, he retained many of the Italian's patrician ways, with the cultivated mind and social graces, but mellowed and softened with the rustic traditions of provincial England. If Elizabeth I is the English version of the Renaissance prince, Sir

Philip Sidney, soldier, poet, courtier, patron, is the native version of the Renaissance aristocrat.

There was also another and fundamental difference in the English response to the Renaissance as compared with that of Italy. Machiavelli, it is true, had seen the vision of Italian nationalism and unity, a nationalism which would be fulfilled by the skilful use of Renaissance political methods employed by a great prince in the service of the state. But the age of the Renaissance in Italy began and ended with national unity still centuries away. Machiavelli's scheme needed one great prince. In Italy, in fact, there were too many princes, none of them great. In England there was in the second half of the sixteenth century, one prince who, whether great or not, somehow responded to—and herself inspired—a large measure of national feeling. In this the birth of a great national literature also played an important part.

Here, the contrast between the late sixteenth century and its first half is enormous. At the beginning of the century John Skelton had lamented:

> Our natural tongue is rude
> And hard to be ennewed
> With polished terms lusty.
> Our language is so rusty,
> So cankered and so full
> Of frowards and so dull,
> That if I would apply
> To write ornately,
> I wot not where to find
> Terms to serve my mind.

Of the earlier poets, he found the English of Gower 'old', with his matter vastly superior to the manner in which he expressed himself. Lydgate he thought diffuse and difficult to follow. Chaucer, 'that famous clerk', was the great exception. His English was:

... Pleasant, easy and plain
No word he wrote in vain.

Hence, he complained, it was absurd for men of the sixteenth century to take his early English and try to bring it up to date:

And now men have amended
His English, whereat they bark
And mar all they work.

This consciousness, that to the world of literature England had contributed only one great poet, survived right through the sixteenth century until the rise of Spenser. More than two generations after Skelton, and on the eve of the greatest age of English poetry, Sir Philip Sidney in his *Apologie for Poetrie* could write of Chaucer: 'Truly, I know not whether to marvel more, either that he in that misty time could see so clearly, or that we in this clear age walk so stumbling after him.'

But as long ago as 1530 Thomas More had rejected the notion that English was too coarse a language for literary expression. 'For as for that our tongue is called barbarous', he wrote, 'is but a fantasy; for so is, as every learned man knoweth, every strange language to other. And if they would call it barren of words, there is no doubt but it is plenteous enough to express our minds in anything whereof one man hath used to speak with another.' He was here defending the use of a Bible in English (if properly safeguarded against heresy); and it was indeed in sacred literature, the Bible, the Book of Common Prayer, Foxe's *Book of Martyrs*, the homilies and the printed sermons, that, on the eve of Elizabeth's reign, English was already displaying its vigour, flexibility, colour, and resourcefulness as a medium of almost limitless promise.

It is, of course, true that much of the prose of this period could be heavy, sluggish, colourless and insensitive; and we should not forget that even in the golden decades of the 1580s and 1590s more bad than good poetry was written. But there can be little question that these later years formed one of the greatest creative periods in the history of English literature. If Shakespeare had never lived, one would still be astounded at the succession of incomparable masterpieces pouring from the pens of Sidney, Spenser, Marlowe, Ralegh, Bacon, Donne, Jonson and others on into the seventeenth century. We are, of course, not here primarily concerned with a history of English literature but with the society which made possible the expression of such richness and diversity of talents. Part of the achievement is to be explained in the changing character of English patronage.

V

Patronage during the Elizabethan period derived from three main sources: the royal court, the great provincial nobility, and the people of London. Of these, the central patronage of the queen was the most complex and subtle in its operation and in retrospect has long been the most elusive to grasp. To Elizabeth and her contemporaries the court was an instrument for the expression of the personal will of the queen, in politics no less than in culture. The grant of high office to a minister was handled in exactly the same way as the grant of a small reward to some literary man for writing a pamphlet. There was in all this a strong element of caprice but contemporaries also understood this, for they did not forget—as historians sometimes do—how essentially personal government was. Sir John Harington, Queen Elizabeth's godson, who is remembered as a court wit, as well as a pioneer of English sanitation, kept a fascinating notebook in which he entered brief observations about events at the royal court. In one such passage we read that he met the lord chancellor, Sir Christopher Hatton, coming away from the royal presence. Hatton, he says, 'came out from her presence with ill countenance and pulled me aside by the girdle and said in a secret way, "If you have any suit today I pray you put it aside. The sun doth not shine." ' The queen was not in the mood.

Edmund Spenser understood the situation as clearly as did Hatton, the lord chancellor, or Harington, the wit. Here for example is Spenser's dedication of his *Faerie Queene*, published in 1590:

> To the most high, mighty, and magnificent Empress, renowned for piety, virtue, and all gracious government, Elizabeth, by the grace of God, Queen of England, France and Ireland, and of Virginia, Defender of the Faith, etc., her most humble servant, Edmund Spenser, doth in all humility dedicate, present and consecrate these, his labours, to live with the eternity of her fame.

And this is how he says the same thing in verse:

> ... O Goddess heavenly bright,
> Mirror of grace and Majesty divine
> Great lady of the greatest Isle, whose light
> Like Phoebus' lamp throughout the world doth shine,
> Shed thy fair beams into my feeble eyne,
> And raise my thoughts too humble and too vile,
> To think of that true glorious type of thine ...

For good measure, the printed version of the *Faerie Queene* is accompanied by dedicatory sonnets, to the lord chancellor, ten noblemen, three knights, two noble ladies and there is one sonnet finally to 'all the gracious and beautiful ladies in the Court', making seventeen sonnets in all.

Spenser in all this was conforming to an already established pattern, one which was to go on for centuries. It is therefore worth glancing for a moment at the ten noblemen and three knights (apart from the lord chancellor) who were the objects of these verses. They include Lord Burghley, lord treasurer; the Earl of Oxford, lord chamberlain; the Earl of Essex, one of the most influential members of the privy council, and the queen's favourite; Lord Charles Howard, lord high admiral; Sir Francis Walsingham, secretary of state; and Sir Walter Ralegh. Amongst these and the others listed are the greatest patrons of the arts, of poetry and of the drama in England. But they were also the most powerful men in politics, the great channels through which flowed the royal bounty in Church, in state, in culture. Yet even so powerful a minister and favourite as Lord Chancellor Hatton might fail to persuade the queen to grant a suit; but if he failed, then no one else would succeed. For these were the established means and no other existed. That is how politics work in conditions of personal government; and even in modern times, with Western constitutional government, it remains true that patronage in practice is a highly personal thing, though never completely monolithic. In Elizabethan England it was.

Hence arose the bitterness with which unsuccessful suitors assailed the court, the attacks upon the corrupt exercise of monopoly power—attacks not against the queen personally but against Burghley especially, regarded by contemporaries as the most influential adviser of the queen, though he himself minimized his influence. The weakness inherent in any such system of personal government is that it breeds faction and that able men are thwarted from obtaining recognition and reward. It is Spenser again, this time in *Mother Hubbard's Tale*, who gives the most vivid picture of the relationship between suitor and patron:

> Full little knowest thou, that hast not tried,
> What hell it is in suing long to bide;
> To lose good days, that might be better spent;
> To waste long nights in pensive discontent;
> To speed today, to be put back tomorrow;
> To feed on hope, to pine with fear and sorrow;
> To have thy prince's grace, yet want her peers';
> To have thy asking, yet wait many years;
> To fret thy soul with crosses and with cares;
> To eat thy heart through comfortless despairs;
> To fawn, to crouch, to wait, to ride, to run,
> To spend, to give, to want, to be undone.

Spenser belonged to the Essex faction, the faction which ultimately lost in the last grim struggle of the closing years of the reign. In 1601 Essex himself was crushed in a hopeless attempt to gain by force what he had failed to obtain by pleading, by pressure and by all the established processes of the Elizabethan court; and Robert Cecil, son of Lord Burghley, emerged into an unchallengeable position at the centre of power.

But there were also lesser courts scattered over the provinces where the landed aristocracy itself exercised a considerable cultural patronage in several branches of the arts. This took visible form in the building, or vastly extending, of castles and palaces. There was Lord Burghley's expenditure on the great house in Northamptonshire which bears his name; Leicester's on his great castle at Kenilworth; the Sidneys' on Penshurst Place; the Herberts' on Wilton; Hatton's on Holdenby, and scores of others. If they gave work to architects, they also encouraged painters for their halls and galleries, goldsmiths and silversmiths for their plate, furniture designers and tapestry workers and, when they died, sculptors and monumental masons to erect massive tombs for their memory. One of the justifications for the magnificent scale of this building was to be able to receive the queen in a manner worthy of Her Majesty when she came on progress in the shires; and, although this has a strong element of special pleading, it was none the less true. Every summer the queen would go on a tour of some parts of southern England—she never got more than a hundred miles from the capital—and this was an occasion of both political and cultural significance.

All this was, of course, part of the great effort to identify the queen with the nation at a time when communication, in every sense, was poor. It was a great display of monarchy: queen, ministers, servants, hundreds strong, moving slowly through the countryside, staying a few days in the various great houses on the way. Often the full splendours of the masque would be brought into play with its heavy symbolism of monarchy and nation. Here local talent would, for a brief spell, display itself before the queen. On the most famous of these occasions, at Kenilworth in 1575, the queen stayed for three weeks to a veritable festival of the arts; and there were numerous other times and places where her visit proved the opportunity for local poets for the first time — and no doubt the last — to appear before a national audience. In London at the Inns of Court and on Lord Mayor's Day, at the universities during her visitations, the same elaborate ceremonials brought forth an abundance of skills, some of it of a very high order. At Oxford and Cambridge, as at St Paul's School, the plays were often the work of scholars. The Inns of Court put on the work of Shakespeare and Ben Jonson. Apart from this, some noblemen like the Earl of Leicester kept their own company of players. Other leading men in Church and state encouraged scholars to live as tutors and secretaries in their households. Thomas Whythorne, the composer, lived under the patronage of Matthew Parker, Archbishop of Canterbury; John Harte, the antiquary and spelling reformer, lived as a tutor to Burghley's wards, as did other distinguished scholars like Sylvius Frisius and Lawrence Nowell.

But if we think of this complex cultural Renaissance as a response to native inspiration at court, in the country and in the capital, it continued to draw from Italy much of its impetus and form. For a spell in Italy, especially Venice and Padua, was considered an important phase in the education of a patron. To Sir Philip Sidney, as to so many of his contemporaries, such a visit, with its contact with Italian culture — it is possible, but by no means certain, that he met Tasso — proved a great formative period. His work *Arcadia* shows the influence of Sannazaro and also of the Greeks Heliodorus and Homer; and of much else too. 'It gathers up', wrote C. S. Lewis, 'what a whole generation wanted to say.' It is 'medieval, Protestant, pastoral, Stoical, Platonic'. A more striking, and more famous, example of the merging of the Renaissance outlook with English domestic culture is Spenser's *Faerie Queene*. It shows the marks of Virgil's *Aeneid*, of Aristotle but much more of Plato, it shows Christian predestinarianism, it reflects the contemporary Italian epic; yet with it all it reaches back to English Chaucer and Malory and at the same time presents as its central figures an Arthur who is essentially Spenserian and Tudor, and a Gloriana who is Elizabeth.

If court and nobility were, then, of great importance as patrons, the capital itself was in its own way a major impulse in English Renaissance culture. To think of London in the late sixteenth century is to think of the Thames—and of Spenser's *Prothalamion*—and of Shakespeare. The fate of the capital, the nation, the river and the dramatist are intimately interwoven. For the capital (in effect the twin cities of London and Westminster) was now completely dominant in English industry, commerce, finance, law and government. For all this the great line of communication was the Thames with its estuary which gave London direct access by water—the cheapest means of communication—to the coastal region of all England and the continent of Europe. 'All our creeks seek to one river,' lamented Thomas Milles, the customs official at Sandwich, in 1604, 'all our rivers run to one port, all our ports join to one town, all our towns make but one city, and all our cities and suburbs to one vast unwieldy and disorderly Babel of buildings which the world calls London.' It had indeed a stranglehold and Milles was expressing a widespread provincial outcry against its supremacy. To others it had long been a source of national pride. An English propagandist of the mid-century thus spoke of the capital:

And as concerning the ancient and famous city of London ... no city in France is to be compared unto it: first for the most pleasant situation; then consider the magnifique and decorate churches, the godly predications and services in them; the true and brief administration of justice; the strong Tower of London; the large and plenteous river; the beautiful palaces, places and buildings royal, as well all alongest the said river as in every street of the City and round about the same; the rich merchants and other people; the fair ladies, gentlewomen and their children; the godly bringing up of youth and activity of their children to learning; the prudent order amongst the occupations; their beautiful halls; the great number of gentlemen there always studying the laws of the realm; the high estate of the mayor and sheriffs, and the keeping of their sumptuous households; the bridge of London, with the fair mansions on it; the large and mighty suburbs; the pleasant walks without every port, for recreation of the inhabitants; and the exceeding number of strong archers and other mighty men which they may make to serve their king furnished for the wars.

Parliament, the Law Courts, the Inns of Court, the whole administration in Whitehall, the great companies in the City, the foreign merchants, all these brought to London a great and ever-growing concentration of population and therefore a mass of trades and men to serve them. By the end of the sixteenth century London and its suburbs had a population of some 200,000 and a strong, secular demand (and resources to pay) for its own secular culture. In 1577 The Theatre was opened in the suburb of Shoreditch. The Curtain came in the same year, The Swan in 1595, and in 1599 The Globe. The audience, the theatre and the playwright came together; and, though Shakespeare belongs to a timeless world stage, and his plots are drawn from the world literature available to him, he remains also and characteristically the great expression of High Renaissance London. It is not a deterministic view of history to say that without London there could have been no Shakespeare, at least in the full richness that we know him. It is also true that without the Renaissance even Shakespeare would have lacked the wealth of cultural resources upon which his genius drew and which it transmuted into imperishable drama.

Shakespeare's predecessors as dramatists had extensively drawn on classical sources, more particularly Seneca, Plautus, Terence, as well as on the Italian *novella*, the short stories so fertile in comic and tragic plot. *Gorboduc*, a blank verse tragedy with a moral, had been produced in 1562 (written by two parliamentarians, Thomas Norton and Thomas Sackville). John Lyly's comedies began to appear in the 1580s, as did George Peele's and Robert Greene's, while Thomas Kyd broke new ground with his blank verse play *The Spanish Tragedy*, composed on Senecan lines. But it was Christopher Marlowe who exploited the wide range of Senecan tragedy with his *Tamburlaine* and *Dr Faustus* and at the same time gave full and memorable expression to one of the central themes of Elizabethan thought, the nature of power, a theme to which Shakespeare himself returned over and over again. But to think of these men only as forerunners and contemporaries of Shakespeare is to underrate their best work. It was men like Norton, Sackville, Lyly, Kyd who delivered the English drama from the traditions of medieval morality and miracle plays. It was men like Kyd and Marlowe who, as it were, took the drama out of the royal and noble palaces, universities and Inns of Court to the people of London themselves. It was they who began the cultural—and social—revolution which Shakespeare carried forward to a matchless victory.

We can, in one sense, see Shakespeare as the culminating point of the English Renaissance in the whole range of culture. The extensive study of classical models dating back to the impact of humanism upon education earlier in the sixteenth century, the influence of Terence, Seneca, the classical poets, the modern Sannazaro and Petrarch; the abundant material of the ancient histories now available also in North's translation of Plutarch's *Lives*; the whole humanist dream of the perfectibility of human reason; all these, and much else, gave form, thought and substance to the magisterial achievements of Shakespeare. But it was not just the fulfilment of a great humanist tradition. In Shakespeare as in many of his great contemporaries this was combined with the new pressures of his age: the Protestant crisis of the place of the individual soul and will in the universal order; the central problems of kingship and power to which Shakespeare constantly returned in the history plays, and in *Macbeth, Hamlet, Lear*, drawing his material in many cases not from the classics but from the great school of English historians of which the *Chronicles* of Holinshed, published in 1577, was the best example. Shakespeare's comedies likewise show his debt to the Elizabethan rediscovery of the classics but *A Midsummer Night's Dream* is as English as anything that our language has produced.

So Shakespeare, like his contemporaries, reflects the conflict within the humanist compromise between the two faiths, the one in the ultimate fulfilment of man's greatness, the other in the frailty of man condemned by original sin. Thus he confronts the problem of the classical man in the Christian world in a famous passage in *Hamlet*:

> What a piece of work is man! How noble in reason, how infinite in faculties, in form and moving how express and admirable! In action how like an angel, in apprehension how like a god! The beauty of the world, the paragon of animals! And yet, to me, what is this quintessence of dust?

If this tension was felt right through English Renaissance culture — and indeed inspired some of its greatest masterpieces — the same conflict was implicit in the first responses in England to the new scientific thought. The problems raised by the work of Copernicus, which threatened the whole cosmological system of the Church, by the medical researches of Vesalius and his successors, which undermined the hallowed concepts of the human body, the new work being done in mathematics, geography, all bred the grave inner doubts which John Donne in the early seventeenth century was to express so vividly. Science itself did not break the established moulds of English thought. But in the early seventeenth century it lived with increasing unease alongside the traditional doctrines of Church and society. Sir Walter Ralegh, scientist, colonist, politician, poet, historian — the Renaissance virtuoso — could not restrain his doubts and earned himself, unjustly, the name of atheist. Bacon, with still larger vision, under cool intellectual control, set out to establish a system of knowledge of universal compass. Harvey, the scientific analyst of true independence, broke through to the fundamentals of human anatomy. These men each in their own way were outstanding products of the English Renaissance. But they each set limits to its survival in its original form. The classical as well as the Christian concepts were in danger.

A new tension was also emerging. Radical Protestantism, or

Puritanism as it was coming to be known, looked to different authorities than a Renaissance culture or a princely state. To the Puritans the Bible was the unchallengeable source of authority about man, God, the state and the world order. And what they found in the Bible had little in common with the late Elizabethan England in which they lived. In Parliament, pamphlet and sermon they preached on behalf of a different society, pre-dating the Renaissance. Intransigently Puritan and soon to become severely sabbatarian as well, they were intolerant of much that they saw in the secular world around them. And their intransigence was met by severe censorship under episcopal control. Long afterwards, in the middle of the seventeenth century, the Puritans would try to establish a biblical common-wealth which was hostile to much in the English Renaissance. But their commonwealth collapsed and the continuing influence of the late Renaissance outlook was clearly felt.

In the early seventeenth century we have a society which— even with the heavy undercurrent of doubt—manifested the vigour and confidence of a nation entering on the period of its greatness. The nationalism we find in Shakespeare, the imperialism we find in the achievements of Drake and the writings of Hakluyt, the enormous amount of patriotic literature flowing from the presses, much of it focusing on the queen, establish the clear outlines of a nation-state governed by a Renaissance prince. Yet to see it in perspective we turn for a last view of her, not to the familiar passages of Shakespeare and the poets, but to the funeral eulogy pronounced upon her by Dr King at Whitehall: '... There are two excellent women, one that bare Christ and another that blessed Christ. To these may we join a third, that bare and blessed him both: She [Elizabeth] bare him in her heart as a womb, she conceived him in faith, she brought him forth in abundance of good works.' A Renaissance prince yet the mother of Christ! How much longer could this extraordinary com-promise—and the compromise of a whole age—endure?

9

County government: Wiltshire
c. 1530–c. 1660

The capacity of English organs of government to combine continuity with change is nowhere better demonstrated than in the history of local administration between the Reformation and the Civil War.[1] At the end of our period, with a restoration in both local and central government we are, almost without exception, surveying the activities of the same local officials whom we met at the beginning. But the strong elements of continuity and tradition somewhat mask a subtle yet profound shift in the balance of local power. If so many of the local officials bore the marks of their medieval origins, they shouldered, none the less, responsibilities peculiar to a later age. In some respects, indeed, there was something approaching a revolution in the structure of local government. How far these officials proved equal to the new requirements, and the nature of the revolution which occurred, form the central themes of this essay.

The material at our disposal is, unfortunately, very unevenly distributed. What the lord lieutenant did, or rather, what he was told to do, we can often discover from the privy council register and sometimes from the state papers. In addition, a narrow but vivid shaft of light is cast upon his day-to-day activities by a volume of the Earl of Hertford's papers at the British Museum.[2] On the other hand, the crucial minutes of the justices of the peace

NOTE: First published in *Victoria History of the Counties of England: Wiltshire*, ed. R. B. Pugh and Elizabeth Crittall (1957), v, pp. 80–110.

[1] The author wishes to thank Mr H. C. Johnson for reading this article and for making a number of helpful suggestions.

[2] B.M., Add. MS. 5496. This volume has now been edited by my former pupil, Mr W. P. D. Murphy: *The Earl of Hertford's Lieutenancy Papers, 1603–1612* (Wiltshire Rec. Soc. XXIII).

are sadly lacking for the Tudor period: only one volume has survived.[1] We meet them elsewhere in chance encounters in state papers, Ancient Indictments, and Star Chamber proceedings, but our visions of their problems and activities are fleeting ones. It is not until 1610 that we begin a full and continuous series of quarter sessions records, which prove increasingly rewarding as we advance through the seventeenth century. As we penetrate further into local administration, into the hundred and parish in search of petty sessions and court leet, high constable and tithingman, we are, for the whole period, virtually without direct reports and can only piece together from scattered references some impressionistic picture of these minor but important institutions and men. For military affairs the pivotal official was undoubtedly the lord lieutenant, for civil affairs, the justice of the peace.

I

From the time of Edward VI until the outbreak of the Civil War, the lieutenancy of Wiltshire seems to have been the perquisite of successive Earls of Pembroke, with only one interruption. In 1551 we find Sir William Herbert, shortly to be created Earl of Pembroke, granted the lieutenancy of Wiltshire;[2] and in 1552 and 1553 he was again exercising his office under direction from the privy council.[3] The lord lieutenant had not yet become a permanent feature of county administration anywhere in England, and, during Mary's reign and indeed in Elizabeth I's until the Armada, the post was filled only intermittently. During such times as it was filled we know that Pembroke was responsible for Wiltshire.[4] In 1559, the commission of lieutenancy joined two counties, Somerset and Wiltshire, under the jurisdiction of Pembroke;[5] and a contemporary list of November

---

[1] *Minutes of Proceedings in Sessions 1563 and 1574–92* (W.A.S. Rec. Brch. iv), hereafter cited as *Sess. Mins. 1563–92*.
[2] *Acts of P.C. 1550–2*, 258.
[3] Ibid., 1552–4, 48, 277.
[4] *Cal. S.P. Dom. 1547–80*, 108.
[5] Gladys Scott Thomson, *Lords Lieutenant in the Sixteenth Century* (1923), p. 48.

1569 shows him still occupying the lieutenancies of the two counties.[1] Early in 1570 he died and was succeeded in the lieutenancy of Wiltshire by his son Henry, the 2nd earl;[2] but the queen also appears to have been prepared, according to the current practice, to leave it in abeyance for periods. In its place she would establish a commission of musters, composed of the sheriff and certain justices of the peace, charged with the levying of troops.[3] Henry, Earl of Pembroke, was on various occasions a member of these commissions.[4] By August 1586, if not earlier, he was again lord lieutenant of Wiltshire, to which Somerset had been added;[5] and when, in 1587, faced with the gravest threat of her reign, the queen issued new commissions of lieutenancy, we find Pembroke in charge also of Shropshire, Worcestershire, Herefordshire, and the twelve Welsh counties.[6] Thus he reinforced his title of president of the Council of Wales with the lieutenancy over the Principality.

With Pembroke's death in 1601 the succession to the Wiltshire lieutenancy passed from the Herbert family to Edward Seymour, Earl of Hertford, son of the Protector Somerset; and the evidence shows him occupying the office, when called upon, until his death in 1621.[7] Then the lieutenancy reverted to the Herberts, with whom it remained until the Civil War. First it went to William, 3rd Earl of Pembroke, statesman, courtier, and patron of literature and the arts, who was given responsibility for Wiltshire and Somerset, the usual combination, to which Cornwall was subsequently added.[8] When he died in 1630 the

---

[1] SP 12/59, no. 57.

[2] Ibid. He does not appear to have succeeded to the lieutenancy of Som. at this stage.

[3] SP 12/67, no. 25. Cf. *Musters, Beacons, Subsidies etc. in Northants*, ed. Joan Wake (Northants. Rec. Soc. iii), pp. 34–5.

[4] *Cal S.P. Dom.* 1547–80, 335, 377, 464.

[5] *Acts of P.C.* 1586–7, 200.

[6] Thomson, *Lords Lieutenant*, p. 50. For his reappointment in Jan. 1589, see *Acts of P.C.* 1588–9, 25. His commission of 1587 is printed in full in Hist. MSS. Com. *15th Rep. App.* V, Foljambe, 20–22.

[7] e.g. B.M., Add. MS. 5496; *Acts of P.C.* 1613–14, 555; ibid., 1619–21, 378.

[8] *Acts of P.C.* 1619–21, 378; ibid., 1623–5, 10.

lieutenancies for the three counties passed to his younger
brother, Philip, Earl of Pembroke and Montgomery,[1] and these
were accordingly added to the lieutenancy of Kent, which he
already held.[2] His office in Wiltshire went on until 1640 at least;[3]
but soon the lieutenant was heavily committed to his duties as a
parliamentary leader against the king from whom he held his
commission of lieutenancy.

The lieutenancy of Wiltshire was fast becoming a perquisite of
the Herbert family, a practice perhaps unwelcome to the
sovereign, but tolerated perforce on account of the primacy of
the family in the county at that time.[4] It is not always easy to
discover the full details of the office, but it is a straightforward
matter to discover who were the lords lieutenant for the period.
When we come to the deputy lieutenants, however, we reach
more difficult territory. The exact origin of the deputies, like so
much in the administrative history of the period, is obscure.
The commissions of musters, which we have seen operating when
the lieutenancy was vacant, clearly pointed the way. But the
emergence of the deputy lieutenant as an important local officer
in Elizabeth I's reign pays tribute, amongst other things, to the
increasing burden of responsibility descending upon the lieutenant
himself. It was becoming necessary for him to shed the load. It is
not easy, however, to discover upon whom precisely the load
descended. When deputy lieutenants began to be appointed as
recognized Crown officials, probably early in Elizabeth's reign,
their names were entered in the commissions of lieutenancy; but
unfortunately we do not possess a complete series of such
commissions. Our first reference for Wiltshire is a manuscript
list, possibly for 1569, where we find that William, Earl of
Pembroke, had two pairs of deputy lieutenants: Sir Henry
Knyvet and Sir John Danvers for this county, and Sir George

---

[1] *Cal. S.P. Dom.* 1629–31, 324.
[2] Ibid., 181.
[3] Ibid., 1640, 309.
[4] Thomson, *Lords Lieutenant*, p. 49. The lord lieutenancy of Lancaster and
Chester, which passed to the 3rd, 4th, 5th and, after an interval, 6th earls of Derby,
is cited here as remarkable for being in practice hereditary (p. 52).

Sydenham and Sir Henry Barker for Somerset.[1] In 1590 we find Knyvet and Danvers occupying the same posts[2] under the 2nd Earl of Pembroke, now lord lieutenant. By 1597 only Knyvet remained, and a privy council letter to the lord keeper pointed out that the lord lieutenant needed more help than this, more particularly 'by reason of the far absence of our very good lord the Earl of Pembroke ... who is for the most part resident in Wales'. Sir Francis Popham was accordingly added as deputy lieutenant.[3] A year later the number of deputies was raised to three and the name of Edward Penruddock was added to the commission.[4] In 1601, perhaps as a further sign of the times, we find that the number of deputies for Wiltshire was now four, in the persons of Sir James Marvin, Sir Francis Popham, Sir Walter Long, and Sir William Eyre.[5] In 1608 there were four again, the only change being the substitution of Sir Thomas Gorges for Sir Francis Popham.[6] Some time after this Anthony Hungerford must have been appointed a deputy, for we find him, in his turn, retiring in favour of his son, Edward, in 1624.[7] In this year, also, Sir John Dauntsey appears to have been added to the deputy lieutenants; but whether he replaced someone else, or augmented the total, we do not know.[8] Four years later we find that Edward Gorges had replaced Thomas Gorges and Edward Baynton's name appears also in the list.[9] Here only three deputy lieutenants are mentioned; but when we meet them again, in 1633, we find that there are now five of them: Francis Seymour, Edward

---

[1] SP 12/59, no. 61. The dating is by a later editor and it is possible that the list was in fact compiled after 1569. An earlier document in the same volume, no. 57, with a contemporary dating of 1569, gives Pembroke two different deputies for Som. but mentions none for Wilts.

[2] SP 12/234, no. 12. In virtue of this office Danvers asked for his name to be removed from the list of those being considered for sheriff of Glos.: Hist. MSS. Com. *Salisbury*, iv, 416.

[3] *Acts of P.C.* 1597–8, 91–92.

[4] Ibid., 1598–9, 209–10.

[5] SP 12/283a, no. 85. The doc. is incorrectly endorsed 27 Apr. 1602.

[6] B.M., Add. MS. 5496, fol. 8a.

[7] *Cal. S.P. Dom.* 1623–5, 164.

[8] SP 14/178, no. 7; SP 14/179, no. 4.

[9] SP 16/91, no. 84.

Hungerford, Neville Poole, Walter Vaughan, and John Popham.[1]

The leading families of the county, then, were called upon to share, under the lieutenant, in the mounting responsibilities devolving upon him; and if the office of lieutenant of Wiltshire was passing from father to son, the office of deputy lieutenant was tending to develop a similar tradition. It was, no doubt, increasingly sought after. 'All men cannot be deputy lieutenants,' the 2nd Earl of Pembroke once wrote to some suitors of Wales, 'some must govern, some must obey.'[2] Perhaps the increase in the number of deputy lieutenants from two to five testifies not simply to the growing pressure of work but to the growing pressure of the county families. But the posts were no sinecures. With the lord lieutenant the deputies shared the military tasks assigned to him and these remained in the forefront of his obligations; but financial and social duties, themselves manifestly related to the key problem of the maintenance of order, claimed a growing share of his time. His prestige in the county, his relationship with the justices of the peace, and, in some cases, his participation in the central government, marked him out as well suited to carry the will of the government into the shires.

His military duties in Wiltshire displayed the features familiar to the rest of England: the division of the county into its component parts, each under the supervision of a group of justices of the peace with perhaps one or two deputy lieutenants; the preparation of the muster roll and the summoning of the trained bands of array; the supervision of military stores and the provision of part of the funds from local sources for the equipment and movement of troops. Some special aspects of the county, however, merit further consideration.

It was perhaps its geographical situation which determined Wiltshire's role in war and the preparation for war. It was part of what the privy council once described as the 'upland counties'. In other words, it was not in the direct line of an enemy's assault but a hinterland to provide the men and means of resistance.

---

[1] SP 16/247, no. 17.

[2] A. H. Dodd, 'The pattern of politics in Stuart Wales', *Trans. Hon. Soc. Cymmrodorion*, 1948, 10.

Hence we find it called upon to provide levies for the 'maritime counties' as well as for the Isle of Wight, the Channel Islands and Ireland, and to help in the movement of troops to focal points. But amidst the plentiful reports on military affairs flowing in from the lieutenant or the commission of musters, in the Elizabethan period, we detect innumerable signs of the difficulties of organization and supply. In 1562 we learn that a contractor who had received £100 some two years previously for supplies had still failed to deliver the goods.[1] In October 1570 the government was warned of the inadequacy of armour and equipment revealed by the county musters;[2] and three years later it was reported that the cost of training troops was greater than the county, heavily taxed already, could endure.[3] When, in 1577, Wiltshire asked that it should be allowed to restrict the period of training to four days in the year instead of the ten officially laid down, it was abruptly told that 'her Majesty's pleasure is that the days shall not be diminished' and that the money needed for the purpose could be 'levied easily' in the county.[4] The Crown for its part was committed to heavy expenditure. In one month alone, November 1596, it had to find £1,000 to pay for the levies from Wiltshire and Hampshire for the Isle of Wight.[5]

Difficulties arose also about the appointment of officers. When, on an earlier occasion, Pembroke found Sir George Carey appointed, apparently over the heads of the local gentry, to take the musters and appoint the captains for the levies for the Isle of Wight, he spoke up on behalf of the county and protested against the whole arrangement.[6] He did so to good effect. In less than a fortnight Carey was relieved of his charge since the captains were already appointed from amongst 'the chiefest and gentlemen of best quality of the said county, who in case they should be removed from their said charges would think themselves therein to be greatly disgraced', especially as they had already been put

[1] *Acts of P.C.* 1558–70, 125.
[2] *Cal. S.P. Dom.* 1547–80, 394.
[3] Ibid., 464.
[4] *Acts of P.C.* 1575–7, 325–6.
[5] *Cal. S.P. Dom.* 1595–7, 308–9.
[6] Ibid., 1581–90, 390.

to great trouble and expense.[1] On the other hand when, in the summer of 1588, Pembroke replaced Sir John Stoyll, the leader of the levies appointed by the privy council eight years earlier, by his own nominee, Gabriel Hanley, Pembroke was told by the council to restore Stoyll to office, to take note of allegations of corruption against Hanley, and to report.[2]

Soon other complaints were being directed against the county administration. In 1592 Wiltshire was named as one of the five counties which had not sent up the muster rolls in spite of being asked to do so on two separate occasions, 'wherewith we can assure you her Highness is not a little displeased'.[3] In November 1596 the privy council once again referred to the poor quality of the Wiltshire levies;[4] and in the New Year it prepared for vigorous action. In February 1597 the lord chief justice, Sir John Popham, was instructed by the privy council to inquire into the alleged irregularities in the disbandment of levies and the waste of equipment in his county. It was not going to be an easy task, especially as 'upon other occasions of service when like abuses have been committed, the matter hath been so shifted from the county to those that had the government of the soldiers, and from these again to the county that we could hardly find where to lay the fault'. In a postscript he was further directed to investigate the 'great abuse committed in the discharge of divers soldiers for sums of money'.[5] A list of offenders was duly returned and in May the council prepared to haul them up to London.[6] But neither Popham nor the council achieved any lasting success. In 1598 the equipment was reported as inadequate and the men unfit for service.[7] In January 1599 things were no better: the lord lieutenant was told that some were refusing to contribute to the muster and he was asked 'to be the more earnest with them'. Moreover, there had been 'slack attendance' on the

[1] *Acts of P.C.* 1586–7, 363–4.
[2] Ibid., 1588–9, 386–7.
[3] Ibid., 1592, 278.
[4] Ibid., 1596–7, 337.
[5] Ibid., 487–8.
[6] Ibid., 1597, 112–13.
[7] *Cal. S.P. Dom.* 1598–1601, 141. The dating of the document is uncertain.

part of justices of the peace when the Irish expedition was in preparation and Pembroke was asked to 'give them admonition'. On top of all this there was wholesale evasion of military duties and contributions, in Wiltshire as elsewhere, in that 'many gentlemen and others do retain more servants than the law doth allow them'. Others, therefore, had to bear a disproportionate burden.[1]

Under the Stuarts, as is well known, the position still further deteriorated, and opposition to the demands of government, including its military demands, finally flared up into civil war. Yet, if the new century provided ample evidence of resistance, corruption, and inefficiency, it yielded also clear examples of officials trying to make the administrative machine work. The Earl of Hertford, lieutenant under James I, was indeed singled out in a House of Commons debate of 1606 for personal attack on the grounds of favouritism, bullying, and general high-handedness.[2] It so happens, however, that his lieutenancy papers for the year 1608 have survived and here we have patiently recorded, and with a wealth of detail, the day-to-day processes by which the military preparedness of the county was tested.[3] Like the Longleat papers on the preparations for the Armada of 1588,[4] this source gives an admirable picture of the county in military array. Here we can only select some of its salient features. First we have the copy of the commission of June 28th, 1608, appointing the Earl of Hertford lord lieutenant of Somerset and Wiltshire, of Bristol, Bath and Wells, and Salisbury 'and all other corporate and privileged places within the limits or precincts of the said counties'.[5] Two days later the privy council drew up the instruction, which reached Amesbury on July 11th, to hold the muster.[6] A fortnight after its receipt, the earl issued directions to

---

[1] *Acts of P.C.* 1598–9, 501–2. Servants were not normally taken for musters unless necessity required. Cf. W. B. Willcox, *Gloucestershire, 1590–1640* (New Haven, 1940), p. 80.

[2] *The Parliamentary Diary of Robert Bowyer*, ed. D. H. Willson (Minneapolis, 1931), pp. 130, 154–6.

[3] B.M., Add. MS. 5496. See above, p. 236 n. 2.

[4] Printed in part in *W.A.M.* xiv. 243–53.

[5] B.M., Add. MS. 5496, fols. 1a–3a.

[6] Ibid., fols. 3b–6a.

his deputy lieutenants and these, and other appropriate documents, were 'delivered by his lordship's own hands unto Sir Thomas Gorges'.[1]

Not everyone delighted in the military titles falling thick and fast upon Wiltshire. On August 1st Sir Thomas Thynne wrote to ask that, in virtue of his office of sheriff 'and some other important occasions', the rank of colonel should be bestowed elsewhere.[2] The letter was brought, significantly enough, by a servant of Sir James Marvin, father-in-law of Thynne and deputy lieutenant of Wiltshire. Marvin himself supported Thynne's plea. None the less Marvin received a stinging rebuke.[3] 'I marvel', wrote Hertford to him on September 18th, 'that your years and gravity could not divert him from so peremptory and undutiful a resolution.' The colonelcy had indeed been offered in the first place at Marvin's suggestion to raise Thynne's prestige in the county and to prepare him for His Majesty's service. In return Thynne had publicly stated 'with many idle words', in the presence of the lord lieutenant and others, that he would not assume the colonelcy. Thynne was now ordered to appear as instructed: the fact that he was sheriff and the 'poverty which he alleged' were brushed aside. Any further refusal would provoke Hertford 'to lay open his said wilful, peremptory refusal', a thing he 'would be sorry so to do knowing he is not able to answer so high a contempt'. The threat at first appeared to work. Marvin replied that he had assumed that Hertford would appreciate the heavy duties which had fallen to Thynne. But in any case, without this recent prompting from the lord lieutenant, Marvin had succeeded in persuading his son-in-law 'to leave all his former accounts and business upon six and seven and to attend that service of colonel himself'.[4] It was an empty promise. When the time came Thynne took himself and his household off to London and left the lord lieutenant to his own devices.[5] Sir Francis

---

[1] Ibid., fols. 6b–7b.
[2] Ibid., fol. 13b.
[3] Ibid., fols. 36a and b. The letter is dated Sept. 18th and refers to another letter of Thynne's received a fortnight earlier.
[4] Ibid., fols. 37b–38a.
[5] Ibid., fol. 44a.

Englefield, Edward Long, and a Mr Moody, who were also absent, and had indeed for many years made a practice of being absent, were warned that any continued refusal to serve would lead to their being reported to the privy council for contempt.[1]

Meanwhile the county officials had been getting down to business. On August 10th the four deputy lieutenants with five justices of the peace had assembled at Devizes to divide up the county between them, each inspection to be made by two deputy lieutenants over a period of two days. First Sir Thomas Gorges and Sir James Marvin would 'take a view' at Hindon on September 23rd and 24th, and at the same time Sir Walter Long and Sir William Eyre would arrive at Devizes. Gorges and Marvin would then go to Salisbury on September 26th and 27th, while Long and Eyre would go to Chippenham. Finally Gorges and Marvin would appear at Marlborough on October 6th and 7th, while their colleagues would be at Trowbridge on the 10th and 11th of the same month. The justices of the various divisions were to appear with the muster books at the appointed places and one at least of the colonels and captains was to be present with his muster roll. So much for the 'trained men with their armour and furniture'. The justices of the peace were also to report any defects in the store of match and powder; and special arrangements had to be made in addition for the light horse and the lancers to be separately inspected. Preparations were also made to send precepts for the clergy 'to be viewed in every division and in the same manner as the other forces are appointed to be viewed'.[2]

But dealing with the clergy was not as easy as that. In Wiltshire, as in Northamptonshire,[3] they resisted attempts to put them on an equal footing with the laity. On August 6th the Bishop of Salisbury was asked by Hertford to provide a list of his clergy capable of bearing arms[4] and his reply, received on the 12th, expressed his willingness to have his clergy ready. He

[1] B.M., Add. MS. 5496, fol. 42a.
[2] Ibid., fols. 15a–16b.
[3] *The Montagu Musters Book*, ed. Joan Wake (Northants. Rec. Soc. vii), xxx–xxxii.
[4] B.M., Add. MS. 5496, fol. 14a.

pointed out, however, that it was normal to expect an instruction from the Archbishop of Canterbury to that effect, but, whether it came or not, 'according to your lordship's direction I will give them admonition to be provided at the days appointed'.[1] Across the border in Somerset, the Bishop of Bath and Wells showed himself less acquiescent. Hitherto the clergy had mustered before the bishop and he had therefore written to his archbishop for instructions. He assumed, he added with a broad hint, that the Earl of Hertford had no intention of innovation.[2] While, therefore, in Salisbury a list was being drawn up at the end of August and the bishop was being asked to appoint a captain for the horse troop of his clergy,[3] his brother bishop of Bath and Wells was still playing a waiting game. He was willing to allow the 'view' of the clergy to be taken (unless he received meanwhile contrary instructions from higher authority) but they were not to be 'charged', i.e. assessed for contribution, because that was not within the power of the commission.[4] The archbishop had meanwhile taken the matter up with the lord treasurer; and on this issue the bishop was victorious.[5] Hertford accepted the situation and issued appropriate instructions to his deputy lieutenants on September 14th.[6]

So the work of the muster went on through the summer and autumn and, at the end of October, the lord lieutenant began to take stock. As in the past there were serious defects laid bare, with no good prospects of immediate redress.[7]

The next three decades witnessed a worsening situation, hardly unexpected in the county of Ludlow, Strode and Long. In April 1613, Hertford was asking for time to bring the equipment up to the required levels, since the use of borrowed arms had prevented his recognizing the true situation earlier.[8] A month

[1] Ibid., fol. 17a.
[2] Ibid., fol. 18a.
[3] Ibid., fols. 21b–22a and 27a.
[4] Ibid., fol. 29a.
[5] Ibid., fols. 33a and b.
[6] Ibid., fol. 34b.
[7] e.g. ibid., fols. 43b, 44a and b.
[8] Cal. S.P. Dom. 1611–18, 180.

later the position seemed to be improving;[1] but in November of the following year many defects in the muster were recorded which were attributed, this time, to the weather.[2] However, in June 1620, near the end of his lieutenancy, he was able to record, for the moment, an improvement. The foot companies were complete, the horse nearly so. Sir Francis Englefield, however, was keeping up what had become for him a long-standing tradition of withholding his contribution.[3] He was not alone. In the directions for muster, issued in April 1618, Wiltshire, Bedfordshire and Somerset were singled out for special mention since 'citizens or other gentlemen as have seated themselves' there were claiming exemption through being rateable in London or elsewhere. No such exemption, the privy council stated, was valid.[4]

If the gentry proved increasingly reluctant to provide the arms, the money, and the men, the men themselves did not enter joyfully upon their commitments. In 1625 some of the troops sent from Wiltshire to Dover mutinied and ran away.[5] Others bribed their way out of military service, and no less a person than Sir Thomas Sadler, himself a justice, was involved. More men were pressed than were actually required; various sums of money were exacted with a good deal of buying and selling of poor men, and 'these abuses were much spoken of by the country'.[6] For this Sadler was brought before the council, imprisoned, ordered to repay the sums collected, and dismissed from the commission of the peace.[7] But even drastic action to meet a major scandal could not remedy the situation as a whole. In 1627 the Wiltshire levies were again short of their target.[8]

If the county musters met with obstruction, and service beyond the county brought in its train corruption and mutiny,

[1] *Cal. S.P. Dom.* 1611–18, 184.
[2] Ibid., 259.
[3] *Cal. S.P. Dom.* 1619–23, 157.
[4] *Acts of P.C.* 1618–19, 119.
[5] Ibid., 1623–5, 424, 446; see also *Cal. S.P. Dom.* 1623–5, 439–40.
[6] SP 14/185, no. 21.
[7] *Acts of P.C.* 1625–6, 78–9; see also *Cal. S.P. Dom.* 1625–6, 72–3.
[8] *Acts of P.C.* 1627, 304.

there were other unpopular tasks awaiting the high officials of the county: for example, the billeting of troops. In 1627 the lords lieutenant of Wiltshire and other counties were asked to arrange that troops coming from Devon and Cornwall should either be billeted or passed on, the billeting allowance being 3*s.* 6*d.* a week, the lodging and diet allowance for those passing through, 8*d.* a day. Twelve miles were to be reckoned as a day's march.[1] But when, at the beginning of 1628, a regiment from Hampshire appeared in Wiltshire, the deputy lieutenants wrote to Pembroke in alarm saying that for this regiment they had no direction from either the council or the earl. They asked for speedy instructions, especially as many of the local inhabitants were refusing to contribute towards the cost of billeting.[2] On another occasion, when in fact money could be collected, this time for a powder magazine, the difficulty lay in getting hold of the people into whose possession the money had passed.[3]

In the 1630s the deputy lieutenants continued to press on with the work of mustering the shire, with varying degrees of enthusiasm and success;[4] though it is worth recording that in 1634 a member of the Englefield family was at last brought to book, or at least before the council. He faithfully promised to give his share to the musters, but whether he kept his word, and, if so, for how long, we do not know.[5] If he continued to default he did so in good company, for, at the beginning of 1637, we find Henry Ludlow, Henry Thynne, Sir Thomas Hall and Walter Long reported for similar misdemeanours.[6] Walter Long, however, flatly denied the allegation, saying that he had had no request for his contribution.[7] And then, in 1640, came mutiny again. The lord lieutenant himself foresaw the danger and warned the council of many obstinate refusals of coat and conduct money. His deputy lieutenants could not conceive 'what mutinous

---

[1] *Cal. S.P. Dom.* 1627–8, 451.
[2] Ibid., 535; see also 580.
[3] Ibid., 1636–7, 291.
[4] e.g. ibid., 1635, 301–2.
[5] Ibid., 1634–5, 2.
[6] Ibid., 1636–7, 413.
[7] Ibid., 469.

courses these armed men may take not having wherewithal to sustain their present necessities'.[1] Some were committed to prison for refusing to contribute. Others, from amongst the trained bands, broke open the prison to enable them to escape. They, in turn, were brought before the sheriff and lord lieutenant for punishment.[2] For a moment this show of force restored order; but the rot had set in at all levels and three of the constables found themselves in prison for refusing to collect coat and conduct money.[3] Finally resistance spread to the lord lieutenant himself as the country slid into civil war.

II

The sounds of war and the preparation for war entered increasingly, as we have seen, into the public and private life of the county from the 1580s onwards. Yet even in times of acute danger it is not the lord lieutenant or his deputies who provide us with the fullest information about how the county went about its business. For that we must turn elsewhere: to the justices of the peace and their quarter sessions.

For administrative and judicial purposes the county fell into six main divisions, each of which tended to carry the name of the lord lieutenant, a deputy lieutenant, or some senior member of the county hierarchy. Thus, in 1592, for example, we find the six divisions named after the Earl of Pembroke, Sir James Marvin, Sir Thomas Wroughton, Sir John Danvers, Sir Edward Baynton, and Sir Walter Hungerford.[4] The names of the divisions changed, of course, with death, departure or for other reasons. In 1633 we find a reference to 'the division heretofore called the Earl of Pembroke's division but lately termed Salisbury division'.[5] In broad outline, during the late sixteenth century, Pembroke's (Salisbury division) covered the south-eastern part of the

---

[1] *Cal. S.P. Dom.* 1640, 203.

[2] Ibid., 281–2.

[3] Ibid., 309.

[4] *Sess. Mins.* 1563–92, 153.

[5] See e.g. *Sess. Mins.* 1563–92, viii–ix. For 'A charge to be given by [? to] a Justice of Peace in the Quarter Sessions, A.D. 1580', see *W.A.M.* xiv. 208–16.

county, Marvin's (Warminster division) the south-western, Wroughton's (Marlborough division) the north-eastern, Danvers's (Devizes division) the central part, Baynton's (Chippenham division) the north-western, and Hungerford's (Westbury division) the west.[1]

We have seen that the shire marshalled itself in 1608 along the main divisional lines, while the quarter sessions records supply frequent examples of justices of the peace having devolved upon them duties to be performed 'within their divisions', with or without their having to refer the matter back to the sessions. But it was not intended that these internal divisions should provide hard and impenetrable boundaries. When directions were sent to the sheriff and justices of the peace of Wiltshire in 1637 about arrangements for collecting contributions towards the rebuilding of St Paul's, this was pointed out.

> Whereas by a letter sent to you in July last touching contributions ... we directed you to sort yourselves into your accustomed divisions ... for the performance of that service ... We by the same did intend only ... your more ease, but not to restrain you in any sort from setting about that work in any other division or place in the said county and ... shall take it very well from any of you who, out of his affection for so pious a work, shall take pain and employ his endeavour in all or any other of the divisions.[2]

It is clear, however, that for many purposes the division was more significant than the shire.

The meeting-places for the sessions did not become fixed during our period, but from the last decades of the sixteenth century they tended to follow a fairly regular course: Salisbury for the Hilary sessions, Warminster at Easter, Devizes at Midsummer, and Marlborough at Michaelmas. But this routine was

---

[1] This is based on the hundreds allotted by R. W. Merriman to the 6 divisions 'Extracts from the records of Wiltshire quarter sessions', *W.A.M.* xxi. 83.

[2] SP 16/368, no. 46.

far from binding and, for example, between 1575 and 1587, it was very considerably modified. Other towns which were used for these meetings were Calne, Chippenham, Hindon and Trowbridge.[1] The duration of the sessions was restricted by statute to a maximum of three days. For the Tudor period it is not possible to establish the exact duration of each meeting; under the early Stuarts the sessions lasted one or two days and only occasionally three.

We may divide the personnel of the commission of the peace into four main groups. First in seniority were eminent men in the state.[2] For example, the commission of 1562 included Sir Nicholas Bacon, the lord keeper, the Marquess of Winchester, the lord treasurer, and the Earl of Arundel, the lord steward of the household. Similarly, the commission of 1600 included Sir Thomas Egerton, the lord keeper, and Lord Buckhurst, the lord treasurer. That for 1638 was headed by Lord Coventry, the lord keeper, Bishop Juxon, the lord treasurer, and the Earl of Manchester, the privy seal. The Commonwealth commission of 1657 was led by the commissioners of the great seal and the commissioners of the treasury. But these distinguished names normally appeared on the commissions for each county. So far as Wiltshire was concerned they were honorary members and played no active part in its quarter sessions.

Next in seniority were the judges who came on circuit twice a year to hold the assizes, where they would deal with complex, and sometimes more serious, issues and in the process instruct their brother justices of the peace, resident in the county, in the arts of judicial procedure. In 1562 we find on the commission Mr Justice Weston and Richard Harpur, a serjeant-at-law.[3] In 1600 there were four judges, led by Lord Chief Justice Popham,

---

[1] *W.A.M.* xx. 324.

[2] In the following paragraphs, references to the commission of the peace are taken, unless otherwise stated, from: *Cal. Pat.* 1560–3, 443 (for 1562); C 66/1523 (1600); SP 16/405 (1638); C 193/13 (1657).

[3] He became a judge of the common pleas in 1567: E. Foss, *The Judges of England* (1848–64), v., p. 497.

a Wiltshire man. In 1638 we find Chief Justice Finch and a baron of the exchequer. In 1657 there were as many as nine judges on the commission.

Then come the men of rank and distinction in the shire, for example the Earls of Pembroke and Hertford, with whom may be coupled the Bishop of Salisbury; while lower down on the commission we find his diocesan chancellor. There was lastly the main body of the justices, knights, esquires and gentlemen, bearing the familiar names of the leading county families: the Thynnes, Hungerfords, Penruddocks, Danverses, Estcourts, and Ludlows. Forming a kind of inner core of the commission were men senior to the others in status or legal training who were described as 'of the quorum' and, for certain purposes, one or more of them had to be present; but the distinction between them and the rest wore thin and most of the justices were so designated.

The size of the commission of the peace showed, during this period, a marked increase. In 1562 it had a membership of thirty, of whom three were 'honorary' members, one a justice of assize, and one a serjeant-at-law. These five came from outside the shire. The rest consisted of one earl, two barons and twenty-two country gentlemen. By 1600 the total number on the commission had risen to fifty-two of whom two were honorary and four were judges, while the 'local' membership comprised two earls, five barons, thirty-seven country gentlemen, the Bishop of Salisbury and his chancellor. In 1638 the number had risen only slightly, to fifty-five, but there were now five honorary members on the commission and two judges, while the basic structure of the commission remained unchanged. Less than twenty years later, however, in 1657, the total membership had reached seventy-nine; but of these six were honorary, seven were judges and one the attorney-general. If these figures are examined in terms of local members only, omitting the names of the judges and of those who appear in every commission for that year, it emerges that local membership rose from twenty-five in 1562 to forty-six in 1600, to two more than this in 1638, but to as high as sixty-five in the last years of the Protectorate. Even with the intermittent purges of the commission during the period, the numbers continued to rise.

The most senior of the justices, sometimes the lord lieutenant, was appointed *custos rotulorum*. But this was not invariably the case. In 1562, though the Earl of Pembroke was lord lieutenant, Sir John Thynne was *custos*. In 1600, on the other hand, the 2nd earl was both lord lieutenant and *custos*; and in the early seventeenth century the Earl of Hertford likewise combined both offices. Towards the end of Hertford's long life, however, Sir Francis Seymour became *custos*. Similarly, between 1621 and 1640 when the 3rd and 4th Earls of Pembroke were lords lieutenant they were not at the same time *custodes*. Under the Protectorate, the 5th earl was *custos* but he gave place to Francis, Lord Seymour, at the Restoration.[1] Clearly, in Wiltshire as elsewhere, the lord lieutenant had no prescriptive right to be custodian of its quarter sessions records.

These records owed more to the clerks of the peace than to the *custodes rotulorum*, especially as some clerks had long periods of office.[2] Christopher Dysmers, the last to be appointed by royal letters patent before the granting of the office reverted to the *custos*, was clerk for thirty years, from 1537 to 1567, to be followed by the thirteen-year tenure of Walter Berington; under the early Stuarts John Kent was clerk for a quarter of a century to be followed by John Frampton who was in office for twenty years. These were no honorific appointments; and the sessions records, especially for the seventeenth century, show a marked widening of the clerk's responsibilities. Not only the purely administrative tasks, such as the issue of quarter sessions writs and the recording of its business, came his way, but executive and legal duties out of sessions. It was he, for example, who had to handle the wearisome and drawn-out investigation

---

[1] With the exception of the year 1562, for which *Cal. Pat.* has been used, the information about the *custos* has been taken from the surviving Q. Sess. writs at the Wilts. Record Office, Trowbridge (W.R.O.). I am indebted to Mr J. P. M. Fowle for the reference.

[2] For Wilts. clerks of the peace in the sixteenth century see *Sess. Mins.* 1563–92, xviii–xx. The names of the clerks in the seventeenth century I owe to Mr J. P. M. Fowle.

to discover who was responsible for the upkeep of Harnham bridge at Salisbury.[1] Then he had to start litigation on behalf of the county. It was he who had to prepare the county's defence when it was 'indicted' at the assizes for the neglect of another bridge. It was he who handled the money brought in by the treasurers of the north and south parts of the county. Not surprisingly, he had to devolve some of his work upon others. By the 1640s there were two deputy clerks, Francis Bennet and William Coles, of whom the latter subsequently succeeded Frampton as clerk in 1646.

How many of the justices were active in quarter sessions? There are two main sources for this information: the pipe-rolls on which the sheriff claimed allowances for what he had paid in wages to the justices, and the list of attendances recorded by the clerk in his minute and order books. Both sources are, however, defective.

Justices below the rank of 'banneret' were entitled to wages of 4s. a day and this, by means of the pipe-rolls, may provide a clue as to their attendance. But for a number of reasons the evidence is not easy to interpret. In the first place, men on the upper rungs of the commission received no wages and therefore are absent from the list. Apart from this, in Wiltshire as in other counties,[2] the money was not paid to individuals but kept as a special fund for their entertainment. This, however, gave rise to difficulties of its own. 'Whereas the usual and ancient custom within this county' (declares the sessions minute book in 1630[3]) 'hath been heretofore that the clerk of the peace was steward and did provide for all the justices' dinners the first day of every sessions in lieu of wages allowed them by his Majesty, in which respect the said clerk of the peace received the benefit of all such allowance as he could procure for the said justices' diet ...' Now, the

---

[1] See below, pp. 286-7.

[2] S. and B. Webb, *English Local Government* (1906-29), i, p. 423 n. 1.

[3] Q. Sess. Minute Bk. 1626-31, Trin.: 6 Chas. I. (Further references to the unprinted minute books and order books in the W.R.O. will be given as 'Min. Bk.' and 'Ord. Bk.', the years covered and the law term under which the entry appears.)

justices felt, the arrangement had shown itself to be unsatisfactory, though the clerk had apparently continued to pay the usual rate for the meal. 'Yet the remissness or covetousness of the innkeeper where the said diet was provided this present sessions in not providing what was meet gave not that satisfaction to the justices there assembled as was requisite.' As a result, the justices with one voice agreed to abandon the long-standing arrangement of having meals in lieu of wages and henceforth 'would expect their wages due to them according to the law!'. What the Devizes innkeeper had served on that July day in 1630 we cannot speculate; but it was clearly not to the taste of His Majesty's justices of the peace.

But whether the justices claimed dinners or cash, how accurate are the lists on the pipe-rolls? The evidence of the Warwickshire county records shows that there are at least discrepancies between attendances warranted by the pipe-rolls and information obtained elsewhere.[1] For Wiltshire also, during this period, there is an interesting change in the statistics provided by the sheriff.[2] At the beginning of the seventeenth century there is a notable variation in the number of days attended by individual justices. One, Edward Hungerford, is credited with nine days, two others with eight, one with seven, and one with six, four with five days, one with four, three with three and four with two days. John Kent, the clerk, is recorded as having attended on nine days. In 1639, on the other hand, all the justices are credited with three days, or multiples of three, and John Frampton, their clerk, with twelve days. In other words, as the editors of the Warwickshire county records have suggested, it looks as though attendance at the first day of quarter sessions brought an allowance for the full three days.[3] Then in 1658 the pipe-roll credits the twelve Wiltshire justices it lists with the unlikely record of attendance for the full twelve days. The other evidence flatly contradicts this. The quarter sessions order book

[1] *Warwick County Records*, ed. S. C. Ratcliff and H. C. Johnson, ii, p. xxii; iii, p. xx.

[2] For this and the next paragraph the following pipe-rolls have been used: E 372/446 (for 1601); E 372/484 (for 1639); E 372/502 (for 1658).

[3] *Warwick County Records*, vii, pp. xxxix–xl.

shows that of the twelve justices recorded on the pipe-rolls as having attended twelve days, in fact none of them attended all four quarter sessions, five of them attended three of the sessions, one attended two, three attended one of the sessions and three of them did not appear at any of the quarter sessions. By contrast, the order book records no less than sixteen other justices who attended one or more quarter sessions but who – if the pipe-rolls are to be trusted – received no reward whatsoever for their pains.

What is the explanation of this? Apparently what mattered to the justices was not how much each of them was entitled to receive but what was the total sum involved. Whether they resumed the practice of using the money for their dinners or devoted it to some other purpose, it is reasonable to assume that it remained a corporate fund. In that case there was no need to record the exact number of attendances for each individual; the clerk and the sheriff between them might agree upon a reasonable sum to claim and attach to it their list of justices. Later, in Charles II's reign, this practice appears to have been in part abandoned, but the sheriff did not revert to the original method of recording the exact numbers of days attended. He stopped at the half-way house: all the attendance figures are given in multiples of three.

Apart from the pipe-rolls we have information about the justices' attendance in the clerk's minute and order books, now preserved in the County Record Office at Trowbridge. But here too we cannot always discover the exact number of attendances because the clerk was content in some cases to name only some of the justices of the peace and complete his list with the expression 'and others'. Fortunately he did not invariably do this, and where the list seems to be a complete one we have some useful statistics at our disposal. If we take the last quarter of the sixteenth century we find very considerable fluctuations. A fairly common attendance was from eight to eleven but there were cases where it fell far below this. For example, at the St Thomas's sessions held at Devizes in July 1576, there were no more than three justices present,[1] and at the Michaelmas sessions

[1] *Sess. Mins.* 1563–92, 21.

held some fifteen months later in the same town, the attendance came down to two (if the clerk's record is accurate).[1] At the Michaelmas sessions two years later, held this time at Chippenham, again only two justices appeared.[2] There were two also at a special sessions called in August 1584, but in view of its character, and the very small amount of work it appears to have done, this is not surprising.[3] The same applies to the special sessions of October 1586.[4] In other words, these meetings look not like the ordinary quarter sessions but either adjournments or the petty sessions now in process of development. By contrast, the preceding Easter sessions at Warminster saw an attendance of sixteen.[5] The attendance varied a good deal not only in numbers but in membership. Some names appear frequently on the list: for example, Danvers, Hungerford and Penruddock. On the other hand, William, the 3rd Earl of Pembroke, came only three times.[6] Other distinguished names also appear on the records, including the Earl of Hertford, Lord Audley and Lord Stourton, but they too were infrequent attenders.

In the seventeenth century we also notice considerable fluctuations.[7] At the Trinity sessions of 1610 there were six justices present while at the Michaelmas sessions which followed there were fifteen. At the Easter sessions of 1620 there were as many as twenty-nine. At the Trinity sessions of 1644 the attendance fell to two, after which sessions meetings fell into abeyance for two years. Under the Commonwealth and Protectorate the numbers continued to fluctuate. At the Easter sessions of 1660, the last sessions before the Restoration, only three justices appeared; at the Michaelmas sessions of 1660, the first after the Restoration, eighteen attended.

An examination of the clerk's lists shows also that justices did

[1] *Sess. Mins.* 1563–92, 31.
[2] Ibid., 54.
[3] Ibid., 98.
[4] Ibid., 114.
[5] Ibid., 110.
[6] Ibid., 17, 33, 45.
[7] The information in this paragraph is obtained from the sessions minute and order bks. at the W.R.O.

not restrict their attendance to the towns nearest their homes. It is true that a good many attended only one out of the four sessions in the year, but others attended two and a few attended three. It is clear also that, in some years at least, half the members of the commission did not appear at quarter sessions at all.

III

As the sixteenth century wore on the meetings at quarter sessions became more and more the clearing-house for the criminal and civil affairs of the county. Many matters were settled in court, others were sent down to be dealt with by one or more justices in their division, while some matters, administrative and judicial, had to await the judgment of the assizes. This happened, for example, in Hilary term 1642, when, as the order book records, 'because it is a case of difficulty this Court doth order that the Judges of Assizes shall be attended with the plea at the next assizes'.[1] In civil affairs quarter sessions had to deal with licences to victuallers and badgers, the maintenance of highways, bridges, and houses of correction, the apprenticing of paupers, the control of markets, local taxation, recusancy, and anything else which came their way. In the seventeenth century the government taxed still further the energies and pockets of the local justices until the whole system very nearly collapsed during the Civil War. Before examining the nature and effects of that collapse, it is necessary to look a little more closely, first at the judicial, then at the economic and social, responsibilities which were steadily accruing to the sometimes unpaid, and often involuntary, instruments of the Crown.

The treatment of criminal matters by the justices in quarter sessions represents neither the most important nor, from our point of view, the most interesting part of their work. In theory their writ ran widely and their powers were extensive, in practice we find a certain monotony in their proceedings, rendered the more so where we have long lists of penalties with no indication

[1] Three assizes order bks. for the Western Circuit (Assizes 24/20, 21, and 22) are extant for this period, from 1629.

of the crimes which gave rise to them. Where we are told of the offence, we find through the years a long procession of whippings for the parents of bastard children, brandings for vagrants, occasionally punishments for trespass or poaching.[1] We have also the usual undertakings to keep the peace. Once, in 1635, the zealous Bench sent a child aged ten or eleven to the Bridewell to await His Majesty's pleasure, for uttering lewd words against the king.[2] Occasionally the proceedings were enlivened by an indictment for unlawful games as when three men, from as far afield as London and Oxfordshire, were indicted before the Wiltshire quarter sessions for playing 'unlawful and cosening games', in this case 'trolemadame and ryffling for dishes and platters'.[3] One, George Copplestone, in 1584, added assault to his gaming and was fined 5s. for the one and 6s. 8d. for the other, the court apparently taking a more serious view of his gaming.[4] We have also, on another occasion, 'a misguided reveller who forgot himself to the extent of unlawfully tippling before he unlawfully bowled [and] was condemned to forfeit xii*d*. for each of these forbidden pleasures'.[5] Once, in 1587, what appears to be a complete bowling team was fined for their game. But they got off lightly — 2s. for the whole team. And it looks as though one of the justices paid the fine.[6]

In the main it was a rough justice which was meted out at quarter sessions and an even rougher justice here and there, unadorned with the full majesty of the law: hence, perhaps, the frequent allegations against J.P.s in the Star Chamber. Thus, Sir Anthony Hungerford, J.P., was accused by a churchwarden in the Star Chamber, in the fifth year of Edward VI, of showing favour in his official duties. One John Boller had, it was alleged, forcibly resisted the churchwardens of Highworth, who were

---

[1] On one occasion, in 1578, the privy council sent special directions to the J.P.s of Wilts. to take action 'against the unlawful takers of partridges and pheasants': *Acts of P.C.* 1577–8, 330.

[2] *Cal. S.P. Dom.* 1634–5, 562–3.

[3] *Sess. Mins.* 1563–92, 70.

[4] Ibid., 97.

[5] *W.A.M.* xx. 332.

[6] *Sess. Mins.* 1563–92, 119.

taking down the altar on instructions from the privy council. Hungerford, according to the accusation, had not only displayed partiality to Boller but had generally thwarted justice by allowing personal friendship to intervene in various cases of felony. In reply, Hungerford flatly denied the allegations and, in the absence of the Star Chamber decrees, we cannot know the upshot. What we do know, however, is that someone wrote on the back of the churchwarden's petition (though it was subsequently crossed out): 'Matter for the King's Majesty. Worthy to commit the said Sir Anthony and Mr. Boller at least to the Fleet.'[1] In 1614, Sir Henry Moody, J.P., was alleging in the Star Chamber that certain justices had achieved their ends by holding a private sessions at Malmesbury.[2] A similar allegation, however, was to be made against him in 1621 in that he 'most unlawfully and corruptly keepeth a session in his own chamber, and there at his will and pleasure dischargeth offenders and vexeth innocent persons, who are compelled to attend him there to their intolerable vexation'.[3] It may well be, however, that the affairs were not as heinous as they sound and we may be catching in them the intermittent glimpses of the petty sessions.

Inevitably much work had to be devolved upon individual J.P.s, or groups of two or three; and the rise of petty sessions (divisional meetings of justices held between the quarterly assemblies) contributed towards this essential devolution. Unfortunately we have only the scantiest references to these meetings in stray records and it is not easy to tell at which stage these 'private' meetings of J.P.s, sometimes held by direction of quarter sessions to report on or settle matters, took on the more formal character of petty sessions. The practice of holding them was perhaps fairly widespread and in Calne they may go back to as early as 1565.[4] Whether such proceedings were formal or

[1] Sta. Cha. 3/5/77.
[2] Sta. Cha. 8/218/5.
[3] Sta. Cha. 8/184/19.
[4] 'For the justices dinner at Mr Fynamor's, 2s.': *Guild Stewards' Bk. of Borough of Calne, 1561–1688* (W.A.S. Rec. Brch. vii), 8. The first reference that has been traced to a Wilts. petty sessional meeting in a minute bk. is for the year 1580: *Sess. Mins. 1563–92*, 58.

informal, it is clear that they gave rise to opportunities for favouritism, bullying and corruption. But they equally provided opportunities for such accusations; and we must not assume that the lengthy and circumstantial allegations in the Star Chamber had necessarily any basis in fact.

There were also plenty of complaints about illegal detention, which sometimes meant no more than arrests by J.P.s. It was not always easy to draw the fine distinction between what a man did in his private capacity and what he did as an official.[1] Giles Estcourt, J.P., was accused of having 'dealt very indirectly' in a certain case, but the attorney-general and the solicitor-general, to whom the privy council submitted the matter, found him to have been 'very unjustly charged'. The council therefore entirely cleared Estcourt but recorded that they found in the whole matter 'such indirect dealing and working that they think it very necessary to have the same more deeply looked unto'.[2] On another occasion the attorney-general took action in the Star Chamber against the false accusers of a justice of the peace.[3]

We cannot leave criminal matters without referring briefly to the county gaol at Fisherton Anger, in Salisbury. It was the only gaol in the county, and early in Elizabeth's reign had apparently fallen into decay. For a time, in 1568, East Harnham, not far from the palace of the Bishop of Salisbury, was proposed as an alternative site, but, on protest from the bishop, this was abandoned. Instead, either a new site was bought at Fisherton, or else the old gaol was enlarged, for which a county rate was levied. The work was not completed until 1578.[4] In 1642, if not earlier, it was again in need of repair and, on petition from its keeper, John Freeland, the justices of assize ordered the county to do the necessary work, under penalty of a £40 fine.[5] At the next meeting of the assizes, however, the county showed that the statutory responsibility lay with the sheriff,[6] and their plea was

[1] e.g. Sta. Cha. 8/140/2.
[2] *Acts of P.C.* 1586–7, 385–7.
[3] Sta. Cha. 7/1/21.
[4] J. E. Jackson, 'Wilts. County Gaols', *W.A.M.* ix. 82–7.
[5] Assizes 24/21, 2 Mar., 17 Chas. I.
[6] 23 Hen. VIII, c.2.

accepted.[1] In 1649, however, the gaol was still in great decay,[2] which may explain why a number of prisoners had been able to break out during the previous year.[3]

In 1646, during the Civil War, prisoners could not be sent to Fisherton and were committed to the garrison at Malmesbury; a special order had to be made at quarter sessions to reimburse the marshals.[4] The money in this case was to be provided by the treasurer for the King's Bench and Marshalsea, who was at least partly responsible for providing funds for the upkeep of the gaol. He worked, apparently, through the 'collectors for the relief of poor prisoners'.[5] One such collector, William Groome, was involved in a scandal. He combined the office of collector with that of baker for the gaol, in which office he was guilty of various abuses. As a result, the justices deprived him of his monopoly of selling bread to the gaol and decreed that he should henceforth supply it only on alternate weeks. When, however, he pointed out that, as honorary collector, he had over the past twenty-four years saved the county about £100, 'there being formerly given for the collecting of the same money four pounds every year', his monopoly was restored.[6] The sheriff was, as hitherto, in charge of the gaol, but the day-to-day responsibility had obviously passed from the sheriff to the gaoler.

IV

From criminal affairs we turn to the variegated duties of the justice of the peace as a civil officer. The most familiar to us of these is the maintenance of what we may perhaps call, in their crude beginnings, the social services: poor relief, pensions and germane matters. Then a word must be said about their control of trade, especially the food trade, and their general supervision of ale-houses. Finally we must look at fiscal matters, at both local

[1] Assizes 24/21, 1 July, 18 Chas. I.
[2] Ibid., 1 Mar. 1648[9].
[3] Ibid., 31 Aug., 24 Chas. I.
[4] Ord. Bk. 1641–54, Mich. 22 Chas. I.
[5] e.g. Min. Bk. 1610–16, Mich. 8 Jas. I.
[6] Ord. Bk. 1654–68, Hil. 1657 and Hil. 1658.

taxation and the part the J.P.s played, with varying degrees of reluctance, in collecting taxes on behalf of the Crown.

The alleviation of poverty and unemployment seems to have been their greatest preoccupation. It is well known that, after many decades of experiment, the Tudors hammered out a poor-law policy which in broad outline survived for centuries. That policy, as it finally took shape in the closing years of Elizabeth I's reign, and was enshrined in the famous statutes of 1598,[1] divided the indigent into four main categories: pauper children, the aged and infirm, the unemployed, and finally the vagrants or sturdy beggars, that is, those who, it was assumed, did not work because they would not work. It is possible to see the implementation of this policy in the Wiltshire sessions records of the period.

Fear of social disorder, which lay at the roots of so much of the social policy of the time, was reflected in the attitude of the Wiltshire officials to young and old alike. Social policy then, as now, began with the cradle; and we find a good deal of the justices' time taken up in the effort to pin the responsibility for bastard children upon their begetters. Whipping of the parents, which was frequently resorted to, could not, of course, provide the funds for maintaining the child, though it was hoped, no doubt, that exemplary punishment might reduce the incidence of illegitimacy in the future. The next stage was the more practical one of issuing an affiliation order against the father. The matter was frequently remitted to two or more justices who, on one occasion, imposed a maintenance charge upon the father but omitted to inflict the appropriate punishment for the offence. Accordingly, at a later meeting of the full sessions, the sentence was modified to include whipping; and, as an instruction to the justices and a warning to the county, it was laid down: 'This order to continue against all such as shall offend as abovesaid.'[2] The amount imposed by a maintenance order varied from 4*d.* to 8*d.* a week in the Elizabethan period. In one order the justices imposed a charge of 6*d.* a week against a clerk but added that if 'the lord of Hertford and Sir Thomas Wroughton like not of this

[1] 39 Eliz. cc. 3 and 4.
[2] *Sess. Mins.* 1563–92, 36–7.

order, then to pay 8*d*.'.[1] On the other hand, in 1620, an affiliation order for 10*d*. a week was reduced to 6*d*.[2] On one occasion, when the father failed to make the necessary payment, the man who had stood surety for him was bound over to pay on his behalf 'until he bring the said William Neat in place to do the same'.[3] Disobedience to a maintenance order brought imprisonment to the defaulter.

A maintenance order was normally made to last until the child was twelve in Elizabeth's reign, but this changed to seven during the next century. Sometimes the money was to be paid to the mother, sometimes to the churchwardens of the parish, presumably when the child was not in its mother's care. But what was to happen to him after the age of twelve, or indeed to pauper children whatever their age? To this the answer was apprenticeship; and one of the functions of the justices was to persuade local employers to make use of this uncalled-for supply of labour. Thus John Williams was left at the age of eight 'by some unknown beggar' in Bradford. He was accordingly apprenticed to Robert Brouncker, a weaver of Broughton Gifford, to serve until the age of twenty-two.[4] In this way the justices hoped at one and the same time to reduce the potential supply of idle beggars and to shift the financial burden of maintaining paupers off the rates. They did not, however, renounce all responsibility. The justices in quarter sessions exercised their statutory authority, where a master ill-treated his apprentice, to intervene and cancel the indenture.[5]

Fear played an even larger role in the approach to the vagrant or 'sturdy beggar'; and the record of whipping, branding and imprisonment in the sessions minutes reflects the widespread alarm engendered by vagrancy in Tudor and Stuart England. But in this, as in so much else, punishment alone was clearly not enough. So the justices pinned their faith to 'settlement', that is

[1] Ibid., 57.
[2] Min. Bk. 1616–20, Hil. 17 Jas. I.
[3] *Sess. Mins.* 1563–92, 129.
[4] Ibid., 52. He was apparently apprenticed by the 'parishioners' but the record indicates that they were acting under direction of a J.P.
[5] Ibid., 132.

the eviction of paupers, or those liable to become destitute, to the place of their birth or settlement. Secondly, where eviction was not possible, they sought their remedy in 'houses of correction'. The earliest settlement law dates from the late fourteenth century,[1] and the sessions records of our period show us the system fully at work. Sometimes it worked ruthlessly, as is instanced by the laconic note entered by the clerk in 1582: 'Memorandum, the woman Elner Clerke is to remain in the sheriff's custody and the child to be carried from tithing to tithing until it come to the place where it was born, videlicet at Melkesham.'[2] For the same reason a close watch was kept on those who took in boarders, and the justices, if they wished, could direct that boarders be evicted or the cottage pulled down.[3] In 1630 two pregnant women were ordered by the justices to be moved from the place where they were lodging as they were liable to become chargeable to the parish.[4] Sometimes ruthlessness was tempered with humanity. Thomas Revell came from Bromham to make his home with his bride in the neighbouring parish of Melksham. But the inhabitants feared that Revell and his wife might one day become a burden on the rates and, after some eight weeks, persuaded the local justices to order them to return to the place of Revell's origin. But the justices in quarter sessions were in better humour. On petition from the inhabitants of Bromham, they reversed the eviction order and left the couple to enjoy what peace their neighbours would allow them at Melksham.[5]

Where eviction was impracticable, the unemployed had to be found work either by private indenture[6] or in a house of correction. The Act authorizing counties to raise money for such institutions was passed in 1576;[7] and at the Midsummer sessions of 1578 it was decided to levy 4*d*. in the pound upon the

[1] 12 Rich. II, c.7; see *Warwick County Records*, i, p. ix.
[2] *Sess. Mins.* 1563–92, 74.
[3] Min. Bk. 1610–16, Trin. 8 Jas. I.
[4] Ibid., 1626–31, Hil. 5 Chas. I.
[5] Ibid., 1616–21, East. 18 Jas. I.
[6] *Sess. Mins.* 1563–92, 68.
[7] 18 Eliz. c.3.

inhabitants of Wiltshire for the establishment of a house of correction.[1] Later in the year the J.P.s were petitioning the Crown for 'a piece of the castle of the Devizes where the said house is thought fittest to be'.[2] Perhaps they had heard of the petition made years before by the citizens of London to Edward VI which had won them his palace of Bridewell as a house of correction. But where London succeeded Wiltshire failed, and other premises in Devizes had to be obtained.[3] In the new year we find two officials charged with the detailed administration of the house, under the general direction of a committee of the justices.[4] By the end of the century the experiment of a house of correction seems to have justified itself. In September 1600 it was decided at quarter sessions that further houses should be established in each hundred of the county; and in October two places, Urchfont and Great Bedwyn, were selected for the purpose. By now also the administration was taking shape and it was decided that a 'corrector' be appointed for each at a yearly stipend of 30s. at Devizes and 20s. at the other two.[5] It is most doubtful whether the project, apart from Devizes, came to anything. Long afterwards, in 1623, we find the Earl of Pembroke seeking the support of the privy council to induce the justices of the southern part of Wiltshire to build a house of correction, since they had none nearer than Devizes in a county 'now oppressed with the numbers and insolences of vagabond and licentious multitudes'.[6] In 1631, the J.P.s, under pressure from the justices of assize, decided to build three houses of correction, this time at Fisherton Anger, Malmesbury, and Marlborough, and to raise £1,200 for the purpose.[7] But meanwhile catastrophe had descended upon the one at Devizes. Its master had employed the

---

[1] *Sess. Mins.* 1563–92, 42.

[2] Ibid., 45.

[3] In 1606 we read of a 'house and tenement ... commonly called Bridewell ... long since purchased in fee simple'. It was even hoped to make it a repository not only of vagabonds but of the county records: *W.A.M.* xxii. 3.

[4] *Sess. Mins.* 1563–92, 47. The two officials seem to have been appointed on an annual basis: we find their office renewed for a further year in 1580: ibid., 59.

[5] *W.A.M.* xxi. 83–4.

[6] SP 14/145, no. 3.

[7] Min. Bk. 1626–31, Trin. 6 Chas. I. See also Hist. MSS. Com. *Var. Coll.* i. 98.

premises not only as a house of correction but as an 'east' or 'kilne' for drying malt, which was perhaps the stock for setting the unemployed to work. The result was a disastrous fire which took place in 1630;[1] and the justices were now faced with the task not only of searching for money for three new houses but of somehow getting money to rebuild the old one. The records of the decade show the justices wrestling with these ambitious schemes. Houses of correction were indeed established at Marlborough and Fisherton but, before the end of our period, both were in need of repair.[2] In the case of the house at Fisherton, there was apparently some confusion of function between it and the gaol; it is probable that they were adjacent to one another, or they may even have shared a common building.[3]

But not all paupers could be moved either out of the district or into a house of correction. There remained the aged, the infirm, the maimed soldiers and sailors, and the victims of unemployment, fire and plague, all with an urgent call upon the county rates. For the aged and infirm there were 'poorhouses'; while 'guiders', as they were called, were sometimes authorized to collect charitable contributions within the shire, and indeed in neighbouring shires.[4] For maimed soldiers, for whom an Act of 1593 ordered that pensions should be provided,[5] the J.P.s in quarter sessions allocated funds. The claimant had to produce a certificate from some responsible military official as evidence of his service, yet even so he was liable to lose his pension subsequently if the justices were satisfied that he was guilty of some abuse.[6] But on one occasion, in 1597, when the justices refused relief to a wounded veteran, they received instructions direct from the privy council either to grant a pension or explain their refusal.[7] For the victims of fire there were grants from quarter sessions of

---

[1] Min. Bk. 1626–31, Trin. 6 Chas. I. See also *Calne Guild Stewards' Bk.* (W.A.S. Rec. Brch.), 41.
[2] Ord. Bk. 1641–54, Hil. 1650; ibid., 1654–68, Hil. 1657.
[3] Ibid., Hil. 1660.
[4] *Cal. S.P. Dom.* 1591–4, 128.
[5] 35 Eliz. c.4.
[6] *W.A.M.* xxi. 77.
[7] *Acts of P.C.* 1597, 147.

sums of money, never very large, for their rehabilitation. For plague there was isolation of the infected area and the organization of contributions from the surrounding districts.

All these measures of social relief involved expenditure. The country was thus faced with a growing burden of taxation and the justices with the intractable problem of building an efficient system for obtaining and distributing the funds. Voluntary relief was an essential part of the scheme. For example, justices in quarter sessions frequently gave authority to organize a collection on behalf of an area distressed by fire. It was also possible, by authority of quarter sessions, to transfer the cost of maintaining an aged father from the parish to his son.[1] The full extent of private charity, whether in the shape of almshouses, gifts to individuals, bequests, or contributions to voluntary collections, is naturally impossible to assess. But clearly it was not enough; and, from the middle of the Tudor period, the county authorities everywhere, under pressure from the state, had been bound to meet part of the increasing cost of the social services out of some compulsory system of collection. Since 1536 parishes had been obliged to grant relief to the poor[2] and since 1563 magistrates were empowered to demand weekly contributions for the purpose.[3] In 1572 came the full measure of statutory compulsion: and the method of assessment by the justices of the peace was established.[4] The Act of 1598 codified existing regulations and vested considerable powers in the overseers (the churchwardens and two substantial householders), under the supervision of the justices.[5]

The whole of the social service was not maintained out of one county rate administered by one county official; the rise of a local government service and of a uniform system of accounting belong to a later age. For the present, as the county assumed new responsibilities, so it appointed officials ad hoc. An Act of 1552

[1] Min. Bk. 1610–16, Hil. 7 Jas. I.
[2] 27 Hen. VIII, c.25.
[3] 5 Eliz. c.3.
[4] 14 Eliz. c.5.
[5] 39 Eliz. c.3.

had established that there should be two or more collectors and distributors of alms, elected annually for each town or parish.[1] In 1572 we find further legislation about 'overseers' of the poor, to be appointed annually by the justices in quarter sessions.[2] The Wiltshire records of the period provide plenty of evidence of the poor law officials in action and of fines imposed upon those who would not accept office or pay their share.[3] In 1577 we have also what appear to be the beginnings of the allocation of special sums for poor prisoners in the common gaol, 'this money to be taken out of the church box or collection for the poor'. But there was an attempt to spread the burden so that it did not fall too heavily on those parishes least able to bear it: 'the churchwardens in every great parish to gather ii*d.* by the week, and in every meaner parish 1*d.* by the week.'[4] In 1593, when the care of maimed servicemen was added to the local responsibilities, special treasurers, with power to levy a rate, were joined to the unpaid bureaucracy of the county.[5] In Wiltshire there were two, one for the north and one for the south of the county. In 1597 the relief of prisoners in the gaol and the maintenance of the paupers in almshouses and hospitals were by statute made the responsibility of a separate treasurer;[6] and for this purpose also Wiltshire appointed one for the north and one for the south. Even before such legislation, however, the county had been organizing collections of this sort by authority of quarter sessions,[7] and the subsidy book was sometimes laid down as the basis of assessment.[8]

From now onwards the treasurers handled a good deal, but by no means all, of the county rates. The treasurers for maimed servicemen seem to have been restricted to this function, but the

[1] 5 and 6 Edw. VI, c.2.
[2] 14 Eliz. c.5.
[3] e.g. *Sess. Mins.* 1563–92, 64, 67, 69.
[4] Ibid., 29.
[5] 35 Eliz. c.4.
[6] 39 Eliz. c.3.
[7] *Sess. Mins.* 1563–92, 35, 42, 120, 153.
[8] Ibid., 42. For dispute as to whether Maiden Bradley lay wholly in Wilts. or was partly in Som., see Min. Bk. 1616–20, 11 July, 18 Jas. I, and *Cal. S.P. Dom.* 1637–8, 412. Apparently one tything was in Som.: *Kelly's Dir. Wilts.* (1875), 216.

treasurers for relief of poor prisoners were continually widening theirs. Known officially as the treasurers for the King's Bench and Marshalsea (or Upper Bench, during the Interregnum), they had to find funds for a variety of purposes, including hospitals, almshouses, houses of correction and the legal costs of defending the county for non-repair of a bridge.[1] The treasurerships were annual appointments and displayed the familiar features of amateur administration.

In 1588 the justices in quarter sessions strengthened their hands to deal with defaulters by giving to a single justice the right to commit to prison anyone refusing to contribute.[2] But, as Miss Leonard pointed out half a century ago, the distinction between voluntary and compulsory contributions was a shadowy one.[3] The justices had their own ways of dealing with recalcitrants. Thus, at an uneven pace and with the stimulus of Parliament and privy council behind it, Wiltshire under Elizabeth I and James I erected a makeshift and uncoordinated system of local taxation and local relief. If it fell short of its objectives, it at least left its mark everywhere in the social life of the county.

Whatever virtues and vigour the system may have developed, it was suddenly put under heavier pressure by the new instructions issued in January 1631 by Charles I.[4] His purpose in issuing the Book of Orders was to shake up the whole of the local administration in England and bring home to the justices the full measure of their obligations. For example, they were now to meet in groups monthly and they were to make quarterly reports. For Wiltshire a number of these reports have survived but it may be significant that the latest of them extant is dated May 1635.[5] From these reports and from the quarter sessions records two facts clearly emerge. In the first place, it was becoming very difficult to extract the money both from the contributors and the collectors. Here, lack of supervision was

---

[1] Ord. Bk. 1654–8, Trin. 1656.
[2] *Sess. Mins.* 1563–92, 121–2.
[3] E. M. Leonard, *Early History of English Poor Relief* (1965), p. 204.
[4] Ibid., pp. 158–64.
[5] *Cal. S.P. Dom.* 1635, 177.

playing into the hands of corrupt or inefficient treasurers and some remedy had to be sought. 'Forasmuch as it appeareth unto this court', observed the quarter sessions minute of April 6th, 1630, 'that divers inconveniences have already grown unto this county and are like to increase in succeeding times in neglecting the passing of the treasurers' accounts yearly ... ', it was accordingly decided that there should be an annual audit at the first general sessions after Easter.[1] Secondly, it was manifest that social policy was being very unevenly enforced throughout the county.

That there was room for improvement was clear enough. The records of quarter sessions tell a lamentable story of treasurers and constables who cannot collect the money they need: one collector found himself in 1610 out of pocket to the tune of £100. First he petitioned the lord chief justice, who transmitted the petition to the J.P.s, who solemnly appointed a committee of inquiry to go into the whole business.[2] In 1622, during a time of acute depression in the Wiltshire cloth trade and the accompanying disorder, the sheriff and justices were chid by the privy council, 'for, as we understand, those laws both for relieving the poor and punishing of rogues are much neglected, which in such times as this is you must cause to be strictly put in execution'.[3] In 1630, when directed to grant pensions to two ex-servicemen, however, the justices had to point out that they had run out of money for the purpose.[4] In 1631 they, as well as their colleagues in Dorset and Somerset, were warned that the king looked to them for a better performance of their duties against malcontents and would call them to an exact account.[5]

The divisional reports resulting from the Book of Orders show also how unevenly the system was working in Wiltshire.[6]

[1] Min. Bk. 1626–31, East. 6 Chas. I.

[2] Ibid., 1610–16, Hil. 7 Jas. I.

[3] *Acts of P.C.* 1621–3, 215.

[4] *Cal. S.P. Dom.* 1629–31, 229.

[5] Ibid., 1631–3, 107. Draft by the attorney-general of a warning to be sent through the judges of assize.

[6] The system of rating also seems to have been uneven. See e.g. *Cal. S.P. Dom.* 1637, 167.

Warminster reported in June 1632 that the justices 'have met divers times concerning the said directions, as well before the receipt of the said letters as sithence'. They then explained what they had done. '[We] have bound many apprentices, and settled many others formerly bound [but] departed from their masters; we punish alehouses offending, and tiplers in alehouses, contrary to the statute. Our watches are duly kept, the penalties upon tiplers are duly paid and distributed to the poor; by means whereof the country is well cleared of vagabonds and wanderers, and such as are found travelling with counterfeit passes are sent to the house of correction.' 'Which course', the report concluded, 'we intend to continue.'[1] Here was vigour indeed; and a similar report came in a month later from the hundreds of Swanborough and Potterne and Cannings with the additional item that they had levied and spent 'seven score pounds at the least on rebuilding the house of correction at Devizes'.[2] In the same month the Salisbury division sent in a full report, including a list of the poor children bound apprentice. In addition, three 'tiplers' had been fined 3s. 4d. each for 'drinking in an alehouse above the space of one hour' while the innkeeper had been fined 10s. for permitting it, and lost his licence.[3] The report of November 1633 shows the J.P.s of the area pressing on with their work.[4] In this division at least the social dictatorship of the Commonwealth period cast its long shadow before it.

In November 1632 the Marlborough division provided evidence of its treatment of the poor but refrained from submitting details of the number of apprentices bound or vagabonds punished, 'fearing our certificate would prove too tedious'. It added, however, that the keeping of watch and ward 'would do very much good if it were generally observed in all parts of the country alike; otherwise to observe it in one place and not in another it doth but little good'.[5] In March 1633 Swanborough

[1] SP 16/218, no. 41.
[2] SP 16/220, no. 29.
[3] SP 16/221, no. 17.
[4] SP 16/250, no. 17.
[5] SP 16/225, no. 1

and Potterne and Cannings reported that watch and ward had been kept in the hundreds, as the result of which they had been 'very little or nothing at all troubled' with vagabonds. They had met difficulty in finding masters for poor apprentices but that they attributed to their having 'formerly bound a great many'.[1] From Chippenham and Calne in November 1633 came the frank admission by the J.P.s that, though they had done their best to fulfil the privy council's directions, they found 'a great neglect and unwillingness in the country to observe the same'.[2] In its report of May 1634 the same hundred painted an even gloomier picture: in apprenticeship, 'great difficulties to cross our proceedings in that behalf', in watch and ward, 'a great neglect in all sorts of people to observe the same'.[3] May 1635 saw the last of these reports, though how far this is due to the destruction of the records and how far to inefficiency and resistance in Wiltshire it is impossible to say. The character of the later reports, however, suggests that it was defectiveness in Wiltshire rather than destruction of the sources which brought the series to a close.[4]

Closely related to the administration of poor relief were the other economic and social services of the justices. With the fairs and markets they were intimately concerned; and by 1586 it is possible to see the six divisions of the county serving as the administrative units, each under a group of J.P.s. At this time there seem to have been sixteen market-towns in all: Salisbury, Ludgershall, Warminster, Mere, Hindon, Marlborough, Wootton Bassett, Highworth, Devizes, Market Lavington, Trowbridge, Bradford, Westbury, Chippenham, Calne, and Malmesbury.[5] Other places were added from time to time: for example, Amesbury in 1614[6] and Swindon in 1626.[7] On the other hand the Crown had the right, by means of a privy council direction,

[1] SP 16/262, no. 33.
[2] SP 16/250, no. 10.
[3] SP 16/267, no. 40.
[4] Cf. Leonard, *English Poor Relief*, p. 239.
[5] SP 12/191, no. 8.
[6] *Cal. of Antrobus Deeds before 1625* (W.A.S. Rec. Brch. iii), p. 180.
[7] *Cal. S.P. Dom. 1625–6*, 372.

to forbid a fair in time of plague, as it did in the case of Steeple Ashton in 1625.[1]

Famine no less than plague brought the Crown into the market-square. When food was scarce in Bristol in 1586, the Wiltshire justices were instructed to permit the movement of corn there and to prevent a price rise.[2] They were ordered to take similar steps in 1587 when the same threat appeared in Carmarthen.[3] In 1597 they were once again being urged to take in hand the problem of cornering and price raising.[4] Under Charles I the pressure upon them intensified. A report of the period, sent by the Salisbury justices to the sheriff in 1631, gives us some measure of their success, as well as of the resistance they encountered.[5] It is significant that only two J.P.s in the whole division were willing to take on the control of the market. The rest of their colleagues presented various reasons for being unable to play their part. One had 'many urgent occasions' which made it necessary for him to leave at once for London. Four others were also reported to be in the capital. Another was in Wales or Bristol. Someone else was afflicted with lameness; another was 'long sick and diseased'; another, aged and unable to travel. The chancellor of the diocese was away on his official duties. Indeed the two surviving justices had heard about the commission only by chance, since the then sheriff had failed to send the proclamation and orders.

But what they lacked in numbers they appear to have made up in vigour. They summoned, through the high constables, a number of the important inhabitants of the area but noticed that 'very few or none at all of the great farmers of corn or such as had store of grain to sell' made their appearance. They discovered a 'reasonable good store' of wheat and barley, but too many maltsters, 'whereof some we suppressed and others we restrained'; many ale-house keepers and tipplers had been suppressed on a

[1] *Acts of P.C.* 1625–6, 127.
[2] Ibid., 1586–7, 69–70.
[3] Ibid., 1587–8, 66.
[4] B.M., Add. MS. 32092, fol. 145*a* and *b*.
[5] SP 16/182, no. 2 and no. 21.

former occasion. There were few, if any, badgers or corn jobbers. A number of millers seemed to be cornering grain, so some were suppressed or restrained and others bound over to appear at quarter sessions. Most suppliers were willing to bring their corn to market and sell at reasonable prices but a few were 'wilful and refractory', and 'we terrified them a little with conventing them before the lords of the council—and then they seemed very willing and tractable'. No wonder the market was well supplied and 'at the end of the markets buyers have been rather wanting than corn'.

Upon corn and beer the Wiltshire justices bestowed a good deal of their time and energy. Only slightly less important than these, in a cloth county like Wiltshire, were their duties in connection with local industry.[1] For example, between 1575 and 1577 the activities of a certain Peter Blackborowe, an informer, set the privy council hot on the trail of the Wiltshire justices, with instructions to make a thorough investigation of the local cloth industry.[2] The justices also, by means of their own officers, the searchers, were expected to maintain the standard of the material, since the alnagers had long since failed to perform their allotted function.[3] As industrial depression deepened from the 1620s, so heavier pressure was brought to bear on the justices, who, in turn, were somehow expected to see that industrialists kept their men in employment and that dealers bought up at least some of the surplus stock.[4] Meanwhile, oppression by trouble-making informers was growing. The justices prayed the privy council 'to take special notice of one William Hackett, as most notorious for extortion and other misdemeanours, who taketh the boldness to call in question some of His Majesty's said justices'.[5] The appeal was not in vain: Hackett was summoned before the council and

---

[1] For a full study of this subject see G. D. Ramsay, *Wilts. Woollen Industry in Sixteenth and Seventeenth Centuries* (1943).

[2] *Acts of P.C.* 1575–7, 73, 204–5, 220; ibid., 1577–8, 28–9; cf. Ramsay, op. cit., p. 59 and App. I.

[3] Ramsay, op. cit., pp. 52, 64.

[4] *Acts of P.C.* 1619–21, 192–3, 200–201, 205–6; ibid., 1623–5, 436–7; ibid., 1625–6, 161–2; see also *Cal. S.P. Dom.* 1619–23, 144, 343, 382.

[5] *Acts of P.C.* 1619–21, 42.

committed to the gatehouse. The Wiltshire justices were told also to send other informers before the privy council, 'whereupon order shall be taken for easing the country of any grievance in that behalf'.[1] When the informers learnt what was in store for them many fled, but three were taken, sentenced to the pillory and imprisoned. Unfortunately, these were merely the small fry, acting as agents on behalf of their masters in London.[2]

In 1633 we find the justices once again receiving instructions about maintaining the standards of the material;[3] but their duties were not restricted simply to textiles. In 1627 they had been instructed to help put an end to tobacco-growing in the county.[4] Now, in 1633, they were also asked to investigate complaints about the manufacture of saltpetre.[5]

Even less welcome than their duties in industry must have been the fiscal burdens which came their way. To them fell the unwelcome task of organizing the collection of loans and taxes. The privy seal requesting a loan was sent to the sheriff,[6] but the actual collection was done under groups of commissioners, by collectors who, incidentally, received in the early seventeenth century 4d. in the pound (and their clerks, 2d.) for their pains.[7] For the collection of subsidies the commission of the peace divided into groups to assess the different parts of the county; and, though the task did not increase their popularity, it did augment their power. Edmund Long was one such commissioner. He was accustomed, it was alleged in a Star Chamber case in 1621, 'to win applause to himself and to increase an estimation of greatness' at the expense of his fellow justices. Accordingly, during the assessment he spread such a 'false concept of his, the said Edmund Long's unlimited authority by virtue of the said commission, that he

---

[1] Ibid., 85.

[2] *Cal. S.P. Dom.* 1619–23, 113.

[3] Ibid., 1633–4, 150–151; see also ibid., 1634–5, 3–4.

[4] *Acts of P.C.* 1627, 409–10.

[5] *Cal. S.P. Dom.* 1633–4, 290.

[6] A privy seal of 1570 sent to Sir John Thynne, then sheriff, is printed in *W.A.M.* xiv. 201.

[7] *Cal. S.P. Dom.* 1627–8, 345; cf. *Two Sixteenth Century Taxation Lists* (W.A.S. Rec. Brch. x).

might induce ignorant people to believe that he had absolute power and authority in himself to raise or abate their several rates'.[1] But however real or illusory the justices' powers might be in deciding the assessment, they were often unable to collect what they claimed. In 1622 Wiltshire was one of ten counties which had made no adequate response to the appeal for contributions towards the war in the Palatinate.[2] It was not always so remiss: five years later the commissioners were being complimented for their part in collecting a loan.[3]

When it came to ship money, however, the hostility of the local justices undermined the whole machinery of collection. In 1635 the sheriff received the ship-money writ and summoned the J.P.s to meet him at Devizes. They arrived simply to tell him that they possessed no powers to undertake the work. As a result the sheriff had to work through the high constables and the process was a lengthy one.[4] He assessed the county at more than £7,000, and we know that on March 21st he was still at least £500 short of his target. He said that he did not expect to reach the figure of £7,000 because some were dead, some had moved away and some were unable to pay. He had written to the high constables about the contributions of the clergy but, as he was no longer sheriff and was not in the commission of the peace, his letters were being ignored.[5] Meanwhile, if the justices declined the invitation to make the assessment, some constables for their part seemed equally reluctant to hand over the money. In the middle of 1639 the high constable of Malmesbury was still clinging to the money he had collected by the writ of 1637.[6]

A long-standing financial and administrative burden was the royal right of purveyance. In essence, it was a system under which the Crown bought in the counties the provisions for its household

---

[1] St. Ch. 8/50/8.

[2] *Acts of P.C.* 1621–3, 302–3.

[3] Ibid., 1627, 43. They were reminded, however, of the need to make a 'speedy return [i.e. delivery] of those monies which are so willingly lent'; see also ibid., 91–2.

[4] *Cal. S.P. Dom.* 1635, 477.

[5] *Cal. S.P. Dom.* Addenda 1626–49, 527.

[6] Ibid., 1639, 284.

at favourable (and, as far as the supplier was concerned, grossly uneconomic) prices.[1] The evils of the system had been attacked since at least the time of Magna Carta. Sometimes the burden was made more tolerable by replacing the old methods by a contractual arrangement, a composition to supply the Crown on a fixed basis. Under Burghley compositions for various items were, wherever possible, organized on a county basis. For example, in 1568 the Wiltshire justices agreed that the Crown could buy as much wheat as the county could conveniently provide, paying for the best wheat 'after the rate that the third wheat shall be sold in the market at the same day and places'.[2] It was bad enough to have to subsidize the government in this way but, to make matters worse, by 1580 the Crown contractors were in arrears of payment.[3] Then, in 1584, we find the justices being asked to provide oats for the queen's stable at Reading. This they resisted as an innovation, especially as they were in any case yielding 'a continual provision of oats, hay, and litter to the studdery at Cole Park'.[4] This anachronistic and inefficient form of indirect taxation was modified still further in May 1594. The justices reached an agreement with the privy council, over a wider range of commodities, under which the county would yield a quantity of certain provisions at fixed prices and make up the difference between these and actual costs by a tax on the county.[5] In return, the Crown renounced its right to take purveyance of these commodities as hitherto, except when the queen came on progress into the county. This agreement was one of the series made by the counties throughout England. In 1596, however, there seem to have arisen new difficulties over the collection of provisions for the navy, a separate matter from purveyance for the household. The justices, on the grounds that they did not possess sufficient authority, suggested that the duty should be shifted on

[1] For an examination of this problem see Allegra Woodworth, *Purveyance for the Royal Household in reign of Queen Elizabeth* (Trans. Amer. Philosophical Soc., N.S. xxxv, pt. I).

[2] *W.A.M.* xiv. 237; see also ibid., xxi. 98.

[3] Ibid., xiv. 238.

[4] Ibid., 238–9.

[5] Ibid., 239–41.

to the constables, but the privy council, reminding them that this was 'a course taken in no other county but in yours', rejected the proposal.[1] Whether the whole system of purveyance was commuted into an annual sum, as happened in Devonshire in 1622, it has been impossible to trace.[2]

The justices were heavily involved also in keeping the lines of communication open. By a statute of 1531 the county was declared responsible for bridge repairs, unless this duty could be shown to belong to some other authority.[3] By a statute of 1555 the parishes were made responsible for providing labour and funds for their highways;[4] and the sessions records abound with fines for failure to implement the statute. The justices were sometimes required also to supply the means of communication. For example, in 1627 Wiltshire and various adjacent counties were required to see that there were always available 'able and sufficient post horses, well furnished to be ready at the postmasters on all occasions, he paying them the usual rates'.[5] Eleven years later, we find a grand jury presenting a bill of complaint to the assizes against oppression by the postmasters of Salisbury and Shaftesbury. They reported that certain tithings were severely pressed to make available a ready supply of horses which, since they were not in easy supply, had to be hired at heavy rates.[6] The carriage of timber for the navy also brought grievances in its train. In 1613 we find the justices ordered by the privy council to remedy their neglect to organize the carriage of timber from the New Forest.[7] In 1632 they were again rebuked for their failure in this work,[8] but in their defence the justices pointed out that they had been held up by the harvest and the king's visit to the county. Moreover, a great part of Wiltshire was sixty miles from

[1] *Acts of P.C.* 1595–6, 144–5.
[2] E. P. Cheyney, *A History of England, from defeat of the Armada to death of Elizabeth* (New York, 1926), ii, p. 340.
[3] See below, pp. 286–7.
[4] 2 & 3 Phil. & Mary, c.8.
[5] *Acts of P.C.* 1627–8, 145.
[6] *Cal. S.P. Dom.* 1637–8, 576–7.
[7] *Acts of P.C.* 1613–14, 118.
[8] *Cal. S.P. Dom.* 1631–3, 436.

where the timber was to be loaded.[1] A year later we learn that it is not the justices but the carters who, although paid in advance, were lagging in their duties and discouraging other carters from doing their share.[2] But in 1637 it was once again the justices who were alleged to be remiss and threatened by the privy council with a charge of contempt.[3] In 1638 a further ill report was made about them and it was noted that, in particular, Sir Lawrence and Robert Hyde had been more 'peremptorily adverse' than was appropriate to men of their station.[4]

V

In this survey of the work of the Wiltshire justices we have seen their responsibilities extending widely and deeply into the whole fabric of the county. Some of their functions fell into clearly defined categories. Others hovered on the uncertain borderland between their judicial, social and fiscal duties: for example, the enforcement of the recusancy laws and the collection of recusancy fines.[5] The justices could not have endured these growing burdens alone. Upon their clerks and upon the high constables of the hundreds, the parish constables, churchwardens, overseers and the rest they were bound to devolve a good deal of the work, though the ultimate responsibility remained with them.

Unfortunately, for the period under review, the conditions of appointment and the work of these lesser officials were by no means well defined. From the intermittent light which the records shed upon him, the high constable emerges as one of the significant, if minor, figures of local administration. The link between him and the justices was indeed given concrete form by his appointment at quarter sessions. When exactly the link was forged it is impossible to say. In theory the power of appointment lay with the court leet of the hundred; in practice by the late sixteenth century, if not earlier, these powers in Wiltshire, in

[1] Ibid., 449; see also pp. 535 and 586.
[2] Ibid., 1633–4, 110.
[3] Ibid., 1637, 137–8.
[4] Ibid., 1637–8, 480.
[5] e.g. *Sess. Mins.* 1563–92, 44–5, 64; *Cal. S.P. Dom.* 1623–5, 276.

common with other counties, were passing to either quarter sessions or the divisional justices.[1] On the eve of the Civil War the link in Wiltshire was made closer still. By direction of the Michaelmas quarter sessions 1639, it was decided to take firm steps against high constables who 'get out of their office before they have served two years' without being discharged of all 'payments and duties'. Henceforth the clerk of the peace was not to make out a warrant for new constables until the presiding J.P. in open court authorized him, and 'the same new constables are to be elected and appointed by him and the rest of the justices at the end of the sessions'.[2]

To the high constables, we have already seen, the executive responsibility for law and order, the preparation against invasion,[3] the collection of rates, and various other social functions were being committed wholly or partly by the justices. It was a position of respect and trust, though high constables not infrequently betrayed the financial trust confided in them. It was said also that they misused their authority to vent personal feelings, and disguised their own riotous acts under the due forms of the law. For example, it was once alleged in the Star Chamber that, under the stretched authority of a high constable, a group of men forced entry into a private house, and 'having found out two minced pies they suddenly devoured them'. After this, and sundry unmentionable acts, they stole a 'double Holland kerchief and a table napkin' and plunged the house-holder's wife into the river.[4]

The powers and opportunities of the office may have encouraged some to conspire to gain the appointment. Others were at least as eager to decline it, which brought them under threat of a fine by the justices.[5] It was this reluctance, no doubt, which contributed to the decision of the justices in 1592 to limit the constable's term of office to three years.[6]

[1] *Sess. Mins.* 1563–92, *passim.*
[2] Min. Bk. 1636–40, Mich. 15 Chas. I.
[3] *W.A.M.* xiv. 247–8, 251–2.
[4] Sta. Cha. 8/123/16.
[5] *Sess. Mins.* 1563–92, 85.
[6] Ibid., 152.

Below him, the petty constable, or tithingman, represented the parish or tithing to higher authority and carried the instructions of J.P., and sometimes high constable, to the parish. Watch and ward, the guarding of prisoners, the enforcement of settlement, the collection of parish dues and other tasks fell to him. In Wiltshire, as in other counties, the office seems to have passed by rotation amongst the householders, to be confirmed at the court leet. It could apparently be held by women as well as by men, though women appear to have acted through a deputy.[1] But it can have had little attraction for either sex. Hence it had to be laid down at quarter sessions in 1640 that freeholders no less than copyholders could be called upon to serve in the office.[2] Even so, it cannot have been easy to fill the posts. At the Michaelmas quarter sessions of 1630, a man produced evidence that he was merely a household servant, that he did not live in the parish allotted to him, and other arguments. None the less, he was instructed to take his oath as a tithingman within a fortnight.[3] When we consider the nature of the work it is remarkable not that men evaded office but that they could be persuaded to take it on at all.

Of the sheriff, the coroner, the escheator and the other Crown officials there is little to be said in this context, though they must have left their mark on the county. The sheriff was in some respects the servant of the justices as he was of the Crown. Sometimes he appears to have acted in collusion with the J.P.s to defeat the course of justice.[4] At others he was punished by them, for example, 'quia non diligenter attendebat durante curia'.[5] On one occasion, during the Commonwealth period, the sheriff, Hugh Audley, was allowed by special authority of the council to live outside the county on account of his age and indisposition.[6] Either the egregious Audley was much needed for his service or the office was proving difficult to fill in troublous times.

[1] Ibid., 72; Ord. Bk. 1641–54, Mich. 19 Chas. I, Mich. 22 Chas. I.
[2] Min. Bk. 1636–40, East. 15 Chas. I.
[3] Ibid., 1626–31, Mich. 6 Chas. I.
[4] Sta. Cha. 2/23/269; cf. also 2/27/98.
[5] *Sess. Mins.* 1563–92, 82, 120.
[6] *Cal. S.P. Dom.* 1653–4, 403.

The sheriff went on, throughout the period, impanelling juries, taking responsibility for prisoners and the county gaol, sending lists of those who could be called upon for a loan,[1] accounting at the exchequer for the royal revenues still in his care, and making returns of Members of Parliament. But of his tourn and his county court, so far as the extant records are concerned, we hear nothing. We meet him, and his under-sheriff, as well as his bailiffs of the hundreds, when they are charged with mis-demeanours. In 1639, for example, a bailiff was accused of blackmailing the freeholders of Amesbury for money to avoid being summoned to the sessions and assizes at Salisbury, more than forty miles away.[2] Of the coroner we know less,[3] though we meet him in Edward VI's reign in a Star Chamber case where he is alleged to have corrupted a jury to return a false verdict of murder instead of suicide, whereby he robbed the Crown of its title to the goods and chattels of the deceased.[4] In 1655 we find two Wiltshire coroners recommended for dismissal by the justices of assize.[5] But these officials were essentially Crown officials dealing with Crown issues as they affected individual Wiltshiremen, not county officials as such. When, however, sufficient material comes to light to enable their history to be written, it will undoubtedly add detail and understanding to our knowledge of the county framework. What is clear, however, from the available material, is that an impressive transfer of functions, from one group of officials to another, was taking place.[6]

In the century which had elapsed between the Reformation and the Civil War, the lords lieutenant and the justices of the peace had been increasing their powers and widening their

[1] *W.A.M.* xiv. 200–8.

[2] Assizes 24/20, 22 July, 15 Chas. I.

[3] The same is apparently the case in Glos.; cf. W. B. Willcox, *Gloucestershire, 1590–1640* (New Haven, 1940), p. 38 n. 1.

[4] Sta. Cha. 3/6/7; see also *Les Reportes de cases in Camera Stellata*, ed. W. B. Baildon (1894), pp. 61–2.

[5] Assizes 24/22, 11 Apr. 1655.

[6] For a brief survey of county administration in seventeenth century see S. A, Peyton's Introductoin to *Minutes of Proceedings in Quarter Sessions*, i (Linc. Rec. Soc. xxv).

interests. In many respects a revolution had taken place. The medieval sheriff had declined in importance by the sixteenth century and the process continued under the Tudors and Stuarts. He continued to be drawn from the same class as the justice of the peace and he was still an important figure in the county. But he was a servant of the justices and his military significance had largely evaporated before the rise of the lord lieutenant. In another sphere we have seen how the courts leet virtually passed into desuetude while the quarter sessions, voluntarily or involuntarily, assumed some of their functions.

But if the military leadership had passed to the lord lieutenant, he was also called upon to do many things outside his military duties: to collect the loans, to deal with recusancy, to improve local administration and to report upon conditions in the shire. In short, he was representing the Crown to the county and the county to the Crown. He was not yet invariably the *custos rotulorum*, the undisputed head of the commission of the peace, as he was to become in the eighteenth century, but he was nearly there. The lord lieutenant, in Wiltshire as in other counties, was often a privy councillor and a statesman of the first rank; then the bond between central and local government was truly personal. Through the lord lieutenant the privy council forged a major link in the chain of responsibility which reached down through the hierarchy of administration.

But the whole relationship between central and local government was much more complex than this. The privy council directions might also go through the sheriff to the justices of the peace and from them to the high constable. He in his turn would pass the instructions to the parish constable or to the tithingman from whom it would go, where necessary, to the church-wardens. In other words, authority could thus be transmitted from the privy council to the humblest churchwarden in the smallest parish. There was also another route: through the justices of assize coming on circuit twice a year. At the same time, the grand jury, foreshadowing the county council of a later age, would, by judicial presentment at the assizes, in effect suggest a future programme of social policy. The county gaol, through the sheriff, was directly the responsibility of the assizes, but for much the assizes operated through quarter sessions, high constable and the rest. County policy was not always made in London; and in the county administrative machinery there is to be discerned the shape of the local self-government to come.

With all its defects, the county administration seems to have been functioning and, under pressure from the central government, the rough foundations of the social services were in their place. Their testing-time came in the 1640s, which gave the nascent system a fundamental shock. How great that shock was may be seen from the records of the quarter sessions; and the general impression is confirmed from other sources. In brief, two things happened: the local organs seemed to be grinding almost to a standstill, 'in these dangerous and troublesome times' as a contemporary put it;[1] and then, when a new autocracy was established under Cromwell, it called for new organs of government to carry its revolutionary dictatorship into the countryside.

Naturally, some of the most urgent issues arose out of war itself. For example, Harnham bridge near Salisbury was of considerable strategic importance, being 'the roadway from the city of London into all the west part of this nation'.[2] The fact that it was in decay raised not only the problem of finance but a complex legal problem, familiar to justices up and down the country.[3] Under the Statute of Bridges of 1531[4] the county could only allocate funds for bridge repair where responsibility did not belong elsewhere, to a municipality, a hundred or a private person. Thus the normal procedure in Wiltshire was for a committee of justices to inquire into the cost of necessary repairs and find out who should pay for them. They would then proceed by way of 'indictment' against those liable for its upkeep. When it was impossible to establish such liability, the county

[1] Ord. Bk. 1641–54, Mich. 18 Chas. I.
[2] Ibid., East. 1652.
[3] S. and B. Webb, *Story of the King's Highway*, pp. 88–104; cf. *Warwick County Records*, ii, p. xxvi; iii, pp. xxx–xxxv; v, pp. xliii–xlvii.
[4] 22 Hen. VIII, c.5.

had to find the money, though justices fought a rearguard action against the imposition upon the county of burdens of this sort.

But a dangerous bridge in a civil war offered little opportunity for establishing where the responsibility for its upkeep belonged; so in 1642 the justices agreed that Harnham bridge should be repaired from county funds, though they recorded at the same time that this was not to serve as a precedent.[1] From now onwards they pressed on with their efforts to discover who in fact should maintain the bridge.[2] It was a drawn-out affair. In the 1650s the justices were hot on the trail of the master of the Hospital of St Nicholas at Harnham, against whom they brought a lawsuit in the 'Upper Bench'. As that was still unsettled they had to pay for the repair of the bridge though 'without prejudice to the county in point of right'. Meanwhile they instructed the clerk of the peace to try to bring the matter to speedy trial.[3] That was in 1653. In 1661 they were still paying for repairs to Harnham bridge, once more 'without prejudice' to their future claims.[4]

In the 1640s we find frequent reference to the increasing difficulties facing local officials in collecting funds for relief of the poor. It may be that, to meet these mounting difficulties, the justices decided to impose on a clerk of the court the responsibility for collecting and administering the 'surplusage' from the treasurers for King's Bench and Marshalsea and from the fund for maimed soldiers and mariners.[5] We may perhaps see in this official the primitive notions of a county treasurer. At Easter 1642 came instructions from quarter sessions that watch and ward must be properly kept in the county and all who failed in their duty were to be brought to book.[6] By Michaelmas 1643 the position appears to have further deteriorated. No proclamation

[1] Ord. Bk. 1641–54, Hil. 17 Chas. I.
[2] Ibid., East. 1652.
[3] Ibid., East. 1653.
[4] Ord. Bk. 1654–68, Hil. 1661. See also Assizes 24/20, 18 July, 12 Chas. I; 24/21, 31 Aug., 24 Chas. I; 24/22, 12 Mar. 1652.
[5] Ord. Bk. 1641–54, Hil. 17 Chas. I.
[6] Ibid., East. 18 Chas. I.

of the sessions had been possible throughout the county and 'the ways are now very dangerous to travel in by reason of the interruption of soldiers'. Those who had failed to honour their recognizances to appear at quarter sessions were therefore absolved from the penalty.[1] Later, in 1649, one justice excused himself from attendance at the sessions on the grounds that he was un-willing to leave home 'for we have with us a troop of soldiers and those none of the civilest'.[2] It was no doubt in recognition of the hazards of the time that the justices decided in Hilary term, 1643, to buy a 'strong chest ... with two locks and keys' for the preservation of the records, to be kept under the charge of the two deputy clerks of the peace, in the vestry house of Warminster church.[3]

Meanwhile, the practice, already difficult before the Civil War, of holding courts leet to elect high constables and tithingmen, was proving virtually impossible. Men were therefore unable to relinquish office for years on end and the justices in quarter sessions were obliged to intervene to appoint successors. On the other hand, some tithingmen were being elected at courts leet but were refusing to serve: one more indication of the breakdown of local government.[4] At the same time, the collection of funds for poor relief was being neglected by all and sundry as the justices' hold upon the county grew weaker. At the Trinity sessions of 1644 only two justices appeared and the meeting lasted one day. After that we have no record of further meetings until Trinity 1646, when nine J.P.s appeared at the sessions. In 1646 it was reported to the assizes that though there were many justices on the commission 'very few of them are sworn to execute their offices, whereby His Majesty's service and the service of the country is much hindered'. In the same year, and again in 1647, it was also learned at the assizes that many parishes were without churchwardens.[5] But from now onwards we notice

[1] Ibid., Mich. 19 Chas I.

[2] *Extracts from Q. Sess. Great Rolls of 17th Century*, ed. B. H. Cunnington (1932), p. 216.

[3] Ord. Bk. 1641–54, Hil. 18 Chas. I.

[4] Ibid., Mich. 22 Chas. I.

[5] Assizes 24/21, 10 Aug., 22 Chas. I and 15 Mar., 22 Chas. I.

that the system of watch and ward was being tightened up, though not with consistent success.[1] We see also an intensified attack on the 'manifold abuses, inconveniences and mischief which ariseth by reason of the multiplicity of alehouses in this county'. All ale-houses were therefore suppressed and no further ones were to be licensed by the justices unless specially requested by the majority of the 'chief inhabitants' and the constables of the area.[2]

In 1647 food was scarce in Wiltshire and the justices stopped maltsters from buying excessive barley for malt, as well as intervening to control the distribution of corn.[3] Arrears of contributions to poor relief and of payments to county officials were mounting and the justices laid down in Michaelmas 1648 that no high constable was to be discharged until he had paid his dues.[4] Meanwhile masters were resisting the imposition of pauper apprentices on them, while constables, churchwardens and others were sabotaging the regulations laid down for the purpose.[5] Then, at the end of 1650, the J.P.s were forced by the justices of assize to set about tackling the question of 'insufficient juries' arising from the 'great neglect' of the under-sheriffs and their deputies as well as bailiffs of the hundreds, and so began to overhaul the whole apparatus for their listing and summons.[6]

While the traditional machinery of justices and quarter sessions was being operated in a defective and half-hearted manner, new organs were being erected to meet the revolutionary requirements of the Commonwealth. Following upon an ordinance of February 24th, 1643, county committees came into existence for raising money for the Parliamentary forces.[7] That for Wiltshire

---

[1] In at least some parts of Wilts. watch and ward could not be maintained in 1648: *Wilts. Q. Sess. Rec.*, ed. Cunnington, pp. 195–6.

[2] Ord. Bk. 1641–54, Trin. 22 Chas. I.

[3] Ibid., Trin. 23 Chas. I.

[4] Ibid., Mich. 24 Chas. I.

[5] Ibid., Hil. 24 Chas. I.

[6] Ibid., Mich. 1650.

[7] *Accts. of Parliamentary Garrisons of Great Chalfield and Malmesbury*, ed. J. H. P. Pafford (W.A.S. Rec. Brch. ii), 14.

consisted of a good many justices of the peace and operated through local collectors. They in turn called upon the tithingmen for help and were supported also by the armed forces. The work of the committee must have been hampered in 1643 by the bitter feud between two of its leaders, Sir Edward Hungerford and Sir Edward Baynton;[1] while the surviving collectors' accounts for Chalfield and Malmesbury provide evidence of resistance, or at least reluctance, to contribute to the full. There is evidence also of the existence of a royalist committee for the county but not of its activities.[2] In 1644 the Parliamentary committee for Wiltshire was reporting to London on local conditions, though apparently not conforming to instructions.[3] A year later it was itself being rebuked for misdemeanours and maladministration.[4] We find also in 1646 that the sub-committee of accounts for Wiltshire was, with considerable difficulty, collecting funds for the Parliamentary forces.[5] Colonel Ludlow, it was said, 'found a great fainting amongst us and could with all his diligence swear but five of us at that time, and since the business lies asleep'. We hear later of 'collectors for drums and colours' but, as the justices observed, these officials were answerable to the militia and were not 'within the power and cognizance of this court'.[6] Other institutions were also active: the commissioners for assessments,[7] the commissioners for ejecting scandalous ministers and schoolmasters,[8] the commissioners for survey of church livings.[9] And, on top of them, in 1655, there was imposed the rule of Major-General John Desborow, who also held Gloucestershire, Dorset, Somerset, Devon and Cornwall within his jurisdiction.[10] Under these new

---

[1] *Ludlow's Memoirs*, ed. C. H. Firth (Oxford, 1894), i, pp. 440–43.
[2] *Chalfield and Malmesbury Garrison Accts.*, p. 17.
[3] *Cal. S.P. Dom.* 1644, 446, 478.
[4] *Chalfield and Malmesbury Garrison Accts.*, pp. 30–33.
[5] SP 16/514, no. 100, Nov. 1646.
[6] Ord. Bk. 1654–68, Mich. 1654.
[7] *Cal. S.P. Dom.* 1653–4, 625.
[8] Ibid., 1655–6, 104 and *passim*.
[9] Ibid., 327.
[10] Ibid., 1655, 275.

organs of government the justices were expected to perform the manifold duties which the times required.

Indeed their authority widened. The publishing of banns, hitherto the responsibility of the Church, now passed to the Puritan state; and the justices solemnly considered matrimonial disputes, and impediments raised to matrimony, at quarter sessions.[1] At the same time, at the assizes, scandalous living and adultery appear on the indictments.[2] Meanwhile, if the attendance at quarter sessions was sometimes small, the necessary vigour was not always lacking. In 1654 the justices ordered a thorough reform of weights and measures throughout the county.[3] In 1656 there was a renewed onslaught on vagabonds and sturdy beggars, as well as on constables and tithingmen who failed to keep the problem within bounds.[4] In the same year also they somehow found time to consider the troublesome dogs of Mere, who were henceforth to be tied or muzzled.[5] And then, in 1657, they discovered that they had, in at least one respect, acted *ultra vires*. In law, on petition from assizes or quarter sessions, only the Lord Chancellor could authorize victims of fire or other calamity to collect money for their relief. But in recent times the justices had in quarter sessions, and without higher authority, authorized these collections (as happened also in Warwickshire). This they now recognized 'upon better consideration to be not altogether legal' and decided to abandon the practice.[6] From now onwards they made grants for such relief through the treasurers of the Upper Bench and Marshalsea.[7] After the Restoration they reverted to the traditional method of petitioning the Lord Chancellor.[8]

The administrative system of the Commonwealth proved an uneasy marriage between the traditional and the revolutionary,

[1] Ord. Bk. 1654–68, Trin. 1654.
[2] Assizes, 24/22, 31 July, 1652.
[3] Ord. Bk. 1641–54, Hil. 1654.
[4] Ibid., 1654–68, East. 1656.
[5] Ibid., Trin. 1656.
[6] Ibid., Trin. 1657.
[7] e.g. ibid., Mich. 1657.
[8] Ibid., East. 1661.

between the permanent and the provisional; and the county which had resisted the dictation of Charles I did not easily acquiesce in the dictation of Cromwell. Then, in Wiltshire as elsewhere, the Restoration produced a temporary upheaval at quarter sessions. At the Hilary sessions of 1660 only five justices appeared, and at the Easter sessions, the last before the Restoration, only three.[1] The Trinity sessions were not held at all. But the Michaelmas sessions, the first held after the Restoration, attracted as many as eighteen justices. No less significant, none of the three who appeared at the Easter sessions before the Restoration, and only one of the five who appeared at the preceding sessions, came to the first meeting after the Restoration. Of the twelve who came to the Michaelmas sessions of 1659 only one came to the Michaelmas sessions of 1660. Of the sixty-five local members of the last Cromwellian commission extant, that of 1657, only nineteen were named on the first Restoration commission[2] and only three came to the first Restoration quarter sessions. The other fifteen who came were not on the Cromwellian commission at all. Here is clear evidence of a purge; and it is noteworthy also that the Earl of Pembroke and Montgomery gave place to the Marquess of Hertford as *custos rotulorum*.[3]

There are clear signs also of a purge in other aspects of the county administration. Two of the masters of houses of correction were replaced.[4] Pensions granted by the justices were revoked unless specially confirmed by quarter sessions. A new series of pensions were granted to royalist ex-servicemen.[5] But in many other respects the commission, with changed personnel, settled down to the familiar duties of social administration. In Wiltshire, as elsewhere, the Restoration brought relief and hope. Perhaps the borough of Calne reflected the mood of a large section of the county when it devoted £1 4s. for the purchase of

---

[1] The attendances given in this paragraph are obtained from the Ord. Bk. 1654–68.

[2] C 220/9/4.

[3] P.R.O. Index, 4214, p. 17.

[4] Ord. Bk. 1654–68, Mich. 1660.

[5] Ibid., Hil. 1660.

one hogshead of beer 'when we proclaimed our most gracious and merciful sovereign lord Charles the Second'.[1] Only time would show whether the restoration of the county administration would be as speedy as the restoration of the king.

[1] *Calne Guild Stewards' Bk.* (W.A.S. Rec. Brch. vii), 71.

IO

Office-holding and government mainly in England and France

Post-Reformation Europe displayed on the surface a large measure of political diversity. The fragmentation of the universal Church, it would appear, completed a process of political fragmentation which had been going on for centuries. With medieval natural law in decline, and the emergence of the modern sovereign state still in the future, the nations of western Europe became locked in conflict within themselves – and with their neighbours – in search of a system of government which would lead them away from confusion and anarchy. Yet the historian who looks at western Europe at the end of the sixteenth century is, in general, impressed not by the diversity of the political systems in the process of formation but by their striking similarity. In the constitutional issues which confronted them, and in the manner of their solution, all the governments of the day had much in common, because the pressures upon them were more or less the same. The general pressure of economic and social forces burst through and flowed beyond the frontiers of the new nation states.

The whole of Europe was at this time, to a greater or less degree, subject to a double upward pressure: of prices and of population. The rise in population far outdistanced the rise in productivity and inevitably commodity prices were driven sharply upwards. In Spain, for example, the 1540s saw a savage rise in prices, and the succeeding decades would see a tragic worsening of the whole situation as the Spanish economic system

NOTE: This paper is a slightly revised version of 'Social Structure, Office Holding and Politics, chiefly in Western Europe', *New Cambridge Modern History*, Vol. III, ed. R. B. Wernham (1968), pp. 126–48.

sagged under heavy overseas commitments, a debilitating war in the Netherlands, and a war of attrition at sea. In France inflation added its own severe stresses at a time when the country was entering upon four decades of civil war. In England inflation in the middle years of the century gave momentum to the process of social dislocation, at a most delicate time of religious and constitutional experiment. Thereafter the pace of inflation slackened: but it was renewed in the last dozen years of the century at the very period when England's political insecurity in relation to Spain deteriorated into a war for survival itself. Inflation spread on into the third decade of the seventeenth century.

If, then, a relatively underdeveloped European economy proved unequal to the demands of a rising population, there were other social consequences no less powerful. London, for example, during the second half of the sixteenth century doubled its population, in spite of the heavy incidence of endemic disease. It was a pressure on both town and country. 'We have not, God be thanked,' wrote William Lambarde in 1594, 'been touched with any extreme mortality, either by sword or sickness, that might abate the overgrown number of us.' But even when sword and sickness did intervene with tragic force, the rise was still largely unabated. Over a considerable part of Europe the combined effects of war, famine and disease proved inadequate to bank up the social system against the accumulating tide of population, a tide which did not begin to ebb until the fourth decade of the seventeenth century.

The pressures of demand upon the scarce and under-developed resources of Europe were irregular in their effect; some areas might have to endure the powerful thrust of an enclosing landlord, others might remain wholly remote from the uneven stresses of agrarian change. In England the west and north saw little alteration in the traditional agricultural techniques and aims, while the central plains and the home counties were more responsive to contemporary economic demands, especially for wool in the Midlands and dairy and market-gardening products in the satellite regions of the capital. If the changes were not as rapid or extensive as contemporaries were willing to believe, they were more unsettling and socially radical than historians were, until recently, willing to acknowledge. In France the economic pressure was less; there is no story of a movement from corn to sheep or of eviction to meet the requirements of agrarian reconstruction. But politics took a more vigorous hand in the proceedings. With the long devastation of the Hundred Years War still not wholly repaired, the French landscape endured once more during the civil wars the remorseless tramp of the soldiery, more especially in the north-east and south. Hence—in the intervals of peace—the lords themselves sought to repopulate the abandoned lands. The old tenures became increasingly impracticable, as they had been in England for some time. The new men were more free—at least in the tenurial sense. This process could not be significant until the early seventeenth century, when the civil war was over. In the second half of the sixteenth, the pressure was working the other way. War drove men from the land.

But whatever the economic causes and consequences, the social effects were clearly manifest. Population was on the move. The 'push' and 'pull' elements were present in most of western Europe. The push came from the land either because of conversion from corn to wool, with a diminished demand for labour, or simply because numbers grew beyond the capacity of the soil to bear them. The pull came from the demand for labour as industry developed, sometimes in old towns, sometimes in new. That pull, of ever-increasing power, stretched beyond endurance the social services of the recipient towns. For, if many were drawn to the towns in the hope of work, a good proportion did not find any—or did not hold it for long. And some of course did not want work at all. So the great cities of Europe, as well as the smaller ones, were confronted with a settlement problem of ever-growing dimensions. There was shortage of work, shortage of houses, shortage of food, shortage of social relief. The problem respected neither national boundary nor ecclesiastical doctrine. It emerged in powerful proportions whether the monasteries were dissolved or intact. Paris no less than London,

Ypres no less than York, found that the social apparatus was unequal to the calls made upon it; while philosophers and theologians alike sought for the principles which should govern social amelioration. These principles concern us less than the basic facts which evoked them, namely, that population was significantly mobile and that it was impossible to contain the vagrant poor within their local restraints. All this underlined the fears of the governing classes that physical dislocation and social instability would breach the slender walls of their internal political security. The revolt of the *Germania* in Valencia, the Anabaptist rising in Münster—these things had happened in the lifetime of the middle-aged men who held power now in the central years of the sixteenth century. The French civil wars of the second half of the century confirmed their gravest social anxieties.

These anxieties were reflected and reaffirmed in the legislation of the time. In England, the Statutes of Weavers of 1555 and of Apprentices of 1563 looked back to a somewhat imaginary past of settled, socially immobile and unexpanding populations, a past conjured up to justify an impracticable economic conservatism. The English statute book displays a gathering volume of economic and social legislation against a thrusting textile capitalism; against uncontrolled movement from one trade to another or from one district to another and in some cases from one class to another; against the wearing of excess apparel—silk was the status symbol of social aspirants below the rank of knighthood who sought to ape their betters. In Germany and France alike the knightly class was expected to live in a manner appropriate to its rank; while in Spain the social divisions had so hardened as to raise well-marked barriers between the leisured classes, secular and clerical, on the one hand, and all those engaged in commercial and industrial enterprise, on the other.

Here was a paradox. At the very time when an expanding economy—albeit slowly expanding—called for a reservoir of mobile labour, whose freedom to move might therefore have reduced the call for unemployment relief, government opinion was in general hostile to such uncontrolled expansion. And where such hostility was not fully effective, bad roads and generally deficient communications imposed insuperable handicaps. So much stood in the way of the full exploitation of human and physical resources. Meanwhile, unemployment and instability dogged each other's heels round the vicious circle of the contemporary social situation.

There is, of course, no fundamental distinction between social and political instability; and they exacerbate each other. This was clearly marked during the sixteenth century; and of all classes the princes of Europe were most vulnerable to the disruptive forces of the age. For the very inflationary movement which stimulated industry and trade—as well as disturbed order and stability in time of slump—struck the monarchies where it could damage them most: in their treasuries. Faced with the growing cost of armies, of domestic administration and of diplomacy, they found that the revenues from their land, and the taxation from their political assemblies, were woefully inadequate for the needs they were alleged to meet. Hence the bewildering assortment of devices, obscure and contorted, illegal sometimes, to which the governments resorted at a high cost in unpopularity and maladministration; hence the heavy confiscations of the possessions of attainted noblemen and, most of all where possible, of the wealth of the Church; hence the pious calls for retrenchment, faintly heard and rarely answered. Throughout Europe it is the same lamentable story of the increasing impoverishment of the monarchy. In Scotland the young James VI had experienced the greatest difficulty in raising sufficient money to go to Denmark to bring back his bride; and, in due course, the baptism of his son had to be delayed because he could not find the money to pay for a ceremony appropriate to his rank. In England the cautious queen was better supplied but she was also more heavily committed and, when she took measure of the cost of war, and the cost of her household, she bitterly directed against her ministers—at one time the Earl of Leicester, at another the comptroller of her household—the full volume of her horrified surprise. In France Sully seriously tried to carry through a policy of fiscal reform; in England under James I, Robert Cecil. But what could one minister do in England against the extravagance of a glamorous court and an irresponsible king? The Swedish pattern was exceptional. There monetary inflation came lightly and late. The confiscated revenues of the Church proved invaluable. Whereas the Swedish monarchy was poorer than that of Scotland before the Reformation, it was relatively richer than that of England after the Reformation. For when ecclesiastical wealth came to the Swedish king it came to stay—at least until well into the seventeenth century. In Scotland and in England it did not. The Spanish monarchy received substantial taxation from the Church, as well as a vast accession of riches from the confiscated treasures of the Incas and from the exploitation of the American silver mines. But the wealth never stayed; and by the end of the century the Spanish monarchy was, at one and the same time, the most powerful and the most poverty-stricken of all the monarchies of Europe.

A complex of crises emerged in Germany. Here the redistribution of ecclesiastical wealth was of no benefit to the Habsburgs; and it carried one stage further the dissolution of central authority. For it came at a time when the whole constitution was crying out for reform, and the whole notion of imperial rule was under fire. To the princes of northern Germany in particular the Reformation had brought a relative increase in power in two separate senses: against the Church and against the emperor. Such visions as the princes had had early in the century of a federated German nation under a German-orientated emperor had vanished. Instead, the centrifugal process of princely consolidation continued apace. Increasingly, as the Reformation spread in Germany, its hostility to a universal Rome reinforced the hostility to an emperor whose claims to universal rule, however tenuous, confused the aims and issues of German nationalism. But, aggressively Catholic, the Spanish possessions of the emperor—a far greater source of wealth and a far greater reservoir of power than the whole of Germany put together—made it likely that he would choose Rome rather than the Reformation. The Protestant Reformation which might have unified Germany against the pope in fact divided Germany against the emperor. The Augsburg doctrine of *cuius regio eius religio* confirmed and extended political particularism into the sphere of religion. On the eve of the Thirty Years War Germany was divided into a mosaic of principalities which needed only the Treaties of Westphalia to give them the powers of endurance. But, before this, the governments of Germany endured a century of consuming instability.

The instability of the monarchies reflected the deeper instability of the classes with whose fortunes their own were so closely intermingled. For if the new monarchies had to fight hard to retain and extend their hold on power, the old aristocracies found their resources under even greater strain. These two sectors of the governing classes were linked in a curious relationship. The monarchies, it is true, found it hard to rule without the nobility; but they found it equally hard to rule with them. Developments in Scotland made this abundantly clear, where, for example, the office of justiciar was hereditary in the nobility – and justice was therefore hard to come by. But all over western Europe the function of the aristocracy in society was inherently self-contradictory. As barons they had traditional ambitions and rivalries which frequently ran counter to the interests of the king's peace. But as hereditary office-holders – as many of them were – they were expected to enforce a legal and political system whose continuing strength depended upon the curbing of their own selfish powers. In Poland the Crown's authority lay under constant threat of the aristocracy, and here was a barrier to good government as effective as any exercised by the Polish *sejm*. In Sweden the nobility was bent on aggrandizing its privileges at the expense of the Crown. In France during the last years of the sixteenth century there was re-enacted, in conditions of incomparable ferocity, the same factious conflict which had been fought out a century earlier in England during the Wars of the Roses. In England the rising of the Northern earls in 1569 was, in one sense, the rising of an *old* aristocratic group whose political power had been sterilized by the centralization of the Tudor Crown; while the rebellion of the Earl of Essex in 1601 was, in many respects, the rising of the leaders of the *newer* aristocracy who had failed to inherit the powers enjoyed by the first generation, the founders of their line. But the belief that the new monarchs were hostile to the older aristocracies is an over-simplification — and distortion — of their attitudes. Even the first of the new Tudor dynasty, it has recently been shown, far from decimating it, employed the older aristocracy in the service of the state. The last of the Tudors clearly regarded a stable aristocracy as an essential part of her regime. Her refusal to inflate and dilute it with the easy creation of peerages, her policy of reserving some of the major offices of state — so far as possible — for noblemen, were all part of her inherent traditionalism. The divine queen needed the trappings of a high nobility about her throne. But it had to be an aristocracy whose teeth had been drawn. Her declaration to the Earl of Leicester that England would have but one mistress and no master might have been addressed to the whole aristocracy. Yet the fact remains that a pivotal office like the lord lieutenancy tended to become hereditary in the leading aristocratic family in the shire. A large part of the nobility remained loyal to the Stuarts throughout; but it is perhaps symbolic of the dualism and contradictory role of the aristocracy that the lord lieutenant of Wiltshire in the 1640s turned his forces against the king.[1]

In France during this period the tension between monarchy and nobility flared up into a long and bloody struggle. It is, of course, well known that the French civil wars derived from powerful secular no less than religious causes, though the issue has been obscured by the intense religious emotions which intervened in the contest. The Calvinist movement in France had first, in the mid-sixteenth century, taken hold upon the merchant and the artisan; and its early martyrs — as in Marian England — came from the humblest stock. But by the time the civil wars began in 1562 the nobility, both high and provincial, had joined in and indeed taken over control. Contemporaries in France recognized the importance of distinguishing between the two wings of the movement, describing the one group as 'Huguenots of religion', and the other group as 'Huguenots of state'. These latter stood for much more than religious dissent. They represented the long-

[1] See above, pp. 239, 250.

standing hostility of the ruling families of provincial France to the power of Paris; to the Crown and its ally, the Catholic Church; and, above all, to the Guises, the family most closely identified with that Church and most bitterly opposed to the aims and interests of these provincial and often decaying noble houses. (The traditional use of the expression 'provincial nobility' in part confuses the issue: most of its members would be regarded in England as belonging not to the aristocracy but to knightly and gentry families. But there were great *provincial* magnates as well.) It was no wonder that many of them—dissident politically—became the patrons of religious dissidence in the shape of the local Protestant sects; no wonder also, that the Crown, whose control over the Church was considerable, should resist the emergence of an alternative ecclesiastical system which was a federation of self-governing synods. In France, as in England, it could be assumed that 'no bishop' meant 'no king'. The French Crown in the second half of the sixteenth century, like the English Crown, had nothing to gain from a Puritan revolution, and a good deal to lose.

To many members of the provincial nobility who joined the Huguenots, ideology probably meant less than the simple fact that they were impoverished and therefore threw in their lot with one or other of the great aristocratic patrons. The same thing happened in Scotland (as in England a century earlier). In Scotland, however, the threat to the provincial baronage came not from over-mighty Catholic magnates like the Guises but from a pseudo-democratic organization, the Calvinist Kirk. Hence in Scotland there was built against the Kirk a natural alliance between the old baronage and the old Church. In France the tendency was in the opposite direction: but even at a time when Frenchmen's religious emotions were most deeply engaged, the constitutional disorder lay close to the heart of the matter. In France, during these last decades of the Valois rule, bastard feudalism flared up into civil war. In England a century earlier it had been a struggle between two warring houses, in France it was now a struggle between three: Guise, Montmorency and Bourbon, with the feeble government of Catherine de Medici vainly trying to hold the ring. The struggle for power became, in essence, a struggle for the throne. At the end it became also a struggle for the independence of France, more especially as the Guises prepared to lead France into the Spanish orbit. Faced from the 1560s onward with the threat that the French system of government might completely dissolve, men like Jean Bodin sought to shift all authority to the king as father, *la grande puissance souveraine*. Bodin's powerful appeal aimed also at minimizing the differences between the various faiths, an attitude which, to the faithful, looked like minimizing the faiths themselves. The chancellor, l'Hôpital, however reminded his listeners of what he described as the old French proverb, 'one faith, one law, one king'. It is at this time, writes Henri Hauser, that 'the nations, like the princes, remain attached to the barbarous doctrine of unity of faith'. It was a heavy price to pay in the search for unity in the state.

The impoverishment of the French nobility, like that of the Scottish, tempted—or drove—them into military adventures. In all aspects of these French wars, the economic problems of inflation and poverty intervened, although it is impossible to isolate the economic from the other causes of social change, or estimate the part they played in the vast reduction of local self-determination which the Valois sought and the Bourbons achieved. In England, the economic decay of a section of the aristocracy is equally clear. But in the present state of knowledge about the structure of English society, it is impossible to establish how far this decay extended, and what were its major causes. Undoubtedly, as Professor Lawrence Stone has recently brought out with an abundance of evidence, the cost of living, of eating and drinking, of marrying, of building—and even of dying—drained away whole fortunes. The notorious Earl of Oxford, it was said, squandered his inheritance in a bitter and distorted revenge against his wife and his father-in-law, the eminent Lord Burghley. Others lost theirs through incompetence of agrarian administration; and still others may have spent their energies—and perhaps their wealth—in the public service, at a high cost to their private estates. But who precisely composed this latter group it is difficult to establish. For, if the royal service drained their income, it was also the source of their wealth, patronage and power. The Earl of Leicester's complaint that he was sent without resources to fight in the Netherlands for the queen reads strangely when his handling of the war chest is closely examined. The Earl of Essex was given by the queen large grants of land and the profits of office – for example, the farm of the sweet wines – but never enough. The Earl of Oxford was also rewarded by the queen, but in this case at the expense of the Bishop of Ely. It has recently been suggested that such aristocratic decline as took place may have derived from social rather than economic causes, for example, the heavy burden of finding dowries which might face a nobleman unluckily possessed of a group of daughters of marriageable age. Recusancy in religion and the fines that went with it might complete the decline of a nobleman's estate. Yet, whatever the causes of aristocratic decay, there were also powerful causes of aristocratic advance: the fortunate discovery of minerals on the estate; the application to the lands of newer techniques and up-to-date methods of administration, by no means the monopoly of the progressive merchants and lawyers who came out from the towns. But in some cases, undoubtedly, it was the holding of public office which yielded the richest rewards to those who could gain access to it. Office, having been gained by patronage, was itself the instrument of patronage. Patronage meant the ability to build up and hold a following; it meant the access to funds from private suitors. Through patronage, if successfully operated, lay the path to wealth and the extension of power. But it was a delicate and complex instrument of government. If it could add to the strength of a Burghley, its absence could exacerbate the weakness of an Essex. Its full effects upon the aristocracy of western Europe have yet to be assessed. But, whereas in France Henry IV consciously aimed at bringing the provincial aristocracy under a tight, centralized rein, a policy ultimately fulfilled by his descendant Louis XIV, in England James I turned aristocratic patronage into a loose system of courtly favouritism. Patronage and favouritism, on the surface, seem largely the same. In fact, the one, patronage, was a system of rule appropriate and practical for its day. The other, favouritism, was merely the reward from the public resources for irrelevant personal qualities. Favouritism is patronage in a condition of utter decadence. But the causes for the rise or decline of the nobility of Europe are still surrounded by obscurity. Perhaps Thomas Wilson's vague summary, which he recorded at the end of the sixteenth century of the English nobility, is about as far as, at present, we can go: 'Some daily decay, some increase according to the course of the world.'

If the causes are obscure, the slow decline of the role of the aristocracy in the constitution is clear enough. The end of the sixteenth century and beginning of the seventeenth saw in England the continuation of a process which can be traced back to at least the Reformation Parliament of 1529–36. The disappearance of the abbots from the House of Lords, the reduction in status of the bishops, the dilution of the lay aristocracy by large creations of a new peerage—all these played their part. Thomas Wilson declared that the monarchy deliberately helped the middle class in their upward climb at the expense of the aristocracy, and thereby clipped the wings of the aristocracy's insolencies. Wilson's hindsight oversimplifies the issue. It reflects more a situation which had arisen than the policy which caused it. But another commentator on this decline went so far as to say, at the beginning of Elizabeth's reign, that the Crown and Commons alone constituted a Parliament. If this was an extreme, indeed a ludicrous opinion, as was the assertion that a member of the Commons carried greater weight than a peer, it was followed, in the next century, by the more realistic observation that the House of Commons could command three times the wealth of the House of Lords. More significant still, Francis Bacon was arguing in 1593 that the grant of taxation was exclusively the concern of the elected house, a doctrine which, only in the present century, and not without difficulty, was at last written into the British constitution.

Here was the crux of the issue; and it divided the constitutional history of England from that of France. For the English parliamentarians tightened their grasp upon the revenue system at the very time when the members of the French Estates General were forced to relax theirs. The English system of taxation was—at least in theory—based firmly on consent. In France, there remained a good deal of obscurity. Claude de Seyssel, writing at the beginning of the sixteenth century, argued that royal necessity did not have to wait for popular consent: the monarch and people were so bound together by mutual obligation that the royal necessity, and therefore the royal right to taxation, overrode the property rights of the subject. The Crown should, of course, be prudent. But prudence in politics is elusive of definition. In England, extraordinary taxation—that is, taxation beyond what the Crown took by custom—was *ipso facto* within the jurisdiction of Parliament. Extraordinary demands required the special consent of the nation. In France, theorists like Chasseneuz argued the precise opposite. They claimed that extraordinary taxation was determined by the extraordinary conditions of the time and these justified the emergency rights of the Crown to tax without consent. This, it was held, was not arbitrary taxation. Chasseneuz is quite clear that necessity alone justified the royal exercise of this right to taxation; otherwise it was indefensible. But since this opportunity existed—with the prince the sole authority on when an emergency could be said to have arisen—the whole constitutional defence against arbitrary taxation could be washed away. The English parliamentarians saw this danger clearly enough. So did John Bates in the celebrated case of 1606 when, in effect, he resisted the right of the Crown to determine the need for special taxation without Parliament. Bates lost the battle but—when their time came—the parliamentarians won the war. In France constitutional resistance to the fiscal prerogative crumbled. In England constitutional resistance brought deadlock in government for half a century—and then victory to the constitutional opposition. It is true that 1614, the year of the last meeting of the Estates General until the French Revolution, is also the year of the Addled Parliament. (It was called addled presumably because it was even more addled than the others under the early Stuarts.) But in England Parliament possessed impressive powers of recovery and, a quarter of a century later, carried through the greatest constitutional revolution in English history. In France, the Estates General, serving no financial purpose and exercising no financial control, was not summoned again after 1614. Its demise made possible the rise of the Bourbon absolutism of the *ancien régime*: its reassembly in 1789 symbolized the end of the *ancien régime*.

It was on this very issue of taxation that the survival and strength of the assemblies of western Europe depended. For, unless the power to grant taxation was vested in the assembly, the prince had no incentive to summon it. But if it possessed that power, it could use it to extort a share in the Crown's authority to govern. The Crown must either lose money or lose power. The notion of a close marriage between the sixteenth-century monarchies and the parliamentary bourgeoisie scarcely exists outside the textbooks. Theirs was at most a chequered honeymoon. In Spain that partnership never came into being, nor did it in Germany. In France the provincial assemblies were often responsive to the royal demands; but the Estates General arrived without a mandate to grant funds and departed without the gratitude of the monarch or any wish on his part to see it again. Even in England, the so-called love-play between Elizabeth I and her faithful Commons finished up sometimes with the lady in tears. The association between Crown and estates was at best an uneasy relationship and at worst an unseemly brawl.

To meet its administrative bills and pay its official salaries, a government could do one of two things. It could seek to increase its taxes upon the nation; or it could in one way or another leave the officials to collect their own fees from the public. One other possibility was for the government to try a combination of both methods. To increase direct taxation — with or without the approval of the estates — raised formidable problems at every stage. For its impact, uneven and clumsy, often fell heaviest on those least able to bear it. In those countries, such as France and Spain, where the Crown was not dependent on the assembly of the estates for grants of supply, a large proportion of the taxes came from those sections of the community whose resistance was weakest — for example the peasantry — but whose resources were equally slender. From the whole community Crown income came through taxes upon trade and industry: crude expedients, shortsighted, unimaginative, harmful to the national economy. In England the system of direct taxation, with all its faults, fell more broadly upon the nation — here it was not the aristocracy which was exempt but the poorest section of the peasantry — but it was held more tightly within the parliamentary grasp. So the English government, too, had to fall back on indirect taxation.

The Elizabethan and early Jacobean system of indirect taxation had a longer continuous history in this country than had direct taxation. But it had become an unstable amalgam of medieval expedients modernized in a half-hearted way to do service in a later age. The customs dues are a striking example of this. The *ancient customs*, dating back to 1275, provided an export duty on wool, hides, tin and leather. To these had been added the subsidies of the middle of the fourteenth century, better known as tunnage and poundage, on wine and other commodities imported and exported. From the early fifteenth century, the practice was to grant them for the life of the monarch. This was in itself a compromise, for the merchants, as well as the baronial opposition, had resisted the Crown's sporadic imposition of these taxes upon trade without the consent of Parliament. By this compromise, the Crown acknowledged that such consent was necessary while Parliament acknowledged the royal necessity to enjoy these taxes for life. But there were still loose ends in the system. The Hanseatics had the special privilege of paying lower rates than the native English. At the same time goods were universally underestimated for customs purposes. Valuations were made somewhat more realistic by the new book of rates issued shortly before the end of Mary's reign in 1558. But they were not significantly raised again until 1608. Meanwhile the whole customs system, quite apart from smuggling, was riddled with mismanagement and corruption. Hence the development of customs farming, by which the Crown leased out some of these indirect taxes for a lump sum for each year and left the lessee to seek greater rewards from customs than the Crown had hitherto been able to obtain. Farming was employed during the middle years of Elizabeth's reign, then more or less discarded, revived at the end of the reign, and used extensively under James I. And then in 1625, at the beginning of Charles I's reign, Parliament broke an old precedent by granting him tunnage and poundage for only one year. He ignored it, but the basic political weakness of the whole revenue structure was laid bare for all to see.

This marshalling of the forces by both sides in the matter of taxes upon trade was merely one of many signs that the Commons recognized that the central weakness of the early Stuart monarchy lay in its revenue system; and that the monarchy recognized it too. The other taxes upon trade were of less importance. Purveyance and pre-emption (rights of the royal household to obtain transport and to purchase provisions at favourable prices) caused a good deal of irritation for a very limited reward to the Crown. Some revenue came also from the issue to private individuals of monopolies in industry and trade. But these bred for Elizabeth I a major constitutional crisis in the last Parliament of her reign and fed the discontents of the opposition throughout the whole of the next reign. Meanwhile, on the one side resistance and on the other incompetence and corruption cut back sharply whatever modest expectations from indirect taxation the government still clung to. On top of this the severe depressions in trade, for example at the end of the sixteenth century and in the second decade of the seventeenth, drained at the source the inadequate revenue from commerce. In Spain the burden was heavier, in the shape of the notorious *alcabala*, a 10 per cent tax on nearly all commercial transactions. It had, at various times, been converted into an annual lump sum, the *encabezamiento*, which under Philip II came to be worth the equivalent of well over half a million pounds sterling. It bled white the state of Castile, the most industrious of the Spanish kingdoms; and when in 1572 a comparable system was imposed in the Netherlands, it tore to shreds the threadbare patience of the Netherlanders. Already a rebellious Calvinism had taken root in a number of industrial and commercial centres, including Antwerp; but in the *alcabala* the whole merchant class saw their very economic existence laid under menace. Freedom, autonomy and prosperity thus shared a common peril and bred a doughty and unconquerable resistance. As a result, war and the heavy cost of maintaining distant armies shifted the Netherlands from the credit to the debit side of the Spanish fiscal balance sheet. Netherlands unity in resistance proved ephemeral but the drain upon Spain's resources lasted on into the next century.

In France, as in metropolitan Spain, the Crown's revenues were limited less by constitutional restraints than by its physical incapacity to gather in its revenues. The Estates General could neither grant nor withhold taxes but could only recommend their grant by local estates. From the Estates General of 1560 the Crown came away without even the promise of this aid. Instead it was given gratuitous advice from the second and third orders that the first order, the clergy, could be called upon to play a larger part in meeting the national debt. The clergy took the warning and made a substantial contribution. The king, too, drew his own conclusion and without ado — since consent was not forthcoming — imposed a wine tax as an executive decision and, at the same time, continued to collect the *taille*. The Estates General of 1576 recited anew the lessons of its predecessor and indeed went a good deal further. But it was itself trapped in a contradiction. Representing as it did aggressive Catholic opinion and committed to a policy of extinguishing the Huguenot forces, it displayed no comparable zeal in recommending funds for the purpose. (In this its members resembled the English parliamentarians of the early seventeenth century who wanted an aggressive foreign policy without yielding the supply to sustain it.) In an assembly confronted with this dilemma, Jean Bodin emerged as the spokesman in the third estate of that minority opinion hostile to a religious uniformity imposed by force, and as a spokesman also of that majority opinion hostile to the fiscal immunities enjoyed by the nobility and the clergy. If in the first of these objectives Bodin failed to carry the third estate with him, in the resistance to taxation he succeeded. The polite refusal to grant the royal demands for funds was couched in language which made the constitutional position plain beyond dispute: 'The deputies were *without the power* to act otherwise.'[1] It was a categoric declaration of *non possumus*.

That, too, had its price. The Estates General never came to a true maturity in any way comparable to the English Parliament. Instead provincial autonomy, deeply embedded in the French constitution, history and psychology—and shown in the unwillingness of the local electors to allow their deputies to be anything more than delegates—starved the Estates General of the life-blood of power. Hence, lacking the authority to grant money, the Estates General never gained the capacity either to make political bargains with the Crown or to enter into any share in political control. Having no authority to pay the piper, it never acquired the right to call the tune. The great incursions into the sphere of the prerogative, so characteristic of late Elizabethan and early Jacobean England, were impossible in contemporary France. The struggle around and against the French throne took place instead on the battlefield in the last third of the sixteenth century; and as victory went to the Bourbons, the prospects of effective national self-government were extinguished for centuries. In England, too, in the middle of the seventeenth century, the issue was fought out on the battlefield; but the cause had already been won in the first months of the Long Parliament. Victory had gone the other way.

In Spain, the constitutional conflict took another form. In both Castile and Aragon the Spanish kings had been faced with assemblies which made far more extensive claims than did the Estates General of France. The Cortes of Castile traditionally claimed that no new tax should be imposed without its being consulted; but in general it was not obstructive, although a group of proctors might declare that the grant would not be upheld in their own province. Yet, although the Cortes of Castile was much less representative than the French Estates General— only some of the towns were represented and the nobility and clergy were in practice not summoned—its deputies none the less *could* commit the towns which had sent them. However, the amounts received from these sources were proportionately small

---

[1] My italics.

compared with the total commitments of the Spanish Crown. In Aragon there was a sharp contrast. There were four estates in the Cortes (with the nobility divided into a greater and lesser section) and its powers were considerable. Led by the vigorous, politically conscious nobility, the Cortes had stubbornly and successfully held fast to its privileges and its purse-strings. But, by the end of the century, after the collapse of the Aragonese rebellion, the king seized the opportune moment to reduce its self-determination, exploited in any case for noble interests. The aristocracy's rights of voting, though not of representation, in the Cortes were diminished. More important, the Cortes's control over the use of the national revenue — essential to any control of policy — was largely reduced.

The governments of sixteenth-century Europe found themselves faced with relatively slender resources against ever-mounting commitments. Philip II had begun his reign with a virtual declaration of bankruptcy; Henry II of France was likewise hastened towards the treaty of Cateau-Cambrésis by the yawning deficit in his revenues. Elizabeth I of England inherited a large debt from her sister and a corrupt currency to make things worse. It was possible, during the middle years of her reign, to combine stringent economies at home with minimal commitments abroad; but, even so, the balance between income and expenditure was a fragile one and did not survive until the end of the reign. Yet even this modest achievement never came into sight for other monarchies. The French civil wars sapped the limited resources of the Crown and bled the monarchy white; the Spanish king's imperial burdens far outweighed even the heavy yield of bullion coming in from the New World. Flung hither and thither in search of ready cash, driven to piecemeal expedients of the most primitive kind, the governments were obliged to seek relief by putting up for auction the machinery of government itself. The distortion of public office for fiscal gain — a phenomenon familiar throughout western Europe — was a desperate and bankrupt device, in part to run government on the cheap, in part to make a profit — if not a virtue — out of necessity. Such a clumsy manœuvre was inescapable. For the governments of Europe were faced with a situation in which the middle classes could not, or would not, carry the major share of the costs of national government.

But if the middle classes proved uncooperative, the behaviour of the monarchies themselves, in relation to the middle classes, was ambiguous to a degree. In France the Crown sometimes opposed the oligarchical powers of the gilds and aimed at bringing them more directly under national control. But the policy was only unevenly carried through. And at other times the Crown quite simply sold *lettres de maîtrise* which in fact gave men the necessary authority to set up as masters of gilds. In Spain the history of the Mesta—the powerful corporation of sheep-breeders—in the later sixteenth century provides an interesting example of the government on the one hand, and the powerful sheep-trading gilds on the other, endeavouring to profit at each other's expense. For example, the Mesta had purchased outright from the exchequer the sheep-tolls collected for the Crown. In time of inflation this arrangement showed a handsome return to the Mesta. So did various other privileges purchased from the impoverished exchequer. But having sold privileges to the Mesta, the government now proceeded also to sell privileges *against* the Mesta, that is, to independent sheep masters. At the same time, having sold exemptions to the Mesta from old dues, it proceeded to impose new taxes upon sheep, thus requiring the whole process of exemption purchase to begin all over again. This process was useful at first but it was killing the goose which was laying the golden eggs. The early seventeenth century saw the emergence of a thoroughly decadent Mesta, with no compensatory improvement in agriculture outside the corporation to set in its place.

These manœuvres are merely examples of a widespread series of attempts made throughout Europe to tax the economy by subterfuge; to use existing commercial and industrial processes as a fiscal sponge. They necessarily involved the distortion of the economy; and this was proceeding on a massive scale. The obvious manifestation is the widespread sale of office. The term itself is a very broad one. It covers a variety of different procedures instituted for a variety of different purposes. In its simplest form it meant the sale of existing public offices by the government, or indeed the erection of special offices simply in order to sell them. It could take the more indirect form of the sale of economic controls—for example, customs farming or monopolies—so that the purchaser guaranteed a capital sum or an income in return for a free hand to use his executive and administrative skills to extract such profits as he was able. Finally, it could take the form of the canalization of the grant of office through ministers or their dependants, who charged fees for their services—fees variously and loosely described as gifts, rewards, perquisites and bribes. In practice the existing system, if so diffuse and diverse a method can be thus described, often partook of more than one of these processes. But it owed its importance fundamentally to its dual purpose: it brought in a revenue to the Crown at the same time as it transferred the burden of administration to private persons. For example, the customs system was notoriously inefficient and the government was forced to resort to customs farming. Thus, the farm allotted to Mr Customer Smythe in 1570 extended over all the import duties of London and its satellite ports. It lasted nearly twenty years and proved rewarding to both the Crown and Smythe. But critics of the farm considered that the government was being underpaid and the farm was brought to an end in 1588. There followed a thoroughly disappointing period of direct government control, with the result that the end of the century saw a reversion to customs farming. Here was a clear admission that an indirect civil service could prove more useful to the exchequer than one operated by the government itself. This, of course, does not apply to the creation of a sinecure or to the grants of patents of nobility. They brought in revenue but they rendered no service.

The need for a bureaucracy was, of course, nothing new. But in the post-Reformation period the problem assumed urgent and growing proportions. The medieval monarchies always, as it were, had at their disposal a bureaucratic reservoir. But the bureaucrats had been supplied and paid elsewhere, namely, by the Church. This was less true of the payments to the military class, which had to be met largely out of feudal lands or the king's revenues—or out of those of a conquered people. But the administrative class had consisted of churchmen and was paid for by the Church; and without this rudimentary framework of a civil service, the king's government could never have gone on. But the sixteenth century saw a severe weakening of the Church, in Catholic as well as Protestant nations—with exceptions such as Spain on the one hand and Geneva on the other. The natural reservoir of administrators began to go down; in any case, the mood of the time made intolerable the whole notion of an ecclesiastical monopoly of government office. In other words, the Crown could no longer hope to run the state with a civil service paid for by the Church. At this very time, also, the volume of administrative duties vastly increased, as the governments assumed enlarged responsibilities at home and abroad, in Church and state, locally and centrally. The sixteenth century saw, therefore, the rise of the secretary of state all over Europe. Through him flowed a mass of directives to all corners of the realm; back to him came a mass of information from all parts of the Continent. In England in the second half of the century the office of the secretary of state became a highly sophisticated, elaborate machine; in France it remained primitive, with the secretaries leading a wretched, overworked, hand-to-mouth existence. Meanwhile the output of official papers reached staggering proportions. If Philip II of Spain is rightly called *le roi paperassier*, the surviving manuscripts in the English Public Record Office, and in the Archives Nationales in Paris, give some measure of what was going on elsewhere. Administration multiplied itself, grew diversified, technical—and costly. Each government in its turn was faced with the appalling task of meeting a spendthrift demand for manpower and money with the ancient and restricted revenues of government. This indeed was the crisis of government in the late sixteenth century. It formed an intimate part of the political crisis of the age.

It was perhaps natural enough that the holder of a public office, if the grant was for life or if he held it for a long period, should come in time to regard his office as almost a piece of property, a kind of freehold which he could pass on to his heirs. This was all the more likely when, in spite of the protocol and extreme formality of the documents produced, the important part of the work was in fact done on an informal, intimate basis between monarch and minister, or between minister and trusted assistant. This was the case with the secretary of state in both France and England. It was a common practice in the France of Catherine de Medici for the secretaries of state to bring in their relations to carry some of the burdens of administration and to be trained as their successors. In England in the later part of Elizabeth's reign, Lord Burghley brought in his younger son, Sir Robert Cecil, to help in the general work of political management, as well as in the more specialized duties of the Court of Wards. An able and apt pupil, Robert Cecil became secretary of state in 1596 and, after his father's death, Master of the Court of Wards in 1599. Within that same institution the family of Hare held the office of clerk for several generations. The succession from father to son could, in some cases, be defended since the funding of experience in one family could make for the more efficient conduct of affairs. But the sixteenth century had seen the increasing use of 'reversions', with officials disposing of their appointments to other men—at a price. This widespread practice alarmed the monarchies who saw the control of appointments, in effect, passing from their hands without any certainty as to the ability or probity of the successor. Elizabeth I was hostile to the practice but could do nothing to stop it. In France, in spite of restraining legislation, the practice continued. Indeed here, having failed to stop it, the government decided to take a share in the proceedings, as for example did Charles IX in 1568, by imposing a tax on the transfer of office. But more important than any share that the government might have in the profits of the business conducted privately was the profit to be gained by itself selling—and creating for sale—numerous offices of state. The *Paulette* of 1604 was not an innovation but completed this process, and under it the holders of many offices were virtually guaranteed their right of inheritance in return for an annual fee to the Crown. Since the profits of office came from the public at large, this was one more example of the Crown taxing the nation at one stage removed. But this process had a considerable influence on the economy and structure of contemporary society. The creation of an elaborate vested interest in officialdom which was self-regarding was often of no help to the Crown. It necessarily set bounds to the advancing autocracy of the early seventeenth-century kings; and the Crown was forced in France to discover new officials and new taxes outside the existing bureaucracy. The office of *intendant* was the answer; but the imposition of the new taxation in the middle of the seventeenth century was one of the causes which turned the established bureaucracy against the Crown in the internal struggles of the period.

In Spain, where the Crown had been selling offices over a wide field, central and local (but not senior administrative ones or any judicial offices), numerous inessential posts were created simply in order that they might be sold. In France, likewise, this process became so extensive that Loyseau could allege that half the citizens of towns were functionaries. In England the sale by the Crown of local offices was unknown; but in Switzerland the bailiffs of the Grisons, who had bought their appointments for substantial sums, proceeded to mismanage their offices in pursuit of gain. This commerce in administration reached up into the heart of government itself: Henry III of France sold four seats in the council at 15,000 francs apiece. Moreover, the general rise of the *noblesse de robe* to a veritable fourth estate in the realm carried also tax exemptions, as it did in Spain; while the sale of patents of nobility was one more of the disastrous ways of selling the future for immediate gains. (On the other hand, the sale in Spain of patents of legitimacy to the children of clerics was at least fiscally innocuous.) In England the sale of titles did not begin until the coming of James I, and it was then that the hereditary title of baronet was created, specifically for revenue purposes. But these sales were not at the expense of the future, for nobility in England carried no exemption from tax. Indeed, the sale of baronetcies, significantly enough, began only in 1611, after a major attempt at fiscal reconstruction, the Great

Contract, had collapsed. But if the English government never put any of its offices of state up for auction, throughout its lesser officialdom and its quasi-civil service private enterprise was rampant.

A striking example of the interplay of government and private enterprise in fiscal matters was displayed in the right enjoyed by the English Crown in wardship and the related feudal dues. The end of the Middle Ages had of course not seen the end of feudalism in Europe: in varying degrees the holders of feudal rights extracted where they could the increasingly irrelevant profits from these ancient tenures. But only in England were the rights of the Crown as feudal overlord raised to a significant position in the revenue system and given a special court to develop and safeguard them. The mere possession of land held in chief by knight-service imposed upon the heir, if under age, the full burden of feudal wardship, including the obligation to marry at the will of the Crown or of the person who had purchased the wardship: a refusal could mean a crushing forfeit. Thus the right of feudal marriage survived beyond its feudal context and was imposed, in irrelevant circumstances, upon a considerable number of landholders. This was largely a royal right—with scattered relics surviving among other lords; and it was a right which was on many occasions sold to strangers for a capital sum, and for a further rent charge for the wards' lands. It led in some cases to grave social abuses and it raised a considerable outcry. But it brought in money to the Crown and it brought in even more in fees and profits to the Crown servants. In very many cases the Crown was simply transferring to the landed classes the task of paying the salaries of the civil service. But far more was involved than this. For, in exploiting these sources of indirect and un-parliamentary taxation, the Crown was parrying the increasing efforts of the opposition, especially in the early seventeenth century, to bring policy—and ministers—under parliamentary control. Such fiscal contortions on the part of the Crown were particularly necessary in a country like England where parlia-mentary consent was essential for direct taxation as well as for new taxes upon trade. Hence the increasing importance of disguised indirect taxation, of which monopolies furnish one example and wardship another.

A further consequence followed from this extension of private control in public administration: the distrust of public administration itself. For it looked like the subversion of public interests to private ends: in short, corruption. But the word corruption is rarely defined and has been as much bandied about by historians as it was indiscriminately used by contemporaries. There were of course numerous examples of justice being subverted by fraud or force. 'The law is ended', said a contemporary rhyme, 'as a man is friended.' There were examples of the despoiling of the Crown by those who had been called to its service. These practices are, of course, corrupt; and an immature – or ill-paid – administration anywhere in the world, at any time, displays precisely these qualities. But the expression corruption, as used of the sixteenth and seventeenth centuries, has been extended and applied to the whole range of official perquisites, gifts and favours; and the structure of society and government has thereby been obscured. For, in many cases, these gifts were virtually fees, and no more than another facet of that indirect and inefficient taxation upon which the governments perforce depended. In all cases they were a double sign, of the rudimentary and incomplete control of the Crown over its civil service and of the gross inadequacy of the public revenues to provide sufficient taxes to sustain its civil service by direct salaries. It is true that many of these gifts were made in order to obtain favours at public expense. But far more were routine payments, made by all and taken by all. This was not corruption but something inherent in the faulty revenue system of the day. In any state in the modern period, the extent to which this defective system survives varies inversely with the success of the government in taxing the nation.

But what happened when the recipients of gifts were not civil servants but royal favourites – the *mignons* of Henry III of France, the Carrs and Villiers of James I of England? It was only then that the system was indeed distorted into corruption. It was only then that these indirect revenues seeped away into the thirsty soil of luxury and greed. Then the system became barren and twisted;

and national interests were sacrificed to a decadent court. As a result the very word courtier acquired the attributes of corruption itself. But that, too, is to confuse the whole with the part. For the court in the age of personal government meant two things. It meant, in its narrow sense, that section of the aristocracy and the household servants called to the immediate service of the palace, with all its luxury, ceremonial and gilded artifice. In this milieu the personal favourite flourished. But the court meant also the whole substantial body of ministers and civil servants called to the public service of the Crown. Sometimes a man was a personal favourite as well as a minister, as was the case with the Earl of Leicester in Elizabethan England. Many contemporaries correctly understood this, as did, for example, the journalists of the eighteenth century who spoke of 'court' and 'country'. By 'court' they meant simply that party which was in public office. 'Court' meant the palace at Westminster; but it also meant the civil service of Whitehall.

The pattern of politics at the centre was reproduced on a smaller scale in the provinces. A local magnate had enormous resources of power and profit both in offices under him on his estates and in his recommendation for public office in the capital. Such a man was the Duke of Norfolk in the first decade of Elizabeth I's reign; but with his execution in 1572, no aristocrat emerged in East Anglia to take his place. Instead, the whole patronage system became the battlefield for bitter local feuds among the upper gentry, with prestige no less than profit in the balance. For example, to be placed on the commission of the peace – or to be evicted from it – raised or reduced a man's social standing to an impressive degree. In the west country the Earls of Pembroke were continually pressed by suitors for office. On the other hand the office of deputy lieutenant was in some counties difficult to fill, while in others it was much sought after. The degree of patronage in English local society is difficult to assess; but it was clearly widespread and served to nourish a flexible yet firm relationship on a local territorial basis. That is to be seen in religion as well as politics, where the country house might serve as a local centre for religious dissent, whether Catholic in

England or Huguenot in France. This quality is reflected no less in the economic than in the social structure of the provinces. In western Europe at this period there was a far greater measure of free cultivation than in eastern Europe and beyond. In those regions a new and tougher form of agrarian feudalism was emerging at the very time when in western Europe many of its harsh qualities were passing away. None the less, the power of the local gentry in the west survived and sometimes grew stronger, but it was power sustained by their role as *rentiers* and by a new kind of social cohesion. It is true that the pressure of rent could in its way be as burdensome and inexorable as the earlier pressure of personal serfdom; but the quality of society was changing. The lord of the manor was becoming the squire of the village.

In France those with vested interests in office—at least in its upper ranges—emerged as a fairly distinct class, the *noblesse de robe*: but this applied to only one sector of the administration. It could not link them as a class to the holders of the innumerable petty offices diffused throughout France. In England, even at the centre, the government servants lacked that constancy of interest and attitude needed to ensure a stable following to the privy council, in Parliament and in the country. Parliamentary patronage, and patronage of office, could guarantee no certain support to a magnate in a Commons debate over some great religious or other issue which divided the nation. Lord Burghley gathered into his clientage men like James Morrice, who later on embarrassed the government by taking a minority view. In successive decades in the first half of the seventeenth century, as the conflicts between their loyalty to Crown and to principle intensified, many officials followed principle—or interest—against the will of the king. In France likewise, at the time of the Fronde, many office-holders identified themselves with the local population against the government, for the mixed reasons of interest and tradition. The lesson of these years and what went before demonstrates the social complexity of office-holding. The office-holders of the governments of Europe formed neither a coherent body of vested interests nor a uniform class or caste. In England the local government was in the hands of amateurs from the lord lieutenant down through the justices of the peace and on to the parish constable. In France it was much more professionalized from the *intendant* downwards. But in neither case could a national directive override the interests of the provinces without splitting the loyalty of those officials drawn from the region. Moreover, men without access to the profits of office had cause to deepen their discontent; and this was especially strong against court favourites with little to commend them except their charm. But in the absence of party politics, patronage provided – however inadequately – the broad channels of political command.

It is the practice to speak of this large and growing body of bureaucrats drawn to the service of the government as belonging to the middle class. The term is quite imprecise; but it has some utility in that it differentiates its members from the older aristocracy who, by a rapidly fading tradition, claimed an hereditary right to govern and advise. It also differentiates the bureaucracy from the artisan and peasant classes. But it was essentially an open class, not a caste. It led on quite often to fairly rapid promotion into the aristocracy at one end (cemented often by marriage), and at the other end it gave access to the talented man of humble birth. The medieval Church had always supplied a channel such as this, of which the career of Cardinal Wolsey is the best and last exemplar in England; but by the end of the sixteenth century the secularization of political power had proceeded far. It was still possible in the middle of the seventeenth century for ecclesiastics like Laud and Juxon to rise high in the Protestant state, and for cardinals to rule in Catholic France. But in most high offices the cleric was giving way to the lawyer and the businessman. After Wolsey came Thomas More, Thomas Cromwell, Gresham, the Seymours, the Dudleys and the Cecils. In France secretaries of state such as de Laubespine, Pinart and Villeroy were laymen. John Maitland of Thirlstane, appointed chancellor of Scotland in 1587, was the first to hold that office without being either a bishop or a great lord. Against this process there was an outcry, not from the weakened Church but from the older aristocracy and their dependants. In England, the rising of the northern earls in 1569 had as one of its declared objects the elimination of the corrupting influence of upstarts like Cecil, thereby echoing the slogan of a generation before when the Pilgrimage of Grace aimed at eliminating the upstart Cromwell. In Sweden, Charles IX was criticized by the aristocracy for relying on secretaries of menial birth. It was, indeed, in Sweden, a nation far less supplied with lawyers, merchants and industrialists than were England and the Netherlands, that the growth of a professional bureaucracy was too long delayed. In this Sweden resembled Catholic Spain rather than Protestant England or Holland. But in western Europe the situation was changing decisively in favour of the professional middle class. In contrast, a state like Poland, with no bureaucratic middle class at the disposal of the government, was obliged to function mainly through an irresponsible aristocracy, with results which are well known.

All over western Europe the monarchies suffered a severe decline of wealth, either absolutely, or relatively to the wealth of the leading sections of the commercial, industrial and landed classes. The disparity between the monarchs and their wealthier subjects was intensified as the governments found themselves obliged to take on the heavier, and more expensive, tasks of domestic administration, diplomacy and war. In the second half of the sixteenth century, England, France, Spain and the Netherlands assumed burdensome military commitments and, in its last two decades, they were continuously at war. By one means or another taxation had to be increased; and, in all cases, indirect taxation (either on trade or by exploiting technical anachronisms, like wardships) offered the most promising source. But it could be stretched beyond endurance, as the response of the Low Countries to the *alcabala* showed, in which case it could hasten the advance towards costly and disastrous war. In Spain, resistance to indirect taxation was weak, but the whole economy of the nation was already enfeebled, with its society distorted into preferences for non-productive pursuits, of which the most important were the Church and the armed services. Yet if this period saw the beginning of the decay of the Spanish economy, it saw also the culmination of the decay of the Spanish Cortes, as the Crown emancipated itself from its consent for taxation. The same thing was happening in France. In England the constitution allowed to the monarchy only limited powers of manœuvre in the field of taxation. Hence the advent of war in 1585, with its call for money, gave Parliament an increasingly strong claim to influence government policy, a claim it would never again renounce. Elizabeth tried to counter this by economies in expenditure, the early Stuarts by stretching to breaking-point the dubious devices of the prerogative. Indeed so fragile was the fiscal prerogative of the early Stuarts that it needed only a minor war on the Scottish border in 1638–9 to shatter it beyond hopes of recovery.

In England the aristocracy never became a caste and the landed gentry never became a lesser nobility. Hence the middle and upper classes stood in much closer relation to each other than they did to the monarchy; and, in time of crisis, had much more in common with each other than they had with the Crown. That was the case in the shires, and it was the families of the same men who felt at ease with each other in the House of Commons. The institution of justices of the peace, said Francis Bacon,

> knits noblemen and gentlemen together, and in no place else but here in England are noblemen and gentlemen incorporated: for abroad in other countries noblemen meddle not with any parcel of justice, but in martial affairs; matter of justice that belongs to the gownmen; and this is it that makes those noblemen the more ignorant and the more oppressors; but here amongst us they are incorporated with those that execute justice, and so being warriors are likewise made instruments for peace; and that makes them truly noble.

This, of course, was an idealistic picture; but, as ever, Bacon put his finger on the crucial point. There can be little doubt that English society was more closely knit at this time than was true of most countries in Europe. This was a major social fact. Alongside it was the major constitutional fact that direct taxation required parliamentary consent and indirect taxation was relatively inelastic. These two things preserved the English Parliament at a time when comparable institutions elsewhere were passing into desuetude.

A Retrospect:

Gunpowder Plot and the politics of dissent

At the end of the period that we have been considering there occurred an incident, minor in itself, which enables us to explore, in retrospect, some of the problems of liberty as they emerged in the Tudor period. The incident was the Gunpowder Plot of November 5th, 1605, the 'Powder Treason' as it was known to contemporaries.

'Sir Thomas Parry,' wrote Robert Cecil, Earl of Salisbury, James I's secretary of state, on November 6th to the English ambassador in Paris, 'it hath pleased Almighty God, out of his singular goodness, to bring to light the most cruel and detestable practice ...'[1] *The most cruel and detestable practice* was nothing less than a plan to blow up Parliament at a time when the royal family and the nobility, the leading ministers, the clergy and judges and Members of Parliament were assembled for its opening. And already on November 5th the government had in its hands an important conspirator, 'one Johnson', as they had put it, 'a Yorkshire man'. There was, in fact, no such person. On November 7th they knew indeed that this man was Guy

NOTE: Part of this paper was broadcast by the B.B.C. and published in the *Listener*, 80, pp. 625–7 (November 14th, 1968), under the title 'The Causes and Consequences of Mr. Guy Fawkes'. The whole was published in *Early Stuart Studies*, Essays in honour of David Harris Willson, ed. Howard S. Reinmuth (University of Minnesota Press, 1970), pp. 95–121.

[1] Cited in S. R. Gardiner, *What Gunpowder Plot Was* (1897), p. 22. There is some doubt whether the letter was sent off on November 6th. A similar letter, dated November 9th, was sent by Salisbury to Sir Charles Cornwallis, English ambassador to Spain. *Memorials of Sir Ralph Winwood*, ed. Edmund Sawyer (1725), II, pp. 170–72. An unprinted copy of a similar letter, addressed to Sir Thomas Edmondes, English ambassador in Brussels, is at Hatfield House (see HMC, *Cal. Salisbury MSS*, XVII, 481–2), of which the original is at the British Museum (*Stowe MSS*, 168, fol. 213).

Fawkes. What had brought Guy Fawkes out of his Yorkshire obscurity to the very centre of the political scene? It is impossible to tell the whole story here but the central events must be briefly recalled.[1]

On October 26th Lord Monteagle, a Catholic peer, while at supper with some guests, was handed a note which had been brought to his door. The note was unsigned but Monteagle quickly grasped its importance. Yet, instead of hastily putting it safely away, he handed it to a member of his household to read with him. The letter was a warning to Monteagle not to attend the opening of Parliament, and it went on, 'for though there be no appearance of any stir, yet I say they shall receive a terrible blow this Parliament and yet shall not see who hurts them'. Monteagle hurried with the letter to the Earl of Salisbury, who hardly needed to exercise any great analytical skill to detect that this language almost certainly meant a plan to blow up Parliament by means of gunpowder. However, Salisbury went through the pantomime, several days later when he showed the letter to King James I, of leaving it to that kingly Solomon to unravel its meaning, to the admiration of his ministers and courtiers.

It is clear that, once the letter had been read, first by a member of Monteagle's household and then by Salisbury, the whole Plot and all the plotters were in jeopardy. Yet they held to their purpose, this strange band of men gathered together in an extraordinary conspiracy. They were led, not by Guy Fawkes, but by Robert Catesby, a man of great charm, strength and personal magnetism. There is reason to think that he may have been a convert to Catholicism and, as is sometimes the case, he may have carried an inherited guilt over the treatment of the Catholic Church by his forbears. Certainly he was single-minded and idealistic, deeply resentful of the inequality and injustice inflicted upon members of his faith by the established order. Many men felt as bitterly as he did about the persecution of the Catholic Church in England but few were so brave—or so foolhardy. But some of these few were drawn to Catesby's

[1] I follow here the narrative as set out in Willson, *James VI and I*, pp. 223–6, and Gardiner, *What Gunpowder Plot Was*, pp. 14–37.

leadership and remained loyal to him until the last. There were two brothers, Thomas and Robert Winter, and their brother-in-law, John Grant; there was Thomas Percy, a member of a distinguished Catholic family; there were the brothers John and Christopher Wright; and Sir Everard Digby, Ambrose Rokewood, Francis Tresham, these three men wealthier than the rest; there was Bates, Catesby's servant; and there was Guy Fawkes, the experienced soldier, in the Plot almost from the start. At the fringe of the Plot there were three Jesuit priests, who knew something about the Plot as it developed but were not directly involved in either its preparation or execution.

The plot itself had two simple components: the first was to be the destruction of Parliament and government in London; the second was to be a summons to arms of the Catholic gentry. Hence for part one, there was the provision of gunpowder at Westminster; for part two, there was the hunting party at Dunchurch in Warwickshire, in the heart of a Catholic complex of estates, although it must be at once observed that the Catholic gentry had no notion of the role reserved for them. All this, and a good deal more, we now know, but little of this was known to the government. Hence, as often happens, even when they had knowledge of the Plot they waited until the last possible moment for fuller information and evidence to come in before they took the decisive step.

It is probable that Tresham, who is widely—and, I think, correctly—believed to have been the writer of the Monteagle letter,[1] wrote it to warn the plotters rather than the government, in the hope of persuading the plotters to abandon the whole thing while there was time. In that case, Monteagle himself may have been part of the conspiracy within the conspiracy—that is, resolved to save the plotters from themselves. That would explain why he asked a member of his household to read it: to warn the plotters that their secret was no longer a secret. But this is still hypothesis.

What is clear, however, is that the plotters rejected so easy an

---

[1] In HMC, *Cal. Salisbury MSS*, XVII, xvii and 550, there is a suggestion that the writer may have been Percy.

escape. Even on November 2nd, when Catesby, Fawkes and three of the others were told that Salisbury and the king were familiar with the Plot, they held fast to their commitment. Tresham's manœuvre, if it was such, went in vain.

On November 4th the government organized a search of the cellar below Parliament. On the first visit they found nothing but coal and wooden faggots, in the care of a certain John Johnson. On the second visit that night barrels of gunpowder were found underneath the coal and faggots, and Johnson was arrested. That was the end of the business. The Plot was unmasked before a tinder could be struck. On the following day, November 5th, Catesby and the others fled, hoping somehow that the second part of the plan, the Catholic rising, might yet be put into effect. But the Catholic gentry to a man rejected the call and would have nothing to do with the enterprise. On November 8th at Holbeche in Staffordshire, Catesby and the Wright brothers were killed by the sheriff's troops. Percy mortally wounded and Thomas Winter and Rokewood wounded and taken prisoner. Those who survived were taken to London for trial. Inquiries were pressed forward, with torture and the threat of torture at hand. The trial followed in January, and at the end of that month and the beginning of February the conspirators were executed.

But the government from the start had been resolved that the affair would not end in anticlimax. The king addressed Parliament, an official account of the whole business was issued, the surviving conspirators were, after trial, barbarously executed in public, and an Act was passed ordaining that November 5th should henceforth be celebrated for ever as a day of national deliverance.[1] This Act was in force until the middle of the nineteenth century; and still now, a century after its demise, November 5th each year continues to bring profit to the pyrotechnics industry and delight to small boys of all ages. And here is another paradox. For every one person who recalls the name of the Earl of Salisbury, regarded in his own day as the most powerful statesman in Europe, a thousand now recall the name of Guy Fawkes, the minor Yorkshire gentleman and captain who

[1] 3 Jac. I c.I.

was more brave than he was wise, more devout than he was intelligent. There is really no need for street urchins – in search of contributions to the cost of their fireworks – to appeal to passers-by to 'remember the Guy', for our folk-memory has preserved him. Guy Fawkes believed that his plans for November 5th, 1605, would give him a secure place in history. He was right.

And yet, it might be said, surely this brief tragedy – which has also something of comedy in it – is hardly worthy of lengthy historical investigation? Nothing could be further from the truth, for we are only at the beginning of our understanding of what Guy Fawkes signifies in the history of England. The developments which prompted him to attempt what he did form part of the tragic story of European liberty: as such, it is a worthy theme for the historian. For this microcosmic situation, the events leading up to November 5th, 1605, has in it the basic ingredients of the whole human order. Any consideration of the Plot in its larger historical context prompts two questions. The first is: what brought Guy Fawkes to that tragic moment in Westminster when, as he stood at the door of his cellar, the Westminster magistrate put out his hand and arrested him? The second question, closely relevant to our own age, is: can such a situation ever again recur in various parts of the civilized world? (I mean, not the Plot but the situation in which gunpowder seems, to brave and honest men, to be the only answer.) This second question falls outside our context but the first – what brought Guy Fawkes to Westminster – is germane to any study of modern history.

The story of Gunpowder Plot is, then, the story of an explosion which never took place. But behind this story there lay long years of bitterness and despair. For Guy Fawkes belonged to an oppressed, disfranchised and dispossessed minority, the English Roman Catholics who, for half a century, since 1559, had been increasingly isolated from their fellow countrymen. How this arose is, of course, well known. The mid-sixteenth century saw the outbreak of religious struggles of great intensity and intolerance in many places in Europe, which were to culminate in the Thirty Years' War from 1618 to 1648. In

ideological warfare mercy is neither expected nor given. Moreover, religious struggle was identified with national survival:
those who did not accept the established faith were, it was held,
enemies of the existing order, perhaps even agents of an enemy
power. We recall, too, that in 1570 the pope formally deposed
Elizabeth from the English throne and thereby set free her
Catholic subjects from their due obedience; and in 1588 a
Catholic crusade in the shape of the Spanish Armada was
launched against England. We know also that several attempts
were made to assassinate her, as they were made to assassinate her
fellow Protestant, William of Orange; and that in 1584 the
attempt against William proved successful. In 1610 James I's
contemporary, Henry IV of France, was also assassinated.

Aware of these things, we are able to explain the savage
penalties which the English government inflicted on Catholics.
I shall mention only a few examples. All Catholic services were
prohibited; and failure to attend the Anglican Church on Sunday
and Holy Days was punished with 1s. fine per week in 1559,
raised in 1581 to £20 a month.[1] In some cases failure to pay the
fine could lead to the seizure of two-thirds of a recusant's lands
for the whole period of his recusancy, and to imprisonment.
After 1585 any Catholic priest found in England was *ipso facto*
subject to the penalties for high treason; and even harbouring a
priest carried the death penalty.[2] The Oath of Supremacy,
required of all men in any branch of public service, barred
Catholics from access to office. The same oath was intended to
keep them out of office in the universities;[3] and the only schools
to which they could send their children would instruct them in
the Protestant faith. Nor was there any available outlet for honest
dissent. The heavy hand of official censorship reached out relent-
lessly to every corner of the kingdom.

In the historical context we can understand how such savage
measures came to be introduced. For this was an age when independent thought, outside the official channels of Church and

[1] 1 Eliz. c.2.; 23 Eliz. c.1.
[2] 27 Eliz. c.2.
[3] 1 Eliz. c.1.

state, was suspect. Heresy—that is, dissent—corrupted the soul just as coining corrupted the currency. The penalty for coining was death; how much more necessary then was it in the contemporary outlook that he who attempted to corrupt the soul and deprive it of eternal life should be punished by death? Nor should we, who live in the twentieth century, be surprised at this Draconic policy. The power of political censorship (with the severest penalties for dissent) in many parts of the modern world needs no illustration.

The function of government is to govern and to preserve the security and independence of the state and the existing order. But it would be a grave lack in the historical imagination not to see that a fervent Catholic minority could not accept an order of society in which their faith was proscribed, their sons and daughters sent into exile for their education, their priests executed, their leaders imprisoned, their lands sequestered. On top of this, the new king, James I, having promised all things to all men found it impossible to fulfil any promise to any man. James was not himself vindictive against the Catholics but he was under heavy pressure in Parliament and elsewhere. In any case, the exchequer was short of funds, and recusancy fines—the fines for not attending church—were a wonderful means for serving God and the exchequer. But they were imposed sporadically, and Catholics continued to be fed on hopes that better times were coming. *Hope deferred maketh the heart sick.* So the English Catholics swung wildly between optimism and despair; and it was in the downward swing of despair that Guy Fawkes threw in his lot with the conspirators.

It is significant that the plotters were all country gentlemen, mostly of moderate means and limited prospects. Such estates as they or their families retained were under continuous threat of savage exactions and, as recusants, they lived under severe disabilities in education and in professional advancement. They were also officially barred from the whole government service. This is not to suggest for one moment that it was with the aim of improving their individual fortunes and prospects that they embarked on conspiracy. It was simply that they could not live at peace in a community which reduced a whole section of that community to the level of second-class citizens, criticized, distrusted and, where occasion served, denounced by any influential demagogue who chose to set fire to false rumour and dark prejudice. Guy Fawkes—so he told his captors—had from the beginning prayed that 'he might perform that which might be for the advancement of the Catholic faith and saving of his own soul'.[1] Here indeed was an alienated minority in what was becoming a multi-religious society, a minority rejected by that very society to which they claimed to belong as equals.

But before examining the consequences of the Plot, we must face a question which has dominated its historiography almost from the start. Everyone who has worked on the materials for the reign is aware that for centuries it has been suggested that the Plot was an invention of the government; and these allegations have been repeated, enlarged, refurbished, all the while building up to a mountainous indictment of the man who is said to have been its true author, the Earl of Salisbury. I cannot in my own lifetime recall a time when there was not someone, somewhere, announcing the discovery of new evidence to confirm these dark suspicions. Of this new evidence I only want to say one thing. Some of it is old; the rest is very old. Guy Fawkes was on trial for one day; the Earl of Salisbury has been on trial for three and a half centuries.

Let us admit at once that the man who should have benefited most from the plot was the Earl of Salisbury. This extraordinary man, one of the subtlest politicians in the whole history of England, had been advanced to office, late in Elizabeth's reign, in the shadow of his famous father, Lord Burghley, minister of the queen for thirty-seven years. Salisbury himself was a hunchback, some five feet tall, with an inordinate ambition for power and wealth. He also had an unrivalled capacity for making enemies. He had a few close friends who worshipped him, but outside his narrow circle he must have been the most unpopular man in England, loathed by the people, never in the full trust of the

[1] HMC, *Cal. Salisbury MSS*, XVII, 479.

king. Moreover, his greatest prospect, to become lord high treasurer of England, was in 1605 as yet unfulfilled.

If there was anything that would bind his monarch to him — and perhaps even win some measure of gratitude from the people at large — it was the dramatic rescue of the king, his ministers and therefore the nation itself from some dastardly plot to plunge the country into blood and confusion. There was, moreover, a religious aura to be gained. Salisbury would emerge as the saviour of Protestantism, protecting the guardians of the reformed faith against the horrible machinations conceived in Rome and designed for England. Long regarded by Catholics as their principal scourge, what he needed was just such a plot to discredit the Jesuit activists, divide Catholic from Catholic, and reduce the moderates to subjection.

We are aware, too, that some of the confessions were obtained by torture or the threat of torture; and that parts of these confessions were never made public at all — as is sometimes the case today when treason trials are held *in camera*. Apart from this, at various times writers have come forward to point out that from their examination of the topography of Westminster they consider it impossible for anyone to have carried the gunpowder without being seen. Others have found mysterious callers at Salisbury's house who, they think, were his *agents provocateurs* among the plotters. Some have satisfied themselves — but no one else — that the confessions were forgeries. Much of this was thrashed out more than seventy years ago in a celebrated debate between Father Gerard and the historian S. R. Gardiner.[1] Not a single piece of major evidence has since been brought forward to alter the case as made out by Gardiner and as accepted by the independent scholars who have worked in this field.

Much of the debate, then, has focused upon the career of the Earl of Salisbury. The view which contemporaries formed of him — and it is a view shared by many historians — is that he, like his father, Lord Burghley, was an inveterate enemy of the Catholics and bent on their destruction. No manœuvre, his

[1] J. Gerard, *What Was the Gunpowder Plot?* (1897). Gardiner, *What Gunpowder Plot Was.*

enemies believed, was too complex or too villainous to be unacceptable to him. Indeed, it was said that his peculiar genius lay
in fabricating these devices with a spectacular degree of success.
Michael Drayton's poem, 'The Owl', written in 1603, may almost
be taken as an anticipatory charge of Salisbury's guilty involvement in the Plot of 1605.[1] In his poem Salisbury is the vulture,
who employs a bat as his agent with a special capacity

> To urge a doubtful speech up to the worst
> To broach new treasons and disclose them first,
> Whereby himself he clears, and unawares,
> Intraps the fowl, unskilful of these snares ...

If this is what Drayton could write in 1603, we should not be
surprised to learn, according to one report, dated November
13th, 1605, that the whole Gunpowder Plot has been described in
Paris as 'a fable'.[2]

Yet this approach is simplistic. It is hard to discover, for
example, whether the same opinion was widely held in French
government circles or whether Dudley Carleton, who transmitted
the news, had special reasons for sending such a report. We know
that he had a link with the plotters—as the Earl of Northumberland's secretary he leased them the vault in Westminster where
the gunpowder was stored. He was subsequently under suspicion
of being involved in the Plot; but there is no evidence to support
this allegation.[3] Nor should we forget that most conspiracies
from Gunpowder Plot to the murder of President Kennedy have
been taken by someone to be the work of government agents.
However, I have found no other record by either an English or a
foreign diplomat at this time to indicate that similar suspicions of
government involvement existed elsewhere. Molin, the Venetian
ambassador, reporting home on December 8th, says that the

---

[1] *The Works of Michael Drayton*, ed. J. W. Hebel (5 vols, Oxford, 1932), II,
p. 493. Ibid., ed. Kathleen Tillotson and B. H. Newdigate (Oxford, 1941), V,
p. 179.

[2] *CSPD*, 1603–1610, 255.

[3] *The Letters of John Chamberlain*, ed. N. E. McClure (Philadelphia, 1939), I,
p. 12.

government would be delighted to be able to prove that the Earl of Northumberland was the leader of the plotters. He reports that Salisbury would be glad to establish this because of the personal enmity between the two men; but as to the authenticity of the plot itself, the ambassador expresses no kind of doubt.[1] Father John Gerard, who wrote his narrative of the Plot in 1606 — not under torture but in freedom and in a report to the papacy — makes no such charge against the government. He expresses doubts about the Monteagle letter and goes on: 'But although many were of opinion that this [the letter] was not the first means of this discovery [of the Plot], yet none that ever I could hear of was able to give a certain judgement which way indeed it was discovered.'[2]

In these early days it was widely believed that the government was aware of the plot before the officials began their search of the vault on November 4th and perhaps aware of it before the Monteagle letter. There is nothing unreasonable in this supposition, for there is something dramatic and contrived about the delivery of the letter; and at least two people, Monteagle and Tresham, may have hoped that way to end the Plot or, failing that, to clear themselves. This hypothesis is, however, quite different from the charge that the government (i.e., Salisbury) organized the Plot, that it was a fabricated affair into which a few innocent Catholics were drawn. We do meet this allegation openly debated, but not until a generation had passed, although his involvement was being rumoured before then.[3]

The argument is sometimes put forward that Shakespeare's *Winter's Tale* was a commentary on the Plot and, in its title, a reference to the confession of Thomas Winter, one of the conspirators; but there seems to be no evidence, either internal or external, to support this interpretation. On the other hand, Ben Jonson's *Catiline His Conspiracy* does by implication deal with the

---

[1] *CSPV*, 1603–1607, X, 301–2.

[2] John Gerard, *The Condition of Catholics under James I*, ed. John Morris (1871), pp. 101–2.

[3] See, for example, [William Lloyd], *The Late Apology in the Behalf of the Papists* (1667), p. 32. See also below, p. 338 nn. 2 and 3.

allegations that the Plot was not genuine, and comes to the conclusion that it was. Jonson, however, enjoyed for a time the patronage of Salisbury and was involved, too, in informing on the plotters.[1] The surviving evidence, therefore, shows widespread rumours of Salisbury's prior knowledge of the Plot and somewhat later allegations of his instigation of it, which is a separate and more serious charge. In the mid-seventeenth century when Godfrey Goodman was writing his memoirs, he said of Salisbury: 'The great statesman had intelligence of all this [Catholic plotting]; and because he would show his service to the state, he would first contrive and then discover a treason; and the more odious and hateful the treason were, his service would be the greater and more acceptable.' He goes on: 'some will not stick to report that the great statesman sending to apprehend these traitors gave special charge and direction for Percy and Catesby, "let me never see them alive," who, it may be, would have revealed some evil counsel given.'[2] A tract of 1642 reports, though it discounts as false, 'that there was no such treason intended but that it was an invention of him, whom in reverence I forbear to name'.[3] By the time of the Restoration, amid the controversy over the emancipation of the Catholics, the charge of instigation is openly laid against Salisbury, though one of his defenders dismisses it as 'a very groundless and impudent fiction'. 'Others perhaps', he says, 'have spoken this in raillery; yet you are the first, that we know of, that has asserted it in print.' Then he goes on to present his argument against the whole thesis:

Bellarmin[e] and his fellow Apologists in that age never pretended it. The parties themselves, neither at their trial, nor at their execution, gave any intimation of it. Can you tell us which of the conspirators were Cecil's instruments to draw in the rest? Or can you think he was so great an artist

[1] Cf. B. N. De Luna, *Jonson's Romish Plot* (1967).
[2] G. Goodman, *The Court of King James I*, ed. J. S. Brewer (1839), I, pp. 102, 106-7.
[3] *Plots, Conspiracies and Attempts ...* , collected by G. B. C. (2nd edn, 1642), p. 5.

that he could persuade his setters to be hanged, that his art might not be suspected? For 'tis well known that he saved not any of those wretches from suffering. And they which did suffer charged none other but themselves in their confessions.[1]

His opponent (thought to be Roger Palmer, Earl of Castlemaine), returning to the controversy, reaffirms that the Plot 'was made, or at least fomented, by the policy of a great statesman'. His reason was to destroy any prospects of improved conditions for Catholics under James; and it was no difficult task for a secretary of state to get hold of 'turbulent and ambitious spirits' to join in the scheme. Indeed, as a reward Cecil was made an earl.[2] (This last observation may be taken as a measure of the evidence now coming forward, sixty years after the event. Gunpowder Plot was centred on the early days of November; Salisbury had been made an earl six months before on May 4th.[3])

By now we are entering the apocrypha of the Plot. The men who were alive at the time had died, and it was becoming possible to attribute a string of fantasies to people who were no longer available to contradict them. Father John Gerard—not the contemporary priest, but the nineteenth-century controversialist—gathered together some of this material in his book *What Was the Gunpowder Plot?*, published in 1897. The following are some examples of his evidence. We have a confession by the second Earl of Salisbury to William Lenthall that 'it was his father's contrivance which Lenthall soon after told one Mr. Webb, a person of quality, and his kinsman, yet alive'. Or again, we have the opinion attributed to Sir Henry Wotton that it was 'usual with Cecil to create plots, that he might have the honour of the discovery, or to such effect'. Here is another witness: Sir Kenelm Digby, son of one of the conspirators, 'would often say it was a

---

[1] *The Late Apology in the Behalf of the Papists*, p. 32.
[2] [Roger Palmer], *A Reply to the Answer to the Catholique Apology* (1668), pp. 203, 208.
[3] G. E. C., *Complete Peerage*, XI, p. 403.

state design, to disengage the King of his promise to the Pope and the King of Spain, to indulge the Catholics if ever he came to be king here; and somewhat to his purpose was found in the Lord Wimbledon's papers after his death'—Lord Wimbledon was a nephew of Salisbury. Here is yet another: 'Mr. Vowell, who was executed in the Rump time, did also affirm it.' Finally, we may learn that 'Catesby's man [George Bartlet] on his death-bed confessed his master went to Salisbury House several nights before the discovery, and was always brought privately in at a back door.'[1]

It only needed a deathbed statement to complete the series; and it is manifest that, like the rest of the evidence, it can hardly attract serious examination. Perhaps the most useful comment upon this kind of material comes from a contemporary of these men, Thomas Fuller in his *Church History of Britain*, first published in 1655: 'there is a generation of people who, to enhance the reputation of their knowledge, seem not only, like moths, to have lurked under the carpets of the council-table but, even like fleas, to have leaped unto the pillows of princes' bed-chambers—thence deriving their private knowledge of all things which were, or were not, ever done or thought of.'[2]

To sum up, there are odd and puzzling things about some of the plotters, Tresham in particular; but if one tries, as some writers have tried, to demonstrate that this shows the government to be the instigator of the Plot, then this hypothesis is riddled with far more contradictions and improbabilities than the traditional, and I think reasonable, view that the plot was the work of brave but incompetent idealists who wasted their lives in a noble cause. In short, the question of the authenticity of Gunpowder Plot is no longer a rewarding subject for historical research. Nothing of major significance has emerged since Gardiner examined the Plot in 1897. Trying to prove that it was a fabrication has become a game, like dating Shakespeare's

[1] Gerard, *What Was the Gunpowder Plot?*, pp. 160–61. These are drawn from Bodleian Library, CCC. 297/no. 50 Corpus Christi, *Fulman MSS*.

[2] T. Fuller, *The Church History of Britain*, ed. J. S. Brewer (6 vols, 1845), V, pp. 353–4.

sonnets: a pleasant way to pass a wet afternoon but hardly a challenging occupation for adult men and women.

If, then, this one-time lively controversy has now run into sand, it releases the subject for much larger consideration. For one of the most interesting historical questions in this context is: what was the social framework of English dissent (in which I include *all* dissent, Catholic, Protestant nonconformist, Jewish, agnostic, atheistic)? And with this I join the related and still broader question of the historical causes of social alienation. Many historians are scarcely aware of this question; and those who are trying to work on it find their materials rich but their tools blunt. It will be decades before we come within sight of an answer, but the subject cries aloud to be studied.

The problem of Guy Fawkes, as we have seen, goes back at least to the Reformation. That fundamental movement—or series of movements—in human affairs no longer admits of a single or simple all-inclusive explanation. It is too complex in its social, cultural, religious and political origins to submit much longer to the narrow bounds into which textbook writers have confined it. Nor can we find in it, as some have too often implied, a straight highway from medieval to modern times. Instead there is a vast labyrinth of roads, some of which turn back on themselves and others of which vanish inexplicably into desert. One winding path, badly marked and very obscure in places, leads toward a notion of toleration. In that respect, the Reformation is one major phase in this story.

Arising from new evidence and new approaches now at the disposal of historians, some of us are no longer able to see the Reformation as a gigantic struggle between two great religious movements, Catholic and Protestant. To us the Reformation is part of a large and longer struggle within religion as a whole and extending beyond Christianity itself.[1] In short, it is part of the long-lasting, never-ending struggle between the laity and the priesthood, or, conceived even more broadly, between order and dissent. If this is so, then the Reformation period sees one of the

[1] The best recent discussion will be found in H. R. Trevor-Roper, *Religion, the Reformation and Social Change* (1967), chs. 1–4.

great rebellions against the priestly order. The fundamental change in the doctrine of the mass, which the Reformers carried through, deprived the priest of his special role of indispensable intercessor between God and man. To put the matter in its most extreme form, the Anglican Church was in essence secularized. For the first time in English history a king, Henry VIII, became its supreme head. The bishops were reduced almost to the role of clerical civil servants. But the victory over the priesthood was by no means complete; English Puritans lamented that in the Protestant Church of England the power of the priest had returned in the shape of the bishops. Hence Peter Wentworth's celebrated rebuke to the Anglican Archbishop Parker: '... That were but to make you popes. Make you popes who list, for we will make you none.'[1] This explains, too, those famous satirical tracts which their authors wrote under the pseudonym Martin Marprelate.[2] But the Puritans — or certain sections of them — in time developed their own priesthood. In spite of all the trappings of spiritual equality, Calvin's Geneva gave enormous powers to the minister, and the Calvinists in Scotland under John Knox tried to establish the same system. James I — 'I that was persecuted by Puritans there' — was perfectly familiar, from his years in Scotland as king, with this struggle for power by a new priest-hood: 'Jesuits', he cried, 'are nothing but Puritan-papists.'[3] Milton put it better when he said, 'New presbyter is but old priest writ large.'[4] When the priesthood is strong and the laity weak, orthodoxy and intolerance flourish; factions of the faith are exclusive; one religious community is spiritually segregated from another. This has nothing to do with the validity of faith but with its government.

This process, then, is clearly visible. But Roman Catholicism,

---

[1] Cited in J. E. Neale, *Elizabeth I and Her Parliaments: 1559–1581* (1953), p. 205.

[2] See for example, *An Introductory Sketch to the Martin Marprelate Controversy, 1588–1590*, ed. E. Arber (London: published by the editor, 1895); W. Pierce, *An Historical Introduction to the Marprelate Tracts* (1908); *The Marprelate Tracts* (1589 edn), ed. W. Pierce (1911).

[3] *The Political Works of James I*, ed. C. H. McIlwain (Cambridge, Mass., 1918), p. 126.

[4] 'On the New Forcers of Conscience under the Long Parliament.'

even though it won back and held large parts of Europe, was experiencing the same tensions. Catholicism without a priesthood would, of course, not be Catholicism at all; and it is to the credit of the Jesuit order—but not to it alone—that it identified this danger to the faith and took vigorous measures to counter it. It is possible that without the Jesuits, and other ecclesiastical missionaries, Catholicism in England might not have survived the Tudor period, save in an attenuated and demoralized form. The Jesuits also realized that survival depended itself on the preservation of Catholic separateness, indeed isolation. Hence they forbade their followers ever to attend the Anglican Church even though the fines for non-attendance were heavy. So we see persecutors and persecuted pursuing the same policy; so in Elizabethan England we see the ghetto walls rising, not those of bricks and mortar but the more impregnable ghettos of the mind.

Lord Burghley, though a deeply religious man, had seen in the Anglican Church the power of the priest reviving, and he had gone out of his way to warn Archbishop Whitgift that there were limits to his power; he gave broad hints elsewhere that he favoured restraints upon episcopal authority. His son, the future Earl of Salisbury, different from his father in many ways, shared his views on this. He sought to restrain the power of the Anglican bishops and reduce their wealth, making a profit in the process; and he also directed his attention to the Jesuits. At the end of the sixteenth century there was a curious and complex manœuvre, sometimes described as the Archpriest Controversy, in which Salisbury played a prominent part.[1] Salisbury, along with Bancroft and others, had tried to drive a wedge between the Jesuit section of the Catholic leadership in England—that section which looked to the papacy and Spain to carry through the reconversion of England—and their rivals, especially some of the secular priests, who hoped to negotiate terms from the English

---

[1] T. G. Law, *A Historical Sketch of the Conflicts between Jesuits and Seculars* (1889); P. Renold, *The Wisbech Stirs* (Catholic Record Society LI, 1958). Cf. J. Hurstfield in *Elizabethan Government and Society*, ed. Bindoff *et al.*, pp. 382–9; above, pp. 115–26.

government which might make their position more secure as a tolerated minority. The terms offered to the moderates did not – in spite of some transient hopes – grant toleration: if they had, then English history might thereafter have taken a different shape. At most there was an informal understanding with a small section of the secular priests that persecution would diminish, and they, in turn, pledged themselves not to obey papal instructions to help depose the queen.

The sincerity of Salisbury and Bancroft in these negotiations is very doubtful. In essence, Salisbury's aim had been to break the hold of the Jesuit priests, separate the leaders from the led, and somehow bring the moderate Catholic priests and laity into some measure of conformity with the established order. He had failed; and his struggle against the priesthood went on. He told the Venetian ambassador in 1605,

> These are the laws, and they must be observed. Their object is undoubtedly to extinguish the Catholic religion in this kingdom, because we do not think it fit, in a well-governed monarchy, to increase the number of persons who profess to depend on the will of other Princes as the Catholics do, the priests not preaching anything more constantly than this, that the good Catholic ought to be firmly resolved in himself to be ready to rise for the preservation of his religion even against the life and state of his natural Prince. This is a very perilous doctrine, and we will certainly never admit it here, but will rather do our best to overthrow it, and we will punish most severely those who teach it and impress it on the minds of good subjects.[1]

Salisbury failed; the power of the priests was not broken; but they recognized their true enemy. And it is not surprising that Salisbury holds a special place in the Jesuit historiography of Gunpowder Plot.

[1] Cited in Gardiner, *What Gunpowder Plot Was*, p. 166. An alternative translation will be found in *CSPV*, X (1603–1607), 230–31.

This is what one of his Catholic opponents wrote to him in 1606: 'We know no other mean left us in the world, since it is manifest that you serve but as a match, to give fire unto His Majesty ... for intending all mischiefs against the poor distressed Catholics.'[1] To this Salisbury replied that he was no enemy of the Catholic faith itself. Nor did he wish to charge the Catholics as a whole with treason for, as he said, he knew of their loyalty to the Crown: 'I do remember, upon the death of the late Queen of happy memory, with what obedience and applause both professions [Catholic and Protestant] did concur to His Majesty's succession, and now observe how little assistance was given to these late savage Papists.' None the less, he went on: 'my prayers shall never cease that we may see the happy days when only one Uniformity of true Religion is willingly embraced in this Monarchy.' But he would avoid persecuting Catholics as such. 'Yet I shall ever (according to the law of God) make so great difference in my conscience between seeing sins, and sins of ignorance, as I shall think it just by the laws of men.'[2] He said more or less the same thing to the Venetian ambassador, in the passage earlier quoted. 'Sir,' he said, 'be content as to blood so long as the Catholics remain quiet and obedient.'[3]

The overwhelming majority of Catholics did remain 'quiet and obedient'. Only a tiny minority saw treason as the only way out of a desperate situation. But here was the crux of the matter. The Catholic defence movement could not write off its past history. Even if, wrote a Catholic two generations later, 'the design [the Plot] had been suggested by papists alone, and unanimously approved by all, *yet we that live now are guilty of no sin*'—and he underlined the words as he wrote them.[4] By his act Guy Fawkes transmitted the taint of guilt to the unborn innocent generations who suffered for an irresponsible decision in which they had played no part; just as throughout the long centuries those of the Jewish faith expiated an ancestral act done

[1] R. Cecil, Earl of Salisbury, *An Answere to Certaine Scandalous Papers* (1606), Sigma B 4.
[2] Ibid., Sigma F 1.
[3] Gardiner, *What Gunpowder Plot Was*, p. 165.
[4] [Palmer], *A Reply to the Answer*, p. 203.

at the beginning of the Christian era, in which they, too, had played no part. In both cases it was the organized faiths opposing them which fastened a charge of guilt upon the innocent and the unborn. *Tantum religio potuit suadere malorum*: the bitter words of Lucretius after so long return to taunt us.

Nothing should be taken to suggest, however, that, if the Plot had succeeded, if Parliament had been blown up, the king and his ministers murdered or in flight and the surviving members of the royal family seized, Catesby, Fawkes, Tresham and the rest would have inaugurated an era of religious toleration under the benign patronage of the papacy and Spain. Granted the contemporary belief that there was only one true religious faith and that all heresy was an offence to God and a threat to the soul of man, everything else followed: injustice, persecution, plotting, assassination. There is no reason to believe that the Catesbys in power would have been any more humane or tolerant than the Salisburys in power. Catesby and Salisbury alike were prisoners of the same harsh dogma of the uniqueness of religious truth and the identification of ideological unity with political security. For this inexorable doctrine many thousands would have to give up their lives in the bloody decades now beginning in Europe, compared with which Gunpowder Plot was no more than a trivial incident in the wings.

It is necessary, therefore, to ask: could the government have tolerated with safety a minority in its midst when that minority belonged to a different faith? The government did not believe that it could, but this was probably a misjudgment of the situation as we now see it in the larger perspective of time. The evidence which was emerging by the early seventeenth century was that the Catholics in England were not likely to bring in a foreign power to wage war on their behalf. There was a tiny intransigent wing which was prepared to attempt anything, but this was contained and restrained; and its efforts were wholly neutralized. The overwhelming majority of Catholics rejected these hotheads on every single occasion when any contact was made. Salisbury, in trying to split the Catholics, had glimpsed the possibility of an agreement with the moderates. But he had no intention of establishing religious toleration, nor did anyone else in the government envisage such a settlement. The question of blame or praise for holding these views does not arise. These men were caught up in the web of their time, as we are in ours, and they could not envisage a time when all men of all races and faiths would live in equality and peace with their neighbours. Because neither they nor their successors could foresee such an age the succeeding centuries would accumulate a vast, bitter record of suspicion, injustice and bloodshed, all transmitted from one innocent generation to another until, at last, in the nineteenth century the whole apparatus of repression began to be dismantled.

I come now to my final question: what were the consequences of Guy Fawkes? His importance lies not in what he did, or tried to do, but in what he was taken to symbolize. Having destroyed the plotters, the government made the maximum political capital out of the Plot. Hence the address to Parliament, the publication of an official record, the inclusion henceforth of a special service in the Book of Common Prayer, and the establishment of November 5th as a day of national salvation. Nor should we think of Guy Fawkes Day in the seventeenth, eighteenth or a good part of the nineteenth centuries as merely an excuse for gathering a few friends in the back garden to entertain the children. All too often in provincial England it was an occasion for whipping up hostility against the Catholics; and in the capital itself the same was often the case. In 1850 when the Catholic hierarchy was restored in England by the papacy, one mob omitted the customary effigy of Guy Fawkes and replaced it with one of Cardinal Wiseman.[1]

So, in the seventeenth century and beyond, English Catholics carried the inherited taint of the plotters' guilt. 'Sir,' said one such critic of them, 'I condemn you not all; but I condemn the religion of you all: for your religion bindeth you all to attempt the like ... your religion bindeth you all to play the traitors.'[2]

[1] *The Book of Days*, ed. R. Chambers (2 vols, 1864), II, p. 550.
[2] Cited in De Luna, *Jonson's Romish Plot*, p. 40.

And Catholicism was indeed easily identified with the foreigner by those who wished to denigrate it. In the sixteenth century it was said that the Catholics would bring in Spain; in the seventeenth, at first they were identified with Spain, then with barbarous and treasonable war in Ireland, and then with submission to the France of Louis XIV. In the eighteenth century it was still France until almost the end; and in the middle of the nineteenth century the Catholics were, by their enemies, linked with the dark forces of repression anywhere. The existence of a minority looking to other traditions provided marvellous material for demagogues to whip up xenophobia, never far below the surface in a modern nation-state. Lord George Gordon, whose name will always be associated with the anti-Catholic riots of 1781, was not the last of his line.

The consequence of these centuries of repression was a grievous impoverishment of the whole nation. We recall that there was nowhere in England where a Catholic — or any other nonconformist — could gain a university degree. Until 1797 they could not vote in local elections; until 1829 they could not vote in parliamentary elections. It was not simply that Catholics were the losers: the whole nation lost, persecutors and persecuted alike. It is true that many nonconformists, Catholics and others, found outlets in those activities for which the 39 Articles or the Oath of Supremacy were not required: in medicine, in commerce and industry. Many sought in settlement overseas the right to practise their faith in dignity and peace. Of these Catholic settlements, Maryland is the most famous and it goes back almost to the time of Guy Fawkes. This process continued, culminating in the great Irish Catholic settlements of the nineteenth and twentieth centuries in Boston, New York, Chicago and elsewhere, settlements which recall a long, bitter ancestry of repression and humiliation, and whose consequences may still be detected in Anglo–American relations of our own day.

History (alas!) does not fall neatly into the dates and epochs of textbooks and examinations. Long after battles have been fought and won, the scars refuse to heal, the memories decline to fade, and new generations are summoned to defend a cause which no one any longer wants to attack. To these surviving memories of injustice and persecution may be attributed a good deal of the meretricious and tendentious writing on Guy Fawkes which has plagued the study of the seventeenth century for so long.

Here then is a situation familiar enough throughout the whole history of organized religion in Europe: the doctrine of the uniqueness of religious revelation, that only one religion or one form of a religion has access to divine truth; and the consequent fragmentation of European society, the persecution, the martyrs, the oft-repeated cycle of war and oppression, the ineradicable memories of injustice. And here is the final paradox. Even as one admires the deep courage, the noble service and devotion of the priesthood to their faithful, one knows also that they were themselves a divisive force, separating by laws against inter-marriage, by dietary laws, by ritual, one member of the European community from another. They were men of great ideals, and they did what they believed to be right. Those within their own community who dissented were ostracized, ex-communicated, and, if they were priests, forbidden to minister to their own people. So we see, if we consider any minority or persecuted faith, that the isolation at first imposed from without was, in due course, perpetuated from within. It was the priest-hood which performed this special role of continuing the isola-tion of their own faithful from other creeds. The fragmentation of Europe was not caused simply by the Protestant Reforma-tion, as has so often been said, but by the leaders of all branches of the Christian faith; and the same pattern is to be seen beyond that faith in the long, chequered and tragic history of the Jews. This is the high price that is paid for believing in the uniqueness of revealed truth, in the superiority of one faith or one com-munity over the rest. Isolation thus becomes welcome to persecutor and persecuted alike. In any history of a ghetto there are two stages. The first is the erection of the wall from without, the second is the renewal of that wall from within. Many recent examples of this second stage can be seen all over the world.

The movement of Catholic protest in England thus passed through two stages, familiar enough in our own times though in a different context. The first stage saw the attempt to win recognition as a tolerated minority among majority groups. This phase ended in failure and Catesby emerged in 1605 as the leader of the party of action, the party which would take its rights by force. But it was a tiny party, and the events of November destroyed it. The movement now entered on its second phase when in despair it turned inward, emphasizing its distinctiveness as a community within the nation, passionately resolved to preserve its separate identity. In gunpowder few of the Catholics believed and in any case it was discredited. They turned instead to a different weapon, the press; and the vast amount of polemical literature is a measure of their devotion and resourcefulness. Meanwhile, many of them withdrew into themselves. But it would be quite false to imagine that all over the British Isles a patient minority endured their disabilities until a better time would dawn. In one area continuous repression was answered with endemic violence: the tragic history of Ireland since the sixteenth century, where racial and religious protest were combined, provides a perfect casebook of how not to treat a dissenting minority.

Deep below this controversy, inseparable as it is from the history of England, is the issue of liberty: the liberty of a minority within society, but the liberty, too, of an individual within that minority, his liberty from the ideological domination of the priestly caste. The rationalist movements of the eighteenth and nineteenth centuries took up again the work of the sixteenth century in weakening the power of the priestly order in all faiths; and they achieved a remarkable degree of success. But success did not last. The second half of the nineteenth century saw the emergence of a whole series of secular theologies, comparable in inspiration, ideals — and intolerance — to the greatest religions in the world; and in the twentieth century pressures of ideological commitment have intensified. Just as the old priestly order was relaxing its grip, a new priestly order asserted its authority, backed now by all the apparatus of the printing-press and the mass media. In many cases the state triumphed over the Church and assumed its powers. Nor should one think of this solely in terms of government. The intolerance of minority leaders in many cases measures up to or exceeds that of the men who sit in the seats of authority. The events of the centuries since Guy Fawkes, seen in this general context, underline for us the tragic destiny of man: for how brief a time he enjoys his liberty and how precarious is his hold upon it.

Yet there are grounds for hope. In the 1530s under Henry VIII, two measures were passed by Parliament. The first was designed to end the official use of the Welsh language in every part of Wales, the second, as it said, to abolish diversity of opinion in religion.[1] But diversity of opinion survives, so does the Welsh language; and as we read those two Acts after so long we marvel at the pretentious littleness of some who lead us, and at the courage and power of those who dissent.

[1] For example, 'And also that from henceforth no person or persons that use the Welsh speech or language shall have or enjoy any manner office or fees within the realm of England, Wales or other the King's dominions upon pain of forfeiting the same offices or fees unless he or they use and exercise the speech or language of English.' 27 Hen. VIII c.26; 31 Hen. VIII c.14.

Index

Index

Blackwell, George, 122
Bluet, Thomas, 118
Bodin, Jean, 303, 310
Bodley, Thomas, 127
Boke named the Governour, The, 220
Boller, John, 260–61
Book of Common Prayer, 225, 347
Book of Martyrs, see Acts and Monuments
Book of Orders, 271–4
Boston, 348
Bourbon, House of, 302–3
Bowes, Martin, 168
Bradford (Wilts.), 265–74
Brandon, Charles, 1st Duke of Suffolk, 108
Brandon, Mary, Duchess of Suffolk, 108
Bribery, 143, 146, 151, 156, 162, 314; *see also* Gifts
Bridewell, 260, 267
Bridges, maintenance of, 259, 280, 286–7
Brinklow, Henry, 176
Bristol, 201, 244, 275
British Museum, 140, 142
Broadcasting and television, 7
Bromham, 266
Brooke, George, 92
Broughton Gifford, 165
Brouncker, Robert, 265
Browne, Anthony, 1st Viscount Montagu, 117
Browne, Mrs John, 180
Browning, Andrew, 157
Browning, Robert, 50, 58, 62
Buckhurst, Baron of, *see* Sackville, Thomas
Buckingham, Duke of, *see* Villiers, George
Buckingham, faction of, 186, 191
Bull of deposition (1570), 81, 89, 116, 332
Bureaucracy, *see* Office; Officials
Burghley, Lord, *see* Cecil, William
Burke, Edmund, 158
Burns, Robert, 50

Caesar, Sir Julius, 188

Calne, 252, 292–3
Calvin, John, 83, 342
Calvinism, 81–2, 301–3
Calvinists, 81–2, 90
Cambridge University, 88, 203, 206
Cambridge University, Chancellor of, 88
Canterbury, 201
Canterbury, Archbishop of, 247; *see also* Cranmer, Thomas; Parker, Matthew; Whitgift, John
Cardinal's College, *see* Christ Church, Oxford
Carew, George, 131
Carey, George, 242
Carleton, Dudley, 336
Carmarthen, 275
Carmeliano, Pietro, 205
Carr, Robert, Earl of Somerset, 153, 193, 318
Cartwright, Thomas, 82, 89
Castiglione, Baldassare, 215, 223
Cateau-Cambrésis, Treaty of, 312
Catesby, Robert, 328–30, 340, 346, 350
Castlemaine, Earl of, *see* Palmer, Roger
Catherine de Medici, 302–3
Catholics: denigration of, 347–8; emancipation of, 338; and Gunpowder Plot, 328, 330–32; persecution of, 63–4, 98, 116–18, 232, 332–3, 348
Catiline His Conspiracy, 337–8
Cavaliers, 51, 157
Cecil, House of, 322–3; manuscripts of, 142
Cecil, Edward, Viscount Wimbledon, 340
Cecil, Robert, 1st Earl of Salisbury, 33, 61, 108, 183–96 *passim*, 218, 247, 316; attitude to Henry VIII, 23; and Catholics, 97–8, 102, 115–18, 123–6, 335–6, 343–6; character of, 132, 185–90, 193–5, 334–5; and corruption, 142, 160, 162, 187–8, 193; ecclesiastical policy, 79–80, 92–103, 104–34 *passim*, 343–5, 346; economic policy,

Index

Index

Index

361

Index

McIlwain, C. H., 102
Measure for Measure, 57, 60–61
Medicine, 203
Melksham, 265
Merchant of Venice, 66
Merchants, 27, 138, 142, 184, 202, 211, 223
Mere, 274, 291
Merriman, R. B., 31–2, 34
Mesta, the, 313
Metham, Thomas, 119
Middle class, nature of, 322–3; *see also* Gentry; Merchants; Lawyers
Middlemen, 140
Middlesex, Earl of, *see* Cranfield, Lionel
Milles, Thomas, 231
Milton, John, 50–51, 342
Missionaries, Catholic, 81–2
Molin, Niccolo, 336
Monarchy: divine attributes of, 65, 69; debts of, 170; feudal rights of, 163–82 *passim*; limited, 27, 39, 49; medieval, 27–8, 47, 154, 201; personal, 191, 193; power and weakness of, 43, 47, 69, 106, 138, 201, 215–16, 324; prerogative of, 188, 324; religious authority, 82, 91; resistance to, 69, 102, 189, 244, 260, 311; succession, 104; Tudor, 23–49, 65, 199, 213, 299
Monasteries, 210
Monks, 201
Monopolies, 309, 319
Monopolists, 160
Montagu, Henry, 1st Earl of Manchester, 252
Montagu, Viscount, *see* Browne, Anthony
Monteagle, Baron, *see* Parker, William
Monteagle letter, the, 328, 337
Montmorency, House of, 302–3
Moody, Mr, 246
Moody, Henry, 261
Morality, public, 93
More, Thomas, 28, 49, 64, 203, 207–9, 216, 219–20, 225, 322
Morrice, James, 83, 321
Morrison, Richard, 45, 206
Mother Hubbard's Tale, 228

Muster rolls, 243, 246
Musters: abuses of, 243–4, 248; commissions of, 238–9, 242
Mutiny, 250

Nashe, Thomas, 200
Nationalism, 224, 235
Navy, Royal, 184, 280
Neale, Sir John, 19, 42, 55, 105, 149
Neat, William, 265
Netherlands, The, 309–10, 323
Neufville, Nicolas III, seigneur de Villeroy, 322
Neville, Henry, 123, 127
New Cambridge Modern History, 140
Newcastle, 210
Newcastle, Duke of, *see* Pelham-Holles, Thomas
New Forest, 280
New Year gifts, 134
New York, 348
Norfolk, Duke of, *see* Howard, Thomas
North, Thomas, 233
Northampton, Earl of, *see* Howard, Henry
Northamptonshire, 229, 246
Northumberland, Earl of, *see* Percy, Henry
Norton, Thomas, 232–4
Norwich, 201
Norwich, Bishop of, 83–4
Nowell, Lawrence, 230

Oath of Allegiance, 97–8, 102, 132
Obedience of a Christian Man, 45
Office: corruption of, 139, 147–62; grant of, 94, 151; growth in numbers, 154–6, 172; nature of, 139, 147–8, 314–15, 321–2; profits from, 138–9, 151, 161, 186, 194, 322; sale of, 155, 312–14, 317
Officials: baronial, 201; ecclesiastical, 154; gild, 154; government, 179, 186, 192, 314–18, 321–2; manorial, 154
Old Testament, 69
Oldham, Hugh, 216
Opinion: local, 25; public, 17
Order, maintenance of, 12, 72, 241

362

Index

Index

Index

Index